Christian Bauer

**Secure and Efficient IP Mobility Support
for Aeronautical Communications**

Secure and Efficient IP Mobility Support for Aeronautical Communications

by
Christian Bauer

Dissertation, Karlsruher Institut für Technologie (KIT)
Fakultät für Informatik
Tag der mündlichen Prüfung: 18. Januar 2013

Impressum

Karlsruher Institut für Technologie (KIT)
KIT Scientific Publishing
Straße am Forum 2
D-76131 Karlsruhe
www.ksp.kit.edu

KIT – Universität des Landes Baden-Württemberg und
nationales Forschungszentrum in der Helmholtz-Gemeinschaft

KIT Scientific Publishing 2013
Print on Demand

ISBN 978-3-7315-0001-8

Secure and Efficient IP Mobility Support for Aeronautical Communications

zur Erlangung des akademischen Grades eines

Doktors der Ingenieurwissenschaften

der Fakultät für Informatik
des Karlsruher Instituts für Technologie (KIT)

genehmigte

Dissertation

von

Christian Bauer

aus Brixlegg

Tag der mündlichen Prüfung: 18. Januar 2013

Erster Gutachter: Prof. Dr. Martina Zitterbart
                                      Karlsruher Institut für Technologie (KIT)

Zweiter Gutachter: Prof. Dr. Dieter Hogrefe
                                        Georg-August-Universität Göttingen

Zusammenfassung

Die Luftfahrtindustrie befindet sich am Anfang einer Modernisierungsphase mit dem Ziel, ein auf dem Internetprotokoll (IP) basierendes modernes Netzwerk aufzubauen welches die mobile Kommunikation zwischen dem Flugzeug (mobiles Netzwerk) und verschiedenen Kommunikationspartnern am Boden (korrespondierende Knoten) unterstützen soll. Durch die Verwendung unterschiedlicher terrestrischer und Satelliten-basierender Funktechnologien kann es zu mobilitätsbedingten Übergängen zwischen diesen Technologien kommen (*Handover*).

Das Internetprotokoll wurde jedoch ohne Unterstützung für mobile Knoten entworfen: Durch einen Handover eines der beteiligten Kommunikationspartner ändert sich auch dessen IP Addresse. Applikationsdaten können somit nicht mehr an die korrekte Addresse weitergeleitet werden. Mit *Mobile IP* (*MIP*) existiert ein bereits standardisiertes Protokoll zur Lösung dieses Problems. Ein dezidierter Netzwerkknoten im Heimnetzwerk, genannt *Home Agent*, weist dem mobilen Knoten eine konstante IP Addresse (Heimaddresse) zu, die topologisch im Heimnetzwerk verankert ist. Der mobile Knoten teilt dem Home Agent stets seine aktuelle, von der topologischen Position abhängige IP Addresse mit. Indem die Adressierung von Applikationen über diese Heimaddresse erfolgt, werden Datenpakete der kommunizierenden Netzwerkknoten über den Home Agent korrekt weitergeleitet. Das Mobilitätsprotokoll *Network Mobility* (NEMO) erweitert MIP dahingehend, dass nicht nur einzelne mobile Knoten sondern mobile Router, inklusive eines dazugehörigen mobilen Netzwerkes, unterstützt werden. Der Nachteil eines MIP/NEMO basierten Ansatzes liegt in der zentralen Komponente des Home Agents. Diese birgt nicht nur das Risiko eines *Single-Point-of-Failure*, sondern erhöht auch die Latenz der Ende-zu-Ende Kommunikation zwischen mobilem und korrespondierendem Knoten bei zunehmender Distanz zum Home Agent. MIP bietet, im Gegensatz zu NEMO, eine Komponente zur *Routenoptimierung*, die es erlaubt, Datenpakete direkt zwischen den beiden Kommunikationspartnern auszutauschen und den Home Agent damit zu umgehen.

Mehrere Faktoren erschweren die direkte Verwendung dieser Mobilitätsprotokolle im Umfeld der Luftfahrtkommunikation. Ein Flugzeug ist kein einzelner mobiler Knoten sondern ein mobiles Netzwerk mit mehreren unterschiedliche Bordnetzen, die unter anderem sicherheitsrelevante Dienste unterstützen: von der Flugverkehrsführung über Fluglinien-interne Kommunikation bis hin zur Passagierkommunikation. Zudem bestehen Anforderungen bezügl. möglichst niedriger Latenzzeiten für die Kommunikation mit dem Boden. Dies bezieht sich nicht nur auf die Flugverkehrsführung (z.B. Alarmmeldungen), sondern auch auf die Überwachung der Integrität eines Flugzeuges (z.B. Triebwerksdaten). Weiters bestehen hohe Sicherheitsanforderungen, insbesondere für die Netze zur Unterstützung der Flugverkehrsführung, welche robust gegenüber diversen Angriffen sein müssen. Durch die relativ begrenzte Bandbreite der verwendeten drahtlosen Funktechnologien ist der Signalisierungsaufwand im Protokoll zudem so gering wie möglich zu halten.

Im Rahmen dieser Dissertation wird ein sicheres und effizientes Routenoptimierungsprotokoll zur Verwendung mit NEMO entwickelt, welches für den Einsatz im Bereich der zivilen Luftfahrtkommunikation geeignet ist. Der Schwerpunkt der Arbeit liegt hierbei auf der Unterstützung der sicherheitsbezogenen Netze, insbesondere für die Flugverkehrsführung.

Das Correspondent Router (CR) Protokoll wird als geeignetster Ansatz für die NEMO Routenoptimierung identifiziert. Ein CR kann stellvertretend für korrespondierende Knoten in der selben Netzwerkdomäne einen routenoptimierten Pfad direkt zum mobilen Router anbieten. Dieses Protokoll bietet überwiegend positive Eigenschaften, wie z.B. gute Signalisierungseffizienz an, beinhaltet jedoch einen negativen Aspekt im Bereich der Sicherheitseigenschaften. Es werden *neue Maskeraden- bzw. Hijacking-Angriffe* identifiziert, die es einem Angreifer erlauben, sich als mobiler Router oder CR auszugeben und somit den für die legitimen Knoten bestimmten Datenverkehr umzuleiten bzw. zu blockieren (Denial of Service).

Den Kern der Dissertation bildet daher der Vorschlag für ein *sicheres CR Protokoll* namens SeNERO, das es erlaubt, einen direkten Kommunikationspfad zwischen dem mobilem Netzwerk und dem korrespondierenden Netzwerk mit seinen korrespondierenden Knoten am Boden aufzubauen. Im Rahmen des neuen Protokolls findet hierbei eine gegenseitige Authentifizierung statt, in welcher IP Adressen des mobilen Routers und CRs durch Zertifikate autorisiert werden. Eine zugrunde liegende Public Key Infrastruktur (PKI) ermöglicht diese Vorgehensweise.

SeNERO ist dabei resistent gegenüber den bereits erwähnten Angriffen. Der Nachweis der erhöhten Sicherheit erfolgt durch eine Untersuchung basierend auf einem für diesen Zweck definierten, mobilitätsspezifischen Angreifermodells. In diesem werden sowohl unterschiedliche Angreiferklassen (z.B. Off-Path oder Man-In-The-Middle) als auch unterschiedliche Angriffsarten (z.B. Replay oder Reflexionsangriffe) berücksichtigt. Hiermit kann nachgewiesen werden, dass die im alten CR Protokoll identifizierten Probleme bezügl. Maskeraden- bzw. Hijacking-Angriffe für SeNERO keine Gültigkeit mehr besitzen.

Im Vergleich zu alternativen Ansätzen benötigt SeNERO eine geringere Anzahl an Signalisierungsnachrichten. Dadurch wird die *Handoverlatenz* verringert. Diese Metrik entspricht der Zeitspanne, die ein mobiler Router benötigt, um nach einem erfolgten Handover einen optimierten Pfad basierend auf der neuen, aktuellen IP Address aufzubauen. Die Verbesserung der Handoverlatenz von SeNERO wird im Vergleich zum bestehenden CR Protokoll gezeigt. Diese Evaluierung erfolgt durch unterschiedliche Ansätze und Werkzeuge, einerseits durch ein analytisches Modell, andererseits durch Implementierungen in einer Simulations- und Versuchsumgebung. Einheitliche Szenarien ermöglichen einen Vergleich zwischen den unterschiedlichen Methoden. Die Versuchsumgebung setzt auf eine bereits vorhandene Linux-basierte Implementierung von MIP bzw. NEMO auf, die im Rahmen dieser Arbeit mit den CR Funktionalitäten und Signalisierungen erweitert wurde. Durch die Erweiterung einer Simulationsumgebung mit einer MIP Implementierung wurde eine Ausgangsbasis für die Simulationen geschaffen. Basierend darauf wurden schließlich NEMO, das ursprüngliche CR Protokoll sowie SeNERO implementiert. Zusätzlich wurde in den Simulationen eine für die Luftfahrt realistische zukünftige Funktechnologie eingebunden, wodurch der Realitätsgrad der Szenarien nochmals erhöht wird. Durch diese Untersuchungen kann eine Verbesserung der Handoverlatenz für SeNERO nachgewiesen werden. Abhängig vom Szenario zeigen die analytischen Ergebnisse eine um 9–50% reduzierte Handoverlatenz im Vergleich zum ursprünglichen CR Protokoll. Diese Verbesserungen werden durch den Versuchsaufbau bestätigt, mit Werten im Bereich zwischen 13–51%. Gleiches gilt für die Simulationsergebnisse, welche Verbesserungen zw. 12–51% aufweisen. Unter Einbeziehung der realistischen Funktechnologie können zudem die Auswirkungen des Auslastungsgrades der Funkzelle auf die Handoverlatenz genauer untersucht werden: Die dafür verwendeten Szenarien erstrecken sich von niedrigem über mittleres Verkehrsaufkommen bis hin zur Überlast. Es zeigt sich, dass SeNERO weiterhin in allen Situation bessere Performanz erzielt, jedoch sinkt der Grad der Verbesserung von ursprünglich 81% über 58% bis auf 32%.

Die Evaluierung des *Signalisierungsaufwandes* erfolgt ebenso durch analytische Mittel. Dabei kann gezeigt werden, dass der Signalisierungsoverhead von SeNERO 3–70% unterhalb des ursprünglichen CR Protokolls liegt. Diese Wertspanne bezieht sich auf ein Zeitfenster von 21–84 Minuten in welchem der optimierte Pfad zu einem CR aktiv beibehalten wird.

Des Weiteren benötigt SeNERO, im Gegensatz zum ursprünglichen CR Protokoll, keinen aktiven Home Agent um den optimierten Pfad aufzubauen. Dadurch wird der *Single-Point-of-Failure* in Form des Home Agents durch die verteilte Komponente der CR eliminiert. Bedingt durch die zugrunde liegende PKI benötigt SeNERO jedoch einen Vertrauensanker (Zertifikatsautorität), der für die Validierung der Zertifikate miteinbezogen werden muss. Dies kann als als Single-Point-of-Failure wahrgenommen werden. Das häufig anzutreffende PKI-Modell mit einem globalen Vertrauensanker als Wurzel einer Hierarchie entspricht zudem nicht dem Vertrauensmodell der Luftfahrt.

Ein weiterer Teil der Dissertation schlägt daher eine *Erweiterung für Identitätszertifikate* vor. Das hierfür eingeführt verteilte PKI-Modell basiert auf landesspezifischen bzw. regionalen Zertifikatsautoritäten vor. SeNERO verwendet diese Zertifikate, wodurch jeder mobile Router und CR mit einem solchen Zertifikat ausgestattet wird.

Die Verifikation eines solchen Zertifikates zur Laufzeit, d. h. während der Authentifizierung zw. mobilen Router und CR, erfolgt hierbei ohne Miteinbeziehung eines zentralen Vertrauensankers. Stattdessen wird hierfür eine lokale Zertifikatsautorität verwendet, welche sich in der Domäne eines jeden CRs befindet.

Der mobile Router verwendet bei der Authentifizierung gegenüber einem CR ein Zertifikat, welches durch den lokalen Vertrauensanker des CRs ausgestellt wurde. Die Verifikation eines solchen Zertifikates durch den CR beschränkt sich auf eine Prüfung von Signatur und Zertifikatswiderrufsinformationen eben dieses lokalen Vertrauenankers. Umgekehrt basiert die Verifikation des Zertifikats des CRs durch den mobilen Router ebenso auf dem lokalen Vertrauensanker des CRs.

Die Zertifikatsprüfung zur Laufzeit basiert somit nur auf dem lokalen Vertrauensanker des CRs und auf keiner weiteren Zertifikatsautorität. Durch diese Vorgehensweise wird der Single-Point-of-Failure eines zentralen Vertrauensankers durch die verteilte Komponente der lokalen Zertifikatsautoritäten ersetzt. Das Vertrauensmodell der Luftfahrt lässt sich zudem mit diesesm Modell abbilden, wenn jedes Land oder Region eine solche lokale Zertifikatsautorität betreib. Mit der Ausgabe eines Zertifikats an einen mobilen Router bestätigt das jeweilige Land bzw. Region, dass sich eben dieses Flugzeug in der lokalen Domäne aufhalten darf.

Die Evaluierung der vorgeschlagenen Zertifikatserweiterung erfolgt durch eine theoretische Herangehensweise, basierend auf Maurers logischem Kalkül. Dieses wird erweitert um auch Cross-Zertifikate modellieren zu können, welche zwischen Zertifikatsautoritäten der gleichen hierarchischen Ebene ausgestellt werden. Ebenso erfolgt eine Erweiterung des Kalküls um die erweiterten Identitätszertifikate modellieren zu können. Durch logisches Inferenzieren kann schließlich die Authentizität der in den erweiterten Zertifikaten enthaltenen Informationen nachgewiesen werden. Diese Verifikation erfolgt für eine Authentifizierung in beiden Richtungen: Es wird sowohl die Authentizität des Zertifikats des mobilen Routers aus der Sichtweise des CRs nachgewiesen als auch die Authentizität des Zertifikats des CRs aus der Sichtweise des mobilen Routers.

Contents

List of Figures

List of Tables

List Of Abbreviations

AAC	Aeronautical Administrative Communication
ACSP	Air Communication Service Provider
ANSP	Air Navigation Service Provider
AOC	Aeronautical Operational Control
APC	Aeronautical Passenger Communication
AS	Autonomous System
ATN	Aeronautical Telecommunications Network
ATS	Air Traffic Services
BA	Binding Acknowledgement
BER	Bit Error Rate
BGP	Border Gateway Protocol
BU	Binding Update
CA	Certificate Authority
CGA	Cryptographically Generated Address
CN	Correspondent Node
CoA	Care-of Address
CoT(I)	Care-of Test (Init)
CR	Correspondent Router
CRL	Certificate Revocation List
CRP	Correspondent Router Prefix

DoS	Denial of Service
ECC	Elliptic Curve Cryptography
ECDSA	Elliptic Curve Digital Signature Algorithm
ECIES	Elliptic Curve Integrated Encryption Scheme
EGP	Exterior Gateway Protocol
FER	Frame Error Rate
HA	Home Agent
HMAC	Hash-based Message Authentication Code
HO	Handover
HoA	Home Address
HoT(I)	Home Test (Init)
IETF	Internet Engineering Task Force
IKE	Internet Key Exchange Protocol
IP	Internet Protocol
IPsec	IP security
IQR	Interquartile Range
L-DACS	L-Band Digital Aeronautical Communication System
MAC	Media Access Control
MH	Mobile Host
MIP	Mobile IP
MN	Mobile Node
MNN	Mobile Network Node
MNP	Mobile Network Prefix
MR	Mobile Router
NEMO	Network Mobility
OCSP	Online Certificate Status Protocol
PKI	Public Key Infrastructure

RO	Route Optimization
RTT	Round Trip Time
SeNERO	Secure NEMO Route Optimization
SHA	Secure Hash Algorithm

1. Introduction

The current air transportation system is experiencing significant stress due to the continuously increasing number of worldwide flights. Current forecasts predict air traffic to double in the time frame from 2009 to 2030 [60]. The number of flights in Europe will increase to 20.9 million per year, with 5.9 million in Germany itself. Similarly, the world passenger aircraft fleet[1] will increase from 15.000 at the beginning of 2011 to over 31.000 by the year 2030 [5]. The increase in air traffic will especially affect long-haul flights, which are expected to increase 2.8 times from 2010 to 2030. On top of this, another challenge is the future integration of Unmanned Air Vehicles (UAVs) that have to be supported within civil air space [86].

The current air traffic management system is, however, unable to support this growth. The tools and procedures used today are not only inefficient but also approaching their bandwidth limits. This is especially the case for air traffic services communication between the cockpit and an air traffic services controller on the ground that is still primarily based on analogue voice communications [72]. But also airlines are attempting to improve the effectiveness of their operations: hardware is replaced by software, paper information is replaced by electronic deliveries, etc. Even flight operations, reporting and maintenance is supposed to be performed between the airplane and ground-based airline systems during a flight via "real-time" network connectivity [181, 182]. At the same time, providing in-flight (Internet) connectivity to passengers is considered being an important customer service [81, 107]. A commercial service for in-flight voice, Short Message Service (SMS) and General Packet Radio Service (GPRS) has been used by over 240.000 customers within a time period of 2 years [208].

---

[1]Considering passenger aircraft with at least 100 seats.

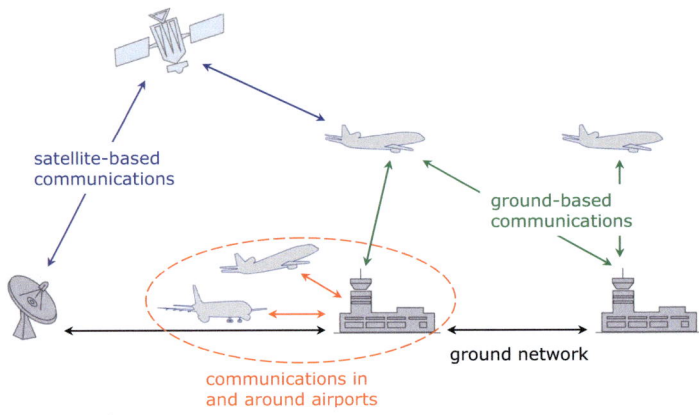

satellite-based
communications

ground-based
communications

ground network

communications in
and around airports

Figure 1.1. Future aeronautical communications network with different wireless communication technologies.

The necessity for a paradigm shift has been acknowledged at the highest level, with the Council of the European Union adopting a resolution that endorses the European Air Traffic Management Master Plan. This plan also specifies the development of new technologies that will be "embedded into a harmonized and interoperable technical architecture" [194]. In order to support this shift to information technology systems and the goal of a networked aircraft, digital communication systems are currently being developed. The future aeronautical communications system will consist of a variety of wireless communication technologies, both terrestrial and satellite links, that are integrated by an Internet Protocol (IP) based network, cf. Figure 1.1. Passenger and purely administrative airline communications will rely on the public Internet. Air traffic services and aeronautical operational control communications, which are related to the safety and regularity of a flight, will be transported in a dedicated aeronautical telecommunications network. This network will support safety related mobile communications between the aircraft and its communication peers in the ground network.

Moving aeronautical safety related communications to an IP based network will raise justified security concerns.

The US national airspace is considered being a high value target that is part of the U.S. Critical Infrastructure and Key Resources (CIKR) [192]. Audit work with penetration testing has therefore been performed for US based air traffic control (ATC) systems. A large number of vulnerabilities has been identified, leading to the conclusion that "it is likely to be a matter of when, not if, ATC systems encounter attacks that do serious harm to ATC operations" [64]. Other operational systems for high-security environments relying on IP are continuously experiencing – often successful - cyber attacks. This includes governmental systems [82], security related companies [83], satellite systems [84] and even military networks [80, 85]. The future prospects are not getting better either, as high-profile attacks on major organizations and significant targets continue to evolve [201]. In addition, insider attacks might be possible, as according to security experts, "employees are a far greater threat to information security than outsiders" [202].

It has therefore been acknowledged that the future air transport system will require aircraft to be "resilient by design to current and predicted on-board and on-the-ground security threat evolution, internally and externally to the aircraft" and that there is a need for a "fully secured global high bandwidth data network, hardened and resilient by design to cyber attacks" [67].

1.1. Problem Statement

Due to its physical mobility, an aircraft will use different wireless communication technologies throughout the different phases of a flight. It is therefore necessary to perform *handovers* between the different terrestrial and satellite based networks.

However, the Internet Protocol (IP) has been designed without any support for mobile nodes. A handover will cause a change of the mobile node's associated IP address. Application data can then not be forwarded anymore to the current, correct address of the mobile node.

The *Mobile IP* protocol [108] has been standardized within the Internet Engineering Task Force (IETF) in order to solve this problem. A dedicated network node within the home network, called *home agent*, provides the mobile node with a persistent IP address (home address) that is topologically anchored within the home network. The mobile node always informs the home agent about its current, topologically correct address that is associated to the visited network, the *care-of address*. The mobile node establishes application sessions based on the home address. Data between the mobile node and its correspondent nodes will therefore be forwarded to the home network. These packets are then intercepted by the home agent and forwarded to the current care-of address of the mobile node.

Mobile IP has been extended with the *Network Mobility* (NEMO) protocol [50] to support a mobile router with an associated mobile network and a large number of mobile network nodes instead of only a single mobile node.

The disadvantage of a Mobile IP/NEMO based approach is the centralized component in form of the home agent. As all traffic has to be routed via this intermediate network node, the end-to-end communications latency between mobile node and correspondent node is increased. This is especially the case if the distance to the home agent continually increases due to the mobility of the mobile node. Additionally, the home agent also introduces the risk of a *single point of failure*. Routing from and to the mobile router will fail if the home agent is not available. In contrast to NEMO, Mobile IP provides a *route optimization* component that permits data to be exchanged on a direct path between mobile node and correspondent node, thereby omitting the home agent on the forwarding path.

A direct application of the Mobile IP and NEMO mobility protocols within the aeronautical communications environment is hampered by several factors. First, an aircraft is not a single mobile node but instead a mobile network consisting of different domains: from air traffic services over airline internal communication up to passenger communications. There are high requirements with respect to security, especially for the safety related domains, which have to be protected against a variety of attacks. Furthermore, it is necessary to keep the latency for the communication between the aircraft and the ground systems as small as possible. This is not only relevant for air traffic services, e. g. emergency information services, but also for aeronautical operational control communications that includes services for monitoring the physical integrity of an airplane, e. g. engine reporting. A small latency is especially critical for Voice over IP based communication, that has already been envisaged for future use [110]. Safety related applications and services also require a high level of availability, with the highest demand being 99.99995% [61]. Finally, due to the limited bandwidth provided by the aeronautical wireless links, the amount of mobility protocol related signaling should be as small as possible.

Simply adopting the NEMO protocol for use within the aeronautical setting is therefore not sufficient. This has already been identified within the appropriate standardization bodies, which resulted in a NEMO route optimization requirements document specified within the IETF [55]. A solution satisfying these requirements has not yet emerged though.

1.2. Goals and Contributions

The goal of this thesis is the development and evaluation of a route optimization protocol for NEMO that is secure, efficient and does not suffer from the single point of failure problem. The work is focused towards supporting the safety related communication domains in the civil aviation environment, especially air traffic services. It is assumed that the safety related domain is segregated from the non-safety related domain for security reasons and therefore served by a dedicated NEMO based mobile router.

The specific contributions of this thesis are as follows:

- Identification of security problems in the existing correspondent router protocol.

- Design of a secure route optimization protocol for NEMO, called SeNERO, that is based on the already existing correspondent router protocol. The core of the new protocol is a secure authentication and signaling mechanism based on certificates.

- Security analysis of SeNERO:

  - Definition of a threat model and its application on the aeronautical environment.
  - Security analysis of SeNERO, based on the defined threat model.
  - Security analysis of the original correspondent router protocol based on the threat model for showing the improvements provided by SeNERO.

- Efficiency analysis, showing the improvements of SeNERO in comparison to the original correspondent router protocol:

  - Handover performance analysis based on an analytical model, simulations and a test-bed environment.
  - Signaling overhead analysis.

- Design of an extended identity certificate model for addressing the single point of failure problem within SeNERO. The new certificates rely on a set of distributed trust anchors instead of a single authoritative trust anchor. This approach also follows the trust model of the aeronautical environment.

- Verification of the extended identity certificates:

  - Extension of Maurer's calculus [133] to support modeling cross-certification and the extended identity certificates.
  - Verification of the extended certificates based on Maurer's calculus.

An evaluation of already existing proposals for NEMO route optimization classifies the different protocols into four categories. Of these, the correspondent router [212] is identified as the most suited approach. A correspondent router can provide an optimized forwarding path between the correspondent nodes located within the same administrative domain and the mobile network served by a mobile router, cf. Figure 1.2. The protocol convinces with multiple advantages, but most suffers from security deficiencies. Within this thesis, new masquerading and hijacking vulnerabilities are identified that allow an adversary to masquerade as either mobile router or correspondent router. It is then possible for the adversary to redirect or drop data traffic destined to the legitimate mobile router or correspondent router.

The core of this thesis is the *proposal for a secure correspondent router protocol* that permits establishing a direct forwarding path between mobile router and corre-

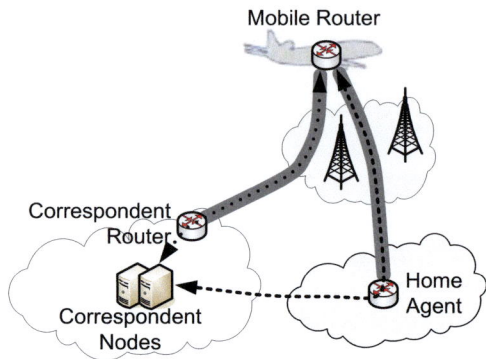

Figure 1.2. NEMO protocol with an optimized forwarding path established between mobile router and correspondent router.

spondent router. The protocol, called SeNERO, is resistant with respect to the already mentioned IP address hijacking attacks. This is achieved through a mutual authentication of the two routers by relying on a public key infrastructure. The IP address prefixes of mobile router and correspondent router are authenticated by certificates that have been extended with the IP addresses of the respective router. Mobile IPv6 based proposals for address authentication are not applicable at all to the prefix authentication required in the NEMO context [15, 37, 124]. The mutual authentication provided by SeNERO can usually not be found in other related work for NEMO [36, 122] or Mobile IP [37, 174, 225]. Those proposals that do provide mutual authentication [119, 125, 170, 227] require a larger amount of signaling than SeNERO. It is a significant advantage of SeNERO to provide a *higher level of security* while keeping the number of *signaling messages smaller* than the related work. This allows to reduce the handover latency, a performance metric that corresponds to the amount of time a mobile router requires to establish an optimized routing path to a correspondent router. Additionally, SeNERO does not require an active home agent in order to establish and maintain an optimized path. This is in contrast to a large number of previously proposed protocols, e.g. [36, 119, 174]. The *single point of failure* of the home agent has therefore been addressed in terms of a distributed set of correspondent routers. Hence, the level of availability has been increased for end-to-end communications between the mobile network node in the aircraft and the correspondent node on the ground. Other related work on NEMO or Mobile IP not requiring a home agent [122, 227] does either not provide mutual authentication, suffers from cryptographic/security problems or requires a larger number of signaling messages. The original correspondent router protocol [212] relies on a reachable home agent for establishing a direct forwarding path between mobile router and correspondent router.

The detailed security analysis performed for both SeNERO and the original correspondent router protocol is based on a mobility protocol specific threat model that has been specified for this purpose. This model considers different adversary positions (e. g. off-path or man-in-the-middle) and attack types (e. g. replay or reflection). The analysis shows that the security deficiencies of masquerading and hijacking, which have been identified for the original correspondent router protocol, have been resolved by SeNERO.

The efficiency analysis considers handover latency and protocol signaling overhead. The evaluation of the *handover latency* is performed as a comparison between the original correspondent router protocol and SeNERO. It is based on an analytical model and implementations within a test-bed and simulation environment. The different results obtained from these three approaches are also compared to each other. This is possible due to using the same scenarios throughout all evaluation methods. The test-bed environment is based on the already existing Linux-based implementation for Mobile IP/NEMO. Within the work conducted for this thesis, this implementation has been extended with correspondent router functionality and signaling for both the original and new protocol. Similarly, the simulation framework OMNeT++ [209] and its INET framework has been extended with a Mobile IP implementation to allow the simulation of mobile nodes within IP based networks. Based on this work, NEMO, the original correspondent router protocol and SeNERO have been implemented. Furthermore, a realistic aeronautical wireless link technology has been embedded to increase the level of realism of the simulations. The signaling overhead evaluation is performed analytically, comparing the original correspondent router protocol and SeNERO against each other.

Due to the underlying public key infrastructure, SeNERO requires a certificate authority that is trusted by both the mobile router and the correspondent router. This trust anchor, especially its certificate revocation service, must be available for certificate validation during runtime, when the authentication in SeNERO is performed. This could be regarded as another single point of failure. This thesis therefore defines an *extension to identity certificates*, which permits verifying an X.509 certificate [45] without relying on a global trust anchor during runtime. Instead, a distributed architecture is introduced. These certificates are constructed iteratively where each certificate authority adds relevant information to the certificate. E. g., an IP address authority adds IP address related information to the certificate. Each certificate authority also adds a signature to bind this information to the public key of the certificate holder. At the end of this process, the certificate authority of each correspondent network domain verifies this information. Such a certificate authority, also called local certificate authority, then signs and issues the certificate. When an authentication to a correspondent router within a certain correspondent network is performed, the mobile router uses the certificate that has been issued by the certificate authority located in the same correspondent network as the correspondent router. The correspondent router can validate this certificate by only verifying the signature and revocation information provided by the local certificate authority, which assures the validity and integrity of the information contained within the certificate. Similarly, the correspondent router can authenticate to the mobile router using a certificate issued by the same local certificate authority. These authentication operations only require the local certificate authority located within the correspondent network as trust anchor, but no other certificate authority/trust anchor. No inter-domain operations with a certificate authority located in another network domain are necessary during the authentication at runtime. The single point of failure represented by a global trust anchor has therefore been replaced by a distributed component, the local certificate authorities located in each correspondent network. This advantage is also preserved by the revocation mechanism that is introduced for use with the extended identity certificate model. In addition, this approach also permits to support the trust model of the aeronautical environment. Every country or region where a mobile router has to authenticate itself can operate a local certificate authority. Prior to the first flight, an extended identity certificate will be requested from each local certificate authority that is then used for authentication within the SeNERO protocol. In case a country does not permit an aircraft to enter its airspace, no certificate will be issued or an already issued certificate will be revoked by the country's local certificate authority. Related work on security in aeronautical communications does not address the single point of failure aspect [22, 164, 178, 180]. Neither does the work in other communication areas, such as Car-to-X communications [161, 171] or grid computing [31, 44]. This is also the case for more generic approaches that do not consider a specific application area [126, 163]. None of the related work specifies a requirement for either a distributed PKI architecture or for avoiding inter-domain operations with a global trust anchor during certificate validation.

The evaluation of the certificate extension is based on a theoretical approach, using Maurer's logical calculus [133]. The calculus has been extended to support the modeling of cross-certification, which is required by the extended certificate model. The calculus has also been extended to support modeling of the extended identity certificates. Using logical inferencing, the validity of the extended identity certificates of Alice (correspondent router) and Bob (mobile router) are shown. More detailed, Alice (correspondent router) can derive the authenticity of the public key of Bob (mobile router) and his associated IP address prefix. Similarly, Bob can derive the authenticity of Alice's public key and her associated IP address prefix.

The contributions of this thesis have been published in:

- Christian Bauer, A Secure Correspondent Router Protocol for NEMO Route Optimization, *Elsevier Computer Networks*, 2013.
- Christian Bauer, X.509 Identity Certificates with Local Verification, In *Proceedings of the International Conference on Communications (ICC) Workshops, International Workshop on Security and Forensics in Communication Systems*, June 2012, Ottawa, Canada.
- Christian Bauer and Martina Zitterbart, A Survey of Protocols to Support IP Mobility in Aeronautical Communications, *IEEE Communications Surveys & Tutorials*, vol.13, no.4, pp. 642-657, Fourth Quarter 2011.
- Christian Bauer, NEMO Route Optimization with Strong Authentication for Aeronautical Communications, In *Proceedings of the 22nd Annual IEEE International Symposium On Personal, Indoor and Mobile Radio Communications*, PIMRC'11, September 2011, Toronto, Canada.
- Christian Bauer, Network Mobility Route Optimization with Certificate-based Authentication, In *Proceedings of the International Conference on Ubiquitous and Future Networks*, ICUFN'09, June 2009, Hong Kong, China.
- Faqir Zarrar Yousaf, Christian Bauer, and Christian Wietfeld, An accurate and extensible Mobile IPv6 (xMIPv6) simulation model for OMNeT++, In *Simutools '08: Proceedings of the 1st International Conference on Simulation Tools and Techniques for Communications, Networks and Systems & Workshops*, 2008, Marseille, France.

The last paper describes the implementation of the Mobile IPv6 protocol within the simulation framework. This topic is not further discussed within this thesis though.

1.3. Structure

The fundamental textbook material necessary for understanding this thesis is introduced in Chapter 2. This covers recent developments in aeronautical communications, wireless communications in IP based networks and information security.

Related work on NEMO route optimization protocols and security aspects for both Mobile IP and NEMO route optimization is discussed in Chapter 3.

Chapter 4 introduces the new correspondent router based protocol for NEMO route optimization that provides strong security properties while still being efficient in terms of signaling when compared to the related work.

Chapter 5 defines a threat model with a focus on mobility specific adversary locations and attack types. This model is then used to evaluate both the new and the original correspondent router protocol.

Chapter 6 provides a handover performance evaluation based on an analytical model as well as test-bed and simulation results.

Chapter 7 specifies an extension to identity certificates and associated certificates for mobile router and correspondent router for use within the SeNERO protocol. The extended certificate model permits a verifier to validate a certificate without requiring a global trust anchor located in another domain. Instead, only a local certificate authority is required.

In Chapter 8, a proof based on Maurer's calculus is used to show the validity of the extended identity certificate defined for the mobile router and correspondent router. These proofs are performed from the perspective of the certificate verifiers, both the mobile router and correspondent router.

Finally, Chapter 9 provides a summary and an outlook on other topics that have not been covered within this thesis.

2. Fundamentals

This chapter provides the background information that is necessary for understanding the content of this thesis. Section 2.1 provides an overview on (future) digital aeronautical information and communication systems. Section 2.2 provides an overview of wireless communications and mobile routing in Internet Protocol (IP) based networks, with a special emphasis on IPv6. Finally, Section 2.3 introduces basic information security aspects, cryptographic schemes and mechanisms for securing communication protocols.

2.1. The Aeronautical Environment

The tools and procedures used today for air traffic management are inefficient and already approaching their limits. They are therefore unable to support the future air traffic growth.

The underlying communication system between an aircraft and the ground is still based on analogue voice. More than 50% of the current air-ground voice communication load is not related to operational exchanges, but instead on repetitions for resolving misunderstandings or instructions related to radio cell handovers, etc. [72]. As a consequence, digital communication systems are currently being developed to provide the capacity for civil aviation that can not be accommodated with the current system [109, 187]. Besides the capacity problems, the intention of the aeronautical community is also to move from analogue technologies (analogue voice, paper notes, etc.) to digital information systems (packet data, software components within the aircraft, etc.) for aircraft operations.

To support the different operational settings for communicating with aircraft in and around airports, over continental areas as well as over oceanic, remote and polar regions, the future communications environment will consist of a heterogeneous set of wireless access technologies. A so called *network-centric* operation can then be supported, where the aircraft will be integrated into a global network [172]. This allows near real-time transport of data between the aircraft and ground based information systems located at air traffic authorities, airlines, etc.

A common network protocol can integrate these different wireless access technologies. The Internet Protocol (IP) is the most widely used protocol in the Internet. It has been adopted for aeronautical communications [104], due to several reasons: a large variety of products and vendors, a high level of maturity when compared to (aeronautical) proprietary solutions, continuous development efforts provided by other industries, etc.

An overview of the envisaged future IP based aeronautical communications system will be provided in the following, starting from the different service classes, the aircraft on-board network, the aeronautical access technologies, ground networks and finally the future applications and services. This summary is restricted to airliners in the context of civil aviation. Such an aircraft will also be called a *mobile network* within the generic context of IP based wireless communications.

2.1.1. Service Classes

Aeronautical communications consists of four different service classes [55, 145]:

1. Air Traffic Services (ATS)
2. Aeronautical Operational Control (AOC)
3. Aeronautical Administrative Communication (AAC)
4. Aeronautical Passenger Communication (APC)

ATS covers communication related to air traffic services including air traffic control, aeronautical and meteorological information, position reporting and services related to the safety and regularity of a flight. Air traffic control communications takes place between the aircraft and one or more ATS controllers. A controller is responsible for a number of aircraft within a certain geographical region. When the aircraft leaves this region, control is handed over to another controller. In today's operations, the ATS controller itself is geographically close to the aircraft it is controlling.

AOC communications is required for the exercise of authority over the initiation, continuation, diversion or termination of a flight for safety, regularity and efficiency reasons. The ground based communication nodes for aeronautical operational control are located at the airline headquarters or at an airline operations center.

AAC is used by aeronautical operating agencies (airlines) to support the business aspects of operating their flights and transport services. This type of communication is used for a variety of purposes, such as flight and ground transportation, bookings, deployment of crew and aircraft or any other logistical purposes that maintain or enhance the efficiency of operation of the flight. The location of the communication peers is similar to aeronautical operational control, but can also include correspondent nodes located at the airports.

APC relates to non-safety voice and data services for passengers and crew members for the purpose of personal communication. The correspondent nodes for aeronautical passenger communication are usually located in the public Internet or inside corporate networks.

ATS and AOC are specified as being *safety related* communications. AAC and APC are considered being non-safety related.

2.1.2. The Digital Aircraft

The most recent generation of aircraft are considered being *digital* [181, 182] due to using recent information and communication technologies. An on-board packet switched network and a wireless access technology allows off-board digital communication with airline systems or airport users for the purpose of AAC as of today. There are also satellite based access technologies in use today for providing APC. In the future, off-board communications will be supported for all four aeronautical service classes (ATS, AOC, AAC, APC).

The Avionics Full Duplex Switched Ethernet (AFDX) standard [7] specifies a packet switching network for use within the aircraft. It is based upon the IEEE 802.3 Ethernet standard [101] with enhancements to provide additional features such as redundancy, deterministic behavior and guaranteed bandwidth. Being based on the Ethernet standard, AFDX is capable of transporting IP packets.

An aircraft does not consist of a single network domain, as illustrated in Figure 2.1. The reference architecture specified in [10, 159] identifies three aircraft network domains.

The "closed" domain contains systems that are used for aircraft control, including air traffic services. The "private" domain consists of systems for operating the aircraft and for informing and entertaining passengers. The "public" domain includes devices that are brought onboard the aircraft by passengers. Segregation has to be enforced between the different network domains. All safety related systems (ATS, AOC) are located inside the closed domain. Non-safety related systems (AAC, APC) are located in the private and public domains.

It is important to note that within currently deployed on-board network architectures, there is a physical separation between the "closed" domain and the other domains. This is for security reasons and also enforced by regulation authorities, cf. [63, 65]. As a consequence, there are two dedicated airborne routers within the aircraft, e.g. one serving the "closed" domain and one serving the "private" domain.

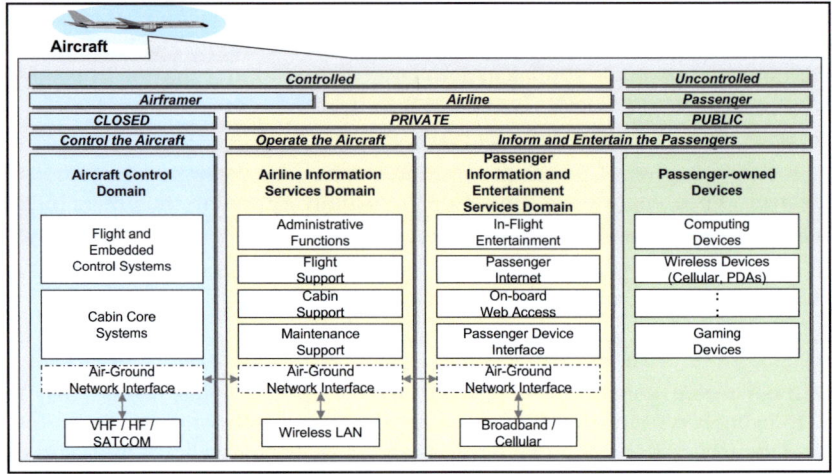

Figure 2.1. Reference architecture for the networked aircraft. From [10].

The Integrated Modular Avionics (IMA) architecture specified in [6] is considered to be an evolution to the current aircraft avionics architecture. It relies on a switched network such as AFDX and provides a modular, distributed architecture. An IMA module is a hardware platform that allows safety compliant sharing of hardware resources (CPU, memory, network access) between several software functions hosted on the same IMA module [186]. This sharing mechanism, specified in ARINC 653 [8], can be considered as a type of virtualization technique where space[1] and time[2] partitioning ensures that a failure in one software module does not affect any other software module. A comparison of ARINC 653 to other virtualization techniques is available in [71].

A single IMA platform can host different virtual network hosts supporting different applications, primarily within the "closed" domain but also within the "private" domain.

2.1.3. Wireless Access Technologies

An aircraft will be connected to the ground via a variety of different wireless access technologies A list of these (future) technologies and their characteristics is provided in Table 2.1. Forward link refers to the direction base station to mobile station and return link refers to the direction mobile station to base station. The

---

[1]The protection of the memory, registers and dedicated I/O assigned to a function.
[2]The protection of processor time and communications bandwidth assigned to a function.

Link Technology	Type	Bandwidth	BER	FER
Gatelink [146]	Short-Range	54 Mbps	10^{-5}	n/a
Inmarsat SBB [146]	Satellite	432 Kbps	FL: 10^{-6} RL: 10^{-4}	n/a
AeroMACS [146]	Short-Range	30 Mbps	10^{-5}	n/a
L-DACS 1 [78]	Long-Range	FL: 1370 Kbps RL: 1000 Kbps	4.81^{-4} to 9.1^{-7}	6.29^{-2} to 6.31^{-5}
L-DACS 2 [48]	Long-Range	275 Kbps	10^{-3} to 10^{-7}	n/a
IRIS	Satellite	FL: 4.85 Mbps RL: 0.76 Mbps	n/a	10^{-2} to 10^{-4}

Table 2.1. Characteristics of (future) wireless aeronautical access technologies for safety related services supporting the Internet Protocol. FL refers to forward link, RL refers to return link.

numbers listed for bandwidth are the maxima and are per radio cell and not per user. Gatelink and Inmarsat SBB are two technologies in use today capable of carrying Internet Protocol packets. The rest of the list is constrained to future access technologies foreseen to support safety related services (ATS, AOC). As this thesis focuses on protocols for supporting safety related services, any other already existing or future technology for supporting non-safety related services is not listed.

The technologies can be separated into three classes, depending on the airspace where the individual technologies are supposed to be used:

- Short-range, for use within the airport area.
- Long-rage, for use during flight over continental areas.
- Satellite technologies, primarily for use when the aircraft is above oceanic, remote or polar regions.

Gatelink [9] is an already existing system based on the IEEE 802.11b/g standard [99]. It is only used for AAC while the aircraft is located at the gate in the airport.

Inmarsat SwiftBroadBand (SBB) is a satellite access technology in use today capable of carrying Internet Protocol packets. It is only used for AAC and APC.

The Aeronautical Mobile Airport Communications System (AeroMACS) is currently under development and will be based on a profile of the IEEE 802.16e [100] standard, also called Mobile WiMAX.

The L-band Digital Aeronautical Communication System (LDACS) will serve as the primary wireless access technology while the aircraft is flying over continental areas. There are currently two candidates, L-DACS 1 and 2, of whom one will be selected in the future. As L-DACS 1 has been used in the simulations in Chapter 4, a more detailed description of this technology is provided later.

The IRIS satellite system is supposed to provide an IP based communication service for safety related services in the European region. No technical specification is available at the time of this writing. The characteristics specified in Table 2.1 are requirements for the future system, as also defined in [139].[3]

Apart from Gatelink and Inmarsat, all of the above mentioned technologies will carry data traffic for both ATS and AOC. It is common to all these technologies that the provided amount of bandwidth is limited. Compared to other wireless communication areas such as personal communications in the 3GPP context, the available capacity in terms of bit/sec is very small. The aeronautical communications environment must therefore consider bandwidth as a scarce resource – it is a *bandwidth constrained* environment. It should also be noted that these technologies, apart from the AeroMACS system, do not provide any security mechanisms at the time of writing.

L-DACS 1

L-DACS 1 is a point-to-multipoint system where a communication service is established between a mobile station (aircraft) and a base station [73, 78]. While this system is optimized for data communications, it also supports air-ground voice communications. It is operated as an Orthogonal Frequency-Division Multiplexing (OFDM) based frequency division duplexing (FDD) system, consisting of an asymmetric pair of forward (base station to mobile station) and return link (mobile station to base station). While data transmission on the forward link is based on OFDM only, the return link uses Orthogonal Frequency-Division Multiple Access (OFDMA) with Time Division Multiple Access (TDMA). In both directions data is sent within OFDM frames, protected by Forward Error Correction (FEC) coding.

The OFDM(A)-based physical layer provides three different time slot types on the reverse link (Random Access slot RA, Dedicated Control slot DC, and DATA slot) and three different time slot types on the forward link (Broadcast Control slot BC, Common Control slot CC, and DATA slot). The assignment of time slots

---

[3]These numbers might be subject to further changes.

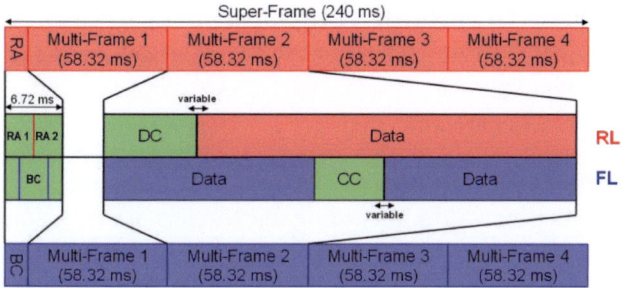

Figure 2.2. L-DACS 1 super frame structure.

to mobile stations for sending data via the return link is performed on demand by the base station.

The slots are embedded into a hierarchical frame structure of a super-frame (time slot length of 240 ms) that comprises four multi-frames (time slot length of each 58.32 ms). The super frame structure is shown in Figure 2.2.

User data between mobile station and base station is exchanged within the logical data channel (DCH) that is transmitted in the DATA frame. Control plane messages for managing the point-to-point connection between mobile station and base station are sent over the logical dedicated control channel (DCCH) that is mapped to the DC slot. Forward link control information is transmitted in the common control channel (CCCH) that is mapped to the CC slot. The random access channel (RACH) and the broadcast control channel (BCCH) are used for radio cell registration and handover signaling and are mapped to the RA and BC slots. A summary of these mappings is provided in Table 2.2.

Depending on the specific coding and modulation scheme used, L-DACS 1 provides a user data capacity starting from 303 Kbit/s on the FL and 220 Kbit/s on the RL and going up to 1373 Kbit/s (FL) and 1038 Kbit/s (RL).

Logical Channel	Time Slot
DCH	DATA
DCCH	DC
CCCH	CC
RACH	RA
BCCH	BC

Table 2.2. Mapping of logical control channels to time slots.

17

2.1.4. The Aeronautical Telecommunications Network

The future aeronautical communications environment will consist of different individual networks:

- Mobile networks (aircraft).
- Ground networks, which also contain the ground based communication partners (correspondent nodes).
- Wireless access networks, providing the wireless access technologies used by the aircraft.

The aeronautical telecommunications network (ATN) is a global network interconnecting all these networks for the purpose of supporting safety related services – ATS and AOC. As part of the International Civil Aviation Organization (ICAO) Convention, ICAO has published Annex 10 which standardizes the aeronautical telecommunications network. An initial definition of the future IPv6 based aeronautical telecommunications network has been published in the ICAO ATN IPS Manual [104]. The aeronautical telecommunications network will not be physically separated network but will instead rely on the public Internet; the ATN can be considered being an overlay network – a network topology that is build on top of the Internet infrastructure.

The networks within the aeronautical telecommunications network are operated by three different actors:

- An Air Navigation Service Provider (ANSP) is a national entity managing air traffic within a country. Usually, each ANSP has its own network that contains the ATS controllers (correspondent nodes). In addition the ANSP might also provide a wireless access network where an aircraft can attach to. The ATS controllers (correspondent nodes) with whom an aircraft is communicating with are located inside the ANSP networks.
- An Air Communications Service Provider (ACSP) operates transit networks and wireless access networks. As of today, there are two ACSPs utilizing terrestrial and satellite access technologies for supporting non-IP based ATS and AOC services. There might be additional providers in the future offering similar services.
- Airline Operations (AO) refers to an airline headquarter or operations center. Within the context of safety related communications, an aircraft will communicate with correspondent nodes that are located inside an AO network.

The current business model [59] foresees that air navigation service providers are responsible for providing wireless access networks to aircraft within their national geographical boundaries. An air navigation service provider might operate this wireless access network by itself or contract an air communications service provider for establishing such a network.

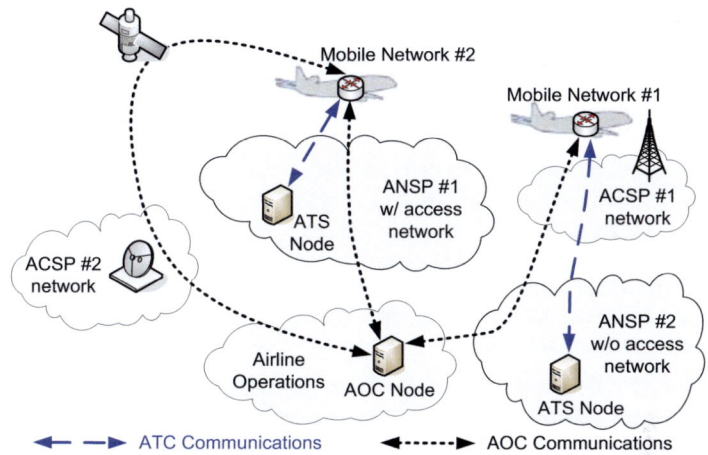

Figure 2.3. Example for aeronautical telecommunications network consisting of mobile networks, ground networks and wireless access networks.

In terms of topology, the ATN has a similar structure as the Internet, based on autonomous systems. An example is provided for illustrative purposes in Figure 2.3. For simplicity, only a single correspondent node is shown in each network. Apart from the mobile networks, five different networks are depicted, each one being an autonomous system by itself. The two air communications service providers (ACSP #1 and #2) operate wireless access networks that provide a point of attachment to the aircraft via either a terrestrial or a satellite based access technology. The airline operations network contains the correspondent node(s) of the aircraft for aeronautical operational control communications (AOC). The air navigation service provider networks (ANSP #1 and #2) contain the correspondent node(s) for air traffic services (ATS) communications. Routing between these different autonomous systems is achieved by using the Border Gateway Protocol (BGP), whose use as inter-domain routing protocol within the aeronautical telecommunications network has been specified in the ATN IPS manual [104].

This example also illustrates the two network attachment options of the mobile network for safety related communications. In the first case, mobile network #1 directly attaches to the wireless access network that is operated by the air navigation service provider. For air traffic control communications, the mobile network and the correspondent node are then located within the same autonomous system. In the second case, mobile network #2 attaches to a wireless access network that is operated by the air communications service provider, on behalf of the air navigation service provider. In that case, mobile network and correspondent node are only separated by a single autonomous system hop.

2.1.5. Applications and Services

Non-safety related applications are not discussed in this section. An initial description of the future applications and services that will be used in the IP-based aeronautical telecommunications network has been specified in [61]. The document provides a list of safety related, ATS and AOC, applications that are supposed to replace the current analogue voice based system as the primary means of air-ground communication. A major fraction of these applications are based on unicast communication.

The defined 32 ATS applications have been grouped into eight categories. These range from data communications management services, flight information services up to emergency information services. The different applications are used for exchanging reports and clearances between a flight crew and the ATS controller, for flight trajectory negotiation between the aircraft and the ATS controller, for providing flight crews with meteorological and operational flight information, offering a flight crew an alternative flight route, etc. Emergency applications are used for notifying appropriate ground authorities when the aircraft is in a state of emergency, when an ATS controller has to establish urgent contact with a flight crew or for sending a collision resolution trajectory from a ground automation system to the aircraft, possibly for execution without human interaction.

ATS applications have high *availability* requirements in the range between 0.999 and 0.9999995. While the former refers to a maximum yearly downtime of 9 hours, the latter refers to a downtime of 1 minute.

Air traffic control voice communication might also have to be supported by the future IP based aeronautical telecommunications network [110]. The latency requirements for Voice over IP state that a latency of up to 150 ms allows to "experience essentially transparent interactivity", while latencies above 400 ms are usually considered as "unacceptable" [106].

For AOC, 21 different applications are defined. They are used for position reports, flight status information (e. g. malfunction reports), fuel reports, engine performance reports, real-time aircraft parameter reporting to the airline maintenance base, weather and map information, etc.

Of increasing importance is the usage of on-board wireless sensor networks for airplane health monitoring [96]. It is expected that some of this health data will have to be sent off-board from the aircraft to ground facilities during the flight. These sensors implement safety related functions, such as monitoring of the structural integrity and avionics status, pressure sensing, smoke and fire detection, etc.

Some of this sensor data is expected to be made available to ground systems in real time, which is defined as "the minimum possible time delay from the time data is generated by a sensor to the time it is delivered to a ground processing facility". Certain data is also expected to meet a near-real time requirement, such that "data is transmitted off-board within several seconds" [96].

2.1.6. IP Mobility in Aeronautical Communications

The typical scenario of ATS communications starts with an end-system inside the mobile network (aircraft) communicating with an ATS controller at the airport tower while still at the gate. In the future aeronautical telecommunications network, this communication is initiated while being connected to the AeroMACS access network. Before take off, the aircraft will perform a handover to the L-DACS access network. The ongoing communication between the on-board end-system within the mobile network and the ATS controller has to be kept alive though. However, due to the handover from AeroMACS to L-DACS, the IP address of the mobile network will change. Such handovers also occur when crossing airspace domains, as each country will have a wireless access network of it's own. In Section 2.2.6, the issue of mobility in IP based networks will be outlined in more detail. In the following, the benefits of using a mobility protocol within the aeronautical communications environment are outlined.

A mobility protocol would provide a "persistent" IP address that is used for end-to-end communication between the end-system inside the mobile network and a ground based ATS controller. This allows to preserve already established communication in the presence of handovers, as this address is independent of the mobile networks current topological position.

Another example for the usefulness of a mobility protocol are future operational concepts where a "personal" ATS controller is assigned to an aircraft. A single controller is then responsible for long durations of a flight, instead of having a series of changing controllers [26]. A similar concept is envisaged for the future European airspace. During low air traffic situations, a flight above France and Germany could be controlled by only a single controller of either Germany or France. This implies that, while performing handovers between the different wireless access networks in Germany and France, the communication between an aircraft and it's personal ATS controller located in one of these two countries has to be kept alive.

Another issue is the availability of globally routable (public) IP addresses within the aircraft: on-board end-systems should be capable of obtaining a global IP address for permitting end-to-end communications. The airborne router obtains such addresses for its off-board network interfaces from the wireless access networks. A Network Address Translator (NAT) would allow sharing of these addresses among all on-board end-systems. This however causes problems as discussed in [141], e. g. with end-to-end security protocols such as IPsec authentication header. Apart from this issue, a NAT is also not capable of preserving already established communication, due to the change of IP address at the off-board network interfaces. In contrast to this, a mobility protocol would provide "persistent" global IP addresses for use within a mobile network that can be used by the on-board end-systems.

Nowadays, ATS communication is always aircraft-initiated. In the future it might become interesting to provide an ATS controller with the means to contact an aircraft that has entered controlled airspace but not yet established communication. A global "persistent" IP address space for the mobile network, independent of the current topological location, would allow for ground-initiated communications.

Summarized, due to the heterogeneous network environment consisting of different wireless access technologies and administrative domains (service and navigation providers), handovers will occur. Without mobility protocol support, this results in the issue that ongoing communication would have to be reestablished due to the change of the aircraft's IP address after each handover.

This implies the need for an IP mobility protocol that permits session continuity, provides global on-board IP address space and offers the possibility to support ground-initiated communications.

However, several constraints are present for supporting IP mobility in the aeronautical scenario:

- An aircraft is not just a mobile host, but instead a mobile network with different network domains that contain more than one end-system.
- A high level of security has to be provided, due to the nature of the exchanged traffic, which includes air traffic control communications. Attacks that jeopardize the routing of packets from and to the mobile network should not be possible.
- Applications and services of the safety related domain have stringent latency requirements, with some of them requiring "real-time" data transport. A small end-to-end latency should therefore be provided when routing data between the aircraft and its ground based communication peers.
- Air traffic services applications have high requirements in terms of availability. The availability numbers of up to 0.9999995 also have to be fulfilled by the mobility protocol as the applications rely on its proper functioning.
- The bandwidth provided by the wireless access technologies is limited when compared to other communication areas. A mobility protocol should therefore attempt to keep the signaling message load small.

2.1.7. Distinction From Other Communication Areas

The aeronautical communications environment is not the only one facing IP mobility problems. It does however differ from other areas, as explained in the following.

Wireless personal communications based on mobile phones, as defined by the 3rd Generation Partnership Project (3GPP), make use of IP mobility management as well [75]. The major differences are that mobile phones are only mobile hosts and not mobile networks like an aircraft. Mobile phones also have a lower degree of mobility.

The Car2Car communications environment has to support several end-systems within a car and thus acts as mobile network. A major difference of the Car2Car protocol stack is the dual-stack approach that not only consists of IP but also relies heavily on dedicated Car2Car protocols for safety related communications [20]. In addition, the degree of mobility and covered distance is smaller when compared to an aircraft – mobility of cars is usually constrained to a single continent.

Summarized, the critical aspects within aeronautical communications, in contrast to other areas, are: a high degree of mobility that will cause delay problems due to routing over large geographical distances as well as a need for high security and availability.

2.1.8. Protocols to Support IP Mobility in Aeronautical Communications

A variety of protocols exist that could be used for supporting mobility of aircraft in the future IP based aeronautical telecommunications network. Those protocols have been investigated and their individual strengths and weaknesses identified, based on a particular set of requirements. A short summary of this investigation is provided in the following. The more detailed discussion is provided in Appendix B.

2.1.8.1. Requirements

The primary requirements that should be fulfilled by the candidate protocols are as follows:

1. Mobile network support: mobility should not only be provided for a single mobile host, but for a complete on-board network. More specifically, instead of providing a single IP address, one or several persistent network prefixes should be provided to the aircraft.

2. Multihoming: the aircraft should be capable of routing data simultaneously over different interfaces/paths from the aircraft to the ground

3. Security 1: an adversary must not be able to claim the IP addresses of an aircraft.

4. Security 2: the mobility protocol itself should not introduce any new denial of service vulnerabilities.

5. End-to-end delay: the delay between the communicating nodes (within the aircraft and on the ground) should be kept minimal.

6. Routing scalability: the impact of the mobility protocol on the global routing infrastructure should be kept to a minimum.

7. Applicability to aeronautical administrative communication/aeronautical passenger communication: the solution should also be applicable to non-safety related services, by avoiding modifications within the protocol stacks of the end-systems. Especially for the passenger domain it is unlikely that popular, frequently visited web servers in the public Internet will upgrade their protocol stacks with mobility extensions.

The requirement "Applicability to AAC/APC" expresses the preference to have a single protocol (family) as a solution for both the safety and the non-safety related network domains. The rationale for this requirement is that a single protocol family used in all domains allows for easier maintenance and reduces costs.

Secondary requirements are desirable and their fulfillment is a bonus:

1. Efficiency 1: the amount of mobility protocol signaling should be limited.

2. Efficiency 2: the overhead imposed upon every individual packet exchanged between the end-systems should be limited.

3. Convergence time: a new routing path from and to the mobile network (e.g. because a new network interface has been activated) should become usable for packet forwarding within the shortest possible amount of time.

4. Support for ground-initiated communications: end-systems on the ground should be capable of sending packets to an aircraft they have not yet communicated with.

2.1.8.2. Protocol Options

The evaluation is focused on protocols on the network and transport layer. Five different approaches have been identified that can be categorized as follows:

- Routing protocol based approach (network layer), with the example of the Border Gateway Protocol (BGP).
- Tunneling based approaches (network layer), with the examples of the IPsec and Mobile IP/NEMO protocol families.
- A transport protocol approach, with the example of the Stream Control Transmission Protocol (SCTP).

Protocol	BGP	IPsec	NEMO	SCTP	HIP
Mobile Network Support	⊕⊕	⊕⊕	⊕⊕	⊖	⊕⊕
Multihoming	⊙	⊖	⊕⊕	⊖	⊙
Security 1	⊕⊕	⊕⊕	⊕⊕	⊖	⊕⊕
Security 2	⊕/⊙	⊙	⊙	⊙	⊙
End-to-end delay	⊕⊕	⊖	⊖	⊕⊕	⊕⊕
Scalability	⊖	⊕	⊕	⊕⊕	⊙
Applicability to AAC/APC	⊕⊕	⊕⊕	⊕⊕	⊖	⊖
Convergence time	⊙	⊕⊕	⊕⊕	⊕⊕	⊕
Efficiency 1	⊖	⊕	⊕	⊕	⊙
Efficiency 2	⊕	⊖⊖	⊖	⊕	⊙
Ground-initiated comms.	⊕⊕	⊕⊕	⊕⊕	⊖	⊕

Table 2.3. Mobility requirements fulfillment of all candidate approaches. Grading can be either completely fulfilled/optimal (⊕⊕), basically fulfilled/fair (⊕), with limitations/average (⊙) or unsupported/poor (⊖).

- Locater-identifier split (IP address as locator that is mapped to an identifier used by the transport layer), with the example of the Host Identity Protocol (HIP).

A summary of the evaluation results is provided in Table 2.3. Again, the more detailed discussion can be found in Appendix B.

The host identity protocol suffers from the major problem that it has to be implemented within end-systems. This causes difficulties for already existing non-safety related airline systems (aeronautical administrative communication) and makes it infeasible for deployment within the passenger domain (aeronautical passenger communication), where public web servers in the Internet would have to be upgraded. The host identity protocol is also unable to fulfill a primary requirement, as it is not able to provide the desired multihoming capabilities.

Similarly, the stream control transmission protocol does also not provide the desired multihoming support. Another critical aspect is the fact that this protocol can only support a mobile host, but is unable to provide mobility for a complete mobile network. It is also necessary to modify the end-systems, thereby causing the same problems as for the host identity protocol with respect to non-safety related systems (aeronautical administrative communication/aeronautical passenger communication).

The major problem of the border gateway protocol is scalability, especially with respect to the non-safety related domains that are routed via the public Internet.

The small number of aircraft would cause a significant impact upon the global routing system. Another issue is the limited multihoming capability.

IPsec and the NEMO protocol are very similar to each other. IPsec suffers from the lack of multihoming capabilities. NEMO, as a generic mobility protocol providing a multitude of features, only suffers from problems with the end-to-end delay.

A close look at Table 2.3 shows that, taking into account all gradings, NEMO is the best rated solution. It is therefore argued that this protocol is the most feasible solution for the aeronautical environment, although one problem remains to be solved: end-to-end latency, which is referred to as the route optimization problem.

2.2. Wireless Communications

The following section provides an overview of wireless communications and the Internet Protocol (IP) suite. Parts of this introduction are based on [24, 120, 184].

A network is a collection of nodes that are inter-connected by *links*. The Internet, as an example for a global network, is not only a collection of nodes but a collection of interconnected networks. Nodes can communicate with each other by sending *packets*. A network node can be either a router or a host. *Routers* forward traffic between different links and networks. *Hosts*, also called end-systems, are the sources and sinks where data traffic originates and terminates.

2.2.1. Addressing

A packet can be exchanged between a pair of nodes or between a larger set of nodes, from the sender to a single or a group of receivers. Either way, a packet is always specifically addressed in order to allow forwarding to the intended recipient or group of recipients. The four most widely used types of addresses are presented in the following.

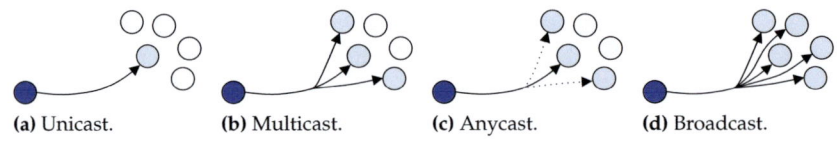

(a) Unicast.   (b) Multicast.   (c) Anycast.   (d) Broadcast.

Figure 2.4. Addressing.

Unicast
Unicast refers to one-to-one communication between two nodes. In unicast transmissions, packets are sent to an address that uniquely identifies a single node. This is illustrated in Figure 2.4a.

For most applications in the Internet, packets are exchanged between two nodes based on unicast addresses.

Multicast
Multicast refers to one-to many communication between one sender and a group of recipients. In multicast transmissions, packets are sent to an address that uniquely identifies the multicast receiver group. Any node wishing to receive these packets has to join the respective multicast group. This is illustrated in Figure 2.4b.

Anycast
Anycast combines elements of unicast and multicast: while a packet is addressed to a group of recipients, the packet will only be forwarded to a particular node of that group. This is illustrated in Figure 2.4c.

Broadcast
Broadcasting refers to another type of one-to many communication. The difference to multicast is the one-to-all relation. If a sender broadcasts a packet, it is sent to all nodes within a certain domain. This is illustrated in Figure 2.4d.

2.2.2. Wireless Links

A link connecting two nodes can be either wired or wireless. Irrespective of the specific type, the underlying physical communication channel can always be considered as a bit pipe: a sender transmits a sequence of bits over the channel to a receiver. At the receiver side, an identical copy of the originally transmitted bits should be received. The transmission of bits is usually not performed as a continuous stream, but instead in blocks of data. The data unit used for sending bits across a link is often called *frame*. While a frame only refers to a data unit on the wireless link, a packet – as introduced on page 26 – refers to a data unit on the end-to-end path.

The transmission of data over a wireless channel is especially prone to transmission errors due to interference, etc. [184, Chapter 2]. A number of bit errors can therefore occur, specifying the number of erroneous bits that have not been correctly received. The *bit error rate* (BER) is calculated by the number of erroneous bits divided by the complete number of received bits. It is often expressed as 10^{-x}, indicating that one erroneous bit has to be expected within 10^x transmitted bits. Similarly, the *frame error rate* (FER) is calculated by the number of erroneous frames divided by the complete number of received frames.

One typical approach for resolving bit errors is to retransmit the erroneous frames in which the error(s) occurred by means of an Automatic Repeat reQuest (ARQ) mechanism. Another approach is the usage of forward error correction (FEC), which provides redundancy within a frame that can be used for reconstructing the original data in the presence of errors. FEC and ARQ can also be combined. A more detailed overview on these approaches is available in [184].

The amount of data that can be transmitted via a communication channel is expressed in (kilo or mega)bit/second, abbreviated as (K/M)bit/s.

2.2.2.1. Wireless Access Networks

In infrastructure-based wireless networks, the *base station* is the point of attachment with whom the host establishes a radio link when inside the radio cell. In Internet Protocol (IP) based networks, a base station will be associated with an *access router* that provides forwarding of IP packets for the hosts that have established radio links to this base station.

A set of base stations and access routers form a wireless *access network*. Such a network is operated by a wireless *access service provider*.

The radio used by the host for attaching to a base station is also called a wireless *network interface*. Each network interface has a unique Media Access Control (MAC) address that is specified in [98]. The address is 48 bit long and used as source address of a frame. The MAC address is also called link-layer address.

Frames are exchanged between host and base station via the radio link using addresses as defined in Section 2.2.1. A frame with the MAC address of a host and base station as source and destination address would conform to the unicast communication model.

2.2.2.2. Base Station Handover

An important aspect of wireless communications is the fact that (mobile) hosts can move between different wireless access networks. Performing a *handover* refers to moving between these networks and preserving ongoing traffic flows upon occurrence of such an event.

A handover can be mobile or network initiated, where either the mobile host or an entity within the access network decides when and to which base station a handover is performed. As this thesis focuses on mobile initiated handovers, a description for network initiated handovers is omitted.

The generic mobile initiated handover procedure for associating to a base station is as follows. Base stations periodically broadcast beacon messages, which include network related information. A mobile host will receive this information. The handover itself then consists of two steps:

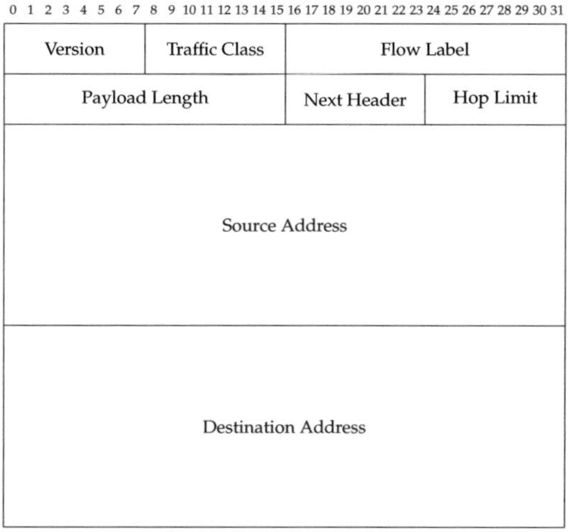

0 1 2 3 4 5 6 7 8 9 10 11 12 13 14 15 16 17 18 19 20 21 22 23 24 25 26 27 28 29 30 31

Version	Traffic Class	Flow Label	
Payload Length		Next Header	Hop Limit

Source Address

Destination Address

Figure 2.5. IPv6 protocol header.

- Handover preparation
- Handover execution

The preparation phase consists of comparing neighbors based on certain metrics (signal strength, pricing, etc.) and selecting a target base station. Once a target base station has been selected, the handover execution phase is entered. The mobile host may send a handover indication message to the serving base station as notification for the imminent handover, which the base station may use to free reserved resources. The mobile host then negotiates basic capabilities, eventually followed by authentication and key exchange procedures before finally registering with the target base station. As soon as registration is completed, the mobile host has successfully established a radio link with the target base station. This link can then be used for transmitting and receiving data.

2.2.3. Internet Protocol Version 6

The Internet Protocol Version 6 (IPv6) has been specified to meet the demands of the Internets growth and to replace the Internet Protocol Version 4 (IPv4). IPv6 does not only provide a larger address space when compared to IPv4, but also has additional features. A short overview of IPv6 will be provided in the following.

An IPv6 header consists of several fields, as specified in [47]. An illustration is provided in Figure 2.5. The *Version* field is always set to 6 for indicating IPv6. The *Traffic Class* and *Flow Label* fields can be used for quality of service purposes

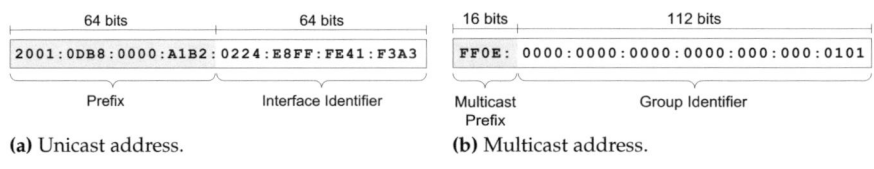

Figure 2.6. IPv6 address structures.

for different packet forwarding treatment, e. g., to prioritize certain packets. The *Payload Length* specifies the length of the IPv6 payload, including extension headers. The *Next Header* field determines the type of protocol that is carried within the IPv6 packet, following the IPv6 header. The *Hop Limit* determines how far a packet can travel: every router that forwards the packet decrements the value by one. As soon as the hop limit is zero, the packet will be dropped. The final two fields are the *Source Address* and the *Destination Address*, which are set to the IPv6 addresses that identify the sender and receiver of the packet.

2.2.3.1. Address Structure

IPv6 addresses have a length of 128 bit and are used to identify a physical interface or a set of interfaces; an interface is associated to a node and serves as point of attachment to a network.

The IPv6 addressing architecture is specified in [88]. Three types of addresses are supported: unicast, multicast and anycast. While a unicast address identifies a single interface, multicast and anycast addresses identify a set of interfaces, which usually belong to different nodes. A node can have more than one interface and is identified by the addresses that are associated with each interface.

All address types have the same basic structure: the leading n bits form the IP address *prefix*. This specifies the type of address and the topological location, indicating in which subnetwork the address owner is located. The preferred textual representation of an IPv6 addresses is based on hexadecimal values.

The unicast address `2001:0db8:0000:A1B2:0224:E8FF:FE41:F3A3/64` is illustrated in Figure 2.6a. Colons are used for separating the consecutive 16 bits blocks. The notation with the number 64 behind the dash indicates that the first 64 bits of the address form the prefix. The remaining 64 bits identify the interface or set of interfaces. A double colon "::" can be used to compress the leading and/or trailing zeros in an address. Similarly, leading zeroes within a 16 bit block can also be omitted. A simplified representation of the example address is therefore `2001:db8::A1B2:224:E8FF:FE41:F3A3/64`.

As of now, the prefix of every globally routable unicast address starts with `2000::/3` [94]. The 64 bit subnetwork prefix is always bound to a specific router, which is uniquely identified by that prefix. The interface identifier is a value that can be generated from the MAC address by the node itself.

IPv6 also defines link-local addresses that, in contrast to a global unicast address, are only valid for use within a subnetwork. The prefix for every link-local address is FE80::/64. Every node usually has at least two unicast addresses per interface: one link-local and one global address.

Anycast addresses are allocated from the unicast address space and are syntactically not distinguishable from unicast addresses.

The multicast address FF0E:0000:0000:0000:0000:000:000:0101 is illustrated in Figure 2.6a. The prefix of multicast addresses always starts with FF00::/8. The set of interfaces that is addressed by this address – the multicast group – is identified by a 112 bit suffix, the group identifier.

IPv6 does not directly support broadcast addresses, instead their function is replaced by multicast addresses.

2.2.3.2. Neighbor Discovery Protocol

IPv6 nodes use the Neighbor Discovery (ND) protocol for discovering the presence of other nodes on the same link, determining other nodes' link-layer (MAC) address, finding routers, etc. An overview of the neighbor discovery protocol is provided in the following. The full specification is available in [143].

Address Resolution
When an IPv6 node sends a packet to another IPv6 node on the same link, the packet can be sent directly to the recipient, without going through a router. The sending node will know that the recipient is on the same link if the IP addresses of both nodes have the same prefix. However, the sender first has to discover the MAC address that is associated to the IP address of the recipient. This is achieved with the neighbor solicitation and neighbor advertisement messages, which allow to establish a mapping between associated IP and MAC addresses.

An illustration is provided in Figure 2.7a. When a node attempts to send an IPv6 packet to a yet unknown node on the same link, the sender will send a neighbor solicitation (NS): this message will contain the IPv6 address of the recipient and is sent to all nodes on the link, e. g. using a broadcast link layer address for transmission. The owner of the IPv6 address in question will respond with a neighbor advertisement (NA) message that contains the MAC address. The NA message can be sent to the sender of the NS directly as both IPv6 and MAC address of the sender have been included in the NS.

The mapping between IP and MAC address is stored by the sender of the NS in order to avoid repeated address resolutions by means of NS/NA message exchanges.

31

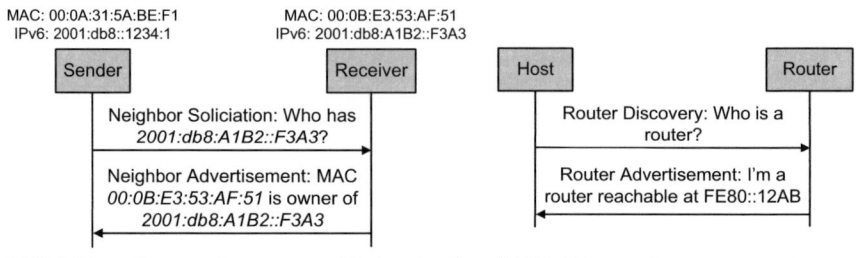

(a) Neighbor discovery between two IPv6 nodes for resolving a MAC address.   (b) IPv6 Router discovery procedure.

Figure 2.7. Neighbor discovery protocol operations.

Router Discovery

If communicating hosts are located within different subnetworks, packets have to be forwarded by routers.

How a host can discover a router that is on the same link is specified by the router discovery procedure in the neighbor discovery protocol. This message exchange is illustrated in Figure 2.7b. The host sends a router discovery (RD) message to the all-routers multicast address FF02::2, e.g. using a broadcast link layer address for transmission on the link. Every router is a member of this multicast group. A router advertisement (RA) is then sent by all routers that are present on this link to the unicast address of the inquiring host. The RA will contain the link-local and the MAC address of the router.

The host can then select among the router advertisements and choose one router that will act as first-hop router. The host can then send traffic destined to hosts located in different subnetworks to the access router, who will forward these packets.

Routers are sending router advertisements in regular intervals, using a broadcast or multicast link layer address for transmission to all nodes on the link. The interface from which the router advertisement is sent is called the *advertising interface*. A host will send a router discovery message only in order to receive an immediate advertisement instead of waiting for the next periodic one.

Routers receiving packets destined to a host on the same link will determine the MAC address of the destination host based on the address resolution that has been described earlier, using neighbor solicitation and neighbor advertisement messages.

Router discovery is also used to learn the subnetwork prefixes and other configuration parameters relevant for IPv6 address configuration.

2.2.3.3. Address Configuration

IPv6 addresses can be configured manually for each interface. IPv6 also provides two protocols as a more convenient option: Stateless Address Autoconfiguration and Stateful Address Autoconfiguration. Both options require a multicast-capable link.

Stateless Address Autoconfiguration will be explained in the following, as it is mandatory for implementation on an IPv6 node [128]. This is in contrast to DHCPv6 [53], which is the stateful option and will therefore not be further discussed.

Stateless Address Autoconfiguration

IPv6 Stateless Address Autoconfiguration [204] allows a host to configure both link-local and global IPv6 unicast addresses without any centralized address management entity or configuration input.

Configuring both link-local and global addresses for an interface consists of several steps:

1. Initially, a link-local address is formed by appending the interface identifier (e. g. `224:E8FF:FE41:F3A3`) to the link-local prefix (`FE80::/64`). The interface identifier is chosen by the node itself, e. g., it can be based on the MAC address of the interface.

2. The resulting link-local address (e. g. `FE80::224:E8FF:FE41:F3A3`) is considered being "tentative" for as long as it has not been verified that this address is not already used by another node on the same link. This verification is performed with the Duplicate Address Detection (DAD) method.

3. If the tentative link-local address has been verified as being unique, it can be assigned to the interface. The node now has IP-level connectivity with all nodes that are located on the same link. The subsequent steps for configuring a global address are only performed by hosts, but not by routers.

4. The host has to obtain a router advertisement (RA) from the access router. The RA will include prefix information that contains information for configuring a global unicast address.

5. A global address is formed by appending the interface identifier (e. g. `224:E8FF:FE41:F3A3`) to the prefix advertised in the RA (e. g. `2001:db8::A1B2::/64`).

6. The resulting global address (e. g. `2001:db8::A1B2:224:E8FF:FE41:F3A3/64`) is considered as "tentative" for as long as it has not been verified that this address is not already used by another node. The verification is performed with the Duplicate Address Detection (DAD) method.

7. If the tentative global address has been verified as being unique, it can be assigned to the interface. The node now has global IP connectivity.

A link-local address can be generated and verified in parallel to waiting for a router advertisement. Step 4 is then parallel to steps 1-3.

Duplicate Address Detection

Duplicate Address Detection (DAD) is part of the Stateless Address Autoconfiguration protocol and verifies the uniqueness of an address among the neighboring nodes on a link. DAD is performed on both link-local and global unicast addresses.

An address is said to be "tentative" for as long as the Duplicate Address Detection procedure has not been completed successfully. Only afterwards, the address can be considered unique and assigned to the interface. While an address is tentative, only neighbor solicitation and advertisement messages can be send and received at the tentative address.

The DAD procedure is as follows [204]: the node sends a neighbor solicitation message containing the tentative address, using a broadcast or multicast link layer address for transmission on the link. If another node is already using that address, it will return a neighbor advertisement saying so. If a node determines that its tentative link-local address is not unique, autoconfiguration fails. If no neighbor advertisement is received within a certain time window, the node ascertains that the tentative address is unique and assigns the address to the interface.

2.2.4. Routing

When packets are exchanged between two hosts across network boundaries, these packets are forwarded by routers. The process of forwarding packets from the source to the destination is called *routing*. Routers contain a *routing table* that specifies the address of the next router (*next hop*) along a routing path. A packet can be delivered to its destination as soon as it reaches the access router of the destination host.

Routing is a two-tier system: *inter-domain* routing is performed between routers of different autonomous systems and uses an Exterior Gateway Protocol (EGP). An autonomous system is characterized by being administrated by a single authority. It can can consist of one or several subnetworks, which in turn include an arbitrary number of network nodes.
Inside an autonomous system, routers perform *intra-domain* routing that uses an Interior Gateway Protocol (IGP).

The routers of an autonomous system often *aggregate* the prefixes that are present within their domain: instead of announcing a large number of individual prefixes, the routers only announce an aggregated, more general route with the shortest possible prefix that is still valid for all prefixes of that domain. This not only reduces the amount of routing information that as to be exchanged among EGP routers, but also reduces the size of the routing tables.

The Border Gateway Protocol (BGP) [173] is the prevailing exterior gateway protocol in the Internet. The most widely used interior gateway protocols are the Routing Information Protocol (RIP), Version 2 [130] and the Open Shortest Path First (OSPF), Version 2 [140].

2.2.5. IP Security

IP security (IPsec) provides "access control, connectionless integrity, data origin authentication, detection and rejection of replays, confidentiality (via encryption), and limited traffic flow confidentiality" for IP packets, where "these services are provided at the IP layer, offering protection in a standard fashion for all protocols that may be carried over IP (including IP itself)" [116].

IPsec can be used for providing IP packet level security between (a) two hosts, (b) two routers ("security gateways") or (c) between a host and a router.

Most of these services are provided by three protocols: the Internet Key Exchange Protocol (IKE), the Authentication Header (AH) and the Encapsulating Security Payload (ESP). A short overview of these protocols is provided in the following. The description of AH and ESP is limited to *tunnel mode*, where the original IPv6 packet is encapsulated into another IPv6 header.

Internet Key Exchange
The Internet Key Exchange Protocol Version 2 (IKEv2) [112] is used for performing mutual authentication and establishing Security Associations (SAs) between a pair of nodes.

IKE makes use of the Diffie-Hellman key exchange for establishing a shared secret among the two nodes. This key exchange is authenticated by using public-private key pairs or a shared symmetric key. Alternatively, another protocol – EAP [2] – can also be used for authentication. IKE also provides *cryptographic agility*, a property that allows negotiating which cryptographic algorithms should be used.

As soon as both authentication and algorithm negotiation have been successfully completed, security associations are established on both nodes, containing information necessary for providing packet level security:

- Type of protocol to be used for packet level security: authentication header or encapsulating security payload.
- Cryptographic algorithms to be used for integrity protection and encryption.
- Keys used for cryptographic operations.
- Sequence numbers.
- ...

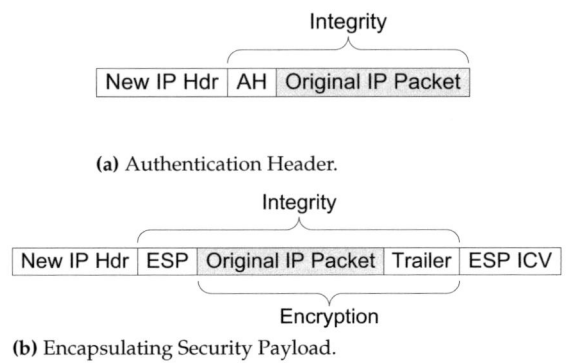

(a) Authentication Header.

(b) Encapsulating Security Payload.

Figure 2.8. IP security protocols used in tunnel mode.

The cryptographic keys associated to a security association are used for performing the packet-level cryptographic operations.

IKE takes also care of maintaining security associations, e. g., it performs a rekeying before the sequence number space becomes exhausted.

Authentication Header
IP Authentication Header (AH) [114] provides IP packet-level integrity and data origin protection.

Figure 2.8a provides an illustration of tunnel mode authentication header: the original IP packet is preceded by an AH header that includes an integrity checksum value (e. g. using a message authentication code), a sequence number and other parameters. The integrity protection covers the entire original IP packet and the AH header. A new IP header is prepended at the front.

Encapsulating Security Payload (ESP)
IP Encapsulating Security Payload (ESP) [115] provides IP packet-level confidentiality, integrity and data origin protection.

Figure 2.8b provides an illustration of tunnel mode encapsulating security payload: the original IP packet is preceded by the ESP header that includes a sequence number and other parameters. A trailer is appended after the original packet for padding, depending on the specific encryption algorithm used. The integrity checksum value (ICV) field at the very end includes the message digest used for integrity protection, e. g., the message authentication code. A new IP header is prepended in the front. The confidentiality protection covers the original IP packet and the trailer. The integrity protection further extends this to the ESP header.

2.2.6. Mobile IPv6

The capability to deal with mobile hosts moving between different wireless access networks has not been addressed in the original IP(v6) architecture. Every time a mobile host moves into a new network and performs a handover to a new base station and associated access router, address configuration is performed and a new IP address obtained. All communication sessions that have been previously established then become invalid, as they have been bound to the old IP address that is topologically incorrect at the new location. This leads to a disruption of the currently active applications that are usually not built to handle a change of the underlying IP address. It is therefore necessary to address the problem of routing packets to the new topological destination of the mobile host.

A network-level solution to this problem is provided by the Mobile IPv6 protocol [108]. It provides *session continuity*, which allows to keep already established communication alive. The protocol has also been adopted by 3GPP [1, 75] for use with mobile phones.

2.2.6.1. Basic Protocol

Mobile IPv6 [108] is a global mobility management protocol that allows a mobile host to remain reachable while moving between different IPv6 networks.[4]

This is achieved by introducing a global unicast *home address* (HoA) that can be used by higher layer protocols and applications as routing end-point. The home address is generated using the home network prefix of the *home link* of the mobile host. The home link is therefore the topological home location of the mobile host, located inside the *home network*. The home network aggregates the prefixes of the home link(s) and announces this aggregate prefix in an exterior gateway protocol (EGP) to other autonomous systems. The home network operator acts as a *mobility service provider* for the mobile host, providing routing from and to the mobile host based on the home address.

As long as the mobile host is attached to the home link, packets addressed to the home address are routed to the home link where they are received by the mobile host. As soon as the mobile host moves into a foreign network, it configures a global unicast *care-of address* (CoA) that is configured from the network prefix advertised by the access router on the foreign link. The care-of address is therefore the mobile host's topologically correct routing end-point inside the foreign access network.

An overview of Mobile IPv6 on the network node level is provided in Figure 2.9. A central component of the protocol is the *home agent*, a special access router

---

[4]The Mobile IPv6 protocol specification [108] refers to mobile node (MN) instead of mobile host (MH). As the term *node* can be either a host or a router, this thesis will use the notion of mobile host when referring to a single mobile device.

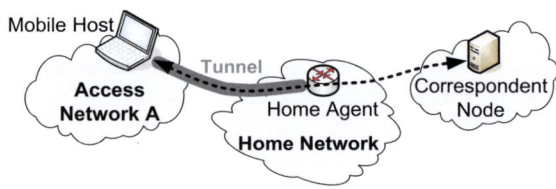

Figure 2.9. Overview of the Mobile IPv6 protocol on the network node level.

located at the home link inside the home network. When moving to a foreign network, the mobile host establishes a *mobility binding* with the home agent: the binding maps the mobile host's home address to its current care-of address. This is achieved by means of a binding update (BU)/binding acknowledgement (BA) message exchange between mobile host (MH) and home agent (HA):

$$MH \rightarrow HA \; (BU) : K_{MH-HA}\{\mathcal{S}, HoA\}$$
$$HA \rightarrow MH \; (BA) : K_{MH-HA}\{\mathcal{S}\}$$

The sequence number $\mathcal{S}$ provides replay protection. HoA refers to the home address of the mobile host. Mobile IPv6 requires to use IKEv2 for authentication and IPsec to provide security for the signaling messages exchanged between mobile host and home agent [49]. The key K_{MH-HA} refers to the symmetric key available from the IPsec security association that exists between mobile host and home agent.

When the home agent receives a binding update, it will update the mobility binding for this mobile host based on the home address and care-of address information contained within the message. The care-of address is the source address of the binding update packet. The response in form of the binding acknowledgement provides confirmation to the mobile host that the binding has been successfully updated at the home agent.

Any correspondent node (CN) communicating with the mobile host will not be aware of the mobile host's movements and addresses packets to the home address. Packets will therefore be routed between home network and the correspondent node. The home agent intercepts packets that are destined to the mobile host and uses tunneling to forward these packets to the current care-of address of the mobile host, as indicated by the mobility binding. On the reverse direction, the mobile host tunnels packets to the home agent that are then forwarded to the correspondent node.

Tunneling refers to encapsulating the original IPv6 packet into another IPv6 header. On the path from the correspondent node to the mobile host, when receiving a

Source: HA	Source: CN	Original IP Packet		Source: CoA	Source: HoA	Original IP Packet
Dest: CoA	Dest: HoA			Dest: HA	Dest: CN	

(a) Correspondent node to mobile host.   (b) Mobile host to correspondent node.

Figure 2.10. Encapsulated packets between mobile host and home agent.

packet destined to a mobile host, the home agent adds an additional header with its own address as source and the mobile host's care-of address as destination – this is illustrated in Figure 2.10a. When this packet arrives at the mobile host, the additional header is removed. On the reverse direction from mobile host to correspondent node, the additional header is present on the path from the mobile host to the home agent, as illustrated in Figure 2.10b. The outermost header uses the care-of address as source and the home agent address as destination. Upon receiving this packet, the home agent will remove the additional header. The packet is then forwarded to the correspondent node by means of normal Internet routing.

The routing of packets between mobile host and correspondent node via the home agent is also called *triangular routing*.

2.2.6.2. Route Optimization

Mobile IPv6 provides a route optimization mechanism that allows establishing a mobility binding with the correspondent node as well. This eliminates the need for routing packets via the home network/home agent. Instead, packets can be routed on a direct path between the correspondent node and the mobile host's care-of address. This however poses a security problem: packets are redirected from their original destination, the home address, to another location, the care-of address. The mobile host therefore has to prove that it actually owns both the claimed home address and care-of address.

The approach followed in the Mobile IPv6 protocol is the return routability (RR) procedure that makes use of the Internet routing infrastructure to verify whether a host actually owns a certain address. This procedure relies on a reachability proof where two cryptographic keys are transported from the correspondent node to the mobile host's home address and care-of address. These keys are then combined for calculating a message digest that authorizes the mobility binding for the mobile host's addresses.

The route optimization procedure will be described in more detail in the following. A message sequence chart showing all involved signaling messages is provided in Figure 2.11.

The first phase is the return routability procedure, consisting of the care-of test and home test messages. These messages contain cryptographic keys that are

39

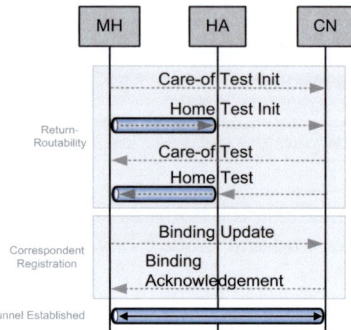

Figure 2.11. Sequence of Mobile IPv6 route optimization signaling messages.

routed via different paths. The care-of test init (CoTI) message contains a nonce N_C and is routed from the care-of address of the mobile host directly to the correspondent node, who will respond with a care-of test (CoT) message:

$$MH \rightarrow CN \ (CoTI): \ N_C$$
$$CN \rightarrow MH \ (CoT): \ N_C, K_C, \mathcal{I}_C$$

The care-of test message contains the nonce N_C, a care-of key K_C as well as a care-of secret index $\mathcal{I}_C$. The key K_C is generated by the correspondent node from a secret key S_C^i that is only known to the correspondent node. $\mathcal{I}_C$ specifies which secret key with index i has been used by the correspondent node for generating the care-of key.

The home test init (HoTI) message contains a nonce N_H and is routed from the home address of the mobile host via the home agent to the correspondent node, who will respond with a home test (HoT) message:

$$
\begin{aligned}
MH \rightarrow HA \ (HoTI): \ & K_{MH-HA}\{N_H\} \\
HA \rightarrow CN \ (HoTI): \ & N_H \\
CN \rightarrow HA \ (HoT): \ & N_H, K_H, \mathcal{I}_H \\
HA \rightarrow MH \ (HoT): \ & K_{MH-HA}\{N_H, K_H, \mathcal{I}_H\}
\end{aligned}
\tag{2.1}
$$

On the path between mobile host and home agent, the home test messages are encrypted with the key K_{MH-HA} from the IPsec security association. The home test init message consists of the nonce N_H. The home test message additionally includes a home key K_H and a home secret index $\mathcal{I}_H$. Similar to the care-of key, the home key is generated from a secret key S_H^i that is only known to the correspondent node. $\mathcal{I}_H$ specifies which secret key with index i has been used by the correspondent node for generating the home key.

This concludes the return routability procedure. The mobile host will only receive the care-of and home keys K_C and K_H if the mobile host is reachable at the claimed care-of address and home address. Once both keys have been obtained, they are combined into a single key K_{bm}:

$$K_{bm} = H(K_H | K_C) \tag{2.2}$$

The two keys K_C and K_H are concatenated and the hash function SHA-1 [153] used to calculate the binding management key K_{bm}.

The next step is the correspondent registration, where the mobility binding with the correspondent node is finally established. The key K_{bm} is used for calculating a HMAC that authorizes the binding update (BU) to the correspondent node. This message is sent with the care-of address as source address.

$$MH \rightarrow CN\ (BU) : K_{bm}[\mathcal{S}, HoA, N_C, N_H, \mathcal{I}_C, \mathcal{I}_H]$$

Upon receiving this message, the correspondent node will recalculate the care-of key K_C and home key K_H with help of the secret keys S_C^i and S_H^i indexed by $\mathcal{I}_C$ and $\mathcal{I}_H$. The binding management key K_{bm} can then be regenerated according to formula (2.2).

The binding is accepted if the correspondent node can successfully verify the HMAC with the regenerated key K_{bm}. The correspondent node will respond with a binding acknowledgement (BA) indicating success:

$$CN \rightarrow MH\ (BA) : K_{bm}[\mathcal{S}]$$

The HMAC on the binding acknowledgement can be verified by the mobile host, as the key K_{bm} is stored locally as session information.

A direct routing path has now been established between mobile host and correspondent node that can be used for sending and receiving packets from and to the care-of address.

If the mobile host performs another handover by moving to a new access network, the entire procedure has to be repeated again. Only if the home key K_H is not older than 210 seconds [108], the key can be reused and the home test init/home test message exchange omitted.

This procedure has a well known security problem that permits an off-path attacker located on the path between home agent and correspondent node to hijack the home address of a mobile node [108, 149, 150, 195]. The notion off-path refers to the fact that the adversary is not on the direct path between mobile host and correspondent node, but instead on a path that is not on the direct communication path between mobile host and correspondent node. The adversary can see the unencrypted home key K_H transported within the home test message (2.1) for a particular (mobile host, correspondent node) pair. The adversary can retrieve a care-of key K_C for his own care-of address. Combining care-of and home keys, the adversary can generate a binding update and send it to the original correspondent node that sent the home key within the home test message. The correspondent node will then establish a binding that redirects all traffic from the stolen home address to the care-of address of the adversary. This constitutes a successful hijacking attack. The Mobile IPv6 specification attempts to limit this vulnerability by limiting the binding lifetime to seven minutes. If the adversary is not capable of maintaining the off-path position between home agent and correspondent node for more then the initial seven minutes, then further hijacking attempts will fail.

2.2.7. Network Mobility

The Network Mobility (NEMO) basic support protocol [50] extends Mobile IPv6 to provide session continuity and global reachability for a mobile router (MR) instead of only a mobile host.

More detailed, instead of providing only a home address, NEMO provides a *mobile network prefix* (MNP) to the mobile router.

The end-systems that attach to the mobile network of the mobile router are called *mobile network nodes* (MNN). They configure their addresses in the standard IPv6 way (cf. Section 2.2.3.3) from the mobile network prefix that is provided in a router advertisement by the mobile router.

The mobility signaling for NEMO is similar to Mobile IPv6, as shown in Figure 2.12a. As soon as the mobile router moves to a foreign network and acquired a *care-of address* (CoA), a home registration is performed with the *home agent* (HA) that is located in the home network. The signaling exchange is performed by means of a *binding update* (BU) / *binding acknowledgement* (BA) exchange, protected by an IPsec security association.

Traffic originating from the mobile network nodes is tunneled by the mobile router to the home agent that forwards packets to their destination, the *correspondent nodes*.

The home network aggregates the mobile network prefixes of all its mobile routers and advertises this aggregate prefix to other autonomous systems using an inter-domain routing protocol. Hence packets originating from a correspondent node addressed to a mobile network node that is attached to a mobile router

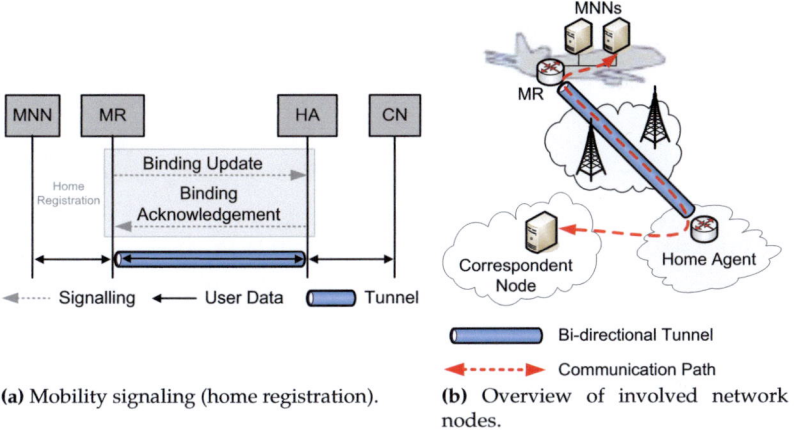

(a) Mobility signaling (home registration).

(b) Overview of involved network nodes.

Figure 2.12. NEMO Basic Support protocol.

are routed to the home agent located within the home network. These packets are then tunneled by the home agent to the current care-of address of the mobile router. The mobile router decapsulates the packet and delivers it to the destination, the mobile network node. This is also illustrated in Figure 2.12b.

The mobility is transparent to both the mobile network nodes and the correspondent nodes as only mobile router and home agent are performing mobility related tasks. The original packets are also not modified, due to the IP-in-IP encapsulation that only adds an additional header on the path between mobile router and home agent.

2.3. Information Security

This section deals with the definition of security properties and cryptographic schemes that can be used to achieve certain security goals. Further information is given on protocol specific security, public key infrastructure and identity certificates. The focus of this introduction is on protocol specific security between a pair of nodes communicating with each other.

The definitions used in the following are based on [30, 111, 113, 196].

2.3.1. Security Attacks

Security attacks can be classified into two different classes: passive and active attacks, as specified in [193]. Either way, an *adversary* or *attacker* Eve will attempt to

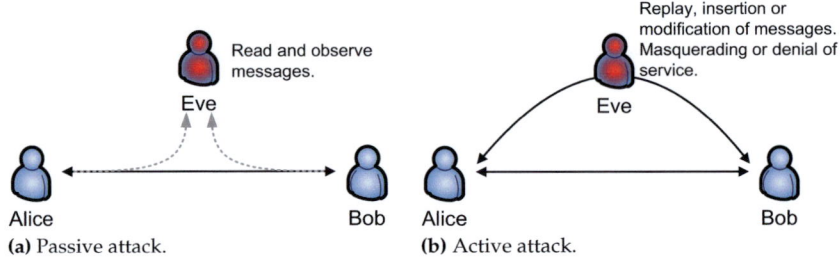

Figure 2.13. Attack classifications.

learn of or influence information exchanged between the communication nodes Alice and Bob. This is illustrated in Figure 2.13.

In a passive attack such as eavesdropping, Eve attempts to learn sensitive information exchanged between Alice and Bob. Additionally, Eve can also perform traffic analysis in order to retrieve information such as the location and identity of Alice and Bob, the frequency of exchanged messages, etc. Another example is cryptanalysis that consists of techniques for, e. g., decrypting a message without knowing the encryption key. In colloquial language, "cryptanalysis is what the layman calls breaking the code" [196].
A general important characteristic of passive attacks is that they are difficult to detect, but relatively easy to circumvent.

Within an active attack, Eve modifies messages exchanged between Alice and Bob. Alternatively, Eve can creates new messages and sent them to Alice or Bob. Active attacks can be categorized into four different classes:

1. Masquerade: For example, Eve pretends to be Bob and engages into a message exchange with Alice. Eve thereby attempts to illegitimately access a system or perform a malicious action.

2. Replay: Eve captures previously observed valid messages and retransmits these messages to the original recipient. This could be used as part of a masquerade attack.

3. Modification: Eve intercepts and modifies parts of or an entire message originating from Alice or Bob.

4. Denial of Service: Eve prevents other (valid) users from authorized access to a system or significantly delays the access to such a system.

Active attacks are often difficult if not impossible to prevent. It is therefore important to detect and recover from such attempts.

An additional issue is whether legitimate nodes act honestly or maliciously, e. g., whether the nodes follow the protocol specification or not. In a weak adversary model, nodes can not be corrupted and therefore act correctly. In a more powerful model, nodes can be corrupted in an attempt to exploit protocol weaknesses by misbehavior with respect to the protocol specification.

A notable type of attacker is the man-in-the-middle, who is located between Alice and Bob. If such an "adversary has control of the intervening communication channel, then E can compromise the communication" [196, Section 10.1] without being detected, if the communication protocol has not been property secured against this type of attacker.

2.3.2. Security Properties

Saying that the communication via an insecure channel for two nodes Alice and Bob is "secure" is not sufficient. Security is usually provided with the goal of preventing any of the attacks listed in the previous section. However, sometimes it might be the case that an attack can only be detected and it's effects on a system only be limited.

Whether a system can be considered secure depends on the purpose and intended robustness of the communication system. Security therefore always has to be defined and assessed with regard to certain requirements.

The property **confidentiality** "ensures that data is only available to those authorized to obtain it" [30, Section 1.4]. Confidentiality can be applied on an entire message or only on parts of it. It provides protection from passive attacks and prevents analysis of observed traffic.

Data **integrity** provides "assurance that data received are exactly as sent by an authorized entity (i.e. contain no modification, insertion, deletion or replay)" [196, Section 1.4]. Integrity prevents the successful attempt of modification, insertion, etc. Integrity can be provided on either an entire message or on parts of it.

Non-repudiation "ensures that entities cannot deny sending data that they have committed to" [30, Section 1.4]. With non-repudiation, the receiver can be assured that the received message has in fact been sent by the alleged entity only.

Authentication provides "assurance that the communicating entity is the one it claims to be" [196, Section 1.4]. Additionally, the entity must actively participate in the protocol exchange, meaning that it must be active at the time of the protocol message exchange(s). This is also called entity authentication. The entity authentication corresponds to a *one-way authentication* if only one of the entities is authenticated to the other. A *mutual authentication* takes place if both entities are authenticated to each other in the same protocol exchange.

Similarly, **data origin authentication** provides "assurance that source of the claimed data is as claimed" [196, Section 1.4]. The property guarantees the origin of the data. Data origin authentication is closely related to integrity, as both properties can be achieved with the same mechanisms.

2.3.3. Cryptographic Schemes

The following section provides an overview on cryptographic schemes that can be used to achieve the above mentioned security properties.

2.3.3.1. Secret Key Cryptography

Secret key cryptography is sometimes also referred to as *conventional cryptography* or *symmetric cryptography*. Secret key cryptography can be used for encryption and decryption of data using only a single key K. Using such an encryption scheme for the communication between a pair of nodes provides *confidentiality* for the exchanged messages.

The definition of such a secret key cryptographic system is as follows [30]:

Definition 2.1. *An encryption scheme consists of three sets: a key set $\mathcal{K}$, a message set $\mathcal{M}$ and a ciphertext set $\mathcal{C}$ together with three functions:*

1. *A key generation function that outputs a valid encryption key $K \in \mathcal{K}$ and a valid decryption key $K^{-1} \in \mathcal{K}$*
2. *An encryption function E, which takes an element $m \in \mathcal{M}$ and an encryption key $K \in \mathcal{K}$ and outputs an element $c \in \mathcal{C}$ defined as $c = E_K\{m\}$. The encryption function may be randomized so that a different c can result from the same m.*
3. *A decryption function D, which takes an element $c \in \mathcal{C}$ and a decryption key $K^{-1} \in \mathcal{K}$ and outputs an element $m \in \mathcal{M}$ defined as $m = D_{K^{-1}}\{c\}$. It is required that $D_{K^{-1}}\{E_K\{m\}\} = m$.*

The input m of the encryption is also called plaintext, while the output c of the encryption is called ciphertext. Alice and Bob are using the shared key K for encrypting and decrypting messages exchanged between them. The usage of the scheme is illustrated in Figure 2.14.

A well known example for such a symmetric encryption and decryption scheme is the Advanced Encryption Standard (AES), specified in [152]. In AES, the size of the key K can be 128, 192 or 256 bits. Another example is Blowfish [185], which allows key sizes between 1–448 bits.

2.3.3.2. Message Digests

A message digest is a one-way function that takes an arbitrary-length input and returns a fixed-length output. A message digest computed from messages exchanged between communicating nodes provides *integrity* to these messages. A

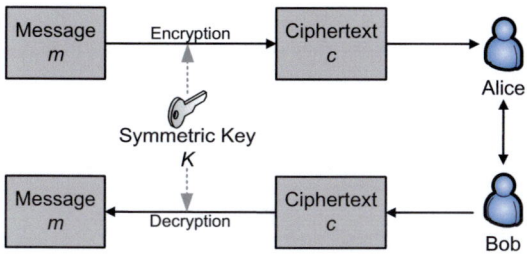

Figure 2.14. Symmetric encryption and decryption using a secret key.

more thorough discussion on one-way function theory, attacks and applications can be found in [136].

Definition 2.2. *A function $f : M \to Y$ allows to easily calculate $y = f(m)$ for a given $m \in M$. Such a function is cryptographically secure if it fulfills the following properties:*

1. *Preimage resistance: it is computationally difficult for the attacker presented with $y \in Y$ to find m so that $f(m) = y$.*
2. *Second-preimage resistance: it is computationally difficult for an attacker presented with random $m_1 \in M$ to find $m_2 \neq m_1, m_2 \in M$ so that $f(m_1) = f(m_2)$.*
3. *Collision resistance: it is computationally difficult for the attacker to find m_1 and $m_2 \neq m_1$ so that $f(m_1) = f(m_2)$.*

Collision resistance implies second-preimage resistance. In practice, collision resistance is considered as the strongest property of all three.

Such a one-way function is also called *hash* function. It takes an arbitrary length input m and computes a fixed length output y. A key feature of such a hash function is that for a given hash output y it is practically impossible to find the original input m from which the hash output was calculated from. Similarly, it should be computationally infeasible to find two different inputs that produce the same hash output.

A hash function can be used to construct a message authentication code that can be used to provide *integrity* and *authentication* for messages exchanged between two nodes. While a message authentication code can also be constructed using symmetric cryptography, the most common approach is the usage of a one-way function as, in general, these execute faster in software. The definition of a message authentication code is as follows [30]:

Definition 2.3. *A message authentication code is a family of functions parametrized by a key $K \in \mathcal{K}$ such that $MAC_K(m)$ takes a message $m \in M$ of arbitrary length and outputs a fixed length value satisfying the following conditions:*

47

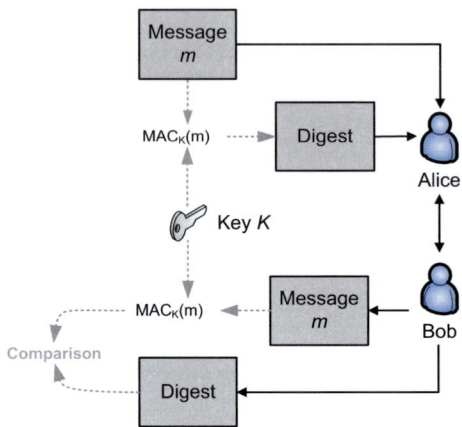

Figure 2.15. Message digest produced with a message authentication code

1. *it is computationally easy to calculate $MAC_K(m)$ given K and m;*
2. *given any number of message authentication code values for a given K for previously observed messages m, it is computationally hard to find a valid message authentication code value for an arbitrary new message m' without knowing K.*

The message authentication code is appended to the message m to be protected. The recipient with the correct key K can then recalculate the message authentication code and verify that it is the same as the one received with the message m. An illustration of this process is provided in Figure 2.15.

A well known example for a message authentication code based on a one-way function is the hash-based message authentication code (HMAC) specified in [154]. A HMAC can use any available hash function and be proven secure if the underlying hash function fulfills the properties listed in Definition 2.2.

Definition 2.4. *A hash-based message authentication code (HMAC) with input key $K \in \mathcal{K}$ and message $m \in \mathcal{M}$ of arbitrary length outputs a fixed length value. Such a HMAC can be expressed as follows:*

$$HMAC(K, m) = H\Big((K \oplus opad)|H\big(K \oplus ipad)|m\big)\Big)$$

where H is a hash function, $\oplus$ refers to the XOR operation, $|$ is concatenation and $opad, ipad$ are constants.

If a HMAC is used for producing a message authentication code, then $MAC_K(m) = HMAC(K,m)$.

A popular hash function, not only for use with HMACs, is the Secure Hash Algorithm (SHA-1) specified in [153]. SHA-1 provides an output length of 160 bits, although other variants, named SHA-x with an output length of x bits, also exist.

2.3.3.3. Public Key Cryptography

Public key cryptography is fundamentally different from secret key cryptography. Instead of relying on a shared secret, a key pair consisting of a private and a public key is used for encrypting and decrypting messages. A public key encryption scheme can provide *confidentiality* for messages exchanged between a pair of nodes. It is defined as follows [30]:

Definition 2.5. *A public key encryption scheme consists of three sets: a key set $\mathcal{K}$, a message set $\mathcal{M}$ and a ciphertext set C together with three functions:*

1. *A key generation function that outputs a pair of keys $(K, K^{-1}) \in \mathcal{K}^2$. The first of these keys is called the public key, which can also be named as K^{PUB}. The second key is called the private key, which can also be named as K^{PRIV}.*
2. *An encryption function E, which takes an element $m \in \mathcal{M}$ and the public key $K^{PUB} \in \mathcal{K}$ and outputs an element $c \in C$ defined as $c = E_{K^{PUB}}\{m\}$. The encryption function may be randomized so that a different c can result from the same m.*
3. *A decryption function D, which takes an element $c \in C$ and the private key $K^{PRIV} \in \mathcal{K}$ and outputs an element $m \in \mathcal{M}$ defined as $m = D_{K^{PRIV}}\{c\}$. It is required that $D_{K^{PRIV}}\{E_{K^{PUB}}\{m\}\} = m$.*

It is practically impossible to obtain the key K^{PRIV} from the key K^{PUB}.

If an entity Alice would like to send an encrypted message m to Bob, Alice has to obtain the public key K^{PUB} of Bob. Using the public key, the message can be encrypted and sent. Bob can decrypt m using his private key K^{PRIV}. This operation is illustrated in Figure 2.16.

An additional feature of a public key system is the possibility to *sign* a message using the decryption key K^{PRIV}. Anyone can verify the resulting signature using the corresponding public key K^{PUB}. Such a signature can not be forged nor can the signer deny having generated this signature.

A signature allows to provide the property of *non-repudiation*. At the same time it can also be used to provide *authentication* and data *integrity* as an alternative to using a message authentication code. The definition is as follows [30]:

Definition 2.6. *A digital signature scheme consists of three sets: a key set $\mathcal{K}$, a message set $\mathcal{M}$ and a signature set S together with two functions:*

1. *A signature generation function that takes an element $m \in \mathcal{M}$ and a private signature key $K^{PRIV} \in \mathcal{K}$ and outputs an element $s \in S$. The notation is $s = K_A^{PRIV}[m]$ where K_A^{PRIV} is the signature generation key of entity A. The signature generation function may be randomized so that a different output can result from the same m.*

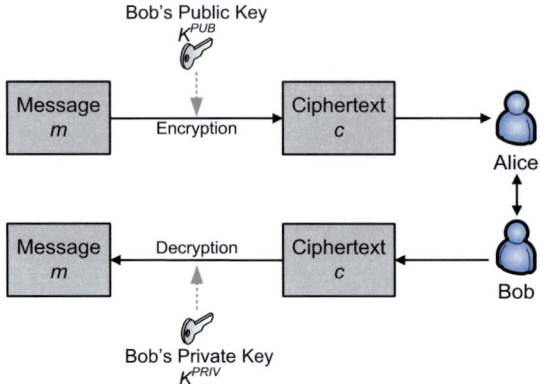

Figure 2.16. Encryption and decryption of a message based on a public-private key pair.

2. *A verification function that takes a signature $s \in S$, a message $m \in M$ and a public verification key $K_A^{PUB} \in K$. The key K_A^{PUB} is the public key of entity A. The function outputs an element $v \in \{0,1\}$. If $v = 1$, then the signature is valid. If $v = 0$, the signature is invalid.*

Signature schemes are constructed using a hash function. The security of the signature depends on the underlying hash function. A signature is considered secure if it is computationally hard to find a valid signature for a previously unsigned message.

The keys used for generating and verifying a signature can be the same as those used for encryption and decryption, cf. Definition 2.5.

Similar to the message authentication code, the signature s is appended to the message m. The recipient with key K^{PUB} can then use the verification function to check whether the signature is valid or not. This asserts whether the message originates from the alleged entity or not. This process is illustrated in Figure 2.17

The most widely used public key system is the one introduced by Rivest, Shamir and Adleman [177], called RSA, which is specified in [155]. It is based on the computational hard problem of prime factorization.

2.3.3.4. Elliptic Curve Cryptography

Another system implementing public key cryptography is Elliptic Curve Cryptography (ECC), which is also specified in [155]. It offers equal security for

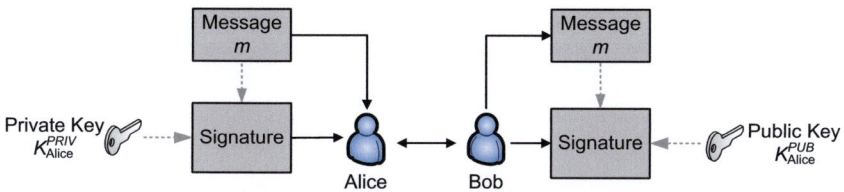

Figure 2.17. Signature generation for a message based on a public-private key pair.

smaller key sizes when compared to RSA. Additionally, it also decreases processing overhead.

ECC is based on the computational hard discrete logarithm problem for elliptic curves. It is necessary to specify global public domain parameters (curve parameters) that have to be supported by all communicating entities. These parameters are used for generating the ECC key pair (K^{PUB}, K^{PRIV}), for encryption and decryption as well as for signature generation and verification.

The signature function used with ECC is the Elliptic Curve Digital Signature Algorithm (ECDSA) specified in [155], which conforms to the signature scheme specified in Definition 2.6.

Encryption and decryption based on ECC is provided by the Elliptic Curve Integrated Encryption Scheme (ECIES) that is specified in [176]. It conforms to the encryption scheme specified in Definition 2.5.

2.3.3.5. Identity-Based Cryptography

Identity-based cryptography [191] is another system implementing public key cryptography. Keys are generated from an arbitrary string, the identity. A key management center plays a pivotal role in such a system as it provides public parameters as well as a master secret for key generation [12].

As an example, the public key K_X^{PUB} and private key K_X^{PRIV} of node X would be generated as follows:

$$K_X^{PRIV} = gen(ID_X, MSK) \qquad K_X^{PUB} = gen(ID_X, PP)$$

where gen is the key generation function, ID_X the identity of node X, MSK the master secret key and PP the public parameters.

The key management center generates a node's private key (e. g. K_X^{PRIV}) from its identity (e. g. ID_X) and the master secret key (e. g. MSK). The latter is only known to the key management center. The key then has to be securely transported to the node (e. g. X).

Security Property	Secret Key Cryptography		Public Key Cryptography	
	Encryption	HMAC	Encryption	Signature
Confidentiality	✓	✗	✓	✗
Integrity	✗	✓	✗	✓
Non-repudiation	✗	✗	✗	✓
Authentication	✗	✓	✗	✓

Table 2.4. Relationship between individual security properties and cryptographic schemes. (✓) indicates supported, (✗) indicates not supported.

Every node within the identity based cryptography system can generate the public key of any other node (e.g. K_X^{PUB}) from this node's identity (e.g. ID_X) and the public parameters (e.g. PP). The public parameters are provided by the key management center.

These keys can then be used within encryption and signature schemes.

2.3.3.6. Summary

To summarize, Table 2.4 shows which security properties can be supported by which cryptographic scheme.

A digital signature provides non-repudiation as the corresponding digital signature can only be computed by using the private key K^{PRIV}, which is only known to the key holder. A HMAC, which is calculated using the symmetric key K, can not provide non-repudiation as the key K is shared between two nodes.

Both a HMAC, according to Definition 2.3, or a digital signature, according to Definition 2.6, attached to a message authenticates this message.

2.3.4. Protocol Security

An attack on a protocol is considered successful if the protocol's correct behavior can not be achieved anymore.

In the following, basic communication protocol security aspects are discussed and a notation for describing protocol exchanges introduced. All symbols used in the protocol message exchanges are also listed in Appendix A.

2.3.4.1. Security Handshake

An initial authentication handshake is usually the very first step in a protocol exchange prior to establishing a protocol session or state. Authentication within this context refers to entity authentication of the involved communication nodes Alice and Bob, cf. Section 2.3.2.

Authentication always requires Alice and Bob to possess information about themselves and the other party. The common approaches are to use either a password, a secret key or a public key system.

Password based authentication will not be discussed in the following; an extensive discussion on this topic can be found in [113, Chapter 10].

Shared Secret
Authentication based on a shared secret requires Alice and Bob to have a pre-shared secret key K_{AB}. An example of such an authentication using a challenge-response mechanism is provided in the following, where A and B denotes Alice and Bob respectively:

$$A \rightarrow B \ (M1): \ Id_A$$
$$B \rightarrow A \ (M2): R \tag{2.3}$$
$$A \rightarrow B \ (M3): \ K_{AB}[R]$$

In the first message (M1) sent from Alice to Bob, Alice provides her identity (Id_A) to Bob. Within message 2 (M2), Bob sends a challenge R, which is a random number, to Alice. Alice proves to be in possession of the shared secret K_{AB} by calculating a HMAC, as defined in Definition 2.4, with the shared key. The final message M3 contains both the original challenge R sent by Bob as well as the HMAC that is calculated as $HMAC(K_{AB}, R)$.

The authentication performed in protocol (2.3) is only a one-way authentication: Alice authenticates to Bob, but Bob does not authenticate to Alice. If an attacker Eve can receive packets sent to Bob and also packets to Alice using Bob's source address, then Eve can masquerade as Bob. This is possible as Eve does not have to proof ownership of the shared secret K_{AB}. After receiving M1, Eve can send an arbitrary R in message M2 and ignore the response provided in M3. Alice will then continue communicating with Eve, assuming that she authenticated to Bob.

An improved version of protocol (2.3), providing mutual authentication, would look as follows:

$$A \rightarrow B \ (M1): \ Id_A, R_2$$
$$B \rightarrow A \ (M2): R_1, K_{AB}[R_2] \tag{2.4}$$
$$A \rightarrow B \ (M3): \ K_{AB}[R_1]$$

Bob now also has to proof ownership of the shared secret K_{AB} by calculating a HMAC for the challenge R_2.

Public Keys
The protocol can also achieve mutual authentication by relying on public key

cryptography. It is required that Alice and Bob know their own private keys as well as the public keys of the other node.

$$A \rightarrow B \ (M1): \ Id_A, R_2$$
$$B \rightarrow A \ (M2): \ R_1, K_B^{PRIV}[R_2] \tag{2.5}$$
$$A \rightarrow B \ (M3): \ K_A^{PRIV}[R_1]$$

For message 2 (M2), Bob signs R_2 by calculating a signature using his own private key K_B^{PRIV} (cf. Definition 2.6). When Alice receives M2, she will verify the signature with Bob's public key K_B^{PUB}. Alice then sends M3 with a signature that is calculated from her own private key K_A^{PRIV}. The signature in M3 can be verified by Bob using Alice's public key K_A^{PUB}.

Note: The notation $K[M]$ refers to message M with either a HMAC or a signature, depending on the context. When using a symmetric key K_X, then $K_X[M]$ refers to message M with an attached HMAC. If using a private key K_X^{PRIV}, then $K_X^{PRIV}[M]$ refers to message M with an attached signature. The same applies for encryption schemes, denoted by $K_X\{M\}$ or $K_X^{PUB}\{M\}$.

2.3.4.2. Freshness Values

The definition of entity authentication in Section 2.3.2 stated that "an entity must actively participate". It is therefore necessary to proof that messages have not been replayed by an adversary, but instead are new or *fresh*. This can be achieved by means of freshness values, for which it can be guaranteed that they have not been used before. There are three types of freshness values that are commonly used in protocols: timestamps, nonces and counters.

Using one of these freshness values in combination with either a HMAC or signature simultaneously provides data origin authentication for the associated message.

Timestamps
Boyd and Mathuria [30] define a timestamp as follows: "The sender of the message adds the current time to the message when it is sent. This is checked by the recipient when the message is received by comparing with the local time. If the received timestamp is within an acceptable window of the current time then the message is regarded as fresh."

An example for a one-way authentication where Alice authenticates to Bob by means of a timestamp is provided in the following:

$$A \rightarrow B \ (M1): \ K_{AB}[\mathcal{T}, Id_A]$$

The timestamp T indicates to Bob that Alice recently sent message M1. The HMAC calculated with the shared key K_{AB} assures that the message has been sent by Alice and not by an adversary.

A problem with timestamps is the need to have synchronized clocks at the sender and receiver.

Nonces
A nonce is random number, also called a random challenge. When Bob receives a request message from Alice, he will return a response that includes a nonce N_X. Alice then has to perform a cryptographic function using N_X as an input and return the result to Bob.

An example for a one-way authentication based on a nonce is provided in the following. It is equivalent to protocol (2.3).

$$
\begin{aligned}
A \to B \ (M1): \ & Id_A \\
B \to A \ (M2): \ & N_B \\
A \to B \ (M3): \ & K_{AB}[N_B]
\end{aligned}
\tag{2.6}
$$

When Bob receives message 3 (M3), he can be assured that Alice interactively responded to Bob's request (M2). It is not possible to replay an old message as M3 must contain a HMAC calculated over the nonce N_B.

A disadvantage of using a nonce is that it usually requires an additional message to be exchanged. Nonces should not be predictable, which requires both a large number space and a good source for obtaining random number sequences in order to prevent an adversary from guessing a nonce in advance.

Counters
A message counter, also called sequence number, is established and kept synchronized between Alice and Bob. When Alice sends a message, she includes the current sequence number. When Bob receives this message, he will verify whether the sequence number used in the message is equivalent to the expected value indicated by his copy of the sequence number. The sequence number is incremented after each message exchange.

An example is provided in the following, based on the mutual authentication protocol (2.4). The sequence number is denoted by S.

$$A \rightarrow B \ (M1): \ Id_A, R_2$$
$$B \rightarrow A \ (M2): \ R_1, K_{AB}[R2]$$
$$A \rightarrow B \ (M3): \ K_{AB}[R_1]$$

Establish state at A,B with $\mathcal{S} = H(R1 \mid R2)$

$$A \rightarrow B \ (M4): \ K_{AB}[Request\ 1, \mathcal{S} + 1]$$
$$B \rightarrow A \ (M5): \ K_{AB}[Response\ 1, \mathcal{S} + 1]$$
$$A \rightarrow B \ (M6): \ K_{AB}[Request\ 2, \mathcal{S} + 2]$$
$$B \rightarrow A \ (M7): \ K_{AB}[Response\ 2, \mathcal{S} + 2]$$

Messages 1-3 are used for authenticating Alice and Bob. Once the authentication phase has been finished, the sequence number $\mathcal{S}$ is derived from the two random nonces provided by Alice and Bob. For each subsequent request-response message pair exchanged between Alice and Bob, the sequence number is incremented.

If messages 4-6 would be sent without a sequence number, an adversary could replay messages that have been observed within previous protocol exchanges between Alice and Bob.

The disadvantage of a counter is the need to keep synchronized state information between the two communication nodes. The sequence number space also has to be very large to reduce the probability of running out of numbers during a protocol session. Reusing sequence numbers is not permitted, as an adversary could then replay an old message when the corresponding sequence number recurs. The common method for avoiding this issue is to change the cryptographic key, as will be discussed in Section 2.3.4.3. Once a new key K_{AB} is available, a reset of the sequence number counter can be performed, as the corresponding message authentication codes are different from those calculated with the previous key.

Another way to proof the freshness of a message is to use a cryptographic key that is known to be fresh. This aspect will be covered in the following.

2.3.4.3. Key Establishment

In a public key system, Alice and Bob could use their public and private keys not only for authentication in the security handshake, but also for signing subsequent messages exchanged within the protocol. Alternatively, when Alice and Bob already share a symmetric key, this key could be used for cryptographic protection of subsequent messages exchanged within the protocol as well.

However, in most protocols the cryptographic keys that are already available between a pair of nodes are only used for an initial (mutual) authentication. Within this authentication, or following it, a shared secret is established among the two communication nodes that is then used for protecting subsequent protocol messages exchanged between the two nodes. Such a shared secret is also known as *session key*.

The process of establishing a session key is defined by Menezes et al. [134] as follows: "Key establishment is a process or protocol whereby a shared secret becomes available to two or more parties, for subsequent cryptographic use".

Boyd and Mathuria [30] further extend this definition to specify the notion of a "good" session key:

Definition 2.7. *The shared session key is a good key for A to use with B only if A has assurance that:*

1. *the key is fresh (key freshness);*
2. *the key is known only to A and B and any mutually trusted parties (key authentication).*

Public-private key pairs can also be used as session keys, but are not further discussed here.

Session Key Generation
A simple example for establishing a session key is provided in the following, where Alice randomly chooses a shared secret and sends it to Bob in encrypted form:

$$A \rightarrow B \ (M1): \ K_A^{PRIV}[Id_A, \mathcal{T}, K_B^{PUB}\{K_{AB}\}] \tag{2.7}$$

The message includes Alice's identity (Id_A), a timestamp $\mathcal{T}$ to ensure freshness of the message as well as a shared secret K_{AB}, randomly chosen by Alice and encrypted with Bob's public key. Finally, Alice attaches a signature calculated from her private key to provide authentication.

The session key K_{AB} can then be used with the respective symmetric cryptographic schemes by Alice and Bob in subsequent message exchanges. This key fulfills the properties specified in Definition 2.7: (1) the key is randomly generated by Alice, with the message itself proved to be fresh due to the timestamp; (2) the shared secret is encrypted with Bob's public key, therefore restricting knowledge of the key to Alice and Bob.

Another possibility for generating a shared secret is to let both Alice and Bob contribute to the key:

$$
\begin{aligned}
A \rightarrow B \ (M1): \ & K_A^{PRIV}[Id_A, \mathcal{T}, K_B^{PUB}\{R_1\}] \\
B \rightarrow A \ (M2): \ & K_B^{PRIV}[Id_B, \mathcal{T}, K_A^{PUB}\{R_2\}]
\end{aligned}
\tag{2.8}
$$

57

Alice and Bob can then each generate a shared secret $K_{AB} = H(R_1 \mid R_2)$. This key also fulfills the requirements of Definition 2.7, as an adversary has no access to either R_1 or R_2.

A widely used protocol for key establishment is the Diffie-Hellman key exchange [51], which provides additional features apart from what is specified in Definition 2.7.

Key Rollover
A session key should be periodically renewed, especially if the sequence numbers used in the protocol message exchanges are about to be exhausted. Otherwise an adversary could replay previously observed messages that have been cryptographically protected with the session key in question.

Changing the shared secret within a protocol run is called *key rollover* or also *rekeying*. The usual approach to achieve this goal is to repeat the authentication procedure and generate a new key, e. g., as in protocols (2.7) and (2.8).

2.3.5. Public Key Infrastructure

The main objective of a public key infrastructure (PKI) is to securely distribute public keys. In the following a simplified overview of the PKIX model as specified in [45] is provided; a more detailed textbook description can be found in [113, Chapter 15].

A public key infrastructure consists of the following elements:

- Certificate: a piece of information that binds a public key to the identity of a public key holder. A certificate is signed by a certificate authority.
- End entity: user of PKI certificates and/or end user system that is the subject of a certificate.
- Certificate Authority (CA): the issuer of certificates and certificate revocation lists (CRLs).
- Repository: a system for storing certificate revocation lists.

The PKIX standard also defines a number of management functions for creating, managing and revoking certificates.

2.3.5.1. PKI Architectural Model

An overview of the individual PKI elements and how they interact is provided in Figure 2.18a. The operations among the different elements are described in the following.

Certification
In order to obtain a valid certificate, the entity first creates a preliminary version

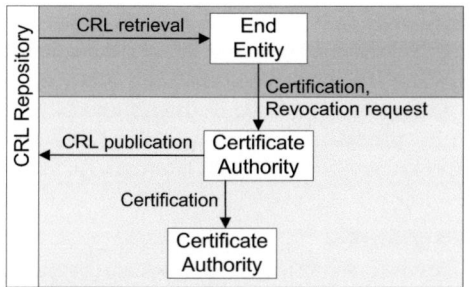

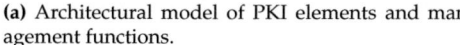

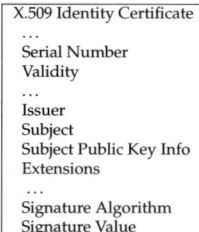

(a) Architectural model of PKI elements and management functions.

(b) X.509 certificate with basic fields.

Figure 2.18. Public Key Infrastructure.

of the certificate containing the entity's public key and identity. This preliminary certificate is then sent to the certificate authority (CA). The CA will verify that the identity provided in the certificate corresponds to the entity's real identity. If so, the CA will add additional information and finally sign the certificate. The certificate has then been properly issued.

An illustration of such a certificate, according to the X.509 Internet standard [45], is provided in Figure 2.18b. The field *"Serial Number"* is specified by the CA and uniquely identifies the certificate within the context of this CA. *"Validity"* specifies the time window in terms of a start and end date, in which the certificate is valid for use. *"Issuer"* refers to the name of the CA that issued the certificate. The *"Subject"* field identifies the entity that is associated with the public key that is stored inside *"Subject Public Key Info"*. A certificate can also include one or several additional, optional fields that are stored inside the *"Extensions"* field. Finally, the *"Signature Value"* contains the signature calculated by the issuing certificate authority, with *"Signature Algorithm"* specifying which scheme has been used for calculating the signature. The signature itself is calculated over the entire certificate using the private key of the certificate authority. Figure 2.18b shows the certificate in human-readable form. For use inside a communication protocol, the certificate would use the Distinguished Encoding Rules (DER) of ASN.1 [105], which is a message transfer syntax representing a certificate in binary form.

A special case are certificates of certificate authorities, where the issuer and subject are the same entity. These certificates are self-signed, meaning that the certificate has been signed with the private key K_{CA}^{PRIV} of the CA that is associated to the public key K_{CA}^{PUB} provided in the Subject Public Key Info field.

ᵉer

It is also possible for a certificate authority to delegate all or parts of its authority to a subordinate certificate authority. For a certificate providing such a delegation, issuer and subject are different entities: the subject refers to the subordinate CA, which is hierarchically below the issuing CA specified in the issuer field. As a result, a tree like structure of certificate authorities is created, with a self-signed CA certificate at the root of the tree and subsequent subordinate CAs further down the tree.

Certification between Certificate Authorities
Depending on the specific public key infrastructure model, several certificate authorities (CAs) might exist. For example, a (root) certificate authority can delegate authority to a subordinate CA. In this case, a corresponding *delegation certificate* is issued by the (root) CA, where the subject of the certificate is the subordinate CA. This process can be repeated by the subordinate CA. This then results in a tree structure of CAs.

There might also be other CAs with self-signed certificates. The set of all these root CAs then forms an oligarchy. It is possible for any root or subordinate certificate authority to issue a certificate to another certificate authority that is located in a tree associated to another root certificate authority. The corresponding *cross-certificate* is another variant of a CA certificate where issuer and subject are different entities.
Cross-certification allows "connecting" distinct trust domains. It permits two entities, which have certificates issued by different certificate authorities belonging to different trust domains, to authenticate to each other.

Revocation Request
A certificate is valid within the time window specified in the validity field. A certificate can however also be revoked explicitly if necessary, e. g., if the private key associated to the certificate has been compromised.

The entity will send a revocation request to the certificate authority that issued the certificate. The certificate authority will then add this certificate, identified by the serial number, to it's certificate revocation list.

CRL Publication
A certificate authority can publish a Certificate Revocation List (CRL). A CRL provides status information about the certificates that have been issued by that CA. The certificate revocation list lists all unexpired certificates, issued by that certificate authority, that have been revoked for any reason.

The certificate revocation list itself is a list of entries consisting of the triple (serial number, time, extensions) for each revoked certificate. Serial number refers to the serial number of the certificate to be revoked. Time refers to the point in time the certificate has been revoked. The extensions field can contain additional

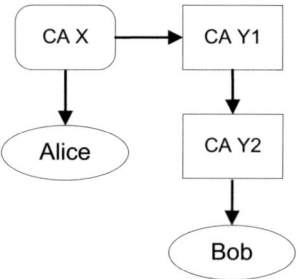

Figure 2.19. Example for a PKI with subordinate certificate authority and cross certification. Arrows indicate certificate issuance.

information, such as the reason for the revocation. The certificate revocation list itself is signed with the private key of the issuing certificate authority.

CRL Retrieval
Before accepting a certificate, an entity has to verify that the certificate has not been revoked. It is therefore necessary to retrieve the certificate revocation list of the certificate authority that issued the certificate. The location from which a certificate revocation list can be obtained is specified within an extension field of the certificate authority certificate.

2.3.5.2. Certificate Verification

Prior to accepting a certificate, it has to be validated. The validation process consists of constructing and verifying a *certification path* between the certificate to be validated and a trusted certificate authority. The entity attempting to verify a certificate is also called *verifier*. The certificate to be validated is also called *target*.

The structure of a certification path depends on the underlying public key infrastructure model: there might only be a single certificate authority that issued certificates to all end entities, but there might also by several certificate authorities, each issuing certificates to a subset of all end entities. An extensive overview of the different PKI models is available in [167]. The model used in the following with two root and one subordinate certificate authority is illustrated in Figure 2.19.

The example is based on the following assumptions:

- Alice attempts to verify Bob's certificate (Alice is the verifier, Bob is the target).
- Alice is in possession of the certificate of the certificate authority X.
- Bob's certificate is issued by certificate authority $Y2$.

- Certificate authority $Y1$ delegated parts of its authority to certificate authority Y2.
- Certificate authority X has cross-certified certificate authority $Y1$.

In order to verify Bob's certificate, a certification path from the target, Bob's certificate, to a certificate authority that is trusted by Alice has to be established. As Alice is in possession of the certificate for CA X and she initially only trusts this certificate, CA X is said to be Alice's *trust anchor*. The certification path to Bob is therefore constructed starting with the certificate of CA X:

$$X \ll Y1 \gg, Y1 \ll Y2 \gg, Y2 \ll B \gg$$

where $Y \ll X \gg$ indicates that certificate of entity X has been issued by certificate authority Y.

Alice can follow the link from X to $Y1$, for which a cross-certificate is available. $Y1$ has issued a CA certificate to Y2, which in turn has issued and end entity certificate to Bob. The verification of this path involves verifying the certificates of $X, Y1, Y2$ and Bob. For each certificate, the following steps have to be performed:

- Verify that that the certificate has not expired (indicated by the validity field).
- Verify that the certificate is not listed in the corresponding certificate revocation list.
- Verify that the signature on the certificate is valid.

If Alice manages to verify each certificate along the certification path, then Alice can trust Bob's certificate.

Bob can verify Alice's certificate via the reverse path, assuming that $Y2$ is Bob's trust anchor and that a cross-certificate from $Y1$ to X exists:

$$Y2 \ll Y1 \gg, Y1 \ll X \gg, X \ll A \gg$$

2.3.5.3. Online Certificate Status Protocol

An alternative to revoking certificates based on a certificate revocation list or for validating certificates in general is the Online Certificate Status Protocol (OCSP) [142].

OCSP is a protocol that allows a client (Alice) to request certificate validity information from a server (X). This is also illustrated in Figure 2.20. The protocol is based on a request-response message exchange: Alice sends a request with the certificate to be validated and the OCSP server will respond with a status message indicating whether the certificate is valid or not. The back-end to OCSP can

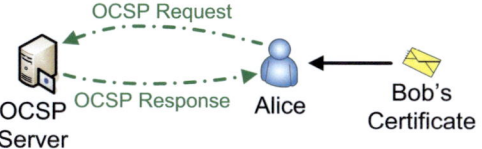

OCSP Request

OCSP OCSP Response Alice
Server

Bob's
Certificate

Figure 2.20. Certificate verification based on OCSP.

be either a certificate revocation list or a database, or a combination of both. The location of the OCSP server is indicated in the certificate of the certificate authority that issued the certificate to be verified. The server can be co-located with the certificate authority. If this is not the case, then the certificate authority must delegate revocation rights to the public-private key pair of the OCSP server. An OCSP server can only provide status information for certificates that have been issued by the certificate authority that is associated with this server.

An OCSP request includes the following information, among others: the serial number of the certificate as well as a hash of the issuer name and public key. The OCSP response includes the serial number of the verified certificate, the status information ("good", "revoked" or "unknown") as well as a hash of the issuer name and public key. The response is signed by the server.

2.3.5.4. Notation

In Chapter 7 of this thesis, certificates will mostly be represented in a formal notation, which is defined in the following.

A serial number S is a positive integer value:

$$S \in \mathbb{N}$$

The name θ of a certificate authority is considered to be an arbitrary length string consisting of characters:

$$\theta \in \{A - Z, a - z\}^n, \ n \in \mathbb{N}$$

A standard identity certificate, issued by certificate authority X to entity Alice, holding Alice's public key A and containing Alice's identity p is written as follows:

$$Cert(X, A, p)$$

The revocation status for a certificate with serial number S is defined by the function ρ:

$$\rho : S \mapsto \{0, 1\}$$

A value of 1 indicates that the certificate with serial number S has been revoked. A revocation service is provided by either a certificate revocation list or an online certificate status protocol server.

A signature σ calculated with the private key K^{PRIV} over the concatenation of arbitrary data is written as follows:

$$\sigma = K^{PRIV}[\text{data}_1 \mid \text{data}_2]$$

3. Related Work

NEMO, a member of the Mobile IPv6 protocol family, will serve as a baseline within this thesis for supporting IP mobility in the future aeronautical communications environment. A rationale for this selection has been provided in Section 2.1.8.

NEMO suffers from the problem of large end-to-end latency due to routing all traffic via the home agent, cf. Section 2.2.7. This chapter therefore provides an overview of related work in the following topics:

- Route optimization protocols for NEMO for providing a shorter end-to-end latency.
- Approaches for providing security within route optimization protocols.

Within the section covering the first item, the correspondent router protocol is evaluated as the most suitable one for the safety related aeronautical environment from a set of candidate solutions. As this protocol suffers from security problems, the section covering the second item will provide an overview of related work for Mobile IPv6/NEMO route optimization security.

3.1. Network Mobility Route Optimization

A disadvantage of the current NEMO protocol is that all traffic between the mobile network nodes and the correspondent nodes suffers from suboptimal routing, since all packets are forwarded through the home agent that is located in the home network. This is in contrast to Mobile IPv6, which does provide a route optimization component for establishing a direct routing path between mobile host and correspondent node.

A significant number of related work proposing route optimization solutions for NEMO is available. An evaluation based on a set of requirements is performed in order to select the most suitable protocol for the safety related aeronautical communications environment.

3.1.1. NEMO Route Optimization Requirements

In the following, requirements are specified that have to be fulfilled by a candidate NEMO route optimization solution for being applicable in the aeronautical environment. These requirements are a refinement and extension of those already specified in [55].

The requirements are as follows:

1. End-to-end latency: the number of intermediate nodes on the routing path between the end-systems in the mobile network and the ground network should be as small as possible.[1]

2. Single point of failure: a new mobility specific node for the purpose of route optimization should not constitute a single point of failure.[2]

3. Separability: it should be possible to apply route optimization only to traffic flows that really require it. For example, route optimization should only be applied to all traffic originating from or destined to one specific mobile network node, while traffic from other mobile network nodes is still routed via the home agent.

4. Multihoming: the route optimization mechanism must be fully usable if several interfaces are present. More precisely, it should be possible to forward a route optimized traffic flow via a particular interface/access network.

5. Efficient signaling: both the size and number of individual route optimization signaling messages that are exchanged over the wireless path should be kept small.

6. Ground network impact: the amount of support necessary from the ground network in order to provide route optimization between the mobile network nodes and correspondent nodes should be limited.

7. Security: the mobility entity on the ground with whom route optimization signaling is performed must be able to validate the aircraft as proper owner

---

[1]A NEMO route optimization protocol can not influence the number of intermediate routers that are present on the intra-domain or inter-domain routing level. This requirement is therefore limited to mobility specific nodes.

[2]The communicating end-systems, the mobile network node and correspondent node, are not considered being single point of failures. The same holds for the mobile router, which is always required as first hop router of the mobile network node, independent of the used route optimization procedure.

of the claimed care-of address and mobile network prefix. In the reverse direction, the mobile router must also validate the claimed address or prefix used by the ground mobility entity.

8. Adaptability: the route optimization scheme should not break applications using new transport protocols or IPsec.

The set of requirements used in this evaluation is partially overlapping with the set that was used for deriving NEMO as the most suitable mobility protocol, cf. Section 2.1.8. The requirement on applicability to aeronautical administrative communication/aeronautical passenger communication has been omitted as this investigation is focused on supporting safety related services. The requirements on routing scalability, convergence time and support for ground-initiated communications have been omitted as they are fulfilled by NEMO, irrespective of the selected route optimization protocol. Additional NEMO specific requirements have been added though, such as separability or adaptability.

The various different proposals for performing NEMO route optimization will be assessed in the following based on these requirements.

3.1.2. NEMO Route Optimization Protocols

Route optimization signaling can be initiated by and performed among different network nodes. Consecutively, four route optimization classes can be established. The classes are defined according to the nodes participating in the signaling:

- Mobile network node to correspondent node.
- Mobile router to correspondent node.
- Mobile router to correspondent router.
- Mobile router to home agent.

An illustration of these categories is provided in Figure 3.1. A compact summary of the individual solutions, categorized by the classes, is provided in the following.

Mobile network node to correspondent node: an example for this approach is [147]. The mobile router relays the router advertisement of its own access router(s) to the mobile network nodes. The mobile network nodes make then use of their own Mobile IPv6 functionality to form a care-of address from this advertisement. They then perform the Mobile IPv6 route optimization signaling with the correspondent nodes themselves. The mobile router is therefore only in a supporting role.

An advantage of this category is that the optimized path is the shortest possible one with direct routing between mobile network node and correspondent node. No single point of failure problem is introduced. The mobile network nodes can

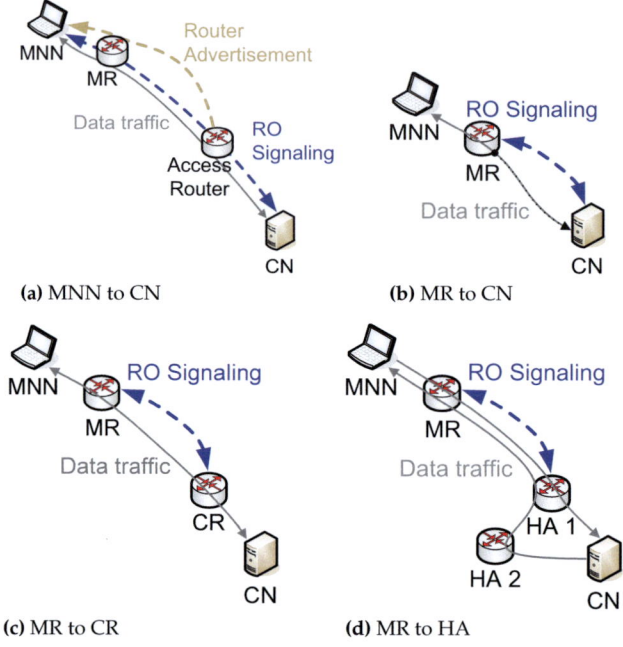

Figure 3.1. The four different NEMO route optimization classes.

also easily decide for which data flows route optimization should be performed. Multihoming can also be supported: for every router advertisement the mobile router is relaying from each access router, the mobile network nodes can configure an additional care-of address. The end-systems can then decide which care-of address should be used for which traffic flow, thereby routing traffic over different access networks.

A significant problem with this approach is overhead, as route optimization signaling is performed between every mobile network node and correspondent node for whom an optimized routing path should be provided.

The mobile router will also have to manage the care-of addresses of the mobile network nodes: packets from the correspondent nodes addressed to the care-of address of a mobile network node have to be retrieved by the mobile router from the access router and forwarded to the respective mobile network node. This means that the mobile router has to act as a neighbor discovery proxy (see Section 2.2.3.2). Depending on the security measures in place in the access network (e. g. Secure Neighbor Discovery [14]), this might not be possible. Apart from these issues, there is no impact on the ground network except for the correspondent nodes having to support Mobile IPv6 route optimization signaling. As the mobile network nodes make use of Mobile IPv6, the security problems of this protocol are also inherited, cf. Section 2.2.6.2. It is also necessary to upgrade the mobile network node protocol stack with Mobile IPv6 functionality.

In Mobile IPv6 route optimization, the packets that are sent over the optimized path are extended with additional headers. This affects the end-to-end integrity and might cause problems with an end-to-end security protocol.

Mobile router to correspondent node: within this class, the mobile router performs the Mobile IPv6 route optimization signaling on behalf of the mobile network node with a correspondent node. The mobile router therefore acts as a route optimization proxy for the mobile network nodes. Several proposals exist [35, 36, 118].

The end-to-end path can still be considered as being optimal with packets being routed directly on the path between mobile router and correspondent node. No single point of failure is introduced, given that the mobile router is always required in a NEMO route optimization context. It is also possible to separate data flows: while certain flows make use of route optimization and are directly routed to the correspondent node, other flows can still be routed via the home agent. The mobile router can decide whether or not to perform route optimization for a certain flow based on IP packet header information, e. g., the source address identifying a certain mobile network node. This is also valid for the subsequent solution classes where the mobile router performs mobility signaling.

The mobile router can also make use of multihoming by registering several care-of addresses with a particular correspondent node. The route optimization signaling overhead is limited to the (MR,CN) pairs for whom an optimized path should be established. As the correspondent nodes within the ground network are participating in the route optimization signaling, they must implement Mobile IPv6 correspondent node functionality.

Due to reusing Mobile IPv6 route optimization signaling between mobile router and correspondent node, this approach also inherits the associated security weaknesses, cf. Section 2.2.6.2. The mobile router also has to extend the original packets with additional headers when performing route optimization on behalf of the mobile network nodes. As this affects the integrity of an end-to-end data flow, a security protocol used between mobile network node and correspondent node (e. g. IPsec) might classify the route optimization operations of the mobile router as a man-in-the-middle attack.

Mobile router to correspondent router was proposed in [212]. A new entity called Correspondent Router (CR), which is located close to the correspondent nodes, is introduced. The mobile router performs mobility signaling with the correspondent router and establishes a bi-directional tunnel that is used to exchange traffic between the mobile network and the network served by the correspondent router. The correspondent router therefore acts as a route optimization proxy for the correspondent nodes.

The optimized path contains the correspondent router as an additional intermediate node. If this node is located within the same network as the correspondent node, the optimized path is at least close to optimal as packets are routed on a direct path to the network of the correspondent node. The correspondent router could be regarded as a single point of failure. This problem is however reduced as there is no single global correspondent router. Instead, every network with correspondent nodes can have its own correspondent router. The mobile router can also register several care-of addresses with the correspondent router and route different traffic flows over different care-of addresses. The signaling overhead has been reduced compared to the previous protocols: the route optimization procedure is now performed for every (MR, CR) pair, where several correspondent nodes can be served by a single correspondent router. It is necessary to deploy a correspondent router as a new component within the individual networks where the correspondent nodes are located.

As the signaling procedure between mobile router and correspondent router is based on Mobile IPv6 route optimization signaling, the associated security deficiency is inherited by the correspondent router protocol, cf. Section 2.2.6.2. Data packets between mobile network node and correspondent node remain unmodified as they are transported within an IP-in-IP tunnel between mobile router and correspondent router. Hence, the route optimization process is transparent to end-to-end transport and security protocols.

Mobile router to home agent: the concept of having only a single home agent has been extended to having multiple, distributed home agents within the home network. The proposal is called Global HA-to-HA [214, 215]. The mobile router binds to the closest home agent (HA 1 in Figure 3.1d) to achieve route optimization. The amount of end-to-end latency reduction depends on the location of the home agents.

The intention of the HA-to-HA approach is to have a home network (autonomous system) where home agents are distributed over the entire world. A large aggregated prefix containing all mobile network prefixes is advertised via an interdomain routing protocol. This inflicts anycast routing, meaning that traffic from a correspondent node to a mobile router or mobile network node will be routed to the topologically closest home agent of the correspondent node. In Figure 3.1d, the mobile router has mobility binding and establishes a tunnel with home agent 1. HA 1 is therefore the primary home agent of the mobile router. All home agents share the binding information among each other. HA 2 is considered being the closest home agent to the correspondent node. When receiving traffic from the correspondent node destined for the mobile router, this home agent will forward packets to the primary home agent, HA 1. This home agent will then forward the packets to the mobile router. In the reverse direction, traffic from the mobile network node to the correspondent node is routed from the mobile router to HA 1 and then directly to the correspondent node.

Global HA-to-HA relies on the home network and its home agents being distributed all over the world. Hence no specific level of route optimization can be guaranteed; instead, the end-to-end latency depends on where and in which numbers the mobility service provider deploys individual home agents. The single point of failure problem has only been partially addressed: while home agents are distributed, they are still located within the home network. In case of routing problems from and to the home network, end-to-end communications is not possible anymore. Multihoming can be supported by having the mobile router register several care-of addresses with its current home agent. However, as the mobile router can only bind to a single home agent, routing different flows simultaneously via different home agents is not possible. Consecutively, the single home agent with whom a binding exists might not be the closest one with respect to all the routing paths from and to the mobile router. An advantage of this protocol is that the signaling overhead is low, as only a binding update/binding acknowledgement message exchange is performed between mobile router and home agent.

The signaling exchanges between mobile router and primary home agent are similar to the basic NEMO protocol. Additional signaling is required though to locate the closest home agent of a mobile router. Synchronization signaling is necessary between all home agents to enable forwarding of traffic to the primary home agent. This inflicts a signaling overhead within the ground network. The synchronization among all home agents can be omitted if a distributed hash table is used for establishing binding servers [228]. With such a scheme, only a particular home agent, called binding server, knows the primary home agent for a certain mobile router. Any other home agent attempting to forward packets to a particular mobile router then refers to the binding server for retrieving the address of the primary home agent.

Global HA-to-HA does not require any mobility functionality in the correspondent nodes or within the correspondent node networks.

Just as in the basic NEMO protocol, the signaling messages between mobile router and home agent are protected by IPsec, which provides a high level of security. Also, due to transporting packets within an IP-in-IP tunnel on the path between mobile router and home agent, end-to-end transport or security protocols remain unaffected.

Requirement	MNN to CN	MR to CN	MR to CR	MR to HA
End-to-End Latency	⊕⊕	⊕⊕	⊕	⊖
Single Point of Failure	⊕⊕	⊕⊕	⊖	⊖⊖
Separability	⊕⊕	⊕	⊕	⊕
Multihoming	⊕⊕	⊕⊕	⊕⊕	⊕
Efficient Signaling	⊖⊖	⊖	⊕	⊕⊕
Ground Network Impact	⊕	⊕	⊖	⊖⊖
Security	⊖⊖	⊖⊖	⊖⊖	⊕⊕
Adaptability	⊕	⊖⊖	⊕⊕	⊕⊕

Table 3.1. Overview of the characteristics of the individual solution classes. Requirements can be either fulfilled (⊕⊕), partially fulfilled (⊕), partially problematic (⊖) or problematic (⊖⊖).

3.1.3. Assessment of NEMO Route Optimization Protocols

A summary of the assessment of the four NEMO route optimization solution classes with regard to the previously specified requirements is provided in Table 3.1. Other, more general discussions on the advantages and disadvantages of these protocols can also be found in [190] and [127].

For the MNN-to-CN class, the property *end-to-end latency* is completely fulfilled (⊕⊕) as an optimal path is provided. As the mobile network node is directly attached to the mobile router, the class MR-to-CN is also considered to provide optimal end-to-end latency. The correspondent router, being an additional intermediate node on the end-to-end path that is close to the correspondent node, can be regarded as sufficiently fulfilling (⊕) the requirement. The need to route traffic via a home agent that is "somewhere" close to the correspondent node has to be considered as only a partial fulfillment of this requirement (⊖).

A single point of failure is not introduced by either the MNN-to-CN or the MR-to-CN solution classes (⊕⊕). A correspondent router can be regarded as a single point of failure, but has the advantage of being distributed across different correspondent node networks (⊖). In the Global HA-to-HA protocol, the home agents are distributed, but still located within the home network (⊖⊖).

The property *separability* is completely fulfilled (⊕⊕) by the MNN-to-CN class and sufficiently fulfilled (⊕) by the other approaches. The reason for the reduced grading is the inability of the mobile router to perform traffic flow identification in case an end-to-end security protocol with confidentiality protection is used. In this situation, the mobile router is unable to inspect the packet content and can therefore not differentiate between different applications.

The property *multihoming* is either completely ($\oplus\oplus$) or sufficiently ($\oplus$) fulfilled. Sufficiently refers to the fact that traffic can be routed via different wireless links, but packets are still routed via the same home agent.

Efficient signaling ranges from very bad ($\ominus\ominus$) up to very good ($\oplus\oplus$), depending on whether mobility signaling has to be performed with a large or small number of nodes.

A certain level of *ground network impact* is present for all solution classes, as either existing nodes have to be modified ($\oplus$), a new network node has to be deployed ($\ominus$) or the home network with its home agents has to be expanded to world-wide scale in order to provide a small end-to-end latency ($\ominus\ominus$).

The *security* requirement has been either fulfilled ($\oplus\oplus$) or not fulfilled ($\ominus\ominus$).

The grading of the property *adaptability* is as follows: it is either not fulfilled ($\ominus\ominus$) because of problems with preserving end-to-end integrity or completely fulfilled ($\oplus\oplus$) because the original payload is preserved due to tunneling encapsulation. It is also possible to sufficiently fulfill ($\oplus$) this requirement in case end-to-end traffic is modified by the end-systems for the purpose of route optimization. In this situation, no problems might be caused if the receiving end-system restores the original packet format before any other (security) protocol operations are performed, in particular integrity checking.

The first two approaches involve either the correspondent node or the mobile network node, or both nodes, in the mobility signaling. This not only causes a burden as these systems must be upgraded with Mobile IPv6 functionality, but these solutions most notably suffer from problems in the areas of efficiency and security. Performing signaling per correspondent node and maybe additionally even per mobile network node causes significant overhead. The security problem refers to the vulnerability to off-path adversaries that has been inherited due to using the Mobile IPv6 route optimization procedure, cf. Section 2.2.6.2.

In the third solution class, MR-to-CR, signaling is performed with a single correspondent router that can then provide a direct routing path to an arbitrary number of correspondent nodes located within the same network. This approach preserves the integrity of end-to-end data packets due to tunneling. However, the protocol suffers from security problems as the Mobile IPv6 route optimization signaling is reused. The single point of failure problem is limited due to the distributed nature of the protocol, considering that a correspondent router only serves a particular network with correspondent nodes.

On the other hand, the Global HA-to-HA protocol (the MR-to-HA approach) provides excellent security properties and also preserves the integrity of end-to-end data packets due to tunneling. However the mobility service provider operating the home agents must have a world-wide network presence. If home agents are not available in close distance to the mobile router, a binding with a distant home agent would again have to be performed. Consecutively, reducing end-to-end latency – the ultimate goal of a route optimization procedure – is not achievable anymore. The protocol does also have a single point of failure in terms of relying on the home network.

The first two solution approaches are discarded due to the need of increased complexity at the end-systems, large signaling overhead as well as security problems. A closer look at the remaining two protocols is taken in the following.

An illustration of the routing paths for the correspondent router and the Global HA-to-HA protocols in a typical safety related aeronautical scenario involving ATS communications is provided in Figure 3.2. As mentioned in Section 2.1.4 on the aeronautical telecommunications network, for ATS communications the aircraft will attach to an access network that is either collocated with the network where the correspondent node is located or is only one autonomous system hop away from the correspondent network.

Hence, for Global HA-to-HA, a "ping-pong" effect is present: packets are tunneled from the mobile network via the correspondent network to the home network, where they are decapsulated by the home agent and forwarded back to the correspondent network. This is not only inefficient, but might also become problematic if firewalls at the correspondent network boundary are configured to drop incoming packets from outside networks.

The introduction of multiple home agents only partially addresses the single point of failure problem that is inherent to the Mobile IPv6 and NEMO protocols. The different home agents are still located within a single, although geographically large, home network. In case of inter-domain routing problems that break the routing path between the correspondent and the home network, end-to-end communication is not possible anymore. Also, in case an airline decides to be its own mobility service provider, it might not be able to operate a large scale home network such that home agents will be close to the aircraft. As a consequence, route optimization can not be adequately provided and end-to-end latency will be larger when compared to other route optimization approaches.

In contrast to this, the correspondent router protocol provides a direct routing path from the mobile network to the correspondent node, assuming that the correspondent router is deployed in the correspondent network. Consecutively, there are no issues with firewalls at the network boundary or with failing inter-domain routing. A single correspondent router provided by the correspondent network operator can provide an optimized path for this entire network domain.

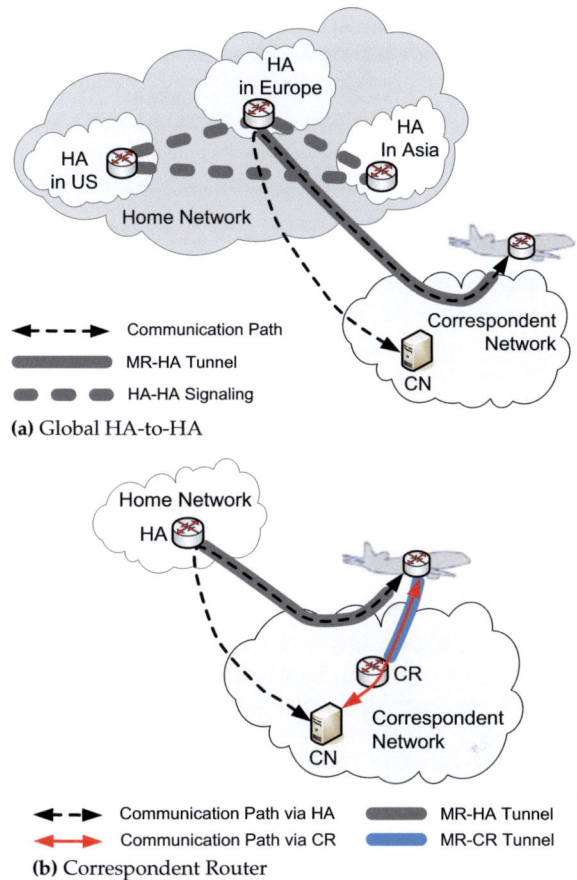

(a) Global HA-to-HA

(b) Correspondent Router

Figure 3.2. Typical air traffic services communications scenario making use of different route optimization protocols.

3.1.4. Conclusion on Protocol Assessment

The correspondent router protocol is the most adequate solution class for *safety related* aeronautical communications. It is especially suitable for ATS communications where the mobile router/mobile network is close to the correspondent node, often being located within the same network. For AOC, where communication takes place between mobile network and ground based airline systems, traffic can be either routed via the home agent (thereby not making use of route optimization) or use a correspondent router located in the airline ground network.

As the focus of this thesis is on safety related communications, especially ATS, the security issues of the correspondent router protocol have to be resolved first. Related work on route optimization security that could be reused for the correspondent router protocol will therefore be discussed in the following.

For *non-safety related* communications, especially aeronautical passenger communications, the Global HA-to-HA protocol is the only feasible solution: it is not possible to modify passenger devices (mobile network nodes), nor servers located in the public Internet (correspondent nodes). Also, it seems unrealistic to assume that content providers in the public Internet will deploy special infrastructure (correspondent routers) to support mobile networks. The only remaining option is to rely on the mobility service provider deploying distributed home agents that can provide a certain level of end-to-end communications latency reduction.

As this thesis is focused on safety related communications, a more detailed overview of the correspondent router protocol and its (security) deficiencies is provided in the following.

3.1.5. Correspondent Router Protocol

The *correspondent router* (CR) acts as a proxy and performs the route optimization signaling with the mobile router on behalf of its locally served correspondent nodes. The signaling exchange is illustrated in Figure 3.3. Traffic destined to the mobile network node or correspondent node can be directly routed between mobile router and correspondent router instead of being relayed via the home agent. Packets addressed to the mobile network nodes associated to the mobile network prefix are routed to the care-of address of the mobile router. Traffic to those correspondent nodes that are in the same network as the correspondent router is routed directly to the address of the correspondent router. These nodes can be associated with the correspondent router as their addresses are configured from the *correspondent router prefix* (CRP). This prefix is the correspondent router equivalent of the mobile network prefix of the mobile router. Forwarding of packets associated to mobile network prefix and correspondent router prefix takes place via a bi-directional IP-in-IP tunnel established between mobile router and correspondent router.

The advantages of this approach are (1) a short end-to-end delay as the correspondent router should be deployed close to the correspondent nodes, (2) an optimized route to several correspondent nodes provided by a single correspondent router simultaneously and (3) the transparency to the end-systems in the mobile network and on the ground due to tunneling.

The protocol was originally proposed by Wakikawa et al. [212]. The authors propose a simple request-response signaling for discovering the correspondent router: the mobile router sends a discovery-request message to the correspondent node. The correspondent router, which is on the forwarding path to the correspondent node, intercepts this message and responds with a discovery response message. Now that the mobile router has the address of the correspondent router, the actual route optimization signaling starts. It is similar to the Mobile IPv6 route optimization procedure (cf. Section 2.2.6) and uses a care-of and home reachability test as shown in Figure 3.3. It is assumed that the IPsec security association between mobile router and home agent provides a symmetric key K_{MR-HA} for packet encryption between mobile router and home agent. In formal notation, the signaling is as follows:

$$MR \rightarrow CR\,(CoTI): \; N_C \tag{3.1}$$

$$MR \rightarrow HA\,(HoTI): \; K_{MR-HA}\{MNP, N_H\} \tag{3.2}$$

$$HA \rightarrow CR\,(HoTI): \; MNP, N_H \tag{3.3}$$

$$CR \rightarrow MR\,(CoT): \; N_C, \mathcal{I}_S^C, K_C \tag{3.4}$$

$$CR \rightarrow HA\,(HoT): \; MNP, N_H, \mathcal{I}_S^H, K_H \tag{3.5}$$

$$HA \rightarrow MR\,(HoT): \; K_{MR-HA}\{MNP, N_H, \mathcal{I}_S^H, K_H\} \tag{3.6}$$

The care-of test message exchange takes place directly between mobile router and correspondent router, cf. message (3.1) and (3.4). The home test message exchange, consisting of messages (3.2), 3.3), (3.5) and (3.6), is routed via the home agent. In contrast to Mobile IPv6, the home test contains and authorizes the mobile network prefix MNP instead of the home address HoA, cf. Section 2.2.6.2.

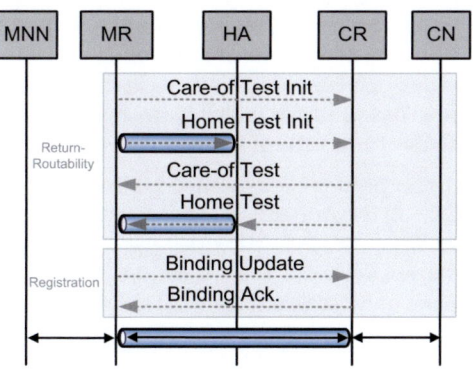

Figure 3.3. Route optimization signaling with correspondent router.

The keys K_C and K_H returned in the care-of test and home test messages are generated by the correspondent router. They are derived from the secret keys S_C^i and S_H^i that are only known the the correspondent router, which keeps a total number of n different keys $S_C^i, S_H^i, 0 < i < n$. These keys are regularly changed by the correspondent router. The index $\mathcal{I}_S^C$ specifies which key $S_C^i, i = \mathcal{I}_S^C$ has been used for generating the key K_C. The key K_H is generated similarly from S_H^i, indexed by $\mathcal{I}_S^H$.

As soon as the return routability procedure has been completed, the binding update/binding acknowledgement messages for establishing the route optimization state are exchanged:

$$MR \to CR\,(BU): K_{rr}[\mathcal{S}, MNP, N_C, N_H, \mathcal{I}_S^C, \mathcal{I}_S^H] \quad \text{where } K_{rr} = H(K_C|K_H) \quad (3.7)$$
$$CR \to MR\,(BA): K_{rr}[\mathcal{S}, CRP] \quad\quad\quad\quad\quad\quad\quad\quad\quad\quad\quad\quad (3.8)$$

The HMAC of binding update and binding acknowledgement are calculated with the symmetric key K_{rr} that is derived from the keys obtained in the return routability procedure. Afterwards packets can be directly routed between mobile router and correspondent router via the bi-directional tunnel.

Deficiencies of the Correspondent Router Protocol

A detailed discussion on the security deficiencies of the existing correspondent router protocol is provided in Section 5.3. Nevertheless a short summary of the problems that are present in the correspondent router protocol is provided in the following. This allows to identify the need for a new and more secure correspondent router protocol.

The correspondent router has to redirect traffic from its original destination (the mobile network prefix of the mobile router, which is routed to the home agent) to another address (the care-of address of the mobile router). A *prefix and address authentication* is necessary before this packet redirection can be performed. The mobile router therefore has to prove that it is the owner of both the claimed mobile network prefix (MNP) and care-of address (CoA).

The correspondent router protocol reuses the Mobile IPv6 route optimization procedure (see Section 2.2.6.2) for authenticating care-of address and mobile network prefix. A *return routability* procedure provides a *proof of reachability* of the mobile network prefix and care-of address. This procedure, as used in the correspondent router protocol, consists of messages (3.1)–(3.6) shown on page 77.

In Mobile IPv6 route optimization, the care-of test init (CoTI) and care-of test (CoT) messages verify that the mobile host can send and receive messages at the claimed care-of address. They are routed directly from and to the care-of address. For the correspondent router protocol, the home test init (HoTI) and home test

(HoT) messages have been extended with the mobile network prefix. These two messages authenticate the mobile network prefix and are routed from and to an address of the prefix, via the home agent. The HoTI-HoT message exchange relies on the home agent only forwarding these two messages to the mobile router if this mobile router is the valid owner of that prefix.

As the correspondent router protocol is based on the return routability procedure, it inherits the well known off-path security problem of Mobile IPv6 route optimization.

Deficiency 1: Mobile IPv6 route optimization has a well known vulnerability allowing an off-path attacker to *hijack the home address* of a mobile host, cf. Section 2.2.6.2. The off-path attacker is located between the correspondent node and the home agent and therefore not on the direct communication path if route optimization is to be performed. The same vulnerability applies to the correspondent router protocol, as the key K_H transported in the home test message authenticates the mobile network prefix instead of the home address. The threat is therefore exacerbated by the fact that all mobile network nodes (the complete *mobile network prefix*) are at stake rather than a single mobile host (one IP address) as in Mobile IPv6.

Additionally, two new security problems have been identified.

Deficiency 2: no mutual authentication is performed in the correspondent router protocol. While the mobile router authenticates its prefix to the correspondent router, the correspondent router prefix is not authenticated to the mobile router. There is no equivalent to the HoTI-HoT message exchange that authenticate the correspondent router prefix. This allows an adversary to masquerade as a legitimate correspondent router and *hijack the correspondent router prefix*. Consecutively, traffic originally destined for the correspondent router can then be redirected to the attacker's address.

Deficiency 3: all types of attackers, which are in possession of a prefix of arbitrary size, can *hijack the mobile network prefix* of a mobile router. Such an attacker only has to claim a prefix that is larger than the one it actually owns. Traffic, originally destined for the mobile router, can then be redirected to the attacker's care-of address. This attack is described in Section 5.3.

There is also another, non-security related, deficiency – the single point of failure problem due to the central home agent component.

Deficiency 4: in case the home agent is not reachable, the route optimization procedure can not be completed. No direct routing path between mobile router and correspondent router can then be established. The root of this problem is the proof by reachability for the mobile network prefix. The home key K_H can not be obtained if the home test messages can not be routed between mobile router and correspondent router via the home agent.

79

3.2. Authentication in Route Optimization

Route optimization security within the NEMO and correspondent router context has to focus on authentication: both care-of address and prefixes have to be authenticated prior to establishing the packet redirection state. Dedicated cryptographic material is required for proving ownership of the respective prefixes and care-of address.

Several options are available for achieving this goal. The vast majority of previous work in this area is focused on Mobile IPv6. However, a mechanism for authenticating a single address (in particular home address) can not be directly applied to the NEMO protocol in general and the correspondent router protocol in particular, where authentication of prefixes is required. Nevertheless, related work for both NEMO and Mobile IPv6 is discussed in the following. This analysis covers more security options and provides a more detailed analysis of the deficiencies of each approach compared to what has been discussed in [91].

A summary of the key characteristics of the protocols discussed in the following is provided in Table 3.2. It indicates whether the authentication is performed on a per-address or per-prefix basis and what kind of authentication approach has been used. If an authentication is not mutual, then the mobile node only authenticates to the correspondent node or correspondent router (one-way authentication), but not vice versa. It is also indicated whether one or several of the route optimization signaling messages has to be routed via the home agent (HA). The table also shows how many individual messages have to be exchanged in total and how many round trip times (RTTs) of signaling this requires. It should be noted that a single round trip time of signaling can consist of more than two messages, e. g., a message from the mobile node to the home agent triggering another message sent from the home agent to the correspondent node. If the same applies to the reverse direction from the correspondent node to the mobile node, than four messages are exchanged within one round trip time within this example.

The individual proposals are categorized into the following classes: pre-shared secrets, reachability test, cryptography based identities, zero-knowledge interactive proofs, identity based cryptography and traditional public-key cryptography. The discussion of each class does not only provide information on related work, but also provides more general remarks on the solution class itself and its possible application to the correspondent router protocol.

3.2.1. Pre-Shared Secrets

The proposal of Perkins [166] does not specify a protocol, but instead discusses how to use pre-shared secret keys S_C^i and S_H^i between a mobile host and a correspondent node. These keys are equivalent to those used in Mobile IPv6 route

Protocol	Authentication			HA Required	Messages	RTTs	Note
	Scope	Type	Mutual				
Wakikawa [212]	Prefix	RR	✗	✓	6	3	3
Calderon [36]	Addr	RR	✗	✓	6	3	3
Koo [119]	Prefix	C	✓	✓	10	2	4
Kukec [122]	Prefix	CBID	✗	✗	n/a	n/a	1,2
Hampel [79]	Addr	RR	✓	✓	6/4	3/2	3
Initial authentication:					6	3	
Subsequent authentication:					4	2	
Ren [174]	Addr	C	✗	✓	6	3	
Qiu [170]	Addr	C	✓	✓	8	3	
Zao [227]	Addr	C	✓	✗	6	3	
Lee [125]	Addr	C	✓	✓	6	2	4,6
Arkko [15]	Addr	CBID	✗	✓	6/4	3/2	1
Initial authentication:					6	3	
Subsequent authentication:					4	2	
Le [124]	Addr	CBID	✗	✓	4	2	5,6
Cao [37]	Addr	IBC	✗	✓	n/a	n/a	7
You [225]	Addr	K	✗	✓	6/4	3/2	
Initial authentication:					6	3	
Subsequent authentication:					4	2	

[1] Problems with short cryptographic output length
[2] Incompatible to IP address auto-configuration
[3] Security problem inherited from Mobile IPv6
[4] Care-of address not verified
[5] Home address (home network prefix) not verified
[6] No binding acknowledgement exchanged
[7] Central key management center for private key calculation required.

Table 3.2. Overview of the characteristics of the individual protocols for address (Addr) or prefix authentication in the route optimization context. The authentication types are crypto-based identity (CBID), return routability (RR), certificate (C), identity-based cryptography (IBC) and Kerberos (K). (✓) indicates supported or yes, whereas (✗) indicates not supported or no.

optimization (cf. Section 2.2.6.2) for generating the care-of key K_C and home key K_H, from which the binding key K_{bm} is derived. The proposal [166] is not listed in Table 3.2 as it does not specify a protocol.

Applied to the correspondent router protocol and prefix authentication, the mobile router would have to keep a table with the entries (CR, CRP, S_H^i). Similarly, the correspondent router has a table with entries (MR, MNP, S_H^i). The mobile router could then use the symmetric key S_H^i for deriving a home key K_H that can then be used to authenticate its mobile network prefix with a certain correspondent router. The correspondent router will use the same key S_H^i to derive the home key K_H that authenticates its correspondent router prefix to the mobile router.

For the care-of address, the mobile router would keep a similar table with the entries (CR, CoA, S_C^i), while the correspondent router has a table with entries (MR, CoA, S_C^i). The mobile router could then use the symmetric key S_C^i for deriving a care-of key K_C that can be used to authenticate its care-of address with a certain correspondent router.

This approach requires a dedicated mechanism for providing mobile router and correspondent router with the keys S_C^i and S_H^i, first initially (bootstrapping) and then for rekeying. Shared secrets are usually not considered to be scalable with a large number of nodes. The information security property of non-repudiation can also not be supported with symmetric keys. An additional difficulty is to know in advance how many and which care-of addresses the mobile router will use.

A special case of pre-shared secrets is a Kerberos-like third-party based authentication as proposed by You [225]. The home agent acts as ticket server issuing tickets to the mobile host that are accepted by the correspondent node. This approach requires a pre-existing trust relationship to be in place between the home agent and the correspondent node. For use with the correspondent router protocol, pre-shared secrets must be provisioned among all (HA, CR) pairs. The proposal also requires a reachable home agent. In the initial authentication, six messages (three round trip times) are exchanged. For subsequent handovers, only four messages (two round trip times) are necessary.

3.2.2. Reachability Test

A reachability test relies on symmetric keys that are transported on-demand instead of being pre-shared. The Mobile IPv6 route optimization procedure relies on such a test, also called return routability procedure. A home test init/home test message exchange transports a symmetric key K_H for home address authentication from the correspondent node to the mobile host. Similarly, the care-of test init/care-of test message exchange transports a symmetric key K_C for authenticating the care-of address.

This approach does not require pre-sharing, as the keys K_H and K_C are sent from correspondent node to the mobile node during the route optimization signaling. The significant disadvantage of this approach is that keys are transported in cleartext between the two nodes. The keys are therefore exposed to an adversary capable of seeing these messages. Hence, in general, this key distribution mechanism is insecure.

With respect to the care-of address authentication, this approach has the advantage of providing the mobile host with a key K_C that is only valid for authenticating the currently used care-of address. A reachability test therefore provides assurance that the mobile host is currently in possession of the claimed care-of address, as the mobile host has to be reachable at this address in order to receive the key.

A specific example for this approach, apart from the Mobile IPv6 route optimization procedure [108], is the proposal by Hampel and Kolesnikov [79]. In the initial handshake, cryptographic keys are exchanged between mobile host and correspondent node. During route optimization signaling, an additional random key is generated and combined with the initial key. The resulting key is then used for authenticating the signaling messages. Six signaling messages are exchanged within three round trip times in the initial authentication, which also requires an active home agent. Subsequent authentications only require four messages exchanged within two round trip times. This proposal provides a security improvement with respect to Mobile IPv6 route optimization: the initial cryptographic key is only exposed during the initial handshake, whereas the random key is only exposed during the subsequent handshake. An adversary must be in possession of both keys though in order to perform a successful attack.

Another example for a reachability test is the original correspondent router protocol proposed by Wakikawa [212]. It adopts the return routability procedure from Mobile IPv6 for authenticating both care-of address and mobile network prefix of the mobile router. The security vulnerability to off-path adversaries is therefore inherited from Mobile IPv6, cf. Section 2.2.6.2. Within this protocol, the correspondent router does not authenticate its correspondent router prefix to the mobile router. Six signaling messages are exchanged, consuming three round trip times. An active home agent is required to successfully complete the signaling procedure.

Another example is MIRON, the proposal of Calderon et al. [35, 36], which provides route optimization for NEMO. However, the authentication is not performed on a prefix basis. Instead, the authors only authenticate the individual addresses of those mobile network nodes that require route optimization. This proposal therefore has to be regarded as a per-address authentication procedure that can be applied to any number of mobile network nodes. The mobile router acts as route optimization proxy, reusing Mobile IPv6 signaling to perform route optimization with the correspondent node on behalf of the mobile network node. Due to reusing the Mobile IPv6 return routability procedure, the security vulnerability to an off-path attacker is inherited. An active home agent is also required. In terms of signaling, a total number of six messages is exchanged within three round trip times. The mobile router authenticates the addresses of the individual mobile network nodes to the correspondent node, but not vice versa.

3.2.3. Cryptographically Generated Addresses/Prefixes

The concept of cryptography-based identities [137] permits to generate an address or prefix from a public key. Given a public key K^{PUB}, auxiliary parameters P_1, P_2 and an identity generation function gen, a care-of address CoA and a mobile network prefix MNP could be generated as follows:

$$CoA = gen(K^{PUB}, P_1) \qquad MNP = gen(K^{PUB}, P_2)$$

The identity (CoA or MNP) is cryptographically bound to the public key. The ownership of the identity can be proven by calculating a signature with the private key that is associated to the public key used in the generation.

Cryptographically Generated Addresses

Enhanced Route Optimization [15] by Arkko et al. relies on using a cryptographically generated address (CGA) for proofing home address ownership of a mobile host in the Mobile IPv6 context. While the 64 bit prefix of the home address corresponds to the home network prefix, its 64 bit interface identifier IID is generated from the public key of the mobile host (cf. Section 2.2.3.3):

$$IID = H(Prefix, P, K^{PUB})$$

where H is a hash function, $Prefix$ is the home network prefix, P refers to auxiliary parameters chosen by the mobile host and K^{PUB} is the public key of the mobile host. Only the owner of the private key that is associated to the public key used to generate the CGA can authenticate himself as address owner by generating a corresponding signature.

As an adversary can use an arbitrary prefix for generating a CGA, Enhanced Route Optimization still requires an initial authentication of the home network prefix that is used in the CGA-based home address. This is achieved with a home test message containing a home key that is sent from the correspondent node via the home agent to the mobile host. In the initial authentication, this key has to be used. Six messages are exchanged within three round trip times. In subsequent authentications only four messages (two round trip times) are required. The authors of [37] argue that the 64 bit cryptographic output used for a CGA should be considered insufficient.

It would be possible for a mobile router to generate a CGA-based care-of address and use it for care-of address authentication in the correspondent router protocol. A CGA can however not provide "real-time" assurance and is therefore prone to *time-shifting attacks*: a CGA with a certain prefix can be generated and used independently of whether the mobile router currently owns that address or not. Once a mobile router has moved to a certain access network and learned of the

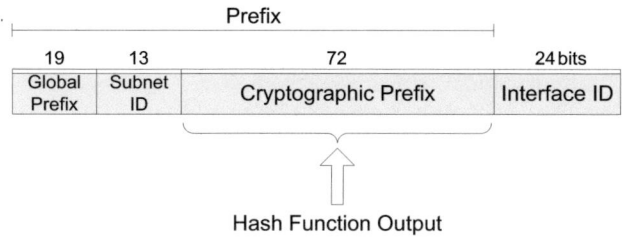

Figure 3.4. IPv6-based Cryptographically Generated Prefix Address.

subnet prefix used in that network, a CGA using this prefix can be generated anytime. The mobile router can then calculate a signature that authenticates the use of the CGA within the route optimization signaling even if the mobile router is currently not reachable at this address.

Cryptographically Generated Prefixes

Kukec et al. [122] have proposed a Cryptographically Generated Prefix Address (CGPA) that is a regular IPv6 address consisting of a cryptographic prefix and an interface identifier.

A mobile router or correspondent router can generate its mobile network or correspondent router prefix from a one-way hash function that takes a public key and auxiliary parameters as input. More detailed, using a hash function H, a public key K^{PUB} and a random number R, the cryptographic prefix $PKHash$ is calculated as follows:

$$PKHash = H(K^{PUB} \mid R) \qquad (3.9)$$

An illustration is provided in Figure 3.4. The cryptographic prefix is 72 bits long. 32 non-cryptographic bits are added in front to permit aggregation of the cryptographic prefixes in order to limit the size of the routing tables (cf. Section 2.2.4). Only the owner of the private key that is associated to the public key used to generate the cryptographic prefix can authenticate himself as prefix owner by generating a corresponding signature.

In this proposal, only the cryptographic prefix with a length of 72 bits is actually bound to the public key. The 32 bits at the front refer to the organization level prefix that is prepended to the cryptographic prefix. This 32 bit prefix is not cryptographically bound to the public key and can therefore be chosen arbitrarily. An adversary could therefore generate a CGPA with a 32 bit prefix that is owned by another organization. Another problem of the cryptographic prefix approach is that the interface identifier is reduced from 64 to 24 bits. This raises an incompatibility with the IPv6 address auto-configuration mechanism that is based on interface identifiers with a length of 64 bits, cf. Section 2.2.3.3. As a consequence, it is not possible anymore to use cryptographically generated addresses (CGAs) at the mobile network nodes or correspondent nodes, as they require 64 bit interface identifiers. The CGPA only leaves 24 bits though.

The route optimization protocol proposed by Kukec [122] using the CGPAs does not include mutual authentication either. The mobile router only authenticates its mobile network prefix to the correspondent router, but not vice versa. Another issue is the question whether a cryptographic output length of 72 bits is sufficient for an intended long-term solution (year 2030+). The author's of [37] argue that the 64 bit output of a cryptographically generated address is already not sufficient – the 8 bit increase for the CGPA is not significantly improving the situation. Another investigation [29] states that a CGA can be impersonated within a time of 2^{59}.

Another issue of CGPAs is the possibility for an adversary to make use of rainbow tables [158]. For each of the possible 2^{72} cryptographic prefixes, the adversary pre-computes 2^{72} public keys that generate said prefixes. The adversary then uses a lookup table to find the key that generates the prefix that should be hijacked. The random number in the prefix generation function (3.9) can only protect from hijacking a prefix for which a route optimization state has already been established. The adversary can however hijack a prefix for which no route optimization state has been established, as the random number can then be chosen by the adversary himself. This attack could be performed right before the prefix owner performs route optimization himself, thereby prevent the authentic mobile router from establishing a route optimization state.

As a final issue, the authors of [122] have only specified signaling for prefix authentication. No care-of address authentication is performed.

3.2.4. Zero-Knowledge Interactive Proof

Based on a zero-knowledge system such as the Feige-Fiat-Shamir scheme [66], mobile network prefix, correspondent router prefix or the interface identifier of the care-of address could be generated from a public key. This approach can therefore be considered as a variant of the cryptography-based identity approach discussed in the previous section.

Le et al. [124] proposed to proof ownership of IP addresses in the Mobile IPv6 context by means of the Feige-Fiat-Shamir scheme. Similarly to a cryptographically generated address, the interface identifiers of the home address and care-of address are generated from the public key of the mobile host. Instead of using a signature as in the case of cryptographically generated addresses, the address ownership proof is based on a 3-pass message exchange. After an initial message sent by the mobile host, the correspondent node responds with a challenge.

This challenge is answered by the mobile host in the third message using the zero-knowledge system.

Similar to the cryptographically generated home address in Enhanced Route Optimization [15], this approach does not authenticate the network prefix used inside the IPv6 address. The authors of [124] have not considered this issue for the home address authentication though. The care-of address authentication can be considered being properly performed as the 3 messages are exchanged via the care-of address. This implicitly provides a proof by reachability and therefore authenticates the address. Such a 3-pass message exchange would also have to be performed for the home address, by routing the messages via the home agent.

The original proposal has been improved to decrease a CPU exhaustion denial of service vulnerability [205]. While the number of messages within the 3-pass message exchange has been increased by two, the number of round trip times necessary for signaling remains the same.

An advantage of this approach is the assurance of the care-of address ownership: successfully completing the 3-pass message exchange is only possible if the mobile node is reachable at the claimed address. This is similar to a reachability test, but is more secure as no cryptographic keys are exchanged between the communication peers. The return routability related vulnerability to an off-path attacker is therefore not existing anymore. The disadvantage of this approach is that the cryptographic operations performed in the zero-knowledge system are more expensive than the symmetric key cryptography used in the return routability procedure.

A prefix generated from such a system, as required for the correspondent router protocol, would suffer from the same problem as cryptographically generated prefixes: the number of bits available for an IPv6 prefix is limited to 64 bits. As aggregation of prefixes has to be supported to limit the size of routing tables, this number would have to be further reduced. As a consequence, the available number of bits could be considered being too small for cryptographic purposes.

3.2.5. Identity-based Cryptography

In identity-based cryptography, public and private keys are generated from an identity, cf. Section 2.3.3.5. Within the correspondent router protocol, both prefix and care-of address could be used as identity – the key management center would generate the private keys from the prefix or care-of address and the master secret and provide them to the mobile routers and correspondent routers. E. g., for the mobile router the private keys for mobile network prefix ($K_{MR_P}^{PRIV}$) and care-of address ($K_{MR_C}^{PRIV}$) are generated as follows:

$$K_{MR_P}^{PRIV} = gen(MNP, MSK) \qquad K_{MR_C}^{PRIV} = gen(CoA, MSK)$$

where gen is the key generation function, MNP the mobile network prefix, CoA the care-of address and MSK the master secret key. The private keys can be used to calculate a signature on a route optimization signaling message. The correspondent router can verify such a signature by independently generating the associated public keys:

$$K_{MR_P}^{PUB} = gen(MNP, PP) \qquad K_{MR_C}^{PUB} = gen(CoA, PP)$$

where PP are the public parameters available from the key management center. The signature therefore provides proof of ownership of either mobile network prefix or care-of address.

Authentication based on identity-based cryptography requires private keys to be distributed by the key management center. The associated public keys can be calculated by any node with help of the identity (prefix or care-of address) and the public parameters, which are obtained once from the key management center.

A problem with the care-of address authentication is the need of the mobile router to know which care-of addresses will be used. The mobile router would have to request the respective private keys in advance. This approach also suffers from time-shifting attacks, similarly to the cryptographically generated addresses. The reason is the lack of assurance that the mobile router is currently in possession of the claimed care-of address: the mobile router will be in possession of the private key that can be used to authenticate the associated care-of address all the time. The mobile router could calculate a signature that authenticates the use of the care-of address within the route optimization process even if the mobile router is currently not reachable at this address.

A more general issue with identity-based cryptography is the pivotal role of the key management center. In case of a security breach of this entity, the private keys of all nodes can be recalculated by the adversary. This is a critical aspect for the global safety related aeronautical communications environment with its multinational structure.

A specific example for this approach is the proposal by Cao et al. [37]. The authors propose to use cryptographically generated addresses in the Mobile IPv6 context based on identity-based cryptography. They propose a modified CGA generation function, but do not specify a route optimization signaling procedure. Similar to Enhanced Route Optimization [15], only the interface identifier of the home address is authenticated with the help of identity-based cryptography. The home network prefix used in the home address would still require an initial authentication, e. g., using a home test message exchange.

A general discussion on using identity-based cryptography for Mobile IPv6 signaling is also available in [68]. The authors modify already existing proposals, such as the one of Qiu et al. [170], to replace traditional asymmetric cryptography with identity-based cryptography. The number of round trip times required for the signaling stays the same though.

3.2.6. Traditional Public-Key Cryptography

Classic public-key cryptography relies on every node generating its own public-private key pair. Certificates as part of a public key infrastructure (PKI) are used for distributing the public keys. The level of security provided by a public key infrastructure depends on the trustworthiness of the individual certificate authorities.

The disadvantage of this approach is the need for a common trust anchor (certificate authority) that is accepted by both mobile router and correspondent router. It is however possible to have an oligarchy structure with several root certificate authorities at the very top of the public key infrastructure hierarchy.

An example for this approach is the proposal of Koo et al. [119] where an optimized route is established between two mobile networks/routers. Certificates for prefix authentication are exchanged between the home agents, which are actively involved in the signaling. A total number of 10 messages is exchanged between different nodes, consuming two round trip times in overall. It should be noted that within the proposed signaling procedure, the care-of address is not verified.

Another public key infrastructure based approach for Mobile IPv6 has been proposed by Ren et al. [174]. The authentication of the home address is achieved with the help of a certificate that is exchanged between home agent and correspondent node. The route optimization signaling of the mobile host therefore still requires active participation of the home agent. The total number of exchanged messages is six, requiring three round trip times. Authentication is only one-way (mobile node to correspondent node).

Qiu et al. [170] proposed a certificate-based home address authentication with the purpose of hiding mobile host movements from the correspondent node. The care-of address and the home address of the mobile host never appear in the same message, thereby providing location privacy. The authentication of the home address still requires message exchanges via the home agent. Eight messages are exchanged within three round trip times. The authentication is mutual.

Zao et al. [227] also proposed a protocol that makes use of a public key infrastructure for home address authentication. A certificate is exchanged between mobile host and correspondent node directly. Due to the usage of the Internet Key Exchange protocol for authentication and for secure transport of signaling messages, the total number of exchanged messages is six (three round trip times).

The proposal of Lee et al. [125] is similar to that, as certificates are used between mobile host and correspondent node. The signaling also requires an active home agent. Six messages are exchanged (two round trip times), although no binding acknowledgement is included in this number and the care-of address is not authenticated to the correspondent node either.

3.3. Summary

The correspondent router protocol has been identified as the most suitable choice for providing route optimization in the NEMO context. The advantages of this protocol are as follows:

- Short end-to-end delay as the correspondent router should be deployed close to the correspondent nodes.
- A correspondent router can provide an optimized route to several correspondent nodes simultaneously.
- Transparency to the end-systems in the mobile network and on the ground.

The disadvantages of the protocol are the security deficiencies with respect to prefix authentication and the need for an active home agent in order to establish a routing path between mobile router and correspondent router.

Within the second part of this chapter, a survey of related work in the area of authentication methods for route optimization for both NEMO and Mobile IPv6 has been performed. This study showed that prior work suffers from one or several of the following issues:

- Vulnerabilities in the authentication of the mobile network prefix, e. g., due to reusing Mobile IPv6 signaling that is vulnerable to off-path attackers.
- Vulnerability to time-shifting attacks, e. g., for care-of address authentication with CGAs.
- Lack of mutual (prefix) authentication, e. g., only the mobile router/host authenticates to the correspondent router/node.
- Home agent is involved in the signaling.
- Inefficiency, due to using a large number of messages and round trip times.
- The need for pre-configuring shared secrets with all correspondent nodes.
- More general problems, such as short cryptographic output, incompatibility to existing IPv6 protocols or the need for private key escrow at a global key management center.

Within the next chapter, a new correspondent router protocol will be defined that resolves these issues.

4. Secure NEMO Route Optimization

The discussion in Chapter 3 showed that the correspondent router protocol is the most suited protocol for providing NEMO route optimization within the safety related aeronautical communications environment, especially for ATS communications. The correspondent router protocol permits to route packets between mobile network nodes and correspondent nodes via a bi-directional tunnel established between mobile router and correspondent router. The discussion in the previous chapter also highlighted the deficiencies of the existing correspondent router protocol: security and dependency on a reachable home agent (single point of failure).

These issues have to be resolved if the protocol is to be used in an environment that has high requirements with respect to security and availability.

The protocol defined within this chapter – SeNERO – is based on the existing correspondent router protocol [212], but addresses its deficiencies. In comparison to the existing protocol, the improvements of SeNERO are as follows:

- Security 1 – it is not possible anymore for an adversary to hijack the mobile network prefix of the mobile router.
- Security 2 – mutual prefix authentication between mobile router and correspondent router. It is not possible anymore for an adversary to steal the correspondent router prefix of the correspondent router.
- No home agent required – the route optimization signaling does not involve the home agent anymore.
- Efficiency – the new protocol is shown to still be efficient in terms of handover latency and signaling overhead.

When compared not only to the original correspondent router protocol but to other related work in the area of route optimization with a security focus, the novel aspects of SeNERO are in the following areas:

- Mutual authentication is provided, which is not the case for most of the previous proposals. This is not only the case for NEMO [36, 122], but also for Mobile IPv6 [37, 174, 225].
- A smaller number of signaling messages is required, especially when compared to those proposals that provide mutual authentication for Mobile IPv6 [119, 125, 170, 227].
- No active home agent is required in order to establish and maintain an optimized path.
- When used with the extended identity certificate model presented in Chapter 7, the authentication can be performed without a single point of failure in terms of a global trust anchor. Instead, a distributed set of trust anchors, located in the same networks as the individual correspondent routers, is used.

The combination of SeNERO and the extended identity certificates eliminates the dependency on both home agent and trust anchor. This eliminates both single point of failures.

4.1. Overview of SeNERO

An overview of the new correspondent router protocol, called *Secure NEMO Route Optimization* (SeNERO), is described.

The basic operation is equivalent to the original correspondent router protocol: the correspondent router (CR) acts as a proxy and performs the route optimization signaling on behalf of its locally served correspondent nodes with the mobile router (MR). Traffic destined to a mobile network node or correspondent node can then be routed between mobile router and correspondent router instead of being relayed via the home agent. Routing of packets takes place via a bi-directional IP-in-IP tunnel established between mobile router and correspondent router.

An illustration of the nodes and forwarding paths of the protocol is provided in Figure 4.1. Packets to the mobile network prefix are routed to the care-of address of the mobile router. Traffic to the correspondent nodes, which are in the same network as the correspondent router, is routed directly to the address of the correspondent router. These nodes can be identified as being associated to a particular correspondent router, as their addresses are configured from the *correspondent router prefix* (CRP). This prefix is the correspondent router equivalent of the mobile network prefix of the mobile router.

The bi-directional tunnel for packet forwarding is only established after an authentication between mobile router and correspondent router has taken place.

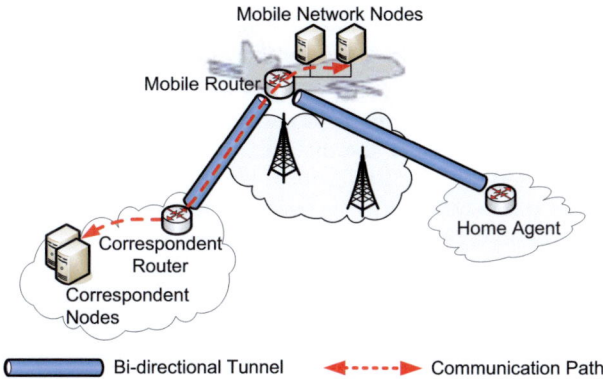

Figure 4.1. Optimized path between mobile router and correspondent router.

4.2. Prefix and Address Authentication in Se-NERO

The core problem of any route optimization protocol is proper authentication, due to being a packet redirection mechanism: packets are redirected from their original destination, the mobile network prefix, to the current temporary location of the mobile router, located by the care-of address. Similarly, traffic to the correspondent nodes that are associated to the correspondent router prefix is routed to the correspondent router, instead of being forwarded to the home agent. A route optimization protocol must therefore include an authentication procedure that authenticates both prefixes and the care-of address prior to establishing the packet redirection state.

The review of related work in route optimization security, cf. Section 3.2, showed the advantages and disadvantages of the individual approaches for both prefix and care-of address authentication.

Public-key cryptography with an associated public key infrastructure and certificates has been chosen for performing the *prefix authentication* in SeNERO. This approach does not require pre-configuration between mobile router and correspondent router (unlike pre-shared secrets) and the private key material is not exposed to anyone except the key owner (unlike reachability tests and identity-based cryptography). No issues with respect to the cryptographic output length exist, as the signature length can be arbitrary (unlike cryptography based identities). The only disadvantage is the need for a public key infrastructure and a common, global trust anchor in place between mobile router and correspondent router. Chapter 7 therefore proposes an extended identity certificate model that can be verified by relying on only a local trust anchor instead of a global trust anchor.

While the feasibility of such a public key infrastructure probably seems unrealistic for the public Internet, it is assumed that it is not just possible but actually necessary for a closed and security critical environment such as the aeronautical telecommunications network. This necessity has already been identified in a more general aviation context [89]. In fact, a global PKI has already been established for electronic passports, based on national trust anchors for the passport issuing countries [103]: Even in the public Internet, a trust infrastructure with a hierarchy based on a single root key has been successfully established: the security extensions for the Domain Name System (DNS) [69, 223]. From a trust perspective, this is similar to a public key infrastructure. It is argued that if a single root key hierarchy was successfully deployed in the public Internet, as in the example of DNS [95], then a public key infrastructure based approach is also possible for the closed safety related aeronautical environment.

For performing the *care-of address authentication*, a reachability test has been chosen for providing the mobile router with a symmetric key during runtime. This approach does not require pre-configuration between mobile router and correspondent router (unlike pre-shared secrets). The mobile router does also not have to know in advance which care-of address it is going to use. Furthermore, a reachability test provides assurance of the mobile router's current ownership of the care-of address (unlike cryptography based identities). In addition, symmetric key cryptography imposes much less processing overhead to the correspondent router then using asymmetric cryptography.

The reachability test based approach only suffers from the disadvantage that the cryptographic key is transported in cleartext. The alternative would be an authentication based on asymmetric cryptography. This approach suffers from time-shifting attacks though and would also pose a denial of service problem to the correspondent router. The reachability test is therefore the preferred choice. While it has a vulnerability, its lightweight cryptography reduces the denial of service exposure for the correspondent router. An additional advantage is assurance of the current care-of address ownership, which prevents time-shifting attacks.

While prefix authentication is mutual, the address authentication is only one-way, with the mobile router authenticating its care-of address. The reason for this is that the correspondent router acts as a server: the route optimization signaling is initiated by the mobile router and performed with an address of the correspondent router. Successfully completing these message exchanges therefore implicitly authenticates the address as correspondent router server address within the route optimization protocol.

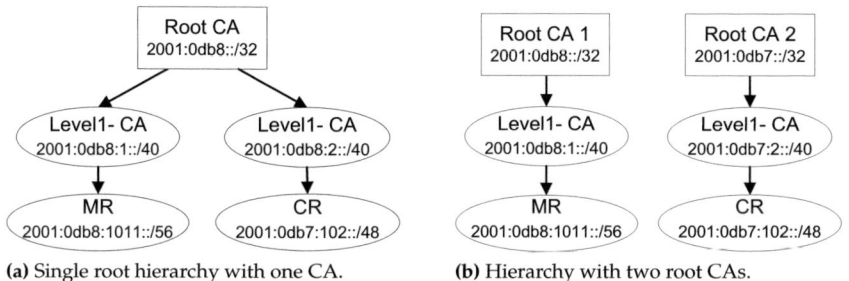

(a) Single root hierarchy with one CA. (b) Hierarchy with two root CAs.

Figure 4.2. Hierarchical Public Key Infrastructure models.

4.3. Public Key Infrastructure Model

The public key infrastructure (PKI) used for authenticating prefixes in SeNERO is described in the following.

Unlike care-of address authentication, prefix authentication is not affected by aircraft mobility. Both mobile network and correspondent router prefix are fixed. The root certificate authority of the proposed PKI is authoritative for the entire aeronautical IP address space. Hence, for every arbitrary pair of mobile router and correspondent router, the certification chain established for mutual authentication will always be based on the same trust anchor, the root certificate authority.

From the different existing public key infrastructure models [167], a hierarchical approach is the most suited one: the overall IP address space is managed by a certain entity that delegates parts of this space to other entities. Both a single-root and an oligarchy-based certificate authority (CA) scheme are suitable, as shown in Figure 4.2.

Whereas Figure 4.2a is an example for a global single root in charge of all IP address space, Figure 4.2b illustrates how the address space for airborne and ground networks could be split among two roots. In both cases, the root CA(s) can delegate parts of their space to subordinate CAs. The level 1 (national) CA correspond to the national air traffic control authorities who are in charge for IP address space management within their national boundaries. A correspondent router will receive its correspondent router prefix from such a certificate authority. Either way, the root CA(s) correspond to aeronautical IP address registries that are in charge of the overall aeronautical IP address space.

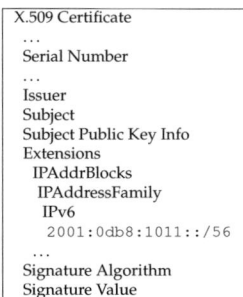

```
X.509 Certificate
 ...
Serial Number
 ...
Issuer
Subject
Subject Public Key Info
Extensions
  IPAddrBlocks
   IPAddressFamily
    IPv6
     2001:0db8:1011::/56
 ...
Signature Algorithm
Signature Value
```

Figure 4.3. X.509 certificate with IP address extension.

IP address space will be reserved by this certificate authority for each airline that is based within this country. Each mobile router will directly receive a mobile network prefix from this reserved space by the level 1 certificate authority. [1]

This IP address delegation chain is implemented by means of X.509 identity certificates. Each CA, MR and CR will receive an X.509 certificate with an extension field [129] that includes the delegated IP address prefix. This certificate permits the public-private key holder to directly use or delegate the specified prefix. The delegation and certification chain from the root(s) of the tree(s) to the mobile router or correspondent router provides the necessary proof for a claim on a certain prefix. For the mobile router, the certificate will include the mobile network prefix whereas for the correspondent router it will include the correspondent router prefix. An example for the mobile router certificate is shown in Figure 4.3. Apart from the public key (Subject Public Key Info), the certificate includes the mobile network prefix in the address extension field (IPAddrBlocks).

The delegation chain can be verified by mobile router and correspondent router by accepting a root certificate authority as trust anchor. In the example in Figure 4.2a, both mobile router and correspondent router must have trust to the root CA. In Figure 4.2b the mobile router must have trust to root CA 2 and the correspondent router must have trust to root CA 1. Only then a certification path to the CR or MR certificate to be verified can be established.

This hierarchical public key infrastructure will be used for prefix authentication and thereby replaces the home test (home test/home test init) signaling component from the original correspondent router protocol (cf. Section 3.1.5).

---

[1]It is assumed that an airline will not operate a PKI with associated certificate authority and revocation services that meet the high availability requirements for ATS. In case an airline nevertheless decides to do so, the responsible level 1 CA will delegate the reserved IP address space to the airline CA. The mobile router then receives its mobile network prefix from the airline CA.

This approach is similar to proposals for securing the Border Gateway Protocol (BGP), where the·mentioned X.509 certificate extension [129] is used as a mechanism to authenticate the public key that is associated with an address prefix or an autonomous system number [93].

4.4. Protocol Description

In the following the signaling and authentication mechanism for SeNERO is described in detail:

- Initial authentication between mobile router and correspondent router.
- Subsequent authentication for updating the mobile router's care-of address.

The *initial authentication* is only performed at the first time the mobile router attempts to establish a bi-directional tunnel to the correspondent router. This authentication consists of four messages exchanged within two round trip times. The first message exchange provides the mobile router with a shared secret for authenticating the care-of address. This message exchange is equivalent to the original correspondent router protocol. The second message exchange carries the certificates and authenticates the prefixes. This is the new prefix authentication used by SeNERO.

The *subsequent authentication* applies when the mobile router performs a handover after a bi-directional tunnel to a correspondent router has already been established. The tunnel then has to be updated with the new care-of address to establish routing to the new location of the mobile router. The subsequent authentication also consists of four messages exchanged within two round trip times. The first message exchange provides the mobile router with a shared secret for authenticating the care-of address; this is equivalent to the first message exchange in the initial authentication. The second message exchange authenticates the mobile router and it's mobile network prefix based on a session key (shared secret). This key has been supplied by the correspondent router in the initial authentication. In the subsequent authentication, certificates are not required anymore as they have been replaced by the session key.

Instead of hard-coding specific cryptographic algorithms into a protocol, it is better to rely on cryptographic agility where an arbitrary algorithm can be chosen. This allows the transition to a more secure algorithms if necessary. This aspect becomes increasingly important, given that vulnerabilities have been discovered in current standard algorithms such as AES [28] or SHA-1 [216]. SeNERO therefore provides cryptographic algorithm agility to allow migration to new algorithms. The assumption has been made that it is possible to standardize a single cryptographic suite as being mandatory for implementation. A *suite* defines a set of algorithms, with one algorithm for each signature, encryption and HMAC scheme.

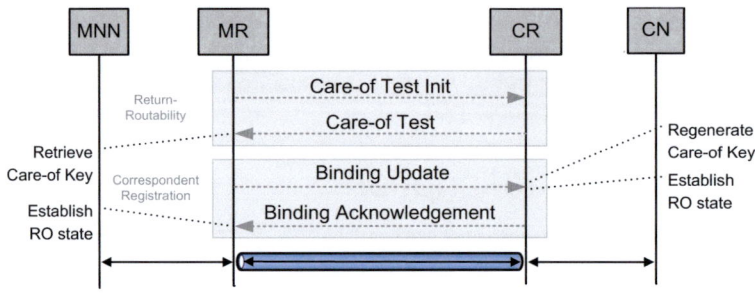

Figure 4.4. SeNERO mobility signaling: initial authentication.

This fall-back suite would be supported by all mobile routers and correspondent routers. This is not an unusual approach but similar to what has also been specified in the Domain Name System Security Extensions [13].

The formal notation that was first used in Section 2.3.4 and also used in the the Mobile IPv6 protocol description in Section 2.2.6, is again used for describing the protocol message exchanges of SeNERO. The used symbols are listed in Appendix A. It is assumed that the reader is familiar with protocol related security mechanisms such as timestamps, nonces, hashed message authentication codes, etc. as introduced in Section 2.3.4.

4.4.1. Initial Authentication

If the mobile router does not yet have a bi-directional tunnel for direct traffic forwarding to the correspondent router, a correspondent registration based on the initial authentication has to be performed.

This signaling procedure consists of two message exchanges. The first exchange is a care-of test for authenticating the care-of address of the mobile router by means of a return routability procedure. The second exchange is the correspondent registration that consists of the binding update (BU)/binding acknowledgement (BA) messages that piggy-back the certificates. These messages authenticate the prefixes of both mobile router and correspondent router. The entire signaling exchange is illustrated in Figure 4.4.

A care-of test init/care-of test (CoTI/CoT) message exchange is used to retrieve the care-of test key K_C. The mobile router sends and receives these messages via the care-of address. By being able to receive the care-of test message at the care-of address, the mobile router proves to be the owner of that address. This allows the mobile router to make use of this address in the route optimization process. This procedure is equivalent to the original correspondent router protocol.

Written in the formal notation, this message exchange looks as follows:

$$MR \to CR\,(CoTI): \; N_C \tag{4.1}$$

$$CR \to MR\,(CoT): \; N_C, \mathcal{I}_S, K_C \tag{4.2}$$

The structure of these two messages is illustrated in Figure C.1 in Appendix C. The correspondent router generates the key K_C in the following way:

$$K_C = H(N_C \mid CoA \mid S_C^i) \tag{4.3}$$

where N_C and CoA refer to the nonce and care-of address from the care-of test init message. S_C^i is a secret key only known to the correspondent router who keeps a total number of n different, randomly generated keys S_C^i, where $0 < i \le n$. Each of these keys has only a limited lifetime. In the care-of test message, the field $\mathcal{I}_S$ specifies which key i has been used in the generation of the care-of key K_C: $i = \mathcal{I}_S$.

This message exchange is stateless for the correspondent router, e. g., there is no need for storing the key K_C for a particular mobile router. No expensive cryptographic functions are performed either.

When the mobile router receives the care-of test message, it will store the key K_C locally.

The next phase is the correspondent registration, whose messages are specific to SeNERO. The first message is the binding update (BU), which includes several fields:

- A sequence number S that is monotonically increasing, as specified in the NEMO protocol [50].
- MNP: the mobile network prefix of the mobile router, as also specified in [50].
- The nonce N_C that was also used in the care-of test.
- The index $\mathcal{I}_S$ of the secret key S_C^i that was used by the correspondent router for generating the care-of key K_C.
- tstamp $\mathcal{T}$: a timestamp with the current time.[2]
- Certificate of the mobile router $\mathcal{C}_{MR}$ with an IP address extension [129] that includes the mobile network prefix.
- Algorithm Identifiers $\mathcal{A}_{MR}$: the mobile router specifies which single signature, encryption and HMAC algorithm it is intending to use. An algorithm is specified with its required parameters, e. g., "ECDSA with the P-384 curve and SHA-384" for the signature algorithm.

---

[2]Due to the availability of GPS receivers at aircraft, a "perfect" time source is available.

- Signature: a digital signature that is calculated with the mobile router's private key K_{MR}^{PRIV} over the binding update message.
- HMAC: a hash-based message authentication code that is calculated with a key derived from the care-of test (CoT) key K_C.

The mobile router uses the key K_{rr} for calculating the HMAC, which is constructed from the care-of key K_C:

$$K_{rr} = H(K_C) \tag{4.4}$$

Both HMAC and the signature are calculated using the algorithms specified in $\mathcal{A}_{MR}$.

The message in formal notation:

$$MR \rightarrow CR\ (BU) : K_{rr}[K_{MR}^{PRIV}[\mathcal{S}, MNP, N_C, \mathcal{I}_S, \mathcal{T}, \mathcal{C}_{MR}, \mathcal{A}_{MR}]] \tag{4.5}$$

The structure of this binding update is illustrated in Figure C.2 in Appendix C.

The binding update therefore carries both a signature and a HMAC, thereby authenticating the use of the prefix and care-of address respectively:

- The signature verifies that the mobile router is in possession of the private key that is associated to the public key in the certificate.
- The HMAC verifies that the mobile router is using a valid care-of key K_C.

When the correspondent router receives the binding update it checks whether the index $\mathcal{I}_S$ refers to a key S_C^i currently available, whether the timestamp $\mathcal{T}$ is recent and whether the algorithms listed in $\mathcal{A}_{MR}$ are valid and supported.[3]

The correspondent router then verifies the HMAC: with help of the nonce N_C contained in the message, the care-of address, which is the source address of the binding update, and the secret key S_C^i indexed by $\mathcal{I}_S$, the care-of key K_C can be regenerated according to formula (4.3). A valid HMAC on the binding update then provides assurance that the mobile router is the proper owner of the claimed care-of address. The correspondent router then has to verify the claim of the prefix used by the mobile router: the mobile network prefix in the binding update has to be equal to the prefix specified in the IP address extension of the certificate $\mathcal{C}_{MR}$. If the certificate is valid and the public key K_{MR}^{PUB} from this certificate can be used to verify the signature on the binding update, the correspondent router can be assured that the mobile router is the proper owner of the mobile network prefix. The correspondent router then accepts the binding update and sets up a route optimization state, which includes the establishment of the IP tunnel for

---

[3]The case where $\mathcal{A}_{MR}$ specifies algorithms not supported by the correspondent router is investigated in the security analysis in Section 5.2

forwarding packets directly to the mobile router. A binding acknowledgement (BA) consisting of the following options is created:

- A sequence number S that is monotonically increasing, as specified in the NEMO protocol [50].
- CRP: the prefix of the correspondent router.
- The nonce N_C that was also used in the preceding binding update.
- tstamp T: the timestamp option copied from the binding update.
- Permanent Home Key K_{PH}: a permanent home key encrypted with the public key of the mobile router.
- Certificate of the correspondent router C_{CR} with an IP address extension that includes the correspondent router prefix.
- Algorithm Identifiers A_{CR}: in addition to the algorithm identifiers specified by the mobile router (A_{MR}), this option includes the identifiers of the algorithms used by the correspondent router.
- Signature: a digital signature that is calculated with the correspondent router's private key K_{CR}^{PRIV} over the binding acknowledgement.

The key K_{PH} is generated randomly by the correspondent router.

Using the formal notation again, the message content looks as follows:

$$CR \rightarrow MR\,(BA) : K_{CR}^{PRIV}[S, CRP, N_C, T, K_{MR}^{PUB}\{K_{PH}\}, C_{CR}, A_{MR}, A_{CR}] \qquad (4.6)$$

The structure of this binding acknowledgement is illustrated in Figure C.3 in Appendix C.

The binding acknowledgement carries a signature that authenticates the use of the prefix – it verifies that the correspondent router is in possession of the private key that is associated to the public key in the certificate. The signature is calculated with the algorithm specified in A_{CR}.

If mobile router and correspondent router are configured with the same preferred set of cryptographic algorithms, the algorithm identifiers in A_{CR} will be equal to those in A_{MR}. In case of different configuration, the mobile router can propose a set of algorithms unknown to the correspondent router. In order to avoid interoperability issues, one cryptographic suite is therefore mandatory for implementation for each signature, encryption and HMAC option. In case the identifiers in A_{MR} are unknown to the correspondent router, the identifiers listed in A_{CR} will then contain the mandatory algorithms, also called fall-back algorithms.

When the mobile router receives the binding acknowledgement, it first verifies whether the sequence number S, the nonce N_C and timestamp T are equal to the ones used in the binding update. It is also checked whether the algorithm identifiers listed in $\mathcal{A}_{CR}$ are supported.[4] The mobile router then has to verify the ownership claim on the prefix used by the correspondent router: the correspondent router prefix in the binding acknowledgement has to be equal to the prefix specified in the IP address extension of the certificate $\mathcal{C}_{CR}$. If the certificate is valid and the public key K_{CR}^{PUB} from this certificate can be used to verify the signature on the binding acknowledgement, the mobile router can be assured that the correspondent router is the proper owner of the correspondent router prefix.

The mobile router will now establish the IP tunnel to the correspondent router and route optimization has been successfully completed. Data traffic between the mobile network nodes and the correspondent nodes, which are served by the correspondent router prefix, can be tunneled between mobile router and correspondent router instead of being routed via the home agent.

The mobile router also decrypts and stores the permanent home key K_{PH} from the binding acknowledgement.

4.4.2. Subsequent Authentication

If the mobile router has already established a route optimization state with the correspondent router and then performs a handover to another access network, the care-of address of the tunnel has to be updated. The overall message exchange is the same as in the initial authentication, consisting of a care-of test and binding message exchange, as shown in Figure 4.4. The authentication is performed without certificates though, but instead using the permanent home key K_{PH}, which acts as a session key. Subsequently, the binding messages are different from those in the initial authentication.

After a handover, the mobile router first performs a care-of test for obtaining a fresh care-of key K_C. This operation is equivalent to the return routability procedure used in the initial authentication.

$$MR \rightarrow CR \ (CoTI): \ N_C \tag{4.7}$$

$$CR \rightarrow MR \ (CoT): \ N_C, \mathcal{I}_S, K_C \tag{4.8}$$

The key K_C obtained from the care-of test message is then combined with the permanent home key K_{PH} stored by the mobile router:

$$K_{rr} = H(K_C \mid K_{PH}) \tag{4.9}$$

A binding update can now be generated. The HMAC for this message is constructed with the algorithm specified in $\mathcal{A}_{CR}$, as learned from the binding ac-

---

[4]In case of an attack on the protocol, the algorithm identifiers listed in $\mathcal{A}_{CR}$ might not be equal to those listed in $\mathcal{A}_{MR}$ and might also not contain the fall-back algorithms. This situation is discussed in the protocol security analysis in Chapter 5.

knowledgement in message (4.6). The newly derived key K_{rr} is used for the calculation. In formal notation:

$$MR \rightarrow CR\,(BU): \; K_{rr}[\mathcal{S}, N_C, \mathcal{I}_S] \qquad (4.10)$$

The structure of this binding update is illustrated in Figure C.4a in Appendix C.

The semantics of the nonce N_C and index $\mathcal{I}_S$ is equivalent to the care-of test init and care-of test messages (4.7) and (4.8) exchanged in the initial authentication. The mobile router can send the binding update without any certificate and signature as the prefix has already been authenticated in the initial authentication.

The correspondent router can regenerate the care-of key K_C with help of the nonce N_C contained in the binding update message, the care-of address, which is the source address of the binding update, and the secret key S_C^i indexed by $\mathcal{I}_S$. The correspondent router can then combine the care-of key with the permanent home key K_{PH}, which is locally stored as session specific information. The keys are combined according to formula (4.9) in order to generated the key K_{rr}. This key then allows the correspondent router to verify the HMAC. Consequently, the binding update is accepted and the tunnel accordingly updated with the new care-of address of the mobile router.

A binding acknowledgement is then sent, with the HMAC being calculated the same way as in the binding update, by using the key K_{rr}. In formal notation:

$$CR \rightarrow MR\,(BA): \; K_{rr}[\mathcal{S}, N_C] \qquad (4.11)$$

The structure of this binding acknowledgement is illustrated in Figure C.4b in Appendix C.

Once the mobile router successfully validated the binding acknowledgement, it updates the tunnel with the new care-of address. Packets between mobile router and correspondent router can now be tunneled from and to the new care-of address.

4.4.3. Signaling Message Details

In case a SeNERO signaling message (CoTI, CoT, BU or BA) is lost during transmission, the mobile router will retransmit the respective message. This is also the case if either a care-of test or a binding acknowledgement is lost – the mobile router will then retransmit the corresponding care-of test init or binding update message that preceded the lost message. The retransmissions performed by the mobile router use an exponential back-off process in which the timeout period is doubled upon each retransmission. This behavior is equivalent to what has been defined in [108].

Parameter	Length (in bits)
Nonces N_C, N_D	64
Secret Key Index $\mathcal{I}_S$	16
Shared Secrets K_C, K_{PH}, K_{rr}	64
Sequence Number $\mathcal{S}$	16
Timestamp $\mathcal{T}$	64
Algorithm Identifiers $\mathcal{A}_{MR}$, $\mathcal{A}_{CR}$	24

Table 4.1. Length of SeNERO protocol parameters.

The length of the individual keys, nonces, etc. contained in the signaling messages is provided in Table 4.1.

The length of these parameters is equivalent to the length of similar properties in other protocols, e. g., Mobile IPv6 [108]. The level of security provided by the number of bits of these parameters can therefore be considered sufficient.

The length of the permanent home key K_{PH} that is used as session key is also sufficient, given that it is randomly generated and only used for a limited amount of time. This key is only required for as long as the bi-directional tunnel to a specific correspondent router has to be kept alive, which will be in the order of magnitude of a few hours within the ATS communication scenario.

The permanent home key has to be renewed when the sequence number space $\mathcal{S}$ has been exhausted – this is the case if a binding update with the largest possible sequence number has been sent. The mobile router then has to perform an initial authentication with certificates again in order to receive a new permanent home key. A wrap-over in the sequence number, e. g., by (re-)using a value of zero, is not allowed. This prevents replay attacks, where an adversary sends previously observed binding messages.

The options $\mathcal{A}_{MR}$ and $\mathcal{A}_{CR}$ containing the algorithm identifiers have a total length of 24 bits each. They list identifiers for the following cryptographic schemes:

- Signatures on binding update and binding acknowledgement.
- Encryption of permanent home key K_{PH} in binding acknowledgement.
- HMAC in binding update/binding acknowledgement exchanges.

8 bits are available for each item, therefore permitting 256 different signature, encryption and HMAC suites. The same number of possibilities has also been defined for the DNS security extensions [13].

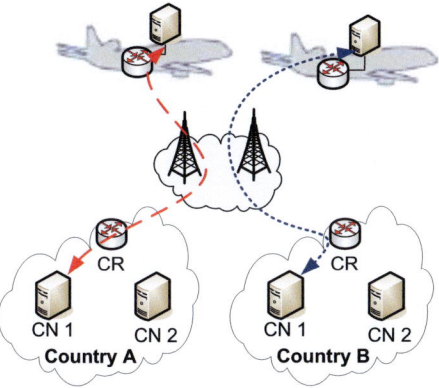

Figure 4.5. Correspondent routers in the aeronautical telecommunications network.

4.5. Aeronautical Communications based on CRs

The following discussion outlines how correspondent routers can be integrated into the aeronautical telecommunications network.

Air traffic control communication takes place between the mobile network node in the aircraft and a correspondent node, the ATS controller. In today's operations, the controller is geographically close to the aircraft it is controlling. There will be each one correspondent node at the departure and destination airport as well as a varying number of correspondent nodes for each crossed country. The aircraft will be communicating with only one correspondent node for the purpose of air traffic control at one point in time. The correspondent nodes are changing in a sequential way, depending on the current location of the aircraft.

Ground networks are organized on a national basis: the correspondent nodes of a country are within the same administrative domain. A single correspondent router located in the same network can therefore provide an optimized route to all correspondent nodes of that country. Each country will have such a correspondent router for providing NEMO route optimization. Another aircraft communicating with a correspondent node of another country will establish an optimized route with the correspondent router located in the respective national network. This is also illustrated in Figure 4.5.

When compared to the original correspondent router protocol, SeNERO offers the advantage of not requiring a home agent for route optimization. The correspondent routers themselves are distributed, as each correspondent router only provides route optimization for a single country/network. The correspondent router and the correspondent nodes located in the same network therefore share the same fate: in case of network problems, the correspondent router is not reachable, but neither are the correspondent nodes of that network. Communication can then not take place anyway, independent of whether SeNERO is used.

4.6. Route Optimization Triggers

As outlined in Section 2.1.5, at least certain safety related data flows will require route optimization. Routing data traffic via the home agent might not be an issue for certain data flows though.

The correspondent router protocol can simultaneously support both types of flows, those requiring route optimization and those not requiring route optimization. It is possible to use route optimization selectively on certain data flows. E. g., while a communication flow with ATS instructions is routed via the optimized path to the correspondent router, other data flows can still be routed via the home agent. This is interesting for flows that have relaxed requirements with respect to end-to-end latency, availability, etc. or for flows where the correspondent nodes are located close to the home agent, e. g., AOC communications.

Initially, no optimized path to any correspondent router is available and all traffic is forwarded via the tunnel to the home agent. It is therefore necessary to classify for which traffic flows route optimization should be performed. For this purpose, *traffic selectors* [207] can be specified that identify the data flows for which route optimization should be performed. Such a traffic selector can be based on a 5-tuple:

(source address, destination address, source port, destination port, protocol)

Before forwarding a packet, the mobile router will match the packet header fields with a list of preconfigured traffic selectors. E. g., using the wildcard character "*", the traffic selectors

```
(2001:0db8:1011::1234,*,*,*,*),(*,2001:0db8:1011::1234,*,*,*)
```

identify all outgoing and incoming packets for the mobile network node with the address `2001:0db8:1011::1234`. Route optimization would then be applied for these packets.

Initially, the first packet of a flow arriving at the mobile router that matches a traffic selector will trigger route optimization signaling. The mobile router will perform signaling with the correspondent router that is serving the correspondent node and establish a tunnel for packet forwarding to the correspondent router prefix. As soon as the tunnel has been established, packets matching the corresponding traffic selector will be forwarded via the tunnel to the correspondent router.

For example, given an established tunnel to a correspondent router with correspondent router prefix `2001:0db8:102::/48` and a packet with IP source address `2001:0db8:1011::1234` (mobile network node) and destination address `2001:0db8:102::abcd` (correspondent node) arriving at the mobile router:

- The source address `2001:0db8:1011::1234` matches the traffic selector defined above, hence route optimization should be applied.
- The destination address `2001:0db8:102::abcd` matches the prefix `2001:0db8:102::/48` of the correspondent router with whom a tunnel has been established.
- The packet will therefore be forwarded via the tunnel to the correspondent router.

Data flows not requiring route optimization will not have a corresponding traffic selector. Hence, associated packets will be routed via the home agent.

Communication can be started by either the mobile network node or the correspondent node. Either way, the first packet of the associated flow arriving at the mobile router will trigger route optimization.

4.7. Summary

Within this chapter, a new route optimization protocol ("SeNERO") for NEMO has been specified. It is based on the existing correspondent router protocol but addresses its deficiencies, which are security and the single point of failure represented by the home agent. The new protocol can therefore be used in the security critical environment of ATS communications.

The core aspect of SeNERO is the mutual authentication performed between mobile router and correspondent router, using certificates for authenticating mobile network prefix and correspondent router prefix. This prevents an adversary from hijacking any of these two prefixes, in contrast to the original protocol.

SeNERO also provides a higher level of resilience: route optimization signaling can be performed in the absence of a reachable home agent. This is not the case for the original correspondent router protocol, where two messages (home test init/home test) have to be routed via the home agent in order to establish an optimized path.

Another advantage of SeNERO is the fact that it only requires two round trip times of signaling. This is more efficient than any other protocol (cf. Table 3.2 in Chapter 3).

More detailed, SeNERO consists of two authentication phases: an initial authentication based on asymmetric cryptography and a subsequent authentication based on symmetric cryptography. The former relies on certificates and is used when the tunnel between mobile router and correspondent router is established for the first time. The latter is used when the mobile router performs a handover and the tunnel has to be updated with the new care-of address of the mobile router. The subsequent authentication is based on the permanent home key K_{PH} that is used as a session key.

Similar to the original correspondent router protocol, a return routability procedure (CoTI/CoT messages) for providing a symmetric key K_C to the mobile router is always used to authenticate the care-of address.

5. Protocol Security Analysis

SeNERO addresses the deficiency of the prefix hijacking attacks that exists in the original correspondent router protocol. A security analysis is performed in the following for providing evidence of these improvements. It is shown that the vulnerability to prefix hijacking attacks has been resolved. With regard to other attacks, it is shown that SeNERO provides the same level of resistance as the original correspondent router protocol.

This chapter first defines a threat model that can be used to analyze mobility and route optimization protocols. The model specifies which types of adversaries have to be expected and what their attack capabilities are. It is also discussed how this model applies to the specific environment of the aeronautical telecommunications network.

Both SeNERO and the original correspondent router protocol are then evaluated based on this model.

5.1. Threat Model for Aeronautical Communications

In the following, a generic threat model is specified that can be used for a security analysis of mobility management and route optimization protocols. The types of adversaries, their locations and capabilities are discussed in a a generic way. How this generic model applies to the aeronautical environment is discussed afterwards.

5.1.1. Generic Threat Model

The following threat model is used for analyzing attacks on the packet redirection mechanism of a mobility protocol. It therefore focuses on attacks on the mobile router and the correspondent router. End-to-end communications security, access network security, etc. are not relevant for the security of a packet redirection mechanism and therefore not addressed within this analysis.

Figure 5.1 illustrates a generic mobile communications network model. For now only the aeronautical overlay network on the top of the figure is considered. This overlay represents the aeronautical telecommunications network (cf. Section 2.1.4), which consists of access networks, correspondent networks and a home network.[1] These different networks are inter-connected by a core network.

The access networks consist of several base stations and an access router. In addition, an inter-domain router provides the inter-connection to the core. The mobile network that is attached to the access network on the left consists of a mobile router (MR1) and an end-system (MNN1). The latter is communicating with a correspondent node (CN1). The communication path from MNN1 to CN1 is an optimized route flowing via a correspondent router. The other mobile network that is attached to the access network on the right consists of a mobile router (MR2) and an end-system (MNN2). The latter is communicating with another correspondent node (CN2). These packets are routed via the home agent.

In the Mobile IP context, attacks are directed against the mobile node or correspondent node. In a NEMO route optimization scenario, the mobility signaling takes place between mobile router and correspondent router– the threat model presented here therefore focuses on attacks on these two routers.

Two basic types of adversaries have to be considered: on-path and off-path. *On-path* refers to a location that is on the optimized, direct forwarding path between mobile router and correspondent router. *Off-path* refers to a location that is not on this direct path. An on-path attacker can be located (a) in the mobile network itself between the mobile router and the radio/modem, (b) within the same radio cell as the mobile router or (c) along the optimized routing path where individual packets between the end-systems are forwarded. In all three cases, the adversaries can be either eavesdroppers or man-in-the-middle attackers. An adversary located between mobile router and mobile network node or between correspondent router and correspondent node can not directly affect route optimization signaling and is therefore not within the scope of this model.[2]

---

[1]The terminology used here, such as access network, has been defined in Section 2.2

[2]An adversary attempting to masquerade, e. g., as a legitimate mobile network node to the mobile router, would nevertheless have to be considered in a non-mobility related, more generic threat model. For example, this should be considered when performing a security analysis of the on-board (airborne) network itself.

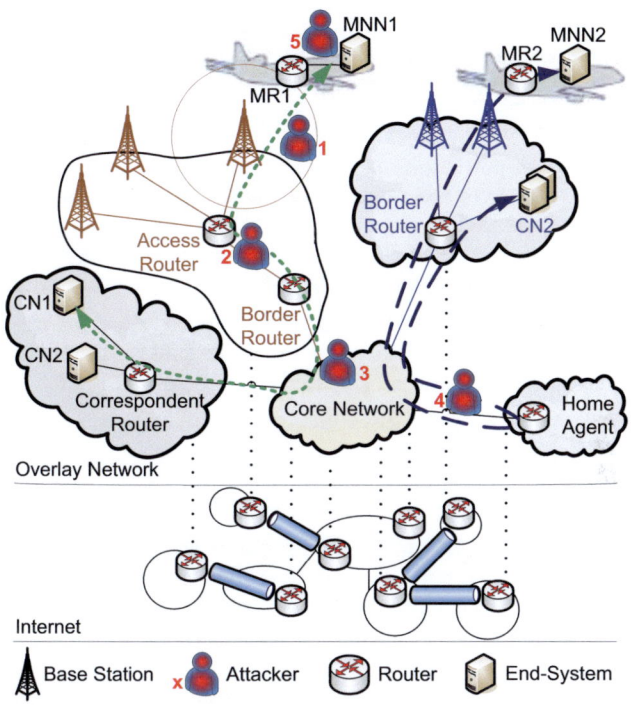

Figure 5.1. Generic mobile communications network model showing attacker locations in overlay network. Topology consists of access networks, networks with correspondent nodes, a home network and a core network.

An example for an on-path attacker of case (a) is illustrated by attacker 5 in Figure 5.1. Inside the mobile network, a wired Ethernet like network is used to connect the mobile network nodes with the mobile router, cf.. Section 2.1.2. An adversary could attempt to attach and compromise this wired network with the goal of gaining control of the wired network part that connects the mobile router with the access technology modem/radio. Only then, attacks on the mobility signaling itself can be attempted.

An example for an on-path attacker of case (b) is illustrated by attacker 1. A lack of security in the access technology (layer 2) allows this attacker to eavesdrop on packets transmitted within the same radio cell. Alternatively, this attacker could also attempt to masquerade as a base station with whom the mobile router connects to.

Examples for an on-path attacker of case (c) are attackers 2 and 3. These can attempt to either compromise an existing router or to masquerade as a router, e.g. as access router directly to the mobile router.

The four exemplary attackers listed above (1,2,3,5) are all on-path attackers.

An example for an off-path attacker is illustrated by attacker 4 in Figure 5.1. This attacker is located close to the home agent, which makes it impossible for this attacker to see packets exchanged on the direct, optimized path. Instead, this attacker only has access to packets that are routed via the home agent. This attacker could have compromised an existing router on the non-optimal routing path.

Apart from the attacker location, the second important aspect are the attacks possible for an attacker. Besides mobility specific attacks, all types of generic protocol attacks are considered, as listed in [30, 175]:

- Hijacking/masquerading: the attacker masquerades as a mobile router or correspondent router and steals the mobile network prefix or correspondent router prefix of the authentic router. The traffic of the hijacked prefix can then be redirected to the attacker's location.

- Flooding/denial-of-service: the attacker runs an application that requests a large volume data stream. The attacker then performs route optimization with the address of a victim node as care-of address. Thereby the large volume data stream is redirected from the attacker's prefix to the victim's address.

- CPU exhaustion/denial-of-service: the attacker overwhelms the correspondent router with a large number of request messages where expensive cryptographic operations have to be performed.

- Protocol interaction: the attacker uses route optimization signaling messages in another protocol to have these decrypted, signed, etc. within the other protocol's session.

- Reflection: the attacker sends a protocol message back to the entity that originally sent it or to another entity involved in a message exchange of the same protocol.

- Replay: the attacker resends an authentic message originally sent by another node (from either mobile router or correspondent router).

- Preplay: comparable to replay, the attacker injects a message in advance. The receiving node could then ignore the proper message because it is classified as a duplicate if the preplayed message arrives earlier. The receiver might also establish a protocol state based on the preplayed message that is undesired at this point in time.

- Delete: the attacker drops packets exchanged between mobile router and correspondent router.

Attack	On-path attackers		Off-path attacker
	MITM	Eavesdropper	
Hijacking	✓	✓	✓
Flooding	✓	✓	✓
CPU exhaustion	✓	✓	✓
Protocol Interaction	✓	✓	✓
Reflection	✓	✓	✓
Replay	✓	✓	✗
Preplay	✓	✓	✗
Delete	✓	✗	✗
Modify	✓	✗	✗

Table 5.1. Attacks that can be attempted by a certain attacker type. The on-path attacker is split into the man-in-the-middle (MITM) and eavesdropping classes. An attack is either applicable (✓) or not applicable (✗) for a certain attacker type.

- Modify: the attacker intercepts, modifies and reinserts an authentic message.

Cryptanalysis has not been included as an attack. Assuming that the underlying cryptographic algorithms are immune to cryptanalysis, this threat only becomes applicable in case weak cryptographic keys are used. This is not the case for SeNERO – the used key sizes are in line with the recommendations for the year 2030 and beyond [21]. The used algorithms can be regularly adjusted due to the cryptographic agility supported by SeNERO.

Table 5.1 lists which adversary can attempt which attacks. This table does not indicate whether such an attack would actually be successful – this will be discussed later in the protocol analysis. An *off-path attacker* is located on the path between correspondent router and home agent. This attacker can initiate route optimization signaling with the correspondent router from an arbitrary location or attempt to perform prefix hijacking. Furthermore this attacker can also initiate route optimization signaling using the mobile network prefix owned by the attacker, but specify an incorrect location (care-of address) for route optimization. Data will then be routed to this incorrect location, where a victim node can be flooded.[3] The off-path attacker can also perform CPU exhaustion attacks by sending a large number of route optimization messages that have to be cryptographically validated by the correspondent router. The attacker can also attempt to run another protocol with the correspondent router or mobile router where, e.g. the mobile router or correspondent router decrypts or signs a message that is

---

[3]This kind of attack is a mobility specific reflection attack: the network node with the incorrect route optimization state (reflector) will redirect the large volume data stream that was originally destined for the adversary to the victim node.

113

then used by the attacker within the route optimization protocol. It is also possible for the attacker to engage in route optimization signaling and reflect authentic messages sent by the mobile router or correspondent router back to them.

On-path attackers (eavesdropper, man-in-the-middle) can launch all attacks possible by an off-path attacker. They can also perform additional attacks though.

An *eavesdropper* is an on-path attacker located either between mobile router and modem/radio or inside the same radio cell as a mobile router. This attacker can therefore usually "see" messages exchanged between mobile router and correspondent router. This allows the attack of replaying old messages that have been observed. Similarly the attacker can preplay a message such that it arrives before the authentic message sent by mobile router or correspondent router.

The *man-in-the-middle* (MITM) attacker usually controls a router on the forwarding path or masquerades as a router to a victim node. This attacker can therefore perform attacks such as modifying or deleting messages exchanged between mobile router and correspondent router. This type of attacker can also launch the attacks possible for an eavesdropper.

The active and passive attack capabilities specified within this threat model can be considered being comparable to the capabilities of a Dolev-Yao adversary [52]. The model used within this thesis is only weakened by the distinction of an adversary having the capabilities of either an on-path or off-path attacker, but not both simultaneously.

5.1.2. Scenario of Aeronautical Communications

It is now discussed how the generic threat model presented in the previous section applies to the aeronautical scenario.

The IP-based aeronautical telecommunications network (ATN) will be a global network operated by entities from different countries and institutions. Due to cost reasons, it will not be physically separated from the public Internet but instead use it as a transit network. This has been visualized in the threat model shown in Figure 5.1 on page 111 – the aeronautical telecommunications network corresponds to the overlay network that is running on top of the Internet underlay.

The ATN packets will not be directly routed via the Internet. Instead, the different ATN networks (the ATN overlay) are connected via virtual private network (VPN) tunnels on top of the Internet. A segregation between the Internet and the ATN is therefore performed at least on the network layer. The ATN will have its own IP addresses space and a dedicated (inter-domain) routing infrastructure for enabling packet forwarding within the aeronautical telecommunications network overlay. The routing infrastructure of the Internet only provides connectivity between the different ATN VPN "islands". The VPN tunnels are established between routers in the Internet underlay in order to connect the ATN "islands", as also shown in Figure 5.1.

The threat model will now be applied on the aeronautical environment.

Attacker Locations and Capabilities in the ATN

In current aircraft network architectures, there is a physical separation between the safety and non-safety related networks (e. g. passenger domain). It is assumed that a physical or logical segregation of the on-board network will also be in place in the future. Access to the safety related network of an aircraft is restricted. However, for this investigation, it is considered as possible for an attacker to attach inside this network.

The on-board packet switched (Ethernet) network only provides direct links between the mobile router and network nodes that are usually already set up by the airframe manufacturer. A prospective on-board attacker that gains physical access to the on-board network might attempt to compromise the network links or attempt to masquerade as mobile router to the mobile network nodes. This enables man-in-the-middle or eavesdropping capabilities.

A compromised link between the end-system (mobile network node) and the mobile router is not affecting the route optimization signaling: an eavesdropper has no attack capabilities at all as signaling messages are only exchanged between mobile router and correspondent router. A man-in-the-middle attacker could successfully prevent communication in general and route optimization in particular by simply dropping packets between mobile network node and mobile router. This vulnerability is a general problem of packet based communication and not specific to a mobility protocol. This attack is therefore out of scope for this model.

However, both man-in-the-middle and eavesdropper are considered at the location between mobile router and radio/modem, as these adversaries are able to influence or observe the mobility signaling.

It is assumed that the ground based networks for safety related communications in the aeronautical telecommunications network overlay are also segregated from non-safety related networks. It is assumed that the ground network infrastructure provided by the (authentic) service providers is in general trustworthy. It might be possible that certain nodes are compromised by either insider or outsider adversaries though. E. g., a security analysis came to the conclusion that it is possible for a non-authorized individual to gain access to safety related ground network systems – the probability was specified with 10^{-3}, which is "likely to occur sometimes" [92].

Eavesdroppers within the wireless access networks have to be expected, as the safety related aeronautical access technologies that exist as of today – with only one exception[4] – do not provide any layer 2 security.

Another threat are hackers that gain access to routers of the aeronautical networks (ATN overlay). Even insider attacks might be possible, as according to security experts, "employees are a far greater threat to information security than outsiders" [202]. Either way, the compromised routers can be access routers, intra-domain or inter-domain routers. Compromising a router of the Internet underlay that is used as VPN gateway for inter-connecting the ATN networks allows an adversary to gain access to the ATN itself.[5] This enables the possibility for both on-path and off-path adversaries.

5.2. Analysis of SeNERO

A security analysis of SeNERO will be performed in the following, based on the threat model defined above. The analysis will regularly refer to the individually numbered SeNERO signaling messages as specified in Chapter 4 on page 97ff. Each attack listed in Table 5.1 is discussed, starting with "modify" and ending with "hijacking". A summary of the results is provided in Table 5.2. The table shows whether an attack can be successfully performed or not against the protocol.

Modify

An attacker can not modify binding update/binding acknowledgement without the receiver noticing this operation. In the initial authentication (cf. messages (4.5) and (4.6)), both messages are protected in two ways: (1) digital signatures generated from the private keys of mobile router and correspondent router and (2) a HMAC calculated from K_C/K_{rr} obtained in the return routability procedure for verifying the care-of address.

In subsequent handovers, the HMAC itself is sufficient for ensuring integrity protection. It is calculated with the care-of key K_C and the session key K_{PH}. The latter is only known to mobile router and correspondent router and can not be accessed by any type of attacker.

The certificates used in the initial authentication can not be modified or replaced, as the signatures on the binding update and binding acknowledgement are calculated from the private key that is associated to the public key in the certificate.

---

[4]The AeroMACS system based on IEEE 802.16e.

[5]Compromised routers are a reality in today's Internet, although to a smaller extend when compared to the number of hacked hosts [203].

Attack	MITM	Eavesdropper	Off-path attacker
Hijacking (CRP)	✗	✗	✗
Hijacking (MNP)	✗	✗	✗
Flooding	∅	∅	✗
CPU exhaustion	∅	∅	∅
Protocol Interaction	✗	✗	✗
Reflection	✗	✗	✗
Replay	✗	✗	✕
Preplay	∅	∅	✕
Delete	∅	✕	✕
Modify	✗	✕	✕

Table 5.2. Vulnerabilities of SeNERO with regard to different adversaries and attacks. The sign (✗) indicates that an attack on the protocol is not successful. It is also possible to have a vulnerability that is of only limited use to an attacker (∅). An attack can also not be applicable for an attacker type (✕).

Another type of modification attack is the attempt to manipulate the cryptographic algorithms specified in the initial authentication. More specifically, the attacker intercepts the binding update and modifies the cryptographic algorithms specified in $\mathcal{A}_{MR}$, cf. message (4.5). If the attacker specifies a signature algorithm that is not supported by the correspondent router, the correspondent router would be unable to validate the signature on the binding update. As a consequence, the integrity of the binding update based on the signature can not be verified and the modification of $\mathcal{A}_{MR}$ not be detected.[6] The correspondent router would then return a negative binding acknowledgement, specifying that the proposed cryptographic algorithms are not supported. The mobile router would be unable to continue as its proposed cryptographic algorithms are seemingly not accepted. No route optimization state could therefore be established and the attacker would be successful with the denial of service attack. To counter this threat in SeNERO, the correspondent router copies the original algorithm specification $\mathcal{A}_{MR}$ from the binding update to the binding acknowledgement (cf. message (4.6)). The binding acknowledgement itself is integrity protected and uses the mandatory-to-implement fall-back algorithms, which are also listed in the message parameter $\mathcal{A}_{CR}$, in case $\mathcal{A}_{MR}$ specifies unknown algorithms. In case of a modification attack, the algorithms specified in $\mathcal{A}_{MR}$ inside the binding acknowledgement are different from those that have been specified by the mobile router in the original binding update message. The mobile router will detect this anomaly and can verify the authenticity of the negative binding acknowledge-

---

[6]The man-in-the-middle attacker can re-calculate the integrity protection provided for the binding update by the HMAC due to seeing K_C in the care-of test message.

ment with the fall-back algorithms specified in $\mathcal{A}_{CR}$. The mobile router can then use these fall-back algorithms when sending the next binding update to the correspondent router.

This behavior also prevents a downgrading attack, where the adversary attempts to force mobile router and correspondent router into using cryptographic algorithms that are weak. The fall-back algorithms will meet minimum requirements with respect to cryptographic strength.

Delete

Deleting route optimization signaling messages results in the inability of mobile router and correspondent router to establish a direct route between each other. Deleting a message of the SeNERO protocol will force the mobile router to resend the original request, either the care-of test init or the binding update. By continuously deleting signaling messages that are (re)sent by the mobile router, the adversary can delay or prevent route optimization from taking place.

This attack is a general problem applicable to all types of communication systems though. There is no mitigation strategy on a protocol level.

Preplay

A preplay can be performed by on-path attackers during the care-of address validation phase, cf. messages (4.1) and (4.2).

A man-in-the-middle attacker can see the care-of test init message sent by the mobile router to the correspondent router. The attacker can then inject a care-of test message with source address of the correspondent router and valid nonce N_C, but an invalid key K_C. The mobile router, due to the valid nonce, will accept the preplayed care-of test. The mobile router will then ignore the proper care-of test from the correspondent router as a key has already been received from the attacker.

This message exchange looks as follows for the initial authentication, with E denoting the attacker:

$$MR \rightarrow CR\ (CoTI):\ N_C$$
$$E \rightarrow MR\ (CoT):\ N_C, \mathcal{I}'_S, K'_C \tag{5.1}$$
$$MR \rightarrow CR\ (BU):\ K_{rr}[K_{MR}^{PRIV}[\mathcal{S}, MNP, N_C, \mathcal{I}'_S, \mathcal{T}, \mathcal{C}_{MR}, \mathcal{A}_{MR}]] \text{ with } K_{rr} = H(K'_C)$$

The mobile router uses the key K'_C for calculating the HMAC in the binding update. This message will not be accepted by the correspondent router due to the wrongly calculated HMAC. In case the attacker is not able to specify a correct index $\mathcal{I}'_S$ in the forged care-of test message, the correspondent router will not even attempt to verify the HMAC of the binding update. Either way, mobile router and correspondent router will not be able to successfully perform route optimization.

The attack is also applicable to subsequent authentications, where the HMAC is calculated from a key K_{rr} that is derived from K_{PH} and K_C. Cf. message (4.10) and the key generation function (4.9).

Preventing mobile router and correspondent router from performing route optimization is already possible for the man-in-the-middle attacker by means of deleting packets. An eavesdropper can only perform this attack if the attacker is capable of sending a care-of test message with a forged source address, namely the address of the correspondent router.

Replay

The replay attacks on the care-of test message, applicable to on-path attackers, fails due to the nonce N_C, cf. message (4.2).

Replay of binding update or binding acknowledgement, applicable to on-path attackers, also fail. In the initial authentication, a replay of a binding update is prohibited by the timestamp $\mathcal{T}$, cf. (4.5). Only a small theoretical window of vulnerability exists for the binding update, which depends on the maximum accepted deviation of the timestamp $\mathcal{T}$ from the current time at the correspondent router. This will however not pose a problem, as binding updates are sent in the order of once per several minutes and not several times per second. The replay of a binding acknowledgement in the initial authentication also fails, as timestamp $\mathcal{T}$, sequence number S and nonce N_C have to match those of the original binding update, cf. (4.6).

For subsequent handovers authenticated with help of the permanent home key K_{PH}, the replay of binding update and binding acknowledgement is prohibited as well. This is achieved by sequence number S and nonce N_C that have to be identical in the binding update and its corresponding binding acknowledgement, cf. messages (4.10) and (4.11).

Reflection

In a reflection attack, an attacker performs two runs of the same protocol in parallel with the same entity: the attacker retransmits a message received in one protocol run back to the originator in the other protocol run. E. g., sending an already received binding acknowledgement back to the correspondent router as a binding update for initiating another route optimization procedure. An example for this is shown in the following, with E denoting the attacker:

$$E \rightarrow CR\ (BU):\ K_{rr}[K_E^{PRIV}[\mathcal{S}, MNP, N_C, \mathcal{I}_S, \mathcal{T}, \mathcal{C}_E, \mathcal{A}_E]]$$
$$CR \rightarrow E\ (BA):\ K_{CR}^{PRIV}[\mathcal{S}, CRP, N_C, \mathcal{T}, K_E^{PUB}\{K_{PH}\}, \mathcal{C}_{CR}, \mathcal{A}_E, \mathcal{A}_{CR}]$$
$$E \rightarrow CR\ (BU'):\ K_{CR}^{PRIV}[\mathcal{S}, CRP, N_C, \mathcal{T}, K_E^{PUB}\{K_{PH}\}, \mathcal{C}_{CR}, \mathcal{A}_E, \mathcal{A}_{CR}]$$

It is assumed that the original message of the attacker (BU) is valid. The response of the correspondent router (BA) is then sent by the attacker as another binding update (BU').

This kind of attack is not possible as binding update and binding acknowledgement have different headers and a different message content, most notably prefixes and addresses. This can be seen in the messages (4.5) and (4.6) for the initial and (4.10) and (4.11) for the subsequent authentication. The protocol headers for all signaling messages are provided in Appendix C.

This attack is also not applicable to the reverse direction: an attacker can send a binding update back to the mobile router that originally sent it, but the mobile router will not accept the message as a binding acknowledgement.

Protocol Interaction

In protocol interaction an attacker could attempt to let a mobile router or correspondent router sign a binding update or binding acknowledgement message within another protocol. This signed message could then be used for the initial authentication with the mobile router or correspondent router. An example for this is shown in the following, with E denoting the attacker and X and Y being request and response messages of another protocol:

$$MR \rightarrow E\ (BU):\ K_{rr}[K_{MR}^{PRIV}[\mathcal{S}, MNP, N_C, \mathcal{I}_S, \mathcal{T}, \mathcal{C}_{MR}, \mathcal{A}_{MR}]]$$
$$E \rightarrow CR\ (X):\ \mathcal{S}, CRP, N_C, \mathcal{T}, K_{MR}^{PUB}\{K_{PH}\}, \mathcal{C}_{CR}, \mathcal{A}_{MR}, \mathcal{A}_{CR}$$
$$CR \rightarrow E\ (Y):\ K_{CR}^{PRIV}[\mathcal{S}, CRP, N_C, \mathcal{T}, K_{MR}^{PUB}\{K_{PH}\}, \mathcal{C}_{CR}, \mathcal{A}_{MR}, \mathcal{A}_{CR}]$$
$$E \rightarrow MR\ (BA'):\ K_{CR}^{PRIV}[\mathcal{S}, CRP, N_C, \mathcal{T}, K_{MR}^{PUB}\{K_{PH}\}, \mathcal{C}_{CR}, \mathcal{A}_{MR}, \mathcal{A}_{CR}]$$

The attacker has to masquerade as legitimate correspondent router to the mobile router, e. g., as man-in-the-middle attacker. After receiving the binding update, the attacker creates a binding acknowledgement and lets the correspondent router sign this message within the other protocol (messages X and Y). The attacker can then send the signed binding acknowledgement (BA') to the mobile router, who will accept the message as it has been signed by the legitimate correspondent router.

This attack can also be attempted by an attacker for retrieving a validly signed binding update:

$$E \rightarrow CR \ (CoTI): \ N_C$$
$$CR \rightarrow E \ (CoT): \ N_C, \mathcal{I}_S, K_C$$
$$E \rightarrow MR \ (X): \ \mathcal{S}, MNP, N_C, \mathcal{I}_S, \mathcal{T}, \mathcal{C}_{MR}, \mathcal{A}_{MR}$$
$$MR \rightarrow E \ (Y): \ K_{MR}^{PRIV}[\mathcal{S}, MNP, N_C, \mathcal{I}_S, \mathcal{T}, \mathcal{C}_{MR}, \mathcal{A}_{MR}]$$
$$E \rightarrow CR \ (BU'): \ K_{rr}[K_{MR}^{PRIV}[\mathcal{S}, MNP, N_C, \mathcal{I}_S, \mathcal{T}, \mathcal{C}_{MR}, \mathcal{A}_{MR}]]$$
$$CR \rightarrow E \ (BA): \ K_{CR}^{PRIV}[\mathcal{S}, CRP, N_C, \mathcal{T}, K_{MR}^{PUB}\{K_{PH}\}, \mathcal{C}_{CR}, \mathcal{A}_{MR}, \mathcal{A}_{CR}]$$

The attacker initiates the route optimization procedure with the correspondent router by retrieving a care-of key K_C. Afterwards, the attacker uses the other protocol (messages X and Y) for signing a forged binding update message (BU') that can be used to establish a route optimization state with the correspondent router. The HMAC on the binding update is calculated from the key K_{rr}, which is derived from K_C that has been validly obtained by the attacker E.

If the public-private key pair used in SeNERO is different from the key pairs used in other protocols, this attack is not possible. In case the key pair is shared, the attacker would have to trick the mobile router or correspondent router into signing a message that has been constructed by the attacker. As the signatures have to be calculated over the entire message, including binding update/binding acknowledgement headers, other protocols can properly identify these message as being from another protocol that should not be signed.

The attack is not applicable at all to subsequent binding update/binding acknowledgement exchanges – cf. messages (4.10) and (4.11) – that are authenticated with the permanent home key K_{PH} that is generated dynamically by the correspondent router within SeNERO.

CPU Exhaustion

A CPU exhaustion attack could be attempted on correspondent routers because of the binding update signature verification in the initial authentication, cf. message (4.5). An attacker could send a large number of binding updates that overwhelm the processing capabilities of the correspondent router who, would be busy with signature verifications. However, the signature verification will not be started before the HMAC has been successfully validated. As a HMAC is almost as efficient as a simple hash function [113, Section 5.2.2], a large number of HMAC protected messages can be verified more easily by the correspondent router.

In order to pass the HMAC barrier prior to signature verification, the attacker has to engage in a care-of test init/care-of test message exchange to obtain K_C

that allows to construct K_{rr}, which is used to calculate the HMAC. The attacker is forced to use the real care-of address for this purpose. Resources in terms of an additional round trip time of signaling have to be committed, cf. messages (4.1) and (4.2). The attacker can also be traced back to the used care-of address. The care-of test init/care-of test message exchange itself is stateless for the correspondent router and does not involve any cryptographic operations. The key K_C can be later regenerated by the correspondent router upon reception of the binding update message according to formula (4.3). The vulnerability has therefore been significantly reduced.[7]

Invalid HMAC Algorithm
The attacker could also attempt to send a large number of binding update messages in the initial authentication with invalid algorithms specified in $\mathcal{A}_{MR}$. The correspondent router will not verify the HMAC of a binding update if the listed HMAC algorithm is unknown.
This behavior could be used by an attacker for sending a large number of binding updates without any preceding care-of test init/care-of test message exchange. Nevertheless, the correspondent router has to return a binding acknowledgement with the fall-back algorithms listed in $\mathcal{A}_{CR}$ that is integrity protected by a signature. Given a large number of binding updates, the correspondent router would then be busy with calculating signatures for a large number of corresponding binding acknowledgement messages.

To counter this attack, in case the HMAC specified in $\mathcal{A}_{MR}$ is invalid, the correspondent router will only return a binding acknowledgement protected by a HMAC and not by a signature.

Flooding

In a flooding attack, an attacker attempts to provide an invalid care-of address to the correspondent router. If this care-of address belongs to another node, then the correspondent router will forward all data, originally destined to the attacker, to the victim node (this is also called as a mobility specific reflection attack in the Mobile IPv6 protocol [150]). The mechanism to thwart this attack is the care-of test init/care-of test message exchange. This ensures that the mobile router can only use a care-of address it currently owns.

The care-of key K_C is only valid for a specific care-of address and within a limited time window. As specified in formula (4.3) on page 99, the key is calculated as follows:

$$K_C = H(N_C \mid CoA \mid S_C^i) \quad \text{where } S_C^i \text{ is indexed by } \mathcal{I}_S$$

---

[7]A similar approach has also been adopted in the Internet Key Exchange Protocol Version 2 [112].

An on-path attacker can not reuse an observed key K_C that is based on a different nonce N_C and/or a different care-of address: the key K_C recalculated by the correspondent router upon receiving the binding update would be different from the key K_C reused by the attacker.

An attacker could also attempt to perform a time shifting attack, where a care-of address is reused although the attacker does not possess this address anymore. The attacker must have obtained a care-of key K_C for a previously owned care-of address. The attacker could later attempt to reuse this key K_C to redirect traffic to the care-of address that is not owned anymore by the attacker. E. g., because the attacker already moved to another location. This is not possible as the key S_C^i is regularly changed by the correspondent router (e. g. every 5 minutes). When the attacker makes use of an old key K_C and associated index $\mathcal{I}_S$ within a binding update, the correspondent router will either (a) not have a key S_C^i available anymore for that index or (b) the key at this index will have already been changed. As a consequence, the correspondent router will not be able to regenerate K_C from the secret key S_C^i indexed by $\mathcal{I}_S$. The HMAC can therefore not be validated and the binding update with the "old", invalid care-of address will be rejected.

Hijacking

An attacker could attempt to hijack the involved prefixes, owned by either the mobile router or the correspondent router. In case of mobile network prefix hijacking, the attacker could attempt to initiate route optimization with the correspondent router and specify an invalid prefix. In case of correspondent router prefix hijacking, an attacker could masquerade as correspondent router to the mobile router, e. g., by means of a man-in-the-middle attack. Both types of attacks are not possible with SeNERO.

In the initial authentication, an attacker can see the certificates with the mobile network and correspondent router prefixes. However, it is not possible for the attacker to calculate a signature for either a forged binding update or a forged binding acknowledgement, cf. messages (4.5) and (4.6): the attacker is not in possession of the private keys K_{MR}^{PRIV} or K_{CR}^{PRIV} that are associated to the public keys in the certificates.

For a subsequent authentication, the attacker would have to know the permanent home key K_{PH} that has been exchanged in the initial authentication. This key has been provided to the mobile router in encrypted form though, as can be seen in message (4.6). An attacker can therefore also not "hijack" an already established mobility binding between mobile router and correspondent router.

Attack	MITM	Eavesdropper	Off-path attacker
Hijacking (CRP)	✓	✓	✗
Hijacking (MNP)	✓	✓	✓
Flooding	∅	∅	✗
CPU exhaustion	✗	✗	✗
Protocol Interaction	✗	✗	✗
Reflection	✗	✗	✗
Replay	✗	✗	✗
Preplay	∅	∅	✓
Delete	∅	✕	∅
Modify	✗	✕	✗

Table 5.3. Vulnerabilities of original correspondent router protocol with regard to different adversaries and attacks. The protocol is either vulnerable to an attack (✓) or is secure from an attack (✗). It is also possible to have a vulnerability that is of only limited use to an attacker (∅). An attack can also not be applicable for an attacker type (✕).

5.3. Analysis of Original Correspondent Router Protocol

To allow comparison with SeNERO, a security analysis of the original correspondent router protocol is performed in the following. A summary of the results is provided in Table 5.3.

The Mobile IPv6 return routability procedure has been reused in the original correspondent router protocol. The mobile router receives a home key K_H and care-of key K_C. These are sent within the home test (HoT) and care-of test (CoT) messages, routed via the home agent and via the direct path respectively. The two keys are combined for calculating the HMAC on the binding update message. This proofs to the correspondent router that the mobile router is the valid owner of mobile network prefix and care-of address.

Due to this procedure, the off-path attacker is more powerful in the original protocol than in SeNERO. The attacks "modify", "delete", "preplay" and "replay" become applicable for the off-path attacker, as the messages home test init/home test that are sent on the path between home agent and correspondent router can now be accessed by the adversary.

The message exchanges of the original protocol are shown in Figure 3.3. The discussion in the following will regularly refer to the individual signaling messages (3.1)–(3.8) shown on page 77.

Modify

An attacker can not modify either binding update or binding acknowledgement without the receiver noticing this operation. As can be seen in messages (3.7)–(3.8), both messages are integrity protected by a HMAC, calculated with key K_{rr}.

Neither an off-path nor an on-path attacker can recalculate the HMAC: the off-path attacker can see K_H in the home test message (3.5), but not the care-of key K_C in the care-of test message (3.4). The on-path attacker can see the care-of key, but does not have access to the home key. Both keys are needed though to derive the key K_{rr} that is used for calculating the HMAC.

Delete

Similar to SeNERO, deleting messages results in the inability of mobile router and correspondent router to properly perform route optimization signaling and establish an optimized route.

Preplay

A preplay could be attempted by both on-path and off-path attackers on the care-of test and home test messages.

The attack possible in SeNERO for on-path adversaries on the care-of test init/care-of test message exchange is also applicable to the original correspondent router protocol. The attacker injects a care-of test message with invalid care-of key K'_C. The binding update message will then not be accepted as the mobile router calculated the HMAC from the wrong key K'_C. Preventing mobile router and correspondent router from performing route optimization is already possible for the man-in-the-middle attacker by means of deleting packets though.

New in the original correspondent router protocol is the possibility for the off-path attacker to inject an home test message with illegitimate home key K'_H. This forged message is sent by the attacker after seeing the home test init message being forwarded from the home agent to the correspondent router. With E denoting the attacker, this attack looks as follows:

$$HA \rightarrow CR\ (HoTI):\ MNP, N_H$$
$$E \rightarrow HA\ (HoT'):\ MNP, N_H, \mathcal{I}'_S, K'_H$$
$$HA \rightarrow MR\ (HoT'):\ K_{MR-HA}\{MNP, N_H, \mathcal{I}'_S, K'_H\}$$
$$MR \rightarrow CR\ (BU):\ K_{rr}[\mathcal{S}, MNP, N_C, N_H, \mathcal{I}'_S]\quad \text{where } K_{rr} = H(K_C|K'_H)$$

The attacker provides an invalid key K'_H inside the home test message HoT'. The home agent will forward this message to the mobile router who will accept the preplayed message due to the valid nonce N_H. The mobile router then uses the forged key K'_H for calculating the HMAC on the binding update. This HMAC will not be accepted by the correspondent router, as the key K_{rr} is invalid. In case the attacker is not able to select a correct index $\mathcal{I}'_S$ in the forged home test message, the correspondent router will not even attempt to verify the HMAC of the binding update. Either way, this attack prevents mobile router and correspondent router from successfully performing route optimization.

The vulnerability to the off-path attacker is serious, as it allows an attacker to block a communication path (the optimized path) on whom the attacker is not located. This is in contrast to the on-path attacker, who can "only" block the communication path where the attacker is also located on (by means of forging an invalid care-of key K_C).

Replay

Replay attacks on the care-of test and home test are not possible due to the nonces contained in these messages, cf. messages (3.1)–(3.6).

The replay attacks on binding update and binding acknowledgement fail due to the sequence number S, the nonces N_C and N_H as well as the corresponding HMAC, cf. messages (3.7) and (3.8).

Reflection

The original correspondent router protocol relies on the same protections against reflection attacks as SeNERO: all signaling messages, such as binding update and binding acknowledgement, have different headers and a different message content. Consequently, these messages would be detected as invalid when sent back to the originator as response.

Protocol Interaction

The keys K_C, K_H and K_{rr}, used in the original correspondent router protocol, are generated and only available within the route optimization protocol.

Hence, feeding either a binding update or binding acknowledgement to another protocol for generating a valid HMAC within the other protocol is not possible, due to the unavailability of the required cryptographic keys K_C, K_H and K_{rr} in these protocols.

CPU Exhaustion

The only cryptographic function used in the original correspondent router protocol is a HMAC, cf. message (3.7). Flooding the correspondent router with a large number of binding updates is therefore not a resource exhausting attack with respect to CPU exhaustion.

Flooding

Similar to SeNERO, the mechanism to prevent an attacker from specifying an invalid care-of address is the care-of test init/care-of test message exchange. This ensures that the attacker can only use a care-of address that is currently owned by the attacker.

Mobile Network Prefix Hijacking

There are two vulnerabilities, a well known one from Mobile IPv6 that also applies to the correspondent router protocol as well as a newly identified attack.

Mobile IPv6 Vulnerability

The vulnerability of Mobile IPv6 route optimization to *off-path attackers* [195] is also applicable to the original correspondent router protocol. The source of the problem is the home test init/home test signaling exchange that authenticates the home address. In the original correspondent router protocol, these messages authenticate the mobile network prefix of the mobile router. In more detail, considering an attacker E, the signaling for such a hijacking attack is as follows:

$$\text{Input}: K'_H \text{ valid for } MNP'$$
$$E \rightarrow CR\,(CoTI): N_C$$
$$CR \rightarrow E\,(CoT): N_C, \mathcal{I}_S, K_C$$
$$E \rightarrow CR\,(BU'): K_{rr}[\mathcal{S}, MNP', N_C, N_H, \mathcal{I}_S] \quad \text{where } K_{rr} = H(K_C|K'_H)$$
$$CR \rightarrow E\,(BA): K_{rr}[\mathcal{S}, CRP]$$

The attacker performs eavesdropping on the key K'_H, which is forwarded within the home test (HoT) message. The key is transported in non-encrypted form on the path between correspondent router and home agent. This key K'_H is valid for a particular mobile router with mobile network prefix MNP'.

Once in possession of the key K'_H, the attacker can initiate route optimization signaling. A care-of test init/care-of test message exchange with the correspondent router is performed to retrieve a key K_C that is valid for the attacker's own care-of address. Afterwards, the attacker can use the stolen key K'_H to hijack the mobile network prefix MNP' of the victim mobile router: the care-of key K_C is combined with the stolen home key K'_H and used to calculate the HMAC on the binding update. This allows the attacker to hijack the prefix, as the HMAC also authenticates the mobile network prefix. Traffic is redirected from the mobile network prefix MNP' to the care-of address of the (off-path) attacker.

Prefix Expansion Attack

A new type of attack has been identified that is applicable to *all types of attackers* (off-path and on-path) within the original correspondent router protocol. No

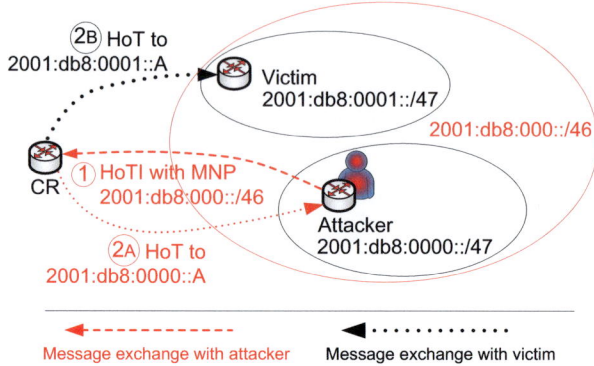

Figure 5.2. Prefix expansion attack where attacker claims a prefix than is larger that the prefix owned by the attacker.

specific location is necessary for the attacker. The attack allows hijacking the mobile network prefix of a mobile router, as long as the attacker is in possession of a valid mobile network prefix by itself. Within a so called *prefix expansion attack*, the attacker claims a mobile network prefix that is larger than the prefix the attacker actually owns. This expanded prefix contains the prefixes of other mobile routers, whose traffic is then redirected to the attacker. An illustration of the attack is provided in Figure 5.2.

The attacker sends a home test init (message 1) with a prefix that is larger than the one it actually owns – e. g., a length of /46 is used in the signaling message instead of the /47 that is owned by the attacker.

In line with the original protocol, the correspondent router will respond with a home test message that is sent to a random address within the /46 prefix. A /46 prefix can be split into two /47 prefixes. In the example it is assumed that one of the two /47 prefixes is a valid subnet of the attacker, whereas the other /47 is in possession of another mobile router (victim). The probability for the correspondent router to send the home test message to either the victim (message 2b) or the attacker (message 2a) is each 50%. If the attacker receives the home test message with home key K_H, a binding update can be constructed that will allow the attacker to redirect all traffic from the /46 prefix to the care-of address.[8] This

---

[8]Similarly to the well known Mobile IPv6 vulnerability to off-path attackers, the attacker only has to engage in a care-of test message exchange to retrieve a valid care-of key K_C. The care-of and the illegitimately obtained home key are then combined to K_{rr}, which is used to calculated the HMAC for authenticating the binding update.

means that all traffic to the /46 prefix is redirected to the attacker, which includes the /47 prefix of the victim.

In a real-word deployment, an attacker will have to expand a prefix by more bits, e. g., from /47 to /42 in order to also include the prefixes of other mobile routers. While this decreases the probability of the attacker to receive the home test message, this can be compensated by sending a large number of home test init messages.

Correspondent Router Prefix Hijacking

An additional vulnerability has been identified in the original correspondent router protocol, which is the lack of mutual authentication. The care-of test (CoT) and home test (HoT) message exchanges authenticate care-of address and mobile network prefix to the correspondent router, but the correspondent router does not authenticate the correspondent router prefix to the mobile router.[9] An attacker therefore only has to masquerade as correspondent router in order to steal the associated correspondent router prefix.

A man-in-the-middle attacker can achieve this by dropping packets destined to the correspondent router and responding with forged packets to the mobile router. Whether an eavesdropper can also successfully perform an attack depends on the mechanism used to discover the correspondent router. In case signaling messages are exchanged between mobile router and correspondent router for discovery (cf. Appendix E), an eavesdropper can see these messages and respond with forged packets to the mobile router.

In both cases (man-in-the-middle and eavesdropper), the mobile router will then perform the return routability procedure and correspondent registration with the attacker. At the end, the route optimization state is established between mobile router and the attacker, who illegitimately claimed the correspondent router prefix.

5.4. Summary

Within this chapter, a threat model has been specified that is suitable for investigating route optimization (packet-redirection) protocols. Different types of adversaries and attacks have been defined and it has been argued where and why the individual types of adversaries can appear within the aeronautical telecommunications network.

---

[9]The address of the correspondent router (CR) does not have to be authenticated. Performing route optimization signaling with the CR implicitly authenticates the CR server address within the route optimization protocol.

A security analysis based on this model has been performed for both SeNERO and the original correspondent router protocol. The most important conclusion of the analysis is that prefix hijacking attacks are not possible with SeNERO. This is in contrast to the original correspondent router protocol, where two new vulnerabilities have been identified that allow hijacking both mobile network and correspondent router prefix. An already known Mobile IPv6 route optimization vulnerability was shown to be applicable to the original correspondent router protocol as well.

The care-of address verification used in both SeNERO and the original protocol has a vulnerability that allows an attacker to prevent mobile router and correspondent router from establishing a bi-directional tunnel between each other. This is already possible for the man-in-the-middle attacker by other means. The vulnerability has to be accepted for the eavesdropper though, as protection against all possible attacks is not possible for care-of address verification. E. g., while the use of cryptographically generated addresses (cf. Section 4.2) would prevent the mentioned attack, it introduces other vulnerabilities such as time-shifting attacks and denial of service problems.

6. Protocol Efficiency Analysis

Providing security within a communication protocol usually comes at a cost, which is is often a decrease in efficiency. It can be shown though that SeNERO, while providing a higher level of security, is more efficient than the original correspondent router protocol. Within this chapter, efficiency in terms of handover performance and signaling overhead is therefore investigated.

Performance in terms of end-to-end latency is not discussed. Both SeNERO and the original correspondent router protocol establish the same bi-directional tunnel for forwarding of traffic between mobile router and correspondent router. The two protocols "only" differ in the signaling procedure that is used for establishing this optimized path. While the end-to-end latency is therefore equivalent for both protocols, the handover latency is different.

Hence, in the first section of this chapter, a handover performance evaluation is performed. A base scenario is defined that is used throughout the different evaluation methods. These methods consist of an analytical model as well as implementations within a test-bed and a simulation environment. While the analytical model relies on a strong level of abstraction, the simulation and test-bed environments increase the level of realism. This is especially the case for the wireless link.

In the second section of this chapter, the overhead incurred by the route optimization signaling will be analyzed analytically.

For both the handover performance and the signaling overhead evaluation, SeNERO is compared to the original correspondent router protocol.

6.1. Handover Performance Evaluation

In the following evaluation, the performance of SeNERO is compared to the original correspondent router protocol. Mobility and route optimization signaling is performed after a handover has taken place. Hence, the relevant performance metric is the *handover delay*.

This delay t_{HO} is usually modeled as a variable consisting of several components [218, Section 16.3]:

$$t_{HO} = t_{L2} + t_{MOV} + t_{MOB}$$

The overall handover process consists of three phases, each contributing to the total handover delay t_{HO}. The access technology specific (layer 2) handover signaling for associating with a new base station is represented by t_{L2}. The process of detecting the new access router and configuring an IP address is captured by t_{MOV}. After both the layer 2 signaling and the IP address configuration have been finished, the mobility protocol signaling is performed – this is covered by t_{MOB}. These signaling exchanges can be the home registration in NEMO Basic Support (cf. Section 2.2.7) or a route optimization procedure such as SeNERO. More details on general IP handover aspects can be found in, e. g. [210]. A handover performance evaluation for the aeronautical wireless access technology L-DACS has been performed by Ayaz et al. in [16] and [17]. The results show that t_{L2} has a value of 90 ms and that movement detection and IP address configuration t_{MOV} can be minimized to 30 ms. The overall handover latency without mobility signaling is therefore 120 ms.

The handover performance investigation performed in the following is focused on the mobility signaling specific latency t_{MOB} only.

Usually, route optimization signaling starts *after* the mobile router has successfully registered with the home agent. When measuring the performance of the original correspondent router protocol in the following, optimistic handover behavior is assumed though: the mobile router sends care-of test init and home test init to the correspondent router immediately after the IP address has been successfully configured (cf. the description of the original protocol in Section 3.1.5). The return routability procedure is therefore performed in parallel with the home registration, as care-of test init and home test init are simultaneously sent with the binding update to the home agent.

6.1.1. Scenario

A basic scenario is defined in the following upon all handover investigation methods will be based on. The topology of this scenario is shown in Figure 6.1.

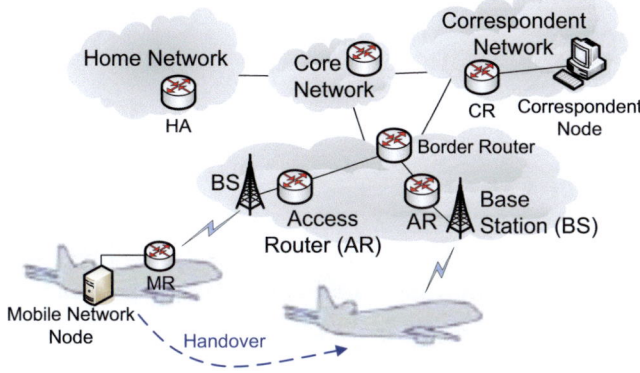

Figure 6.1. Topology used for handover latency evaluations.

The mobile network consists of a mobile router (MR) with one end-system, the mobile network node. The home agent (HA) is located in the home network. The access network consists of two base stations, each attached to a different access router (AR). The correspondent network includes both the correspondent router (CR) and the correspondent node, with whom the mobile network node is communicating with. Packets between access network, home network and correspondent network are routed via the core network.

The mobile router performs a handover between the base stations. Such a handover entails a change of the IP subnet. The mobile router will therefore configure a new care-of address, which triggers IP mobility signaling.

Furthermore, two different scenarios are defined. While both have the same topology, the latency of routing packets from and to the home network varies between the two scenarios.

In the *European scenario*, routing packets between core network and home network takes 18 ms. This describes the situation where mobile router, home agent and the correspondent node are all located in Europe.

In the *Asian scenario*, routing packets between core network and home network takes 148 ms. This describes the situation where mobile router and correspondent router/correspondent node are all located in Asia, but the home agent is based in Europe. Routing traffic between Asia and a Europe based home agent therefore inflicts a larger latency when compared to the European scenario.

The latencies used in the evaluation of the two scenarios are provided in Table 6.1. The delay values for the wired network have been obtained from the

133

Delay (in ms) on/between	Europe		Asia	
	Latency	Deviation	Latency	Deviation
Wireless: Forward Link	99	14	99	14
Wireless: Return Link	162	33	162	33
Access Router - HA	18	0	148	0
Access Router - CR	10	0	10	0
HA - CR	18	0	148	0

Table 6.1. Mean delays for evaluation topology. The deviation is described by a normal distribution. Forward link refers to the direction "base station to mobile", return link refers to "mobile to base station".

service level agreement of an operator with a global IP network/back-bone [157]. The latencies for the wireless link have been obtained from simulation results of the aeronautical access technology L-DACS 1 [74], where a mean delay with a certain standard deviation has been observed. No delay has been specified *inside* each network. The reason for this is the lack of real-world data specifying intra-network (intra-domain) latencies, especially for aeronautical wireless access networks. The delays for routing packets within Europe and between Europe and Asia (latency to home agent) have been obtained from the service level agreement of a backbone network operator [157]. This is a reasonable assumption, as the the aeronautical telecommunications network itself will not operate its own world-wide infrastructure. Instead, it will be implemented as a virtual private network on top of publicly available backbone networks. The service level agreement [157] also defines an average jitter of "500 microseconds or less". Due to this small value, the jitter has been completely omitted. This is indicated in Table 6.1 by a deviation of 0 ms.

The statistical parameters used to describe the evaluation results are defined in Appendix D.1.

In the aeronautical use case of air traffic control communications, the correspondent node is always close to the aircraft (the aircraft is communicating with a node from a certain country if it is flying over that country). The delay between access network and correspondent network is therefore small when compared to the delay between access network and home network. This is due to the fact that base stations will be deployed in close distance to the correspondent node, either within the same network or in a network that is only one autonomous system routing hop away from the correspondent network.

Variable	Explanation
t_{rr}	Delay for return routability procedure
t_{creg}	Delay for correspondent registration
t_{hk}	Delay for HoTI-HoT message exchange
t_{ck}	Delay for CoTI-CoT message exchange
t_{bu}, t_{ba}	Delay for BU or BA message
$t^{(x,y)}$	Delay for sending a message from node x to y

Table 6.2. Variables used for delay analysis.

6.1.2. Analytical Delay Investigation

In the first step, an analytical delay investigation is performed. This analysis is the simplest approach of analyzing the handover latency, ignoring the varying behavior of the wireless link, processing overhead, etc. The analysis is based on the previously presented best-case and worst-case scenarios and compares the handover latencies of the original correspondent router (CR) protocol and SeNERO against each other.

The scope of this investigation has been limited to the route optimization signaling delay represented by t_{MOB}. The other handover delay components t_{L2} and t_{MOV} have not been taken into account. The rationale is that the latter two values are equal for both protocols.

Variables are used for representing the latencies of route optimization signaling messages on the different routing paths between mobile router and correspondent router, mobile router and home agent as well as home agent and correspondent router. The variables are listed in Table 6.2.

Original CR Protocol

The original, return routability based protocol – as described in Section 3.1.5 – is analyzed first. The overall delay t_{MOB}^{rr} is the sum of the latencies of (a) the care-of and home test messages, called the return routability delay t_{rr} and (b) the binding update/binding acknowledgement exchange, called correspondent registration delay t_{creg}.

Both message exchanges take place in a sequential way:

$$t_{MOB}^{rr} = t_{rr} + t_{creg}$$
$$= max(t_{hk}, t_{ck}) + (t_{bu} + t_{ba})$$

This can be rewritten, e. g. t_{hk} refers to the latency on the path $MR - HA - CR$ while t_{ck} refers to the latency on the direct path $MR - CR$.

$$\begin{aligned} t^{rr}_{MOB} =max\Big(t^{(mr,ha)} + t^{(ha,cr)} + t^{(cr,ha)} + t^{(ha,mr)}, \\ t^{(mr,cr)} + t^{(cr,mr)}\Big) \\ + \Big(t^{(mr,cr)} + t^{(cr,mr)}\Big) \end{aligned} \quad (6.1)$$

SeNERO

The SeNERO protocol was specified in Section 4.4. The number of exchanged messages is equivalent in both the initial certificate-based authentication (CBA) and the subsequent authentication. The formula defined in the following therefore applies to both types of authentication.

The delay t^{cba}_{MOB} is the sum of two components. The first component is the return routability delay t_{rr} that consists of the latency for the care-of test message exchange. The second component is the correspondent registration delay t_{creg}, whose latency depends on the binding update/binding acknowledgement message exchange. Summarized:

$$\begin{aligned} t^{cba}_{MOB} &= t_{rr} + t_{creg} \\ &= t_{ck} + (t_{bu} + t_{ba}) \end{aligned}$$

This can be rewritten into the following formula, given that t_{ck} refers to the care-of test init/care-of test message exchange:

$$t^{cba}_{MOB} = t^{(mr,cr)} + t^{(cr,mr)} + \Big(t^{(mr,cr)} + t^{(cr,mr)}\Big) \quad (6.2)$$

Comparison

The protocols can be compared to each other by calculating t^{rr}_{MOB} and t^{cba}_{MOB}, using meaningful values for the individual variables $t^{(x,y)}$ in formulae (6.1) and (6.2). This requires specifying delays for the wireless and wired parts of the overall end-to-end path. The values defined in Table 6.1 have been used for this purpose. These are in line with the European and Asian scenarios that have been defined previously. The obtained results are only valid for the scenarios and corresponding latencies defined in Table 6.1.

The goal of the following comparison is to obtain an idea on how the handover performance of the two protocols varies, depending on the latency of routing packets from/to the home network. The deviation on the wireless link has been omitted for this analysis. As the deviation would increase the absolute handover latency for both protocols equally, the relative performance between the two protocols would remain the same.

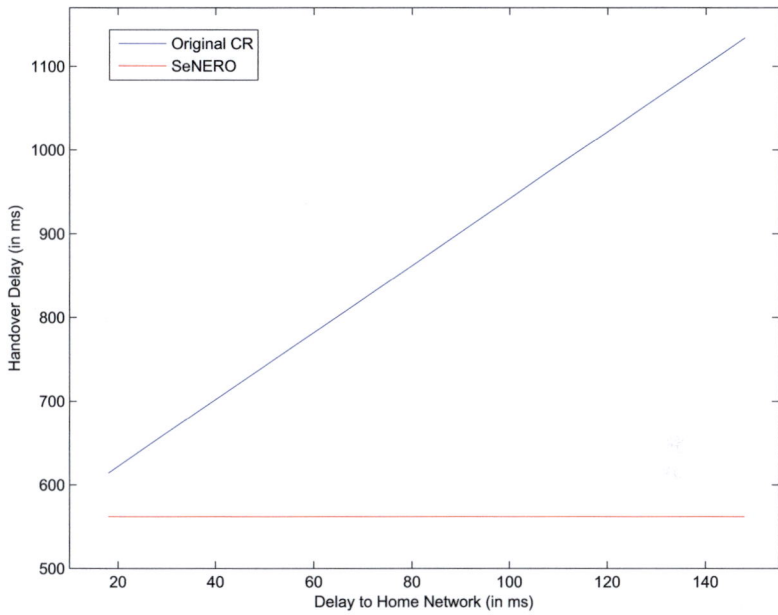

Figure 6.2. Handover latency results of analytical investigation.

For illustrative purpose, the handover latency for both protocols is calculated in the following for the European scenario, where the latency for routing packets from and to the home network is 18 ms.

The delay for the original correspondent router protocol based on formula (6.1) is as follows:

$$
\begin{aligned}
t^{rr}_{MOB} =& max(162 + 18 + 18 + 18 + 18 + 99, \\
& \quad 162 + 10 + 10 + 99) \\
& + (162 + 10 + 10 + 99)\ ms \\
=& max(333, 281) + 281\ ms \\
=& 614\ ms
\end{aligned}
$$

The variable $t^{(mr,ha)}$ refers to the delay on the path from the mobile router (MR) to the home agent (HA). The latency consists of two components: (1) the wireless hop (return link) from the MR to the access network and (2) the path from the border router to the HA. According to Table 6.1, $t^{(mr,ha)} = 162 + 18$ ms.
The variable $t^{(ha,mr)}$ refers to the delay on the same path, but in reverse direction.

The latency therefore consists of (1) the path from the HA to the border router and (2) the wireless hop (forward link) from the access network to the MR. According to Table 6.1, $t^{(ha,mr)} = 18 + 99$ ms.

Similarly, the delays on the direct path between MR and CR, represented by $t^{(mr,cr)}$ and $t^{(cr,mr)}$, are $162 + 10$ and $10 + 99$ ms respectively.

For SeNERO, the delay based on formula (4.5) is as follows:

$$t^{cba}_{MOB} = 162 + 10 + 10 + 99 + (162 + 10 + 10 + 99) \ ms$$
$$= 281 + 281 \ ms$$
$$= 562 \ ms$$

These two calculations have to be performed again for the Asian scenario, using the respective delays from Table 6.1.

Figure 6.2 shows the handover latency for both scenarios, calculated from the mentioned formulae as a function of a linearly increasing delay to the home agent, represented by $t^{(mr,ha)}, t^{(ha,mr)}$. The latency of routing packets to the home network starts at 18 ms (European scenario) and is incremented up to 148 ms (Asian scenario). It therefore also takes into account intermediate latency values of 28–138 ms.

The handover delay values of 614 and 562 ms calculated above can be seen on the very left of Figure 6.2. For the original CR protocol, the handover delay increases linearly to 1134 ms with an increased delay to the home network. This is due to the forwarding path $MR \rightarrow HA \rightarrow CR$ for the home test init message and $CR \rightarrow HA \rightarrow MR$ for the home test message. The varying latency to the home network affects the individual variables $t^{(mr,ha)}, t^{(ha,mr)}, t^{(ha,cr)}$ and $t^{(cr,ha)}$ used in the formulae for calculating the overall handover latency t^{rr}_{MOB}. In contrast to these variables with a home agent component, the delays on the path between mobile router and correspondent router are constant.

More detailed, given a delay to the home network of 18 ms, the latency of routing the home test init message from mobile router to correspondent router is $2 \cdot 18 = 36$ ms. As the delay for home test is the same, only the direction is reversed, the total accumulated latency of finishing a HoTI/HoT message exchange is 72 ms. If the latency to the home network is 148 ms, routing the home test init message takes $2 \cdot 148 = 296$ ms. The total accumulated delay for HoTI/HoT is then 592 ms. The difference between the 18 ms (European) and 148 ms (Asian) scenario for routing HoTI/HoT is therefore $592 - 72 = 520$ ms. This number constitutes the increase in handover latency between the two scenarios for the original protocol.

SeNERO does not perform any signaling exchanges via the home agent and therefore has a constant handover delay with respect to a varying latency to the home network.

Summarized it can be said that for both scenarios, and the intermediate home network latency values in the range of 28–138 ms, SeNERO always performs better then the original CR protocol. The handover latency improvement ranges from 8.5% for the European up to 50.4% for the Asian scenario. SeNERO can therefore be considered being more efficient than the original correspondent router protocol with respect to the handover latency.

From a general perspective, these results show that SeNERO performs better than the original correspondent router protocol if the latency for routing packets from and to the home agent increases. The specific level of improvement depends on the scenario and its defined latencies.

6.1.3. Simulation Results I

The analytical evaluation in the previous section is an abstraction of a real-world setting. Most importantly, the wireless link has been modeled with a fixed delay value. In reality, the latency of sending a packet over a wireless link actually depends on the packet size. In order to address this issue, simulations were performed. This allows to evaluate the handover latency of both protocols based upon a realistic wireless link model.

The simulation environment OMNeT++ [209] has been used together with the INET framework[1], which provides simulation models for IP based network components. In a first step, this simulation environment has been extended with a Mobile IPv6 implementation [226]. This framework has then be further extended with NEMO as well as the original correspondent router protocol and SeNERO.

The evaluation is based on the the European and Asian scenario as best-case and worst-case scenarios, similarly to the analytical investigation. The obtained results are therefore only valid within the context of the assumptions defined for these two scenarios. The simulation topology is equivalent to the one shown in Figure 6.1 on page 133, which has also been used in the analytical investigation. The latencies of the wired and wireless parts of the network topology depend on the scenario, as defined in Table 6.1.

For the wireless link, the IEEE 802.11 [99] implementation of the INET framework has been used with a data rate of 54 Mbit/s. This allows to stay aligned with the 802.11 access points used in the test-bed, which is discussed in the next section. The forward link and return link latency and deviation defined in Table 6.1 are added on top of the latency that is inherent to the 802.11 link model. The latency caused by the wireless link itself is dynamic and depends on the size of the message to be transmitted.

Similar to the analytical investigation, the simulations are performed with a linearly increasing delay to the home agent: starting from the first scenario where

---

[1] http://inet.omnetpp.org

Radio Parameters	Value	Application Parameters	Value
Radio Bitrate	$54 \cdot 10^6$ Bit/sec	Packet Size (w/ UDP header)	56 bytes
Transmitter Power	2.0 mW	Message Frequency	1/100 ms
Carrier Frequency	$2.4 \cdot 10^9$ Hz		
Thermal Noise	-110		
Sensitivity	-82		
Path Loss (Alpha)	2		
SNIR Threshold	4 db		

Table 6.3. Simulation parameters.

the latency to the home network is 18 ms (Europe), the latency is increased in steps of 10 ms up to the worst-case scenario, where the latency to the home network is 148 ms (Asia). 60 simulation runs were performed for each protocol and home network latency. The total number of simulation runs is therefore $14 \cdot 60 = 840$ for each original correspondent router protocol and SeNERO respectively.

Other parameters used within the simulations are listed in Table 6.3. The mobile router is moving from one radio cell into the other one. The constant-bit rate application running on correspondent node and mobile network node uses a periodic request-response signaling for exchanging data. The application is already started when the mobile router is within the first radio cell, thereby triggering route optimization. Once the mobile router performs the handover to the other radio cell, the route optimization state is updated.

The cryptographic operations are not considered in the simulation environment. These results are obtained with a test-bed implementation, introduced later in Section 6.1.4. These results show that the processing time for certificate verification and related asymmetric cryptography in SeNERO is negligible in comparison to the overall handover latency.

For both protocols, the mobility specific handover latency t_{MOB} is measured. For the original correspondent router protocol, a single latency value is measured for the route optimization signaling performed during the handover. For SeNERO, two handover latency values are measured: the first one is measured when the first application packet triggers route optimization signaling – this is the handover latency for the initial authentication. The second latency value is measured for the route optimization signaling performed during the handover– this is the handover latency for the subsequent authentication.

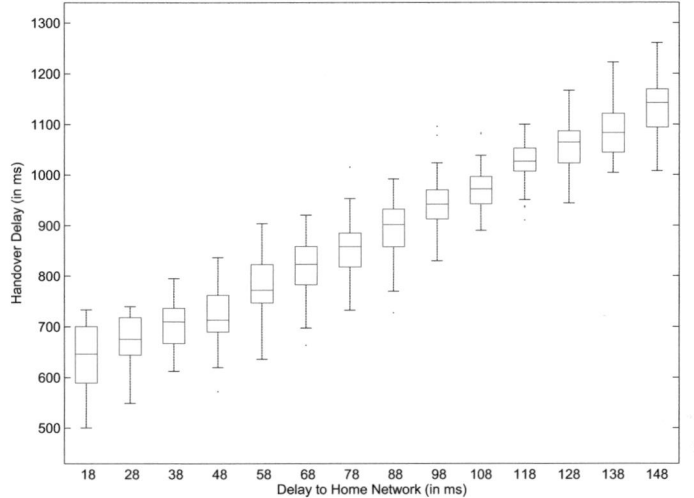

Figure 6.3. Handover delay as a function of the delay to the home network in simulations for original CR protocol.

Results

Figures 6.3 and 6.4 show the results of the simulations, where the handover latency is displayed as a function of the latency to the home network. Figure 6.3 shows the handover latency for the original correspondent router protocol, while Figures 6.4a and 6.4b show the results for SeNERO.

Box-and-whisker plots show the *medians* of the observed results in the center, with the 25th ($q_{0.25}$) and 75th ($q_{0.75}$) percentiles represented by the edges of the individual boxes. The outermost edges are the minima and maxima of the measurement results, excluding the outliers. The outliers, if present, are shown as red dots below or above the minima and maxima.

Appendix D.3 provides more information on the results of these simulations: the statistical properties for each of the two protocols are provided in Tables D.4–D.6. Figure D.3 shows the distribution of the handover latency results.

For the original correspondent router protocol, the handover latency median is increasing linearly from 646 ms up to 1142 ms. Each 10 ms increment in the home network latency increases the mean handover latency by 40 ms. As already explained in Section 6.1.2, this is due to the HoTI/HoT message pair that is routed along the paths $MR - HA - CR$ and $CR - HA - MR$. As each of the two messages

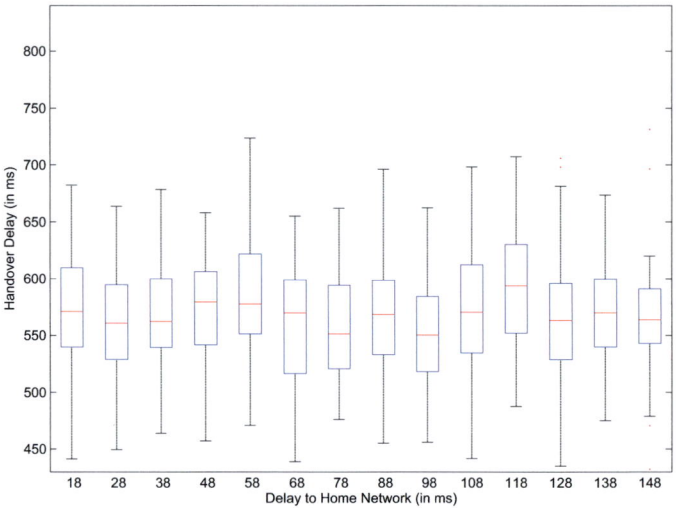

(a) Handover latency for initial authentication in SeNERO.

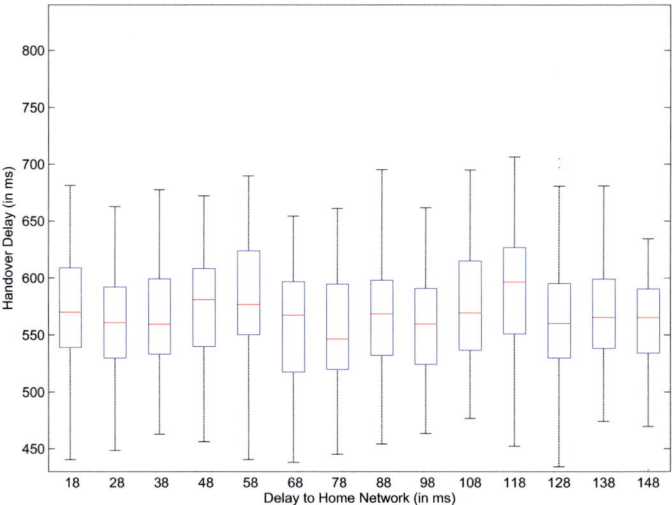

(b) Handover latency for subsequent authentication in SeNERO.

Figure 6.4. Handover delay as a function of the delay to the home network in simulations for SeNERO.

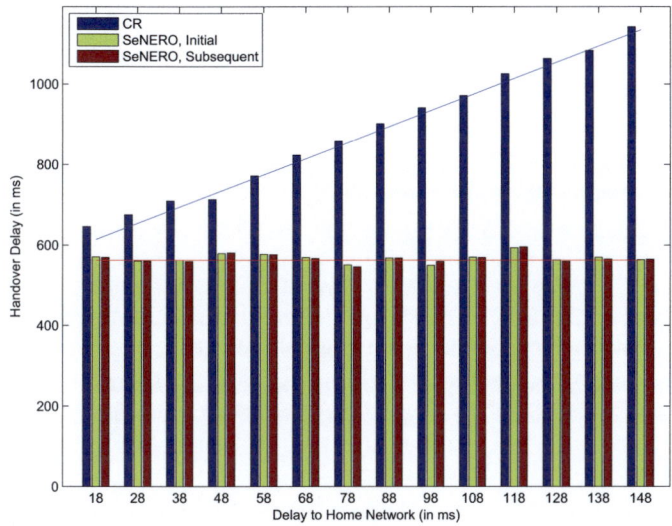

Figure 6.5. Comparison of analytical and simulated handover delay results.

is routed twice via the home agent, the latency to the home network is imposed four times in total.

For SeNERO, the handover latency median is constant with respect to a varying latency to the home network, apart from a certain standard deviation. Hence, a single global median can be calculated among all scenarios – it is 577 ms for the initial authentication and 568 ms for the subsequent authentication.

To summarize, Figure 6.5 shows the grouped handover delay medians of the original correspondent router protocol and SeNERO. The simulation results are shown by the bars, whereas the solid lines represent the results of the analytical investigation.

The handover latencies of the analytical investigation are usually smaller when compared to the simulation results. This difference is up to 32 ms for both Se-NERO and the original correspondent router protocol.

In two situations (latency to the home network: 78 and 98 ms), the handover latency for SeNERO obtained in the simulations is smaller than the respective analytical value. The reason for this is that the analytical model does not consider any standard deviation (jitter) for the wireless link in the handover latency calculation. In contrast to this, the simulations include a standard deviation for the wireless link that increases or decreases the handover latency, cf. Table 6.1. In these two situations, a negative standard deviation added to the mean decreased the handover latency to a value that is smaller than the analytical result.

Detailed Results

A more detailed investigation of the simulation results is performed for the European and Asian scenario. More detailed box-and-whisker plots for home network latencies of 18 and 148 ms are shown in Figure 6.6.

For the European scenario (cf. Figure 6.6a), SeNERO has a handover delay median of 571 ms for the initial and 570 ms for the subsequent authentication, while the original CR protocol it is 646 ms. In relative terms, the handover latency improvement of SeNERO is 11.7% for the initial and 11.8% for the subsequent authentication when compared to the original protocol.

For the Asian scenario in Figure 6.6b, the medians are 564 ms and 565 ms for SeNERO and 1142 ms for the original correspondent router protocol. The corresponding handover latency improvement is 50.6% and 50.5% with respect to the initial and subsequent authentication.

There is a noticeable difference in terms of interquartile range (IQR) between the two protocols: while for SeNERO, the IQR is in the range of 48–70 ms, for the original correspondent router protocol it is between 75–111 ms. Similarly, the standard deviation is only 48–49 ms for SeNERO but 56–419 ms for the original protocol. The significantly larger IQR and standard deviation in the original correspondent router protocol are only present in the European scenario.

The reason for this is the packet reordering introduced by the artificial delay on the wireless link: the delay assigned to the binding update message sent from the mobile router to the home agent can be larger than the delay for the home test init message, due to the standard deviation. Afterwards, even the home test message that follows home test init can arrive at the home agent prior to the binding update sent to the home agent. The home agent is then unable to forward the home test message as the binding update with the new care-of address of the mobile router has not yet been received. The home test message will therefore be lost and the mobile router is forced to retransmit another home test init message after a timeout of 1 second.

This problem will not occur if the latency from the home agent to the other networks is larger, as it is the case for the Asian scenario: the binding update message will then always arrive at the home agent before the home test message, that can then be forwarded to the new care-of address of the mobile router.[2]

The different sizes of the binding update and binding acknowledgement messages in the initial and subsequent authentication of SeNERO show no significant difference in the handover delay: the latencies only differ by 1 ms between

---

[2]Wireless links in a real-world environment usually provide in-order delivery. The described problem will therefore usually not occur in the real-world.

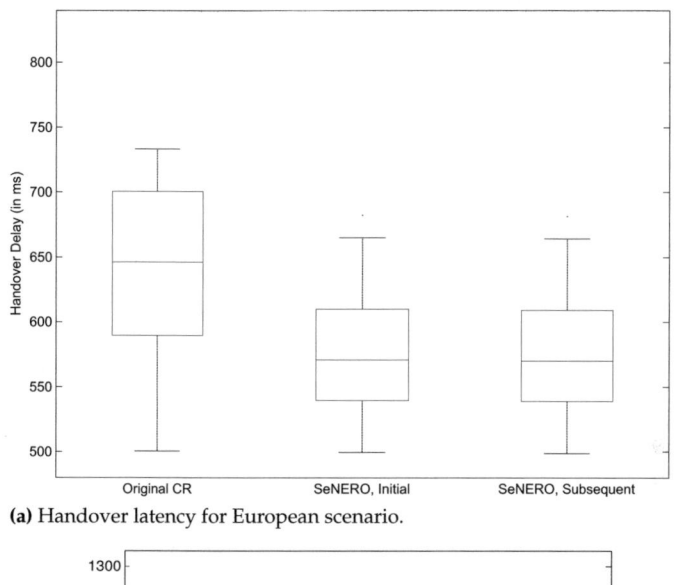

(a) Handover latency for European scenario.

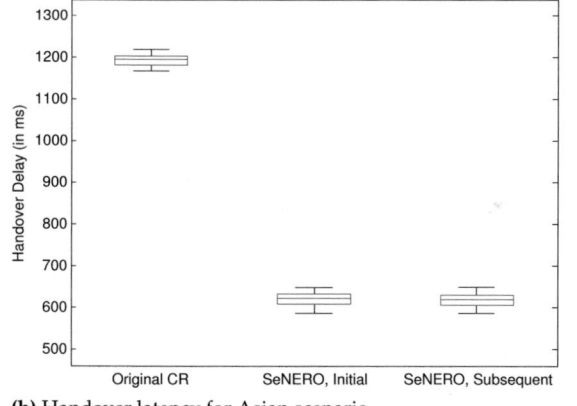

(b) Handover latency for Asian scenario.

Figure 6.6. Handover latency results for simulations.

the two scenarios. Similarly, the handover latency mean values are either equal (European scenario) or only differ by 4 ms (Asian scenario). In fact, for both scenarios, the handover mean of the initial authentication is within the confidence interval of the subsequent authentication and vice versa. It can therefore be inferred, that the handover latency for both authentication phases is the same. A message size difference of 750 bytes does obviously not significantly influence the transmission time on the wireless link within the simulation model.

6.1.4. Test-bed Results

As an additional type of evaluation, SeNERO and the original correspondent router protocol have been implemented in a test-bed environment. The objective of the testbed is to provide (a) a proof of concept of the SeNERO protocol to show its practical feasibility and (b) an evaluation based on a detailed implementation of the protocols. Within a simulation environment, the implementation of a protocol is usually abstracted, e. g., simplified protocol headers, no cryptographic operations, etc. In contrast to this, a test-bed implementation provides the highest level of detail.

The experimental implementation and evaluation was performed based on a standard PC test-bed setup. The Linux-based Mobile IP implementation UMIP-0.4[3] and its NEMO patches[4] have been extended with an implementation of a correspondent router. In addition to that, both correspondent router and mobile router have been extended with route optimization signaling to support the return routability procedure of the original correspondent router protocol and the certificate-based authentication of SeNERO.

The cryptographic operations have been implemented using the OpenSSL library 0.9.8.[5] SHA-1 was used for hash functions, ECDSA for signatures and the Elliptic Curve Integrated Encryption Scheme (ECIES) for encrypting and decrypting the permanent home key, relying on the blowfish algorithm. As OpenSSL did not support ECIES at the time of the implementation, the encryption and decryption scheme have been implemented inside SeNERO, reusing the existing cryptographic schemes provided by the library. The X.509 certificates inside the signaling messages have been DER encoded [105] in order to save bandwidth. The public keys inside the certificates had a size of each 384 bits.

The mobile network consisted of notebooks for mobile router and mobile network node, while standard desktop PCs have been used for the access routers, home agent, correspondent router and the correspondent node.[6] The test-bed topology is equivalent to the one shown in Figure 6.1 on page 133. IEEE 802.11 [99] access points are used as wireless base stations. The latencies of the wired and wireless parts of the network topology depend on the scenario, as defined in Table 6.1. Netem [87] was used to emulate these delays, both on wired and wireless

---

[3]http://umip.linux-ipv6.org/

[4]http://software.nautilus6.org/NEPL-UMIP/

[5]http://www.openssl.org

[6]Ubuntu 9.04 was used on the notebooks and desktop PCs, with Linux kernel 2.6.28. The wireless chip in the notebook was an Intel 5300 AGN. The access points were Apple Airport Extreme.

links. The forward link and return link latency defined in Table 6.1 is added on top of the latency that is inherent to the 802.11 link.

A constant-bit rate application periodically generated data traffic between mobile network node and correspondent node. The application parameters are equivalent to those listed in Table 6.3. The application is started manually while the mobile router is attached to the first 802.11 cell, thereby triggering route optimization. Afterwards, a handover is triggered by manually selecting the other access point, thereby disassociating from the current 802.11 access point.

Similarly to the simulations, the time needed for the route optimization signaling is measured as mobility specific handover latency t_{MOB}. The initial route optimization signaling, triggered by the constant-bit rate application, is measured as handover latency for the initial authentication in SeNERO. The handover performed afterwards is measured as handover latency for the subsequent authentication in SeNERO. The mobility specific handover latency for the original correspondent router protocol is only measured during the handover.

The evaluation is based on the the European and Asian scenario as best-case and worst-case scenarios, similarly to the previous investigations. For each of the two scenarios and protocols (original correspondent router protocol & SeNERO) 30 handovers have been performed, resulting in a total number of 120 measured handovers.

In contrast to the simulations, many steps had to performed manually within the test-bed evaluation. E. g., triggering the handover between the access points as described above. As this is a time consuming process, the latencies to the home network in the range of 28–138 ms have not been evaluated.

Results

The following results and the demonstrated performance improvements of SeNERO are only valid within the context of the assumptions of the underlying European and Asian scenarios.

Tables D.1, D.2 and D.3 in Appendix D.2 provide a full list of statistical properties for the obtained measurement results. Figure D.2 shows the distribution of these results.

Illustrations of the results are shown in Figures 6.7a and 6.7b for each of the two scenarios. For SeNERO, the handover latency for both initial and subsequent authentication is shown.

In both scenarios, SeNERO outperforms the original correspondent router protocol. In the European scenario (cf. Figure 6.7a), SeNERO has a handover delay *median* of 619 ms, while for the original protocol it is 665 ms. The handover delay has therefore been improved by 6.9% in comparison to the original protocol.

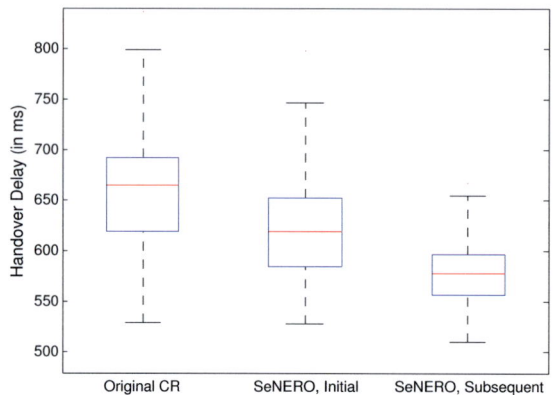

(a) Handover latency results for European scenario.

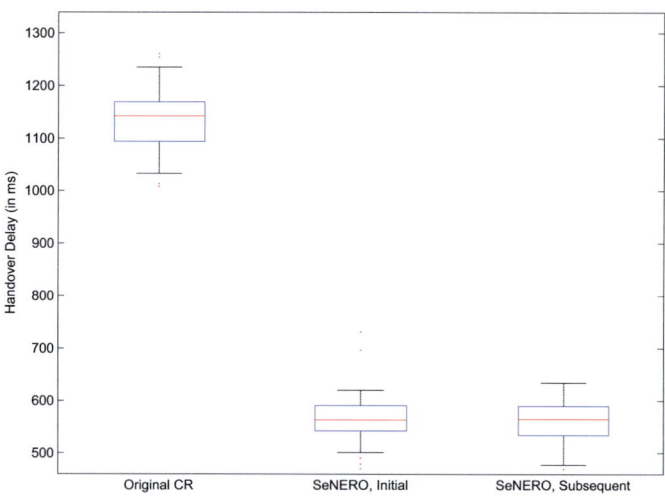

(b) Handover latency results for Asian scenario.

Figure 6.7. Handover latency results for test-bed evaluation.

Considering the subsequent authentication for SeNERO, the handover latency median is further reduced to 578 ms. The improvement to the original protocol is then 13.1%.

The *mean* handover delay for SeNERO is 625 ms and 576 ms for initial and subsequent authentication, while for the original protocol it is 660 ms. This is an improvement of 5.3% and 12.7%.

For the Asian scenario (cf. Figure 6.7b) the median delay for SeNERO is 619 ms and 575 ms for initial and subsequent authentication, while for the original protocol it is 1162 ms. This is an improvement of 46.7% and 50.5%. The mean handover delay for SeNERO is 627 ms and 574 ms, while for the original protocol it is 1166 ms. The corresponding improvement is 46.2% and 50.8%.

The handover latency in the subsequent authentication in SeNERO is roughly 43 ms smaller in both scenarios when compared to the initial authentication.

In all figures, a noticeable IQR of up to 77 ms for SeNERO and up to 75 ms for the original protocol can be observed. The standard deviation for SeNERO is up to 69 ms for the initial authentication and up to 46 ms for subsequent authentications. For the original protocol it is up to 64 ms.

A large part of this "jitter" can be explained by the artificial delay that has been introduced into the test-bed for both wired and wireless links. As specified in Table 6.1, a standard deviation of each 14 and 33 ms is present for forward and return link respectively. In addition to that, several milliseconds have to be accounted for processing delay within the test-bed nodes. Finally, studies [46] showed that, depending on the kind of used equipment, an average jitter of 2.6 ms or 3.7 ms is present for IEEE 802.11b access points. Jitter can even exist within the wired part of a test-bed network, causing individual packets to be delayed by several milliseconds.

The amount of time required for validating the signatures within binding update and binding acknowledgement was 7-8 ms on the test-bed devices. This results in a maximum of 125 verifications/second. This is enough for the aeronautical use case, where the airport, with one aircraft every 20 seconds, is the busiest airspace [58].

Comparison with Analytical Results

A comparison of the test-bed measurements with the analytical results from Section 6.1.2 is provided in Figure 6.8. The medians of the test-bed results are drawn as bars with the European scenario on the very left (delay to home: 18 ms) and the Asian scenario on the very right (delay to home: 148 ms). For SeNERO, the handover latency for both the initial and subsequent authentication are shown.

The analytical results are represented as solid lines. As the analytical model does not take into account message sizes or cryptographic operations that differentiate

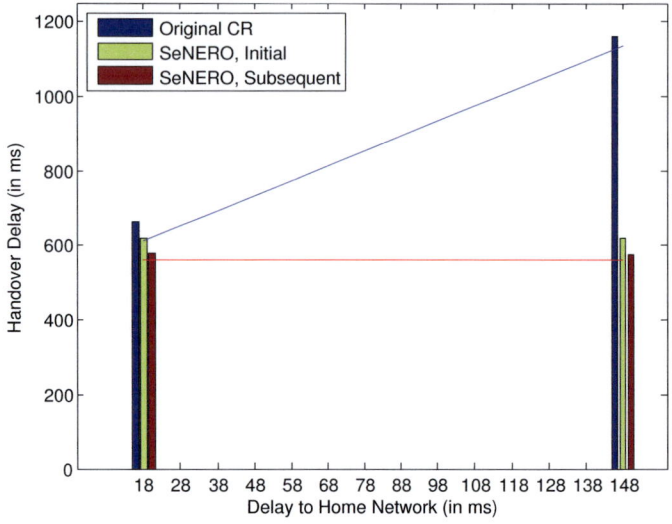

Figure 6.8. Comparison of test-bed with analytical handover results. For Se-NERO, the handover latency for both initial and subsequent authentication are shown.

the initial from the subsequent authentication, there is only a single solid line drawn for SeNERO.

In the European scenario, the offset between test-bed and analytical results is $665 - 614 = 51$ ms for the original correspondent router protocol. For SeNERO, it is $619 - 562 = 57$ ms for the initial and $578 - 562 = 16$ ms for the subsequent authentication.

In the Asian scenario, the offset is $1162 - 1134 = 28$ ms for the original correspondent router protocol, while for SeNERO it is $619 - 562 = 57$ ms for the initial and $575 - 562 = 13$ ms for the subsequent authentication.

A certain offset had to be expected, given that the analytical model does not take into account the jitter of a real-world wireless link, inter-node delays or the processing delays on each node that are present in a test-bed, such as cryptographic operations.

It can also be seen for SeNERO that the handover latency for the initial authentication is larger than for for the subsequent authentication. There are two reasons explaining this behavior: (1) the initial binding update and binding acknowledgement messages include certificates, which increase the overall message size. As a consequence, the transmission time over the wireless link also increases; (2) the initial authentication requires verification of signatures at correspondent router and mobile router. Both aspects are not considered in the analytical model.

Finally, the IQR and standard deviation present in the test-bed results also contribute to the observed offset: for the original protocol, the IQR is 73–75 ms and the standard deviation is 61–64 ms. For SeNERO, the IQR is 67–77 ms for the initial authentication and 67–77 ms for subsequent authentications. The respective standard deviations are 63–69 ms and 42–46 ms. Due to the limited number of samples obtained in the test-bed, the "real" median or mean handover latency might be smaller. This is also in line with the confidence intervals, that have a range of 43–52 ms, by which the mean obtained in the test-bed results could deviate.

E. g., for the original protocol in the Asian scenario, the spread in the handover latency is larger towards the maximum than the spread towards the minimum. The median and mean values calculated from the measurement data might therefore be larger than the "real" median and mean.

Comparison with Simulation Results

The simulation and test-bed results for both protocols in the European and Asian scenario are compared against other in the following. The comparison is based on Figure 6.6 for the simulation results and Figure 6.7 for the test-bed results.

The handover delay in the simulations is smaller than the measurements obtained in the test-bed for both protocols. For SeNERO, the medians deviate by up to 69 ms for the initial and up to 29 ms for the subsequent authentication. For the original correspondent router protocol, the deviation is up to 20 ms.

For both protocols, the smaller handover latency was to be expected for the simulation results. In contrast to the test-bed, no processing delays are present in the simulations. This is most notable in the initial authentication in SeNERO, due to the missing signature verifications. In the test-bed, the difference between initial and subsequent authentication in SeNERO is more than 40 ms (cf. Figure 6.7). This is due to the different cryptographic operations and sizes of the binding update and binding acknowledgement messages in the two authentication phases. In the subsequent authentication, no signature verifications are performed and the messages are smaller.

The different message sizes for the binding messages in the initial and subsequent authentication should result in different transmission times on the wireless link. No noticeable statistical difference in the handover latency of the two authentication phases can be noticed though. The simulation model of the wireless link obviously behaves differently than the real-world devices used in the test-bed, where different message sizes results in a different handover latency.

Channel	Bit Error Rate	Frame Error Rate
RACH	9.53^{-5}	8.7^{-4}
BCCH	6.37^{-6}	1.63^{-4}
CCCH	9.1^{-7}	6.31^{-5}
DCH FL	9.1^{-7}	6.31^{-5}
DCH RL	4.81^{-4}	6.29^{-2}
DCCH	9.1^{-7}	6.31^{-5}

Table 6.4. Bit and frame error rates of individual L-DACS 1 channels.

The standard deviation of the handover latency in the simulation results is similar to the test-bed results. A noticeable difference is only present for the initial authentication in SeNERO. In the simulations, the transmission of the larger messages does not inflict a large standard deviation, as it is the case within the test-bed.

6.1.5. Simulation Results II

Up to now, only the effect of a varying latency to the home network upon the mobility specific handover latency has been investigated. Another component affecting the handover latency is a varying latency on the wireless link, caused by a varying radio cell load.

The performance advantage of SeNERO is due to the eliminated HoTI/HoT message exchange that had to be performed via the home agent in the original correspondent router protocol. The investigation performed in the following shows that SeNERO, despite having larger initial binding update/binding acknowledgement messages, still provides better handover latency even in situations where the radio cell is overloaded. This shows that an increased latency on the wireless link does not eliminate the handover latency reduction achieved by eliminating the HoTI/HoT messages exchanges within the ground network.

For this reason, the IEEE 802.11 wireless link has been replaced with a more realistic access technology, the L-Band Digital Aeronautical Communications System Type 1 (L-DACS 1) [78]. The bit and frame error rates used in the simulations for the individual logical L-DACS 1 channels are provided in Table 6.4.

The others simulation settings are the same as used in Section 6.1.3, relying on the network topology illustrated in Figure 6.1. A constant-bit rate application periodically generates data traffic between mobile network node and correspondent node. The application parameters are equivalent to those listed in Table 6.3. The application is started while the mobile router is attached to the first radio cell, thereby triggering route optimization. Similarly to the previous simulations, this route optimization signaling is measured as mobility specific handover latency t_{MOB} for the initial authentication in SeNERO. The handover performed afterwards to another radio radio cell is measured as handover latency for the subsequent authentication in SeNERO and for the original correspondent router protocol.

The latencies specified for the wired parts of the simulated network topology are in line with Table 6.1. The delays for forward and return link provided in this table have not been included in the simulations as these became superfluous due to the L-DACS 1 link.

Similar to the previous simulations, a linearly increasing latency to the home agent has been assumed: starting from the European scenario with a home network latency of 18 ms, the latency is increased in steps of 10 ms up to a home network latency of 148 ms for the Asian scenario.

The new parameter within these simulations is the varying radio cell load. This has been achieved by having a varying number of L-DACS dummy nodes within the radio cells. This number is also linearly increasing: it starts at 0 and is incremented in steps of 10 up to a maximum number of 170 nodes.[7] The latency within the access network is therefore not defined as a parameter, but instead depends on the number of dummy nodes that are attached to a base station.

The dummy nodes use the same constant-bit rate application as mobile network node and correspondent node for generating additional "background" traffic. This traffic increases the radio cell load and consumes 2420 bit/sec on the forward link (base station to mobile) and 484 bit/sec on the return link (mobile to base station) on the application layer for each dummy node.[8] With 170 dummy nodes within a cell, this results in a peak application traffic volume of 400 Kbit/sec on the forward and 80 Kbit/sec on the return link. Including UDP and IPv6 headers, the peak volume is 529 Kbit/s on the forward link and 207 Kbit/s on the return link.

40 simulation runs are performed for every (home network delay, number of dummy nodes) parameter pair. The total number of simulation runs per protocol is therefore $14 \cdot 18 \cdot 40 = 10.080$. This number of simulation runs is performed for each of the two protocols.

Results

An overview of the results for the original correspondent router protocol and SeNERO are shown in Figure 6.9: the mobility specific handover latency median

---

[7]The number of 170 dummy nodes proved to be a practical upper bound: the radio cell is experiencing high load and the simulation time is very large, with a lower peak of about 0.47 simulated seconds within one second of real processing time.

[8]This traffic volume is derived from values for the ENR medium service volume as specified in [183]

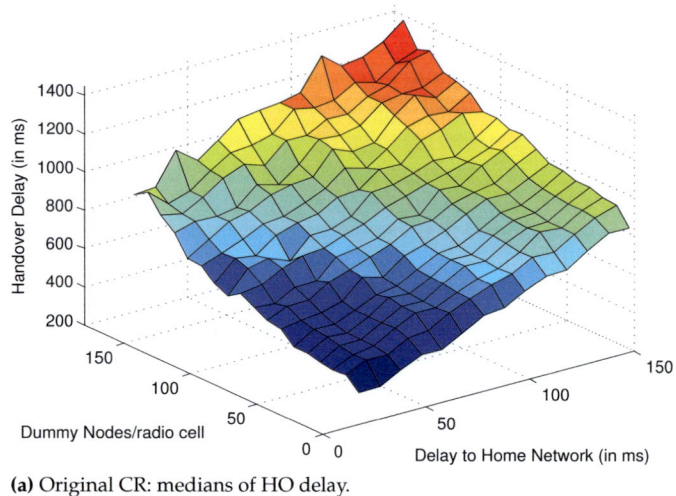

(a) Original CR: medians of HO delay.

Figure 6.9. Overview of handover (HO) delay for original correspondent router protocol in extended simulations with L-DACS 1.

(z-axis) of the two protocols is shown as a function of the latency to the home network (x-axis) and the number of dummy nodes in the radio cell (y-axis).

Figure 6.10 shows side views on the 3-dimensional plots, illustrated as box-and-whisker diagrams. Subfigures (a), (c) and (e) show the handover delay (y-axis) in correlation with the delay to the home network (x-axis). Subfigures (b), (d) and (f) show the handover delay in correlation with the number of dummy nodes in the radio cell.

The statistical properties of the results for each of the two protocols are provided in Tables D.7 to D.12 in Appendix D.4.

Original Correspondent Router Protocol
Figure 6.9 shows that the handover delay for the original correspondent router protocol increases linearly with a larger latency to the home network and a larger number of dummy nodes in the radio cell.

A more detailed view on the correlation between handover latency and latency to the home network is provided in Figure 6.10a. The spread on the y-axis, measured in terms of the IQR, is 236–279 ms. This spread originates from the varying number of dummy nodes within the radio cell. A larger number of nodes produces a higher load on the wireless link – as a consequence, the available capacity for every individual node becomes smaller, therefore increasing the latency for

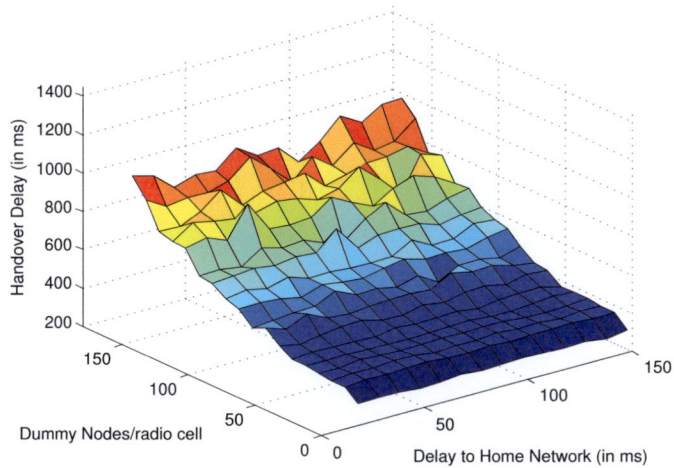

(b) SeNERO, initial authentication: medians of HO delay.

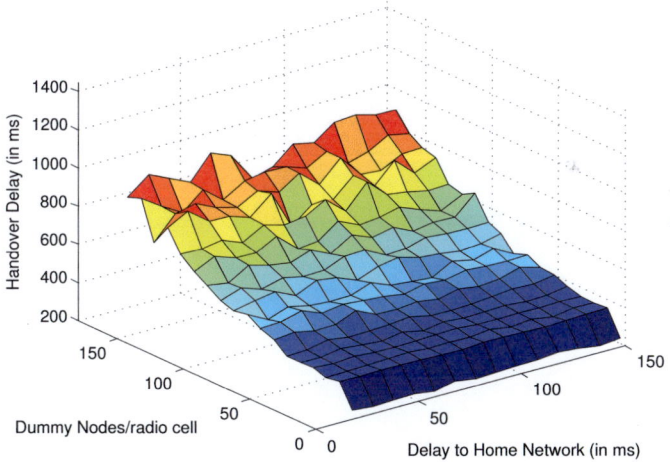

(c) SeNERO, subsequent authentication: medians of HO delay.

Figure 6.9. Overview of handover (HO) delay for SeNERO in extended simulations with L-DACS 1.

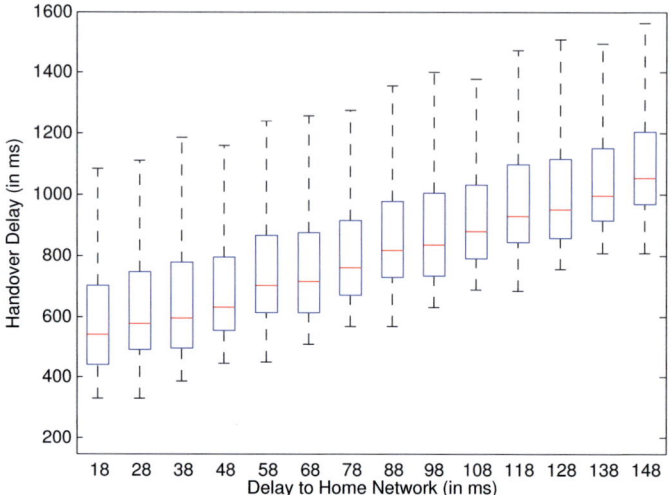

(a) Original CR: HO delay due to varying home network latency.

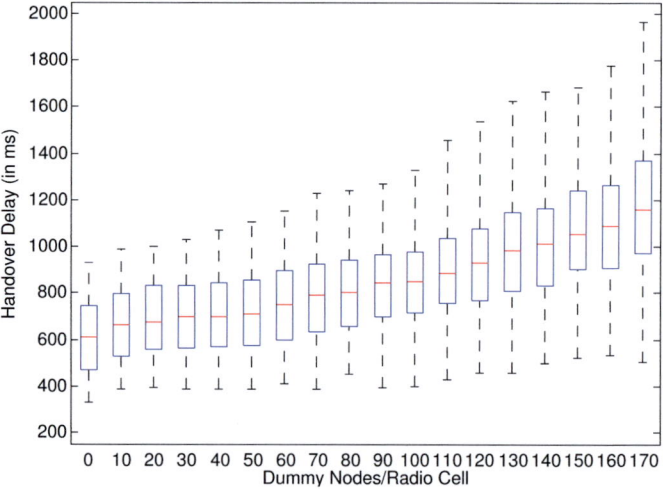

(b) Original CR: HO delay due to number of nodes per radio cell.

Figure 6.10. Handover (HO) delay for original correspondent router protocol and SeNERO depending on the delay to the home network and the number of nodes in the radio cell.

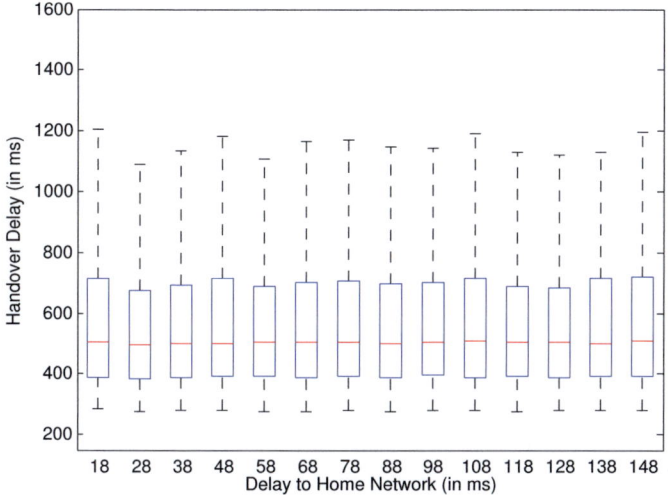

(c) SeNERO, initial authentication: HO delay due to varying home network latency.

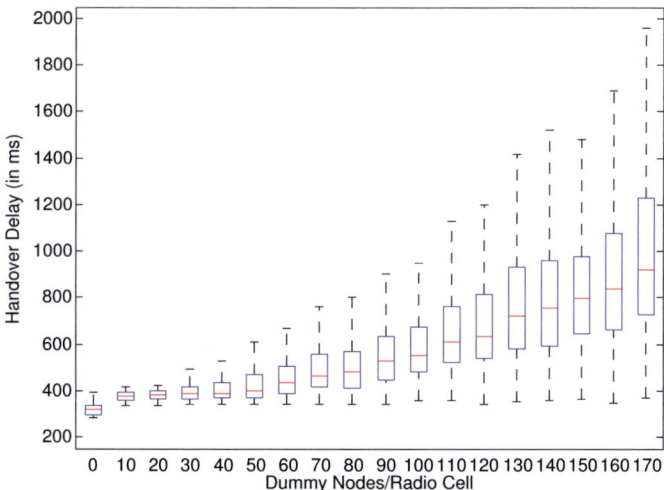

(d) SeNERO, initial authentication: HO delay due to number of nodes per radio cell.

Figure 6.10. Handover (HO) delay for original correspondent router protocol and SeNERO depending on the delay to the home network and the number of nodes in the radio cell.

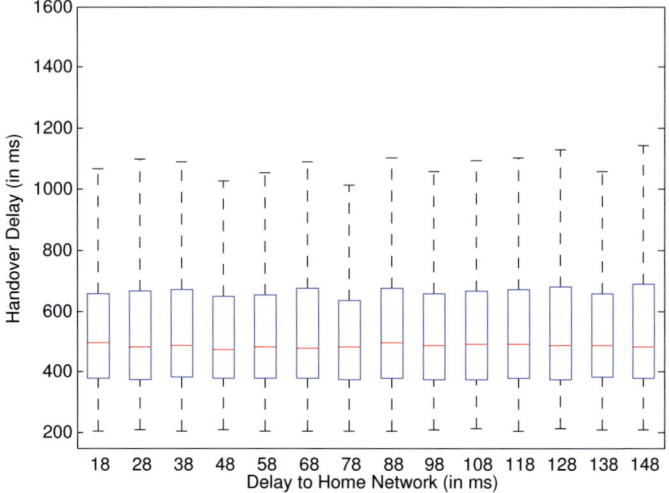

(e) SeNERO, subsequent authentication: HO delay due to varying home network latency.

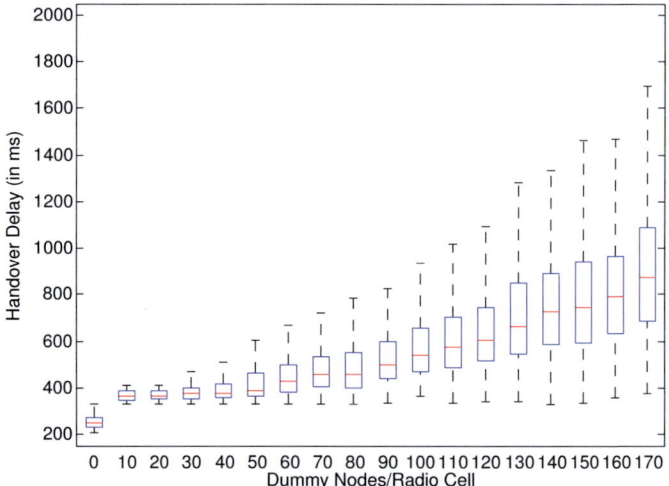

(f) SeNERO, subsequent authentication: HO delay due to number of nodes per radio cell.

Figure 6.10. Handover (HO) delay for original correspondent router protocol and SeNERO depending on the delay to the home network and the number of nodes in the radio cell.

sending packets over the wireless link. This latency increase is most noticeable between the 75th percentile ($q_{0.75}$) and the maximum, which represents situations with up to 170 dummy nodes. The explanation for this behavior is that the increase in latency from 120 to 170 nodes is significantly larger than the increase in latency from 0 to 50 nodes, where the radio cell is underutilized.

Figure 6.10a shows that the handover latency median is 540 ms on the very left (European scenario with home network latency: 18 ms) and 1055 ms on the very right (Asian scenario with home network latency: 148 ms). The difference between the two scenarios is therefore 515 ms. This linear increase of the handover latency has already been explained as resulting from the routing path of the HoTI/HoT message pair. The results of the analytical investigation in Section 6.1.2 showed that a 520 ms increase had to be expected. Given an interquartile range (IQR) of 258–238 ms and a standard deviation of 263–268 ms for these two specific scenarios (home network latencies: 18 and 148 ms), the simulation results are in line with the analytical results.

A different view on the obtained results of the original correspondent router protocol is provided in Figure 6.10b, which shows the handover latency as a function of the number of dummy nodes within a cell.

The vertical spread in the handover latency inside each box is, to one part, due to the varying latency to the home network. The spread is further increased with an increasing number of dummy nodes. The different numbers of nodes can cause an additional latency of 547 ms, considering a handover latency median of 609 ms on the very left (0 dummy nodes) and 1156 ms on the very right (170 dummy nodes). The IQR increases from 271 ms on the very left to 400 ms on the very right. The increasing number of nodes causes a higher utilization of the available bandwidth of the radio cell. Consecutively, less bandwidth is available for every individual node and latency increases. As a consequence, the spread within the handover latency boxes also continually increases with the number of nodes.

Summarized, the handover latency median for the original protocol has a dynamic component of 515 ms due to a varying home network latency, which is in line with the results of the analytical investigation. A 547 ms spread exists for a varying number of dummy nodes in the radio cell.

SeNERO
For SeNERO, results for both the initial and subsequent authentication are provided. Figures 6.9b and 6.9c show that the handover delay for SeNERO remains constant with respect to a varying delay to the home network. It only increases with a larger number of dummy nodes in the radio cell.

A more detailed view on the correlation between handover latency and home network latency is provided in Figures 6.10c and 6.10e.

The medians are in a range of 496–508 ms for the initial and 473–495 ms for the subsequent authentication. As already known from the previous evaluations, the constant handover latency with only a small variation had to be expected, as SeNERO has no signaling dependency on the home network. The overall median in the initial authentication, when aggregating among the different latencies to the home network, is 18 ms or 3.6% larger then in the subsequent authentication. The vertical spread in the handover latency, measured in terms of the IQR, is 289–328 ms for the initial and 256–306 ms for the subsequent authentication. The larger handover latency and IQR for the initial authentication can be explained by the large sizes for binding update and binding acknowledgement. Both messages include certificates, and the transmission of a large message consumes more time, especially on the wireless link.

The impact the number of dummy nodes per radio cell has on the handover delay is shown in Figures 6.10d and 6.10f.

The medians of the handover latency, considering 0 additional dummy nodes in the cell, are 315 and 247 ms for initial and subsequent authentication. In the case of 170 nodes, the medians are 917 and 873 ms respectively. The varying number of dummy nodes therefore causes an additional latency of up to 602 and 626 ms for the two individual authentication phases.

The spread in terms of the IQR increases considerably from 40 ms (for 0 nodes) to 505 ms (for 170 nodes) for the initial authentication. For the subsequent authentication, the spread increases from 41 ms (for 0 nodes) to 406 ms (for 170 nodes). The reason for this behavior is that the traffic caused by the increasing number of nodes consumes all of the available capacity of the radio cell. A fully utilized radio cell causes packets to be queued until they can be transmitted over the wireless link. The latency therefore increases and, as a consequence, the handover delay variance also increases. This is particularly noticeably in the transition from 100 nodes to 110 nodes during the initial authentication, where an IQR increase of more than 50 ms is present. The IQR is smaller for the subsequent authentication due to the smaller binding update and binding acknowledgement message sizes.

Summarized, an important observation is the handover latency median of 485 and 503 ms for the initial and subsequent authentication, considering a varying latency to the home network. A 465 and 365 ms spread exists for a varying number of dummy nodes in the radio cell. This is 82–182 ms smaller compared to the spread of the original correspondent router protocol for a varying number of dummy nodes.

Comparison to Analytical Results

The results of the extended simulations are compared with the analytical investigation from Section 6.1.2 in the following.

The illustration in Figure 6.11 shows the analytical results as solid green lines on top of the box-and-whisker plots showing the simulation results.

As the analytical model only considers the latency to the home network as a parameter of varying value, the comparison is restricted to this single figure, where the handover delay is shown as a function of the home network latency.

The comparison for the original correspondent router protocol is shown in Figure 6.11a. As can be seen, the analytical results are located between the median and the 75th percentile ($q_{0.75}$) of the simulation results.

The reason why the analytical results are 55–96 ms below the medians of the simulation results is as follows: the calculation in the analytical model used a fixed latency value of 99 ms on the forward link and 162 ms on the return link. These two numbers, which have been taken from [74], turned out to be larger than the wireless link latencies obtained in the simulations.

The comparison for the initial authentication in SeNERO is shown in Figure 6.11b. Again, the analytical results are located between the median and the 75th percentile ($q_{0.75}$) of the simulation results. The difference between analytical and simulation results is 29–71 ms. The reason for this difference to the analytical results is the same as explained above.

For the subsequent authentication, the difference between analytical and simulation results is 61–97 ms. The accompanying figure is not shown as no difference can not be noticed when compared to the initial authentication shown in Figure 6.11b.

The latency of the initial authentication is closer to the analytical results than the subsequent authentication. The signaling messages in the initial authentication are large and therefore consume more time during transmission on the wireless link, resulting in a larger handover latency. Consecutively, the handover latency of the initial authentication is closer to the analytical result that has a larger latency on the wireless path than the simulations. In contrast to this, the subsequent authentication has smaller signaling messages that consume less time on the wireless link. As a consequence, the handover latency of the subsequent authentication is smaller and therefore shows a larger deviation to the analytical results.

Radio Cell Load Impact

A more detailed investigation of these simulations results based on a varying radio cell load is provided in the following.

This final comparison between original correspondent router protocol and SeNERO is based on three different load situations:

1. Small load: 50 dummy nodes per cell.

2. Medium load: 100 dummy nodes per cell.

3. Overload: 170 dummy nodes per cell.

This classification is similar to the one used in [74], where comparable scenarios contain 45, 62 and 204 nodes. It should be noted that the radio cell load in the simulations presented here is larger, as the authors of [74] did not consider IP packet overhead.

In the small load case, for the original protocol the handover latency *median* is 706 ms and the *mean* is 723 ms. For the initial authentication in SeNERO, the median is 400 ms and the mean is 433 ms. For the subsequent authentication, the median is 389 ms and the mean is 430 ms. Considering the initial authentication, SeNERO therefore provides an improved handover performance of 77% considering the *median* and 67% considering the *mean* value. With respect to the subsequent authentication, the improvement is 81% and 68%.

For the medium load case, the handover latency median for the original protocol is 849 ms and the mean value is 863 ms. For SeNERO, the median is 552 ms and the mean is 613 ms for the initial authentication, while for the subsequent authentication the median is 537 ms and the mean value is 588 ms. SeNERO therefore provides an improved handover performance of 54% and 41% considering the median and mean values of the initial authentication respectively. With respect to the subsequent authentication, the improvement is 58% and 47%

For the overload case, the handover latency median for the original protocol is 1156 ms and the median is 1243 ms. For the SeNERO initial authentication, the median is 917 ms and the mean is 1041 ms. For the subsequent authentication, the median is 873 ms and the mean is 933 ms. SeNERO therefore provides an improved handover performance of 26% and 19% considering the median and mean values of the initial authentication respectively. With respect to the subsequent authentication, the improvement is 32% and 33% for median and mean.

Summarized, SeNERO always provides a better handover performance, with improvements usually ranging between 26% and 81% for the medians when compared to the original protocol. For the means the range is 19% to 68%. The performance improvement of the subsequent authentication, when compared to the original protocol, is 4-7% larger then for the initial authentication.

That the performance advantage decreases from the small load to the overload scenario is due to the fact that the delay on the wireless link becomes larger. As a consequence, the latency to the home network is not the dominating component of the handover latency anymore. Instead it is reduced by the delay on the wireless link that constitutes a larger part of the overall handover latency.

Message	CR	SeNERO
CoTI/CoT	56/64	56/64
HoTI/HoT	96/104	-/-
Initial BU/BA	92/68	860/879
Latter BU/BA	92/68	92/66

Table 6.5. Route optimization signaling message sizes in bytes for old and new protocol.

6.2. Signaling Overhead Evaluation

In the following, the overhead caused by the original correspondent router protocol and SeNERO is compared against each other. The discussion addresses overhead caused by the mobility signaling itself. The overhead for the end-to-end application data packets is equivalent for both protocols as both use an IP-in-IP tunnel for forwarding user data between mobile router and correspondent router.

The trade-off for the improvements provided by SeNERO is an increase in the size of the mobility signaling messages: public-key certificates have to be embedded within the initial binding update and binding acknowledgement messages. These signaling messages are therefore larger in SeNERO than in the original protocol.

However, a disadvantage with respect to signaling overhead also exists for the original correspondent router protocol: the return routability procedure with its care-of test and home test messages (cf. Figure 3.3 on page 77) has to be periodically repeated every 7 minutes, as specified in [108]. This is to limit the vulnerability to off-path attackers (see Sections 3.1.5 and 5.3). This periodic signaling causes additional overhead, even if the mobile router is not performing any handovers.

The sizes of the individual messages for each of the two protocols are provided in Table 6.5. These values have been obtained from the test-bed implementation, presented in Section 6.1.4. Elliptic Curve Cryptography has been used for public-key cryptography in SeNERO. The associated keys and signatures have a size of each 384 bits and 96 bytes.

Figure 6.12a shows the accumulated signaling overhead of both protocols as a function of time. It can be seen that the initial overhead of SeNERO is larger, but remains constant over time in contrast to the original CR protocol, where overhead increases linearly over time. For the original CR protocol, the signaling consumes 480 bytes every 7 minutes. For SeNERO, the initial overhead is 1859 bytes.

Figure 6.12b shows the signaling overhead per minute, also as a function of time. It can be seen that SeNERO has a high overhead per minute in the initial phase, but becomes more efficient if the optimized route remains established over a longer time period of time. In contrast to this, the original CR protocol has a smaller initial overhead, but remains at a higher overhead level over time.

The initial overhead for the original correspondent router protocol (480 bytes) is 74% *below* that of SeNERO (1859 bytes). Considering the signaling overhead generated per minute, the original protocol requires less bandwidth than SeNERO in the first minutes. For the time duration of the first 7 minutes, the bandwidth consumption per minute of the original protocol is 74% below that of SeNERO.

However, the overhead of the original protocol increases over time due to the periodic signaling. The overhead of SeNERO remains constant, as it is time-independent. After 21 minutes (1920 bytes), the overhead of the original protocol is almost identical to that of SeNERO. The overhead is 3% *above* that of SeNERO, for both the absolute signaling overhead and the signaling overhead per minute.

After 29 minutes, the overhead of the original protocol is slightly above the overhead incurred by SeNERO. After 56 and 84 minutes, the overhead for the original protocol (4320 and 6240 bytes) further increases to 57% and 70% above that of SeNERO, when comparing the absolute numbers. When comparing the signaling overhead per minute, the overhead of SeNERO is 57% and 68% below that of the original protocol for a time duration of 56 and 84 minutes.

These numbers have to be interpreted based on the communication patterns of how often the communication peer is changing. Each time the correspondent node, or rather the associated correspondent router, is changed, route optimization signaling with a full authentication has to be performed again. The following two scenarios describe such communication patterns that are advantageous for either SeNERO or the original correspondent router protocol.

Scenario 1: The correspondent node is not changing frequently or (a large number of) the different correspondent nodes are served by the same correspondent router. The optimized path is then established and kept alive for more than 20 minutes. Only the care-of address of the mobile router has to be updated in case of subsequent handovers. SeNERO is then more bandwidth efficient than the original protocol.

Scenario 2: The correspondent nodes are changing frequently and they are located within different networks, therefore also served by different correspondent routers. For each correspondent router, a route optimization procedure with an initial authentication has to be performed. If this happens every 20 minutes or even less, then the original correspondent router protocol is more bandwidth efficient than SeNERO.

For ATS communications, scenario 1 dominates: an aircraft usually remains for more than 20 minutes within a certain national airspace. During this time, it is communicating with air traffic controllers of that airspace. The bi-directional tunnel established to the correspondent router of a particular national network can be used for forwarding traffic to all correspondent nodes located within the same network. Hence, SeNERO can be considered being more bandwidth-efficient than the original correspondent router protocol within the aeronautical communications scenario.

6.3. Summary

Within this chapter, the efficiency of SeNERO has been analyzed and compared with the original correspondent router protocol. This evaluation was focused on handover latency and signaling overhead. Based on analytical, test-bed and simulation studies it was shown that SeNERO provides better efficiency than the original protocol.

A European and an Asian scenario has been defined as best-case and worst-case scenario for the *handover latency evaluation*. The scenarios differ in the varying latency for routing packets from and to the home network. According to the analytical investigation, based on the above mentioned scenarios, SeNERO provides a handover latency improvement of 8.5%–50.4%. The simulation results show an improvement of 12%–51% with respect to the handover medians. Similarly, the test-bed results show reduced median handover latencies of 13.1%–50.8%. The best results for SeNERO have been obtained for the subsequent authentication, where the signaling messages (binding update/binding acknowledgement) are small.

The handover latency results varied among the different evaluation methods, with the analytical model having the smallest latency, followed by the simulation and then test-bed results with the highest handover latency. This is due to the different model of the wireless link within the different evaluation methods. Also, cryptographic operations have only been implemented in the test-bed.

An extended set of simulations did not only consider a varying latency to the home network, but also a varying radio cell load. These simulations relied on L-DACS 1 as a realistic aeronautical access technology. The results show that the performance improvement of SeNERO is still up to 58% in situations with a medium radio cell load. Even if the radio cell is overloaded, an improvement of up to 32% is possible. In case the radio cell load is small, the improvement can even be up to 81%.

The *overhead evaluation* showed that the signaling overhead of SeNERO is 3–70% below that of the original correspondent router protocol, considering a time win-

165

dow of 21–84 minutes in which the bi-directional tunnel to a single correspondent router is kept active.

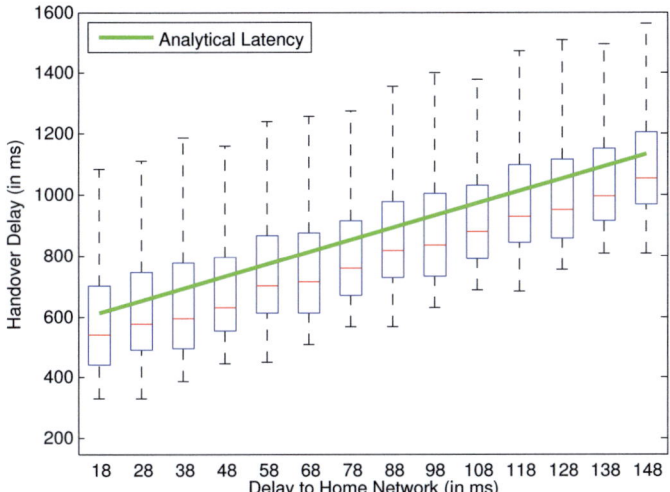

(a) Original CR: handover delay due to varying home network latency.

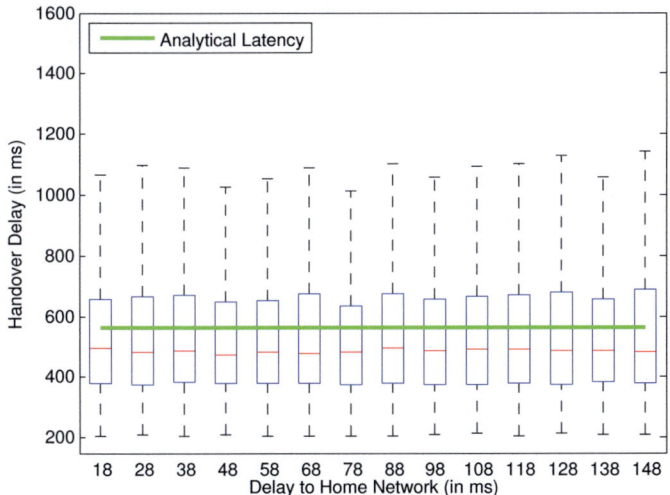

(b) SeNERO, initial authentication: handover delay due to varying home network latency.

Figure 6.11. Comparison of handover delay of the analytical investigation with results from the extended simulations.

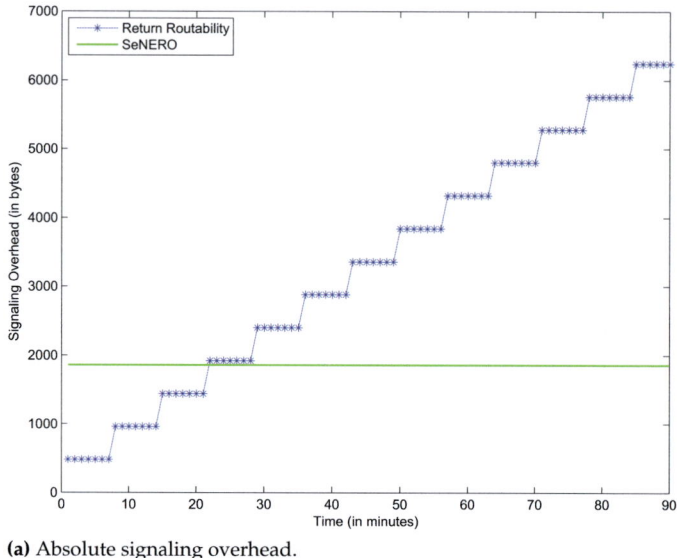

(a) Absolute signaling overhead.

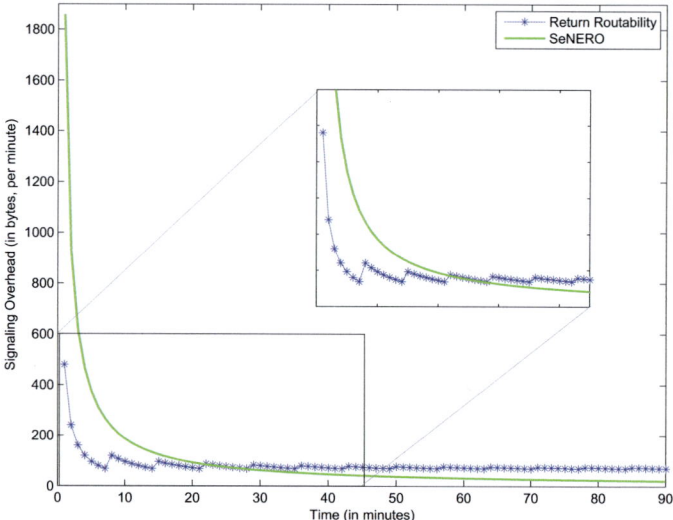

(b) Relative signaling overhead (per minute).

Figure 6.12. Signaling overhead of SeNERO and original correspondent router protocol as a function of time.

7. Identity Certificates With Local Verification

The SeNERO protocol presented in Chapter 4 relies on a public key infrastructure and identity certificates for mutual authentication. The verification of these certificates requires the mobile router and correspondent router to establish a certification path to each others certificate. This certification path will consist of the trust anchor and of additional certificate authorities.

The validation of this certification path requires to verify each individual certificate that is along the path, including its revocation status. In case the revocation service, such as a certificate revocation list or online certificate status protocol server, of any certificate authority along the certification path is not available, the validation can not be successfully completed. The non-availability of such a service would prevent mobile router and correspondent router from authenticating to each other. As a consequence, a bi-directional tunnel between mobile router and correspondent router can not be established.

Given the public key infrastructure defined for SeNERO, both the global trust anchor and the certificate authority issuing the certificate of the mobile router will be located in a network that is different from the correspondent network or mobile network. Mobile router and correspondent router would therefore have to perform *inter-domain operations* for certificate verification. The public key infrastructure could therefore be considered being a *single point of failure.*

In addition, a public key infrastructure model based on a single global trust anchor would not fit the air traffic control communications environment. As of today, prior to establishing a flight route, each country that is along the flight route has to approve such a route. However, in a public key infrastructure model with a global trust anchor, once the trust anchor is accepted, every single certificate issued by this trust anchor can be used for authentication purposes.

To address these issues, an extension to X.509 identity certificates is defined within this chapter. The certificates of the mobile router and correspondent router, for use within the SeNERO protocol, are defined based on this extended certificate model. When used inside the SeNERO protocol, each correspondent router can verify the extended certificate of a mobile router by only performing intra-domain operations; the correspondent router will only rely on the certificate authority and revocation services located within its correspondent network domain, also called local certificate authority. Similarly, a mobile router can also verify the extended certificate of a correspondent router by only relying on the certificate authority and revocation services located in the correspondent network domain where the correspondent router to be authenticated is located.

No inter-domain operations with certificate authorities located outside the correspondent network or mobile network are required anymore. Each country or region where an aircraft has to authenticate to can operate a local certificate authority. For a single mobile router, an extended identity certificate will be issued by every local certificate authority. Such a certificate can be used for authentication within the domain of a local certificate authority. In case a country does not permit an aircraft to enter its airspace, no certificate will be issued or an already issued certificate will be revoked by the country's local certificate authority.

The certificate construction process is based on the assumption that the mobile network knows in advance in which correspondent networks it will authenticate to during a flight. An authentication within a correspondent network for which no certificate is available can only be supported by means of a transitive trust relationship to the certificate authority of another correspondent network. E. g., based on cross-certificates between the certificate authorities of two correspondent networks or via a bridge certificate authority that is trusted by two correspondent networks.

This concept replaces the original centralized (global trust anchor) with a distributed architecture (local trust anchors). The idea is motivated by the "fate-sharing" argument [43], that can be translated into the aeronautical context as follows: if the local certificate authority of a correspondent node is not available due to, e. g., network problems, then no issue arises, as at the same time the correspondent node with whom the aircraft attempts to communicate with will also not be available.

The certificate extension is not tied to SeNERO. It is also applicable to other protocols and applications.

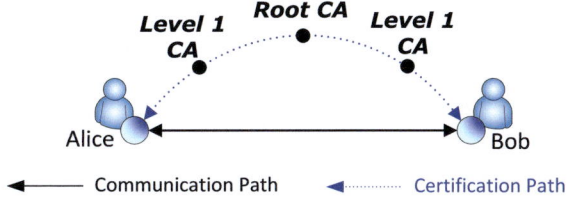

Figure 7.1. Authentication between Alice and Bob based on a root certificate authority as trust anchor.

7.1. Problem Description

In the following, Bob will be used as synonym for the mobile router, whereas Alice will be used as synonym for the correspondent router.

7.1.1. General Problem with PKI-based Authentication

Alice and Bob attempt to authenticate to each other. In the context of SeNERO, the mobile router and correspondent router will authenticate their IP address prefixes. This authentication requires a common trust anchor (certificate authority) that is trusted by both Alice and Bob. Based on the public key infrastructure defined in Section 4.3, this will be the root certificate authority that corresponds to the aeronautical IP address authority. Alice and Bob will then construct a certification path that is based on this root certificate authority and intermediate certificate authorities, cf. Figure 7.1.

Based on this certification path, Alice will verify the certificates of Bob, the intermediate certificate authorities and the trust anchor. She will also check the revocation status of these certificates, by means of the online certificate status protocol or a certificate revocation list provided by each issuing certificate authority. The same is performed by Bob for Alice's certificate. If any certificate authority, in particular its revocation services, are not available, then Alice and Bob are not able to verify the certification path. They are then not able to successfully authenticate to each other. In the context of SeNERO, mobile router and correspondent router are then unable to establish the optimized routing path between each other. is not located along the routing path. that is different from Alice's and Bob's.

The PKI therefore becomes a single point of failure, especially the root certificate authority (trust anchor) due to its pivotal role. Other PKI models [167] do not resolve this problem, as Alice and Bob would still require a particular certificate authority not associated to Alice's or Bob's domain as trust anchor for certification path construction.

171

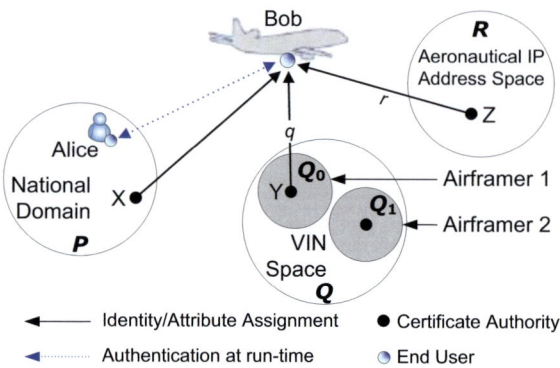

Figure 7.2. Different trust domains in the multi-institutional aeronautical environment.

Another issue is trust on an organizational level: once a trust anchor is accepted, all certificates issued by this trust anchor are accepted. In air traffic control communications, every country should be able to independently decide which aircraft can enter and authenticate themselves to the national air traffic controllers though. An improved PKI model should therefore make a country specific certificate authority the last instance to decide on whether a certificate is accepted in the respective national trust domain.

7.1.2. PKI in the Aeronautical Environment

An illustration of the aeronautical communications environment with a focus on its different trust domains and certificate authorities is provided in Figure 7.2. Bob (mobile router) is a mobile network moving between different local trust domains (countries), which constitute network domains. When located within such a network, Bob will authenticate and communicate with entities located in this network, such as Alice (e.g. ATS controller).

There are additional trust domains with associated certificate authorities. These do not contain any communication partners for Bob from an end-to-end perspective, but are instead only responsible for assigning an identity or an IP address prefix to Bob. These are international organizations.

In the provided example, there is one country specific trust domain as well as two trust domains representing international organizations.

The first trust domain is the vehicle identification number (VIN[1]) space containing the identities that are assigned to an aircraft. The overall VIN space Q will be partitioned among the different airframe manufacturers, e. g., $Q = Q_0 \cup Q_1$. In addition, there is the IP address space $\mathcal{R}$. Both the overall VIN and IP address space are not country specific, but instead managed by international entities. Finally, there is the identity space of a national ground network $\mathcal{P}$. This space is used for assigning identities to local (country specific) entities such as Alice.

The various identity and IP address spaces are disjoint.

A differentiation is introduced between *preconfiguration* phase and *runtime*. During the preconfiguration phase, Bob will receive a vehicle identification number $q \in Q_0$ from CA Y that will be assigned and used as Bob's identity within an X.509 identity certificate. Additionally, the mobile network prefix $r \in \mathcal{R}$ is assigned to Bob by the certificate authority Z that manages the aeronautical IP address space $\mathcal{R}$. Both identity and mobile network prefix are assigned by certificate authorities located in different trust domains. From a general perspective, other authorities might assign additional parameters. Additional assignments are not considered in this example.

At runtime, Bob will attempt to authenticate to Alice using the identity q and mobile network prefix r. The entity Alice is located inside a local domain represented by the certificate authority X. This certificate authority is authoritative for its local identity space $\mathcal{P}$ and for deciding who can authenticate within its domain. In the case of SeNERO, runtime refers to the authentication performed between mobile router and correspondent router.

The standard solution for situations where, e. g., IP addresses are assigned in addition to an identity would be X.509 identity certificates in combination with attribute certificates [62]. An attribute certificate, as illustrated in Figure 7.3b, is issued by an attribute authority and contains attribute information such as a mobile network prefix $r \in \mathcal{R}$. Such a certificate is bound to an identity certificate, illustrated in Figure 7.3a. E. g., the IP address authority Z could issue an attribute certificate that is bound to Bob's identity certificate provided by Y. Within the *holder* field, the attribute certificate refers to the identity certificate, e. g., by listing the issuer and serial number of the identity certificate. The other fields of the attribute certificate are used as follows. The *issuer* refers to the attribute authority that issued the certificate. The attribute or attributes, such as the mobile network prefix $r \in \mathcal{R}$, are stored inside the *attributes* field. The *signature* field at the end specifies the used signature algorithm and contains the signature itself, as calculated by the attribute authority.

---

[1]Such a VIN does not yet exist but discussions have already been started in the respective standardization organization (Airlines Electronic Engineering Committee - AEEC) to specify such an identity in the future.

Attribute Certificate		X.509 Identity Certificate
...		...
Holder		Serial Number
Issuer		Validity
...		...
Serial Number		Issuer
Validity		Subject
...		Subject Public Key Info
Attributes		Extensions
...		...
Signature Algorithm		Signature Algorithm
Signature Value		Signature Value
(a) Identity certificate.		**(b)** Attribute certificate.

Figure 7.3. X.509 Identity and attribute certificates.

Alice, when presented with Bobs pair of identity and attribute certificates, would have to perform *inter-domain* operations: she has to establish a certification path to Bob's certificate via the trust anchors Y (for identity) and Z (for attribute) and rely on the certificate revocation services of these authorities. This is also illustrated in Figure 7.1, where the trust anchors are located in domains that are different from those of Alice and Bob. In this example, the path used for the authentication signaling (e. g. certification path construction, retrieving revocation information) is different from the communication path used by Alice and Bob. If a certificate authority or attribute authority and its revocation services are not available, Alice is unable to verify Bob's certificate and vice versa. The authentication can then not be successfully completed. Each of these authorities therefore constitutes a *single point of failure*; non-availability of such an authority will prevent successful authentication and therefore communication between Alice and Bob. In the context of the SeNERO protocol, mobile router and correspondent router will not be able to establish a bi-directional tunnel between each other.

An additional issue is that a trust relationship with a certificate/attribute authority implies *trust on an organizational level*: if Alice trusts a certain certificate authority or attribute authority, then Alice will accept all certificates that have been issued by these authorities. This is a basic property of public key infrastructures due to the way certificates are validated.

It is argued that both aspects are not acceptable for a safety related environment such as ATS communications. Due to the single point of failure, the non-availability of an attribute or certificate authority can prevent two nodes from communicating with each other. The issue with trust on an organizational trust is in conflict with operational ATS procedures, where aircraft always have to request for individual clearance before entering national airspace. E. g., an airline certificate authority can not be granted authority to decide whether its aircraft can enter a national airspace or not.

7.2. Trust Model

The trust relationships between different aeronautical trust domains as a whole and trust between nodes of these domains is described in the following.

Two types of trust domains exist. The first type are *identity/attribute domains*. Examples for these are: the vehicle identification number space of each airframe manufacturer or the IP address space of an aeronautical Internet registry. The second type of trust domains are the *local domains*, which represent local networks or countries. In the example shown in Figure 7.2, Alice is located in a local domain that is represented by certificate authority X. The local domains also have their own identity space, such as $\mathcal{P}$, from which identities of local nodes are assigned.

Each trust domain has a a certificate authority (CA) that is *authoritative* for the respective domain. Only the authoritative certificate authority can assign and revoke identities or attributes from the identity or attribute space of this domain. The certificate authority that is authoritative for a local domain is also called the local *local certificate authority*.

A ground entity Alice (e. g. correspondent router) only trusts her local certificate authority, also called *national* CA. This certificate authority is Alice's only trust anchor with respect to certification path construction. The local CA as limited trust into certificate authorities located in other domains, also called *foreign certificate authorities* located in *foreign domains*. This trust is limited to only accepting identity or attribute assignments for which the foreign CA is authoritative. Apart from this, certificate authorities of different domains are in general considered to not have trust to each other. National/local certificate authorities are furthermore authoritative with respect to authentication operations within their domain. Considering a ground entity Alice located within her local domain, an arbitrary Bob (aircraft) is not permitted to successfully authenticate to Alice with only a certificate that has been issued by a foreign CA. Instead, Alice's local CA first has to approve Bob's identity and attributes.

Bob (mobile router/aircraft) will trust the national certificate authorities within their respective local domains. Bob will also trust other certificate authorities for assigning identities/attributes from those domains for whom these are authoritative.

It is assumed that Bob will know in advance with whom he will be communicating during runtime. Hence, in the context of the trust model, Bob will know which trust domains he will visit during runtime, the flight phase.

7.3. Identity Certificate Extension

In the following, X.509 identity certificates are extended in such a way that they can be verified based on a local trust anchor only. No global trust anchor, such as the certificate authorities Y or Z (cf. Figure 7.2), is required for certificate verification. Additionally, Bob will only be able to authenticate to a ground node Alice if his certificate has been approved by Alice's local certificate authority. To avoid confusion with attribute certificates, the attributes and associated extension fields are called *properties* within the new certificate extension.

These certificates are only used by Alice and Bob; certificate authorities still rely on the standard X.509 certificate format [45].

The certificate construction itself is performed in the preconfiguration phase, cf. Section 7.1.2.

7.3.1. Bob's Certificate

The certificate defined in the following for Bob (mobile router) is intended for use with the SeNERO protocol.

The different certificate authorities iteratively *extend* Bob's certificate by adding properties for whom they are authoritative. Once all properties have been assigned, Bob will request the individual local certificate authorities of the national domains (e. g. the CA of Alice) to sign and issue this certificate. Such a certificate is written as follows, extending the formal notation introduced in Section 2.3.5.4:

$$Cert(X, B, \{(X_0, p_0), (X_1, p_1), \ldots, (X_n, p_n)\})$$

The extended identity certificate contains an identity p_0 that is issued by X_0, as represented by the superscript notation. The certificate contains several additional attributes p_i assigned by different authorities X_i. For each property holds that $p_i \in \mathcal{P}_i$ and each X_i is authoritative for $\mathcal{P}_i$, $0 \leq i \leq n$. The certificate authority X issuing the certificate does not assign any additional property.

The example used in the following is based on the assignments for Bob shown in Figure 7.2. The different stages of certificate construction are shown in Figure 7.4.

Initial Identity Certificate

In the first stage, the airframe manufacturer CA Y provides an identity q (VIN) for Bob's public key. The following certificate is issued:

$$Cert(Y, B, q^Y),$$

assuming that $q \in \mathcal{Q}$ and Y is authoritative for $\mathcal{Q}$. The superscript in q^Y indicates that q has been assigned by Y.

An illustration of the corresponding certificate is provided in Figure 7.4a. The certificate includes standard X.509 [45] fields that include, among others, the name

```
X.509 Certificate
  Serial Number = S₁, Issuer = Y
  Validity = [t⁴ⱼ,t⁴ₖ]
  Subject
  Subject Public Key Info = K^PUB_Bob
  Extensions
    Subject Alternative Name = Q₀
    Property 1
      Issuer = Y
      Serial Number = S₁
      Validity = [t⁴ⱼ,t⁴ₖ]
      Property = q
      Signature Alg., Signature σ¹ₚ
  Signature Alg., Signature = σ₁
```

(a) First stage with assigned identity.

```
X.509 Certificate
  Serial Number = S₂, Issuer = Z
  Validity = [t⁵ⱼ,t⁵ₖ]
  Subject
  Subject Public Key Info = K^PUB_Bob
  Extensions
    Subject Alternative Name = Q₀
    Property 1
      Issuer = Y
      Serial Number = S₁
      Property = q
      Validity = [t⁴ⱼ,t⁴ₖ]
      Signature Alg., Signature σ¹ₚ
    Property 2
      Issuer = Z
      Serial Number = S₂
      Property = r
      Validity = [t⁵ⱼ,t⁵ₖ]
      Signature Alg., Signature = σ²ₚ
  Signature Alg., Signature = σ₂
```

```
X.509 Certificate
  Serial Number = S₀, Issuer = X
  Validity = [t⁶ⱼ,t⁶ₖ]
  Subject
  Subject Public Key Info = K^PUB_Bob
  Extensions
    Subject Alternative Name = Q₀
    Property 1
      Issuer = Y
      Serial Number = S₁
      Property = q
      Validity = [t⁴ⱼ,t⁴ₖ]
      Signature Alg., Signature σ¹ₚ
    Property 2
      Issuer = Z
      Serial Number = S₂
      Property = r
      Validity = [t⁵ⱼ,t⁵ₖ]
      Signature Alg., Signature σ²ₚ
  Signature Alg., Signature = σ₃
```

(b) Second stage with assigned property.

(c) Final stage with signature from national authority.

Figure 7.4. Different stages of extended identity certificate construction. Red colored fields are new or have been modified by the respective certificate authority when compared to the previous stage.

of the issuing certificate authority ("Issuer"), the time period in which the certificate is valid ("Validity"), the public key ("Subject Public Key Info") as well as the identity q. The latter is stored in an already existing extension field ("Subject Alternative Name") that is specified within the X.509 standard. Furthermore, the certificate authority Y adds a new extension field "Property 1" that contains the identity again as a property. All information necessary to support the revocation of the identity is included inside the property field: name of the issuer, serial number, validity period, the assigned property (identity in this case) as well as a signature σ_p^1. The serial number uniquely identifies the property within the context of the issuing certificate authority. The signature σ_p^1 within the extension field is calculated with the private key of Y, covering Bob's public key in the field "Subject Public Key Info" up to the extension field "Property 1" containing the replicated for the identity:

$$\sigma_p^1 = K_Y^{PRIV}[K_{Bob}^{PUB} \mid Subject\ Alternative\ Name \mid Property\ 1]$$

This signature binds the public key of Bob to the assigned property (identity in this case).

The final signature σ_1 at the end of the certificate corresponds to the standard X.509 signature calculated over the entire certificate, as specified in [45]. It is also calculated with K_Y^{PRIV}:

$$\sigma_1 = K_Y^{PRIV}[Serial\ Number \mid Issuer \ldots]$$

Extension of Initial Identity Certificate with Properties

In the subsequent stage, other certificate authorities extend the initial certificate with additional properties for whom they are authoritative.

In our example based on Figure 7.2, the IP address authority Z assigns the mobile network prefix r to Bob.

Given that $r \in \mathcal{R}$ and Z is authoritative for $\mathcal{R}$, the initial certificate is extended as follows:

$$Cert(Z, B, \{Y^q, Z^r\}),$$

The corresponding X.509 certificate is illustrated in Figure 7.4b. The new property r is added within the extension field "Property 2". The structure of this field is equal to the one used in the previous step for storing the identity.

The serial number S_2 uniquely identifies the property within the context of CA Z. An explicit validity period is also defined for the property $r \in \mathcal{R}$. The signature

σ_p^2 stored at the end of the extension field is calculated with the private key of Z, spanning over Bob's public key and the new property field:

$$\sigma_p^2 = K_Z^{PRIV}[K_{Bob}^{PUB} \mid Property\ 2]$$

The new property is therefore bound to the public key. The certificate authority Z also updates the information stored in the standard fields of the certificate, such as serial number, issuer, validity and the signature σ_2 at the end. This signature corresponds to the standard X.509 signature calculated over the entire certificate, using the key K_Z^{PRIV}:

$$\sigma_2 = K_Z^{PRIV}[Serial\ Number \mid Issuer\ \ldots]$$

In case additional properties should be added by other certificate authorities, this procedure is repeated.

It should be noted that a certificate authority can add more than one property. Each property is then added in a separate step, using a dedicated extension field for each property.

Signing of Extended Certificates by National Certificate Authorities

In the last step, the extended certificate including all properties can be signed by each local certificate authority. These certificate authorities have to verify the signature σ_p^i and revocation status of each property i listed in the extension fields.

In the provided example, the local certificate authority X will issue the following certificate, after asserting that the signatures σ_p^1, σ_p^2, σ_2 and the revocation status for each property i is valid:

$$Cert(X, B, \{q^Y, r^Z\})$$

The certificate authority X does not assign any property and does therefore not add a new extension field.

An illustration of this certificate is shown in Figure 7.4c. Only standard X.509 fields have been updated. This includes the issuer name that is set to the name of the local certificate authority X, the serial number and the validity period. All these fields are set by the local certificate authority X. The signature σ_3 is calculated as defined in the X.509 standard over the entire certificate using the private key of X:

$$\sigma_3 = K_X^{PRIV}[Serial\ Number \mid K_{Bob}^{PUB}\ \ldots \mid Property\ 1 \mid Property\ 2 \mid \ldots]$$

Certificate authority X thereby assures that (1) it verified the validity of the assigned properties and (2) Bob is permitted to authenticate within the local trust domain of X. The certificate authority X hereby also becomes the issuing certificate authority for this certificate.

This final step has to be performed for every local certificate authority in whose domain Bob has to authenticate to. For m different national domains, Bob will end up having m different certificates issued by different national/local authorities. These certificates only differ in the issuing information, such as signature σ_3 and the serial number.

Certificate Usage at Runtime

When Bob attempts to authenticate to Alice (e. g. correspondent router), Bob will present the certificate $Cert(X, B, \{Y^q, Z^r\})$ issued by Alice's local certificate authority X, cf. Figure 7.4c.

Alice could attempt to verify the signature σ_p^i and the revocation status of each assigned property, the identity q and the IP address prefix r. This has already been performed by her certificate authority X though before issuing the certificate. The authenticity and integrity of the properties listed inside the certificate is therefore guaranteed by X. As certificate authority X is Alice's trust anchor, it is sufficient for her to only perform the verification as she would do it with a regular X.509 identity certificate [45]: she will check the outermost signature σ_3 and the certificate revocation status provided by her local certificate authority X for serial number S_0. The authenticity of the properties listed inside the certificate is guaranteed by the signature σ_3 generated by X. The revocation status can be checked based on either the certificate revocation list issued by X or via an OCSP server operated by X.

In case Bob wishes to authenticate with to an entity Charlie that is located in another domain, Bob will use the certificate issued by Charlie's local certificate authority, $Cert(C, B, q^Y, r^Z)$. This is also illustrated in Figure 7.5. In this certificate, the signature σ_3 and a dedicated serial number have been generated by the Charlie's local certificate authority.

The certificate construction process fits the operational ATS environment, where an airline is required to register the aircraft route with the authorities of each country that are along the flight path. This process can be used to request each national certificate authority along the flight path to sign and issue a certificate.

7.3.2. Alice's Certificate

So far, the discussion only considered one-way authentication: Bob was considered to authenticate to Alice, but not vice versa. In case of the SeNERO protocol, a mutual authentication between mobile router and correspondent router takes place though. A certificate can also be constructed similarly for Alice though. The

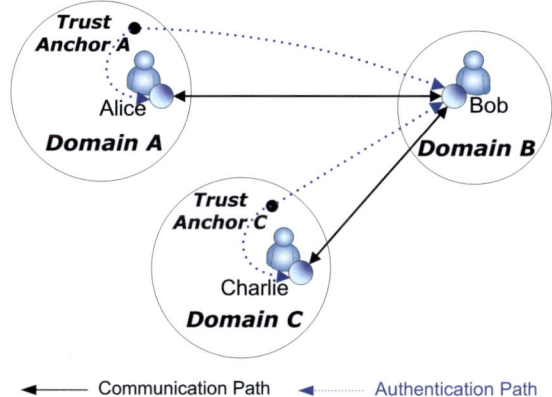

Figure 7.5. Distributed certificate authorities as implemented by the extended identity certificate model.

certificate defined in the following for Alice (correspondent router) is intended for use with the SeNERO protocol.

Bob (mobile router) will accept a national (local) certificate authority such as X as trust anchor for the purpose of authenticating within the domain of X. Alice will therefore use an extended identity certificate issued by her local certificate authority for authenticating to Bob.

An example for Alice's certificate is shown in Figure 7.6. The same property extension fields are used as in Bob's certificate. Alice's certificate contains an identity p assigned by her local certificate authority X from the national name space $\mathcal{P}$. X also assigns the IP address prefix $r \in \mathcal{R}_1$. This is only possible if the certificate authority Z delegates a subset $\mathcal{R}_1 \subset \mathcal{R}$ from the overall aeronautical IP address space $\mathcal{R}$, for whom Z is authoritative, to X. The individual signatures σ_p^i and σ_3 are all calculated with the private key of X.

Alice can use the resulting certificate for authenticating to Bob. In the formal notation, the certificate is written as follows:

$$Cert(X, A, \{p^X, r^X\})$$

Pre-Verification Phase

Prior to moving to any local domain, Bob will retrieve the certificates of each certificate authority that is authoritative for either an property space or for a local domain. The local/national certificate authorities, e. g. X with property space $\mathcal{P}$,

181

```
X.509 Certificate
  Serial Number = S₁, Issuer = X
  ...
  Subject Public Key Info = K_{Alice}^{PUB}
  Extensions
    Subject Alternative Name = p
    Property 1
      Issuer = X
      Serial Number = S₁
      Property = p
      Signature value = σ_p^1
    Property 2
      Issuer = X
      Serial Number = S₂
      Property = r
      Signature value = σ_p^2
  Signature value = σ₃
```

Figure 7.6. Extended identity certificate for Alice.

are well known as they are along the flight route. Any other certificate authority that is authoritative for assigning properties (e.g. Z with property space $\mathcal{R}$) is also well known.

Bob will validate the delegations performed by these authorities, which are implemented by certificates. For example, this can be the (IP address) delegation $\mathcal{R}_1 \subset \mathcal{R}$ from Z to X. Bob will verify the signature and revocation status of the associated delegation certificate. If this succeeds, Bob can be assured that certificate authority X is authoritative for the subset $\mathcal{R}_1$.

Runtime Operation

During runtime, Bob will move into a country (local domain) and authenticate to a local node such as Alice. Bob can verify Alice's certificate based on the signature σ_3 and the revocation information provided the local certificate authority X that issued Alice's certificate, cf. Figure 7.6.

The revocation of the property p can be performed by X, as $p \in \mathcal{P}$ and X is authoritative for $\mathcal{P}$.

The revocation of the property r can also be performed by X, as $r \in \mathcal{R}_1$, and X is authoritative for $\mathcal{R}_1$. The validity of the delegation $\mathcal{R}_1$ to X itself has been verified by Bob during at preconfiguration phase by validating the delegation certificate from Z to X.

Hence, at runtime, Bob can verify Alice's certificate based on information provided by Alice's local certificate authority X, the signature σ_3 and revocation information from a certificate revocation list or OCSP server provided by X. No other certificate authorities are involved during runtime. Bob does therefore not require any inter-domain operations for the verification of Alice's certificate.

7.3.3. Certificate & Property Lifetime

The certificates of Alice and Bob contain properties that might have different life-times. The local certificate authority issuing the certificate will define the lifetime of the overall certificate as the intersection of the individual property lifetimes. The specific certificate lifetime is subject to the decision of the local certificate authority though.

In case a certificate has expired, but the contained properties are still valid, Alice/Bob will request the local certificate authority to re-issue this certificate (final stage of certificate construction, cf. Section 7.3.1).

In case the identity has expired, a new certificate has to be reconstructed from scratch. In case a property i has expired, the certificate construction process is repeated: the certificate from stage $i - 1$ is reused and extended with a new assignment for property i. This certificate is then further extended with additional properties, if existing. At the end, the new certificate is signed and issued by the individual local certificate authorities.

7.3.4. Certificate Revocation

The verification of an (extended) identity certificate is not only based on verifying the signature σ_3 of the issuing certificate authority. It is also necessary to check whether the certificate has been revoked. Certificates can be revoked either implicitly or explicitly.

A short certificate lifetime, expressed in the certificate field validity period, is an *implicit* mechanism that limits the need for other revocation mechanisms. Within the aviation industry, the recommended certificate lifetime is 12–18 months or 3 years [4]. This time period is based on aircraft maintenance check intervals. Already assigned properties should remain valid between maintenance and therefore throughout the proposed certificate lifetime.

An *explicit* revocation is usually achieved by means of a certificate revocation list (CRL) [45] or an online certificate status protocol (OCSP) server [142]. An explicit revocation becomes necessary if, e. g., the private key associated to a certificate is compromised.

Within the context of an extended identity certificate, it is important to note that the certificate authority that issued a certificate or assigned a property is also responsible for providing a revocation service. The mechanism for explicitly revoking an extended identity certificate is described below. The chosen approach preserves the distributed nature of the certificate verification where the verifier only requires the revocation service of a local certificate authority. The introduction of a single point of failure due to a centralized revocation service (certificate revocation list or online certificate status protocol server) is avoided.

An explicit revocation of an extended identity certificate may become necessary due to one of the following reasons:

- Revocation of Alice's certificate by the local certificate authority that issued her certificate.
- Revocation of a property assigned to Bob by the respective authoritative certificate authority.

The first case is a standard revocation. The second case requires a new revocation approach. Both cases are discussed in the following. The examples are based on Bob's certificate shown in Figure 7.4c and Alice's certificate shown in Figure 7.6.

Revocation by Local Certificate Authority

The local certificate authority X of a national domain can revoke a certificate issued to either Alice or Bob the same way as a standard identity certificate. The serial number of Alice's or Bob's certificates are either listed in the respective certificate revocation list or have the status information "revoked" within an online certificate status protocol server response.

Alice's certificate, and all the information included in her certificate, has been issued by her local certificate authority X. The entire certificate can therefore be revoked by using the revocation service provided by X. During runtime, when presented with Alice's certificate, Bob will check the serial number S_1 in the revocation service provided by X. If $\rho(S_1) = 1$, then Bob will consider Alice's certificate being revoked. In case a certificate revocation list is used, certificate authority X will append the serial number of Alice's certificate to this list. The function ρ then refers to an operation where the certificate revocation list is fetched and checked for Alice's serial number. In case the online certificate status protocol is used, then ρ refers to the signaling exchange with the OCSP server that is queried by Bob with the serial number of Alice's certificate.

Bob's certificate has also been issued by a local certificate authority, such as X. It can therefore also be revoked the same way as a standard identity certificate, using the revocation service provided by X. In the final stage of the certificate construction, the local certificate authority X issues Bob's certificate and generates the outermost signature σ_3. The revocation status ρ of Bob's certificate can therefore also be defined by that certificate authority, as it is authoritative for certificates issued within its domain. By revoking Bob's certificate, he will be prevented from authenticating within the local domain of X. Alice will check Bob's serial number S_0 in the revocation service provided by X. If $\rho(S_0) = 1$, then Alice will consider Bob's certificate being revoked. The revocation status can be queried from either an OCSP server or be retrieved from a certificate revocation list issued by X.

The revocation by a local certificate authority does not involve any inter-domain operations, as Alice and Bob only perform operations with the local certificate authority. The scope of the revocation status is limited to the local trust domain represented by the local certificate authority.

Revocation of Individual Properties

The properties assigned to Alice's certificate are entirely assigned by her local certificate authority. This certificate authority can therefore revoke a property assigned to Alice by simply revoking the entire certificate, as described in the previous section.

The situation is different for Bob's certificate. A property $p \in \mathcal{P}$ assigned to Bob can only be revoked by the certificate authority that is authoritative for $\mathcal{P}$. Given Alice attempts to verify Bob's example certificate shown in Figure 7.4c, she would have to use the revocation services provided by the certificate authorities Y and Z for checking the revocation status of the properties q and r. If Alice would contact these certificate authorities during runtime for checking the revocation status of individual properties assigned to Bob, inter-domain operations would have to be performed. The dependency on these revocation services would constitute a single point of failure though. This would counteract the advantages provided by the extended certificate model, where only a local certificate authority is involved in the authentication.

The outline of this solution is as follows:

- For each certificate issued by a local certificate authority (e. g. X): check whether a property of the issued certificate has been revoked.
- In case a property has been revoked that is associated to a certificate issued by X, the certificate as a whole will be revoked via the revocation service of X.
- During runtime, when Alice verifies Bob's certificate, she will retrieve the revocation status from the local revocation service provided by X.

Alice can be assured that the revocation of a property assigned to Bob results in full revocation of Bob's certificate issued by X.

The detailed 3-step algorithm used by a local certificate authority such as X for managing the revocation status of certificates issued by this authority is provided in Algorithm 7.1. The example used in the following for illustrating the algorithm is based on the certificate shown in Figure 7.4c. The local certificate authority X receives Bob's preliminary certificate $Cert(Z, B, \{Y^q, Z^r\})$ that will be issued as $Cert(X, B, \{Y^q, Z^r\})$.

Step 1, specified in lines 1 to 9 of Algorithm 7.1 specifies the operations performed by the local certificate authority that issues a certificate.

185

Require: Preliminary certificate $\mathcal{C}$ with property information tuples $(\theta_i, S_i), 0 <$
$\quad\quad i \leq n$
1: **procedure** CERTIFICATE ISSUING($\mathcal{C}$)
2: $\quad$ Assign serial number S
3: $\quad$ $\Sigma = \Sigma \cup \{S\}$
4: $\quad$ **for all** property tuples (θ_i, S_i) in $\mathcal{C}$ **do**
5: $\quad\quad$ $\Theta = \Theta \cup (\theta_i, S_i)$
6: $\quad\quad$ Update mapping $\mu : \Sigma \rightarrow \Theta$ such that
7: $\quad\quad$ $\mu(S) \mapsto (\theta_i, S_i)$
8: $\quad$ **end for**
9: **end procedure**
Require: Revoked property information tuple (θ_p, S_p)
10: **procedure** PROPERTY REVOCATION(θ_p, S_p)
11: $\quad$ Retrieve $S = \mu^{-1}(\theta_p, S_p)$
12: $\quad$ **if** $S \neq \emptyset$ **then**
13: $\quad\quad$ $\rho(S) = 1$
14: $\quad$ **end if**
15: **end procedure**
Require: Extended certificate with serial number S
16: **procedure** CHECK FOR REVOCATION(S)
17: $\quad$ **if** $\rho(S) == 1$ **then**
18: $\quad\quad$ Return Status Revoked
19: $\quad$ **else**
20: $\quad\quad$ Return Status Valid
21: $\quad$ **end if**
22: **end procedure**

Algorithm 7.1 Certificate status management algorithm.

A serial number S is assigned to Bob's preliminary certificate by the local certificate authority and stored in the local database Σ. The certificate authority also stores the tuples (issuer name, serial number) for each property listed in the certificate within the local database Θ. A function μ provides a mapping between the serial number assigned by the local certificate authority and the property tuples assigned by other authorities to the same certificate:

$$\mu : \Sigma \rightarrow \Theta$$
$$S \mapsto (\theta, S)^n, \ n \in \mathbb{N}$$

The function μ is bijective, meaning that for every $(\theta_p, S_p) \in \Theta$ there is exactly one $S \in \Sigma$ such that $(\theta_p, S_p) \in \mu(S)$. In the example based on Figure 7.4c, the mapping is

$$S_0 \mapsto \{(Y, S_1), (Z, S_2)\}$$

Step 2, specified in lines 10 to 15, defines how a local certificate authority retrieves property revocation information and appropriately defines the revocation status of certificates issued by this certificate authority.

The local certificate authority can retrieve property revocation information from any authoritative certificate authority via a CRL or the OCSP, using the serial numbers stored in the local database Θ. E. g., if the tuple (Z, S_2) is listed by the revocation service, this indicates that certificate authority Z revoked the property r, identified by S_2. Based on the revoked property, identified by the tuple (θ, S), and using the inverse of the mapping function μ, the local certificate authority can retrieve the serial number of the certificate issued by X that contains the revoked property. If the inverse of the mapping function μ returns an empty result set, the revoked property is not associated to any issued certificate. If a serial number is returned, than the certificate containing this serial number will be revoked. In the provided example, it is assumed that Z revoked the property r, hence $\mu^{-1}(Z, S_2) = S_0$. The local certificate authority will then set the revocation status of Bob's certificate to revoked: $\rho(S_0) = 1$.

Step 3, specified in lines 16 to 22, defines how the revocation status of a certificate is provided by a local certificate authority.

Alice will check the revocation status of Bob's certificate based on the serial number assigned by the issuing (local) certificate authority. This certificate authority will simply query the database Σ for the provided serial number, which also contains the property revocation status ρ for a particular certificate. In the provided example, Alice will retrieve $\rho(S_0) = 1$ from the revocation service provided by X. This indicates that Bob's certificate has been revoked.

To summarize, every national (local) certificate authority builds a database consisting of the information which properties have been assigned to which certificate. The database only refers to certificates issued by the local certificate authority. The national authority then retrieves property related revocation information from other certificate authorities. In case a property has been revoked that is listed within a certificate issued by the national certificate authority, the entire certificate is revoked by the national certificate authority.

7.4. Aircraft Key Hierarchy

It is possible for an aircraft to receive numerous properties, all assigned to the same public key/certificate. These properties can be delegated to other certifi-

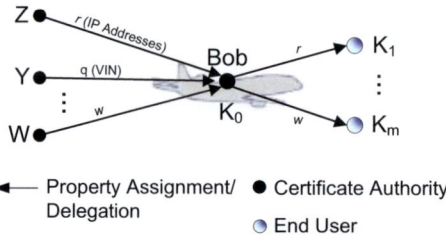

Figure 7.7. Public key hierarchy within aircraft.

cates with associated public keys that are specific to a protocol or application. This results in a tree structure, with the certificate containing all properties at the root and certificates containing the delegated properties as leaves.

This is also illustrated in Figure 7.7. The properties are assigned by the different certificate authorities to Bob's public key K_0. This key is used as the aircraft's certificate authority key. The certificate containing key K_0 and all properties is issued and signed by the individual local certificate authorities. The individual properties are then delegated by the aircraft certificate authority to other public keys. For m different properties, a delegation to m different public keys can be performed. E. g., the property r is delegated from K_0 to K_1. The certificate containing K_1 and r is issued and signed by Bob, using the certificate authority key K_0.

When Bob attempts to authenticate to Alice with property r, she will first verify the certificate with key K_0, containing all properties, issued by her local certificate authority. If successful, she will then verify the certificate with key K_1 and property r. If also successful, the key K_1 can then be used within the protocol for authentication purposes. The certification chain is as follows, using the keys K_0 and K_1 to refer to the different public keys of Bob:

$$X \ll K_0 \gg, K_0 \ll K_1 \gg$$

7.5. Related Work

A standard approach for "connecting" different trust domains is the bridge model [135]. A trust domain represented by certificate authority X can cross-certify a bridge certificate authority, which in turn can issue certificates to the certificate authorities of other domains, e.g. to certificate authority Y. In the certificate verification process, Alice can then establish a path from her own certificate authority X to a certificate issued by Y via the bridge certificate authority. Alice will have to verify certificates from other trust domains. This requires inter-domain operations with a foreign certificate authority during runtime, thereby suffering from the single point of failure problem. The problem with trust on an organizational basis also arises, as every certificate issued by a foreign certificate authority can be verified based on a certification path established via the bridge certificate authority.

The concept of smart certificates [162, 163] was a first attempt of combining identity and attribute certificates. The authors propose to store attribute information within an extension field of a standard X.509 certificate. When presented with such a certificate, Alice will validate each identity and attribute assignment separately. This requires inter-domain operations with the foreign certificate authorities that assigned identity and attribute. This approach therefore suffers from the single point of failure problem. It is also necessary to change the X.509 certificate standard, as the standard signature is changed: in order to support extending an already issued identity certificate with attribute information, the signature is not calculated over the entire certificate anymore. Instead, the extension fields are omitted. The authors do also not address the problem of attribute revocation.

A nested certificate [126] is basically a certificate referring to another certificate. It does not include a public key, but only a reference to another certificate, called subject certificate. A verification of the nested certificate also implicitly verifies the integrity of the subject certificate. Such a nested certificate could only be used to resolve the problem of trust on an organizational level. Bob could only be allowed to authenticate within a local domain based on a nested certificate issued by the local certificate authority. The nested certificate would refer to Bob's identity certificate. An attribute certificate is still required to assign attributes/properties to the public key listed in the identity certificate though. The verification of the nested certificate would implicitly validate the identity certificate. The attribute certificate would still have to be verified though, based on the attribute authority. This requires an inter-domain operation with a foreign authority, which constitutes a single point of failure. This proposal also requires to change the X.509 certificate standard, at least the semantics of certain fields.

The current certificate profile for the aviation industry, as specified in [4], is based on the standard X.509 identity certificate profile [45]. It does therefore not provide any of the features supported by the extended identity certificate model, which are (a) verification without requiring inter-domain operations with a foreign certificate authority (single point of failure) and (b) authentication without the need for organization level trust to a foreign certificate authority. Research work in the area of aeronautical communications relies on standard identity certificates, e. g., for air traffic management [164] or for air-to ground data exchange of wireless sensor network data [180]. In [178], the authors recommend the usage of local certificate authorities with a root or bridge certificate authority for enabling inter-domain authentication. Such a bridge would again introduce a single point of failure, which is avoided by the certificate extension defined within this chapter.

The authors of [22] propose a hierarchical public key infrastructure that requires a root certificate authority and inter-domain operations to establish certification paths with foreign certificate authorities. In fact, the authors acknowledge that problems will arise "when a certificate authority has to manage some aircraft that do not belong to its domain for instance". The certificate extension defined in this chapter addresses this issue.

A lot of research has been performed on security in the Car-to-X communications environment. A requirement with respect to verification of certificates without inter-domain operations does not seem to exist. Instead, a large amount of work is related to providing privacy in the presence of identity certificates. The foreseen vehicular public key infrastructure is based on multiple cross-certified certificate authorities issuing standard identity certificates [161, 171].

Grid computing faces similar issues as the aeronautical mobile communications environment as authentication has to be performed among different trust domains. A process might be executed on hosts that belong to security domains different from original domain where the process was created. Surveys of grid security [31, 44] show that the proposed concepts are usually on-line systems, e. g. [38], to support using attributes from multiple authorities. It is common to all approaches that dedicated proxies or servers from different authorities are queried during the authentication procedure at runtime, e. g., to map global to local rights of the visited domain. Specific examples are [18, 222] where a *domain manager* (DM) or trust manager acts as an introducer for a new process into a federation of individual domains, also called virtual organization. The DM computes trust values between the new and already existing members of the virtual organization. This computation might involve several DMs from different domains at runtime.

Another approach originating from the distributed systems environment is [211]. The authors propose a passport-via system: a mobile agent receives a *passport* (special certificate) from the home domain that is presented upon entering a foreign trust domain. If the authority of the foreign domain successfully verifies the passport, it will issue a *visa* (special certificate) that is valid for authentication of the agent in the visited domain. The problem of this approach is the necessity of an inter-domain trust operation when the foreign authority has to validate the passport that has been issued within another trust domain during runtime.

A Shibboleth protected privilege management infrastructure is presented in [217]. Shibboleth is a protocol for securely transferring user attributes between collaborating sites (the "federation"). The responsibility of authenticating users is delegated to the users home institution. Shibboleth allows to reuse local authentication and authorization information for use within the different institutions of the federation. No centralized authentication mechanism is introduced. When accessing resources of a foreign domain, the user is redirected to the home domain for a logon. If this authentication succeeds, the visiting domain is informed about the successful authentication and the user is granted access to the foreign resources. This protocol therefore also performs an inter-domain operation during runtime, which is the communication with the home domain.

Yet another approach for grid computing based on Kerberos is presented in [138]. A public key infrastructure is proposed as an additional component for authenticating the request to the Kerberos ticket. The authentication between a client (Bob) and a server (Alice) is still performed based on Kerberos. Kerberos requires a third party (ticket server) to be available during the initial authentication.

For all those approaches, inter-domain operations with foreign (certificate) authorities have to be performed during runtime. There does not seem to be any similar requirement for avoiding inter-domain operations within the related work. Consecutively, the related work does not propose an architecture where verification operations are performed in the local domain only.

7.6. Summary

The extended certificate model introduces a distributed architecture based on local trust anchors. Two different time phases have to be considered for the certificate construction and usage: certificate construction time and runtime.

During the *preconfiguration phase* (certificate construction time), properties[2] are appended to an identity certificate. The properties are added by the certificate authorities that are authoritative for the respective property space. Each property (such as the IP address prefix r) is bound to the public key of the certificate holder by a signature σ_p^i (e. g. σ_p^1). This signature is calculated by the certificate authority assigning the property. For Bob's certificate, the properties are added by different certificate authorities. For Alice's certificate, all properties are added by her local certificate authority. In the final step of certificate construction for both Alice and Bob, the local certificate authority verifies the preliminary certificate containing identity and properties. If the validation is successful, the local certificate authority issues the certificate and generates the outermost signature σ_3. This is performed for the certificates of both Alice and Bob.

During *runtime*, when Bob authenticates to Alice, Alice does not have to verify the individual properties listed in the certificate. This has already been performed by her local certificate authority (her trust anchor) at certificate construction time when issuing Bob's certificate. Alice therefore only has to verify whether the certificate has been approved by her certificate authority. This can be achieved by verifying the outermost signature σ_3 and the revocation status

---

[2]The word property is used in order to avoid confusion with attributes and attribute certificates [62].

provided by her local certificate authority. Similarly, an authentication of Alice to Bob can also be supported using a certificate issued by Alice's local certificate authority. This certificate can be verified by Bob based on the outermost signature σ_3 and revocation information provided by Alice's local certificate authority.

Alice and Bob only rely on revocation information provided by the local certificate authority. This also covers the revocation of Bob's properties assigned by foreign authorities. This is achieved by having each local certificate authority revoke a certificate in case a property associated to Bob's certificate has been revoked.

Within the certificate extension and the associated revocation mechanism defined within this chapter, inter-domain operations are only performed during the pre-configuration phase, the certificate construction time. During runtime, a certification path is constructed that only involves the local certificate authority. This addresses the issue of both single point of failure and trust on an organizational level to foreign authorities.

Certificate verification only requires the availability of the certificate authority and associated revocation services of the local domain. The non-availability of a local certificate authority only prevents authentication operations within the domain represented by this authority, but does not affect other domains.

Alice does also not have to accept certificate authorities of other domains as trust anchors. Instead, she will only accept certificates issued by her local certificate authority. The properties listed in the certificate and assigned by foreign authorities will therefore be accepted by Alice without requiring a trust relationship to these foreign authorities.

8. Certificate Verification

An evaluation of the extended identity certificates defined in Chapter 7 will be performed in the following. The aim is to show that the authenticity and integrity of a certificate with its public key and properties can be inferred by the certificate verifier.

Especially for security related evaluations it is important to precisely define both the objectives of an analysis and the means of reliably achieving them. This evaluation is therefore based on a rigorous formal foundation. The advantage of such an approach is that a formally well founded system "provides a setting in which reliability can be rigorously established by mathematical proof" [39].

The first section of this chapter introduces Maurer's calculus, which makes use of logical inferencing. The calculus allows reasoning about certificates, especially with respect to attributes or properties assigned within a certificate. In this section, the calculus is also extended to support modeling cross-certification and extended identity certificates.

In the second section of this chapter, the extended identity certificates of both the mobile router (Bob) and the correspondent router (Alice), as defined in Chapter 7 for use with the SeNERO protocol, are verified.

8.1. Maurer's Calculus

A wide variety of formal methods is available for describing public key infrastructure systems [39]. A deterministic and powerful model has been proposed by Maurer [133]. The calculus allows modeling and reasoning about trust in general and authenticity of public keys in particular from the perspective of an entity such as Alice. More detailed, Maurer's model is a special logic calculus based on propositions (statements) and inference rules that are used for deriving statements from a set of initial axioms. It is comparable to classic propositional logic [144].

Mauer's work has been tailored for use with Pretty Good Privacy (PGP) though. This issue has been addressed by Marchesini and Smith [131] who extended Maurer's original calculus to permit a more powerful reasoning within the context of real-world public key infrastructures.

Maurer's calculus and the extensions of Marchesini have been chosen because they are well suited for the purpose of verifying the extended identity certificate model: (1) the calculus supports reasoning with properties that have been assigned to a public key/certificate and (2) it also supports modeling implicit and explicit certificate revocation.

While others [25] have also extended Maurer's calculus, the extensions of Marchesini are more suitable for the purpose of evaluating the extended identity certificates.

8.1.1. Maurer's (Extended) Calculus

In the following, the extended calculus as defined by Marchesini [131] is introduced. The calculus models the point of view of the verifier Alice, describing whom Alice believes to be *authentic* and whom she trusts for issuing certificates. The term authenticity refers to the authenticity of a binding between a certain entity and a public key and other information contained within a certificate. Certificate authorities are modeled as having authority over a certain domain: they are allowed to issue certificates with properties assigned from this domain.

Given a certificate of Bob, the model permits Alice to conclude whether the public key and the properties inside the certificate are validly associated to Bob. This is achieved by starting from Alice's initial view that contains statements describing whom she trusts and of whose authenticity Alice is already convinced. In addition, this initial view also contains information on which certificates or trust delegations have been issued among different entities. By using inference rules, Alice can then extend her initial view and derive the authenticity of other entities, such as the certificate holder Bob.

When Alice derived the authenticity of Bob's certificate, she believes in the authenticity of Bob's public key and other information contained within the certificate, e. g., the properties assigned to Bob's public key.

8.1.1.1. Statements and Inference Rules

Alice's initial point of view consists of a set of *statements* that can then be extended with the help of *inference rules*.

194

Statements
In general, a statement s is a quadruple consisting of the following four elements:

- The *two* involved entities, which are certificate authorities or network nodes such as Alice or Bob.
- A domain $\mathcal{D}$ indicating the set of properties that may be assigned by a certificate authority or a set $\mathcal{P}$ indicating the set of properties that has been assigned to a certificate authority, Alice or Bob.
- A time interval $\mathcal{I}$ in which the statement is valid.

The domain $\mathcal{D}$ refers to the properties for whom the certificate authority is authoritative. E. g., an airframe manufacturer is authoritative for assigning identities to aircraft and an Internet Registry is authoritative for assigning IP address prefixes. The set of properties $\mathcal{P}$ refers to properties that have actually been assigned to a certificate authority, Alice or Bob.

A time interval $\mathcal{I}$ has a starting time t_j and ending time t_k. It is used to model implicit revocation: a statement is only valid at current time t if it is within the time interval $\mathcal{I} = [t_j, t_k]$. If $t < t_j$, then the statement is *not yet valid*. If $t > t_k$ then the statement has already *expired*.

The individual statements are defined as follows:

- **Authenticity of binding** $Aut(A, X, \mathcal{P}, \mathcal{I})$: A believes that entity X has the properties defined by the set $\mathcal{P}$ bound to the associated public key during time $\mathcal{I}$. X can be a certificate authority or Alice or Bob.
- **Trust** $Trust(A, X, \mathcal{D}, \mathcal{I})$: A believes that entity X is trustworthy for issuing certificates over domain $\mathcal{D}$ during time $\mathcal{I}$. X is always a certificate authority.
- **Certificate** $Cert(X,Y,\mathcal{P},\mathcal{I})$: X issued a certificate to Y that binds Y's public key to the set of properties $\mathcal{P}$ during time $\mathcal{I}$. X is always a certificate authority, whereas Y can refer to either a certificate authority or Alice or Bob.
- **Trust Transfer** $Tran(X,Y,\mathcal{P},\mathcal{I})$: X transfers trust to Y, which binds Y's public key to the set of properties $\mathcal{P}$ during time $\mathcal{I}$. X and Y are always certificate authorities.

The graphical representations of these statements are shown in Figure 8.1. Directed graphs are used to illustrate statements, with the involved entities being represented as vertices.

The *authenticity* statement describes Alice's believe in a certain entity, such as Bob, being validly associated to a public key. Authenticity not only states that this entity holds the respective private key, but in addition also has a set of properties associated to the public key.

Trust describes Alice's believe that a certificate authority is authoritative for assigning properties from within a certain property domain. In addition, the state-

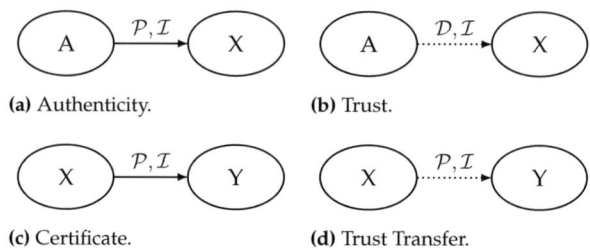

Figure 8.1. Graph representation of calculus statements.

ment asserts that a certificate authority will only issue certificates to properly verified entities.

A *certificate* refers to either a standard identity certificate [45] or to an extended identity certificate as specified in Chapter 7.

A *trust transfer* is a delegation of rights, e. g., by a certificate authority to another entity, which can also be a subordinate certificate authority. In a public key infrastructure, this will usually be implemented implicitly in terms of a certificate; within the calculus, it is modeled as an explicit statement though.

Validity Templates
Before Alice accepts certificates and trust transfers, their validity at evaluation time t has to be evaluated. Whether a certificate or trust transfer is valid depends on several factors, e. g., the certificate should not have expired nor have been revoked.

To cover the multitude of possibilities when a certificate or trust transfer is considered valid or invalid, a *template* is introduced. The template is a meta-statement whose evaluation depends on the argument type.

- **Certificate Validity Template** $Valid\langle A, C, t \rangle$: A beliefs that certificate C is valid at evaluation time t "according to the definition of validity appropriate for C's format" [131].

- **Transfer Validity Template** $Valid\langle A, T, t \rangle$: A beliefs that trust transfer T is valid at evaluation time t "according to the definition of validity appropriate for T's format" [131].

The templates can be instantiated with whatever constraints should be present for the validation. E. g., for a standard X.509 identity certificate the instantiation will verify that the certificate has not been revoked and that the signature of the issuing certificate authority is valid.

Inferencing

Alice starts with an initial view $View_A$ containing a set of statements. On the one hand, this set expresses her initial believe in authenticity and trust to certain entities, usually limited to one certificate authority – her trust anchor. On the other hand, this set also describes which certificates or trust transfers have been issued among other entities.

If Alice (A) attempts to extend her trust to entity Bob (B) who claims to own property p at *evaluation time* t, she has to infer the statement $Aut(A, B, \mathcal{P}, \mathcal{I})$ where $t \in \mathcal{I}$ and $\mathcal{P} = \{p\}$. The derived authenticity of Bob is then only valid at time t, which refers to the point in time when Alice is reasoning on the set of statements.

In general, a statement s is considered valid if it can be derived from Alice's initial view $View_A$. Starting from this initial set of statements, additional statements can only be derived with help of the following inference rules.

$$\forall X, Y, t \in \{\mathcal{I}_0 \cap \mathcal{I}_1\}, \mathcal{Q} \subseteq \mathcal{D}:$$
$$Aut(A, X, \mathcal{P}, \mathcal{I}_0), Trust(A, X, \mathcal{D}, \mathcal{I}_1), \tag{8.1}$$
$$Valid\langle A, Cert(X, Y, \mathcal{Q}, \mathcal{I}_2), t\rangle \vdash Aut(A, Y, \mathcal{Q}, \mathcal{I}_2)$$

$$\forall X, Y, t \in \{\mathcal{I}_0 \cap \mathcal{I}_1\}, \mathcal{Q} \subseteq \mathcal{D}:$$
$$Aut(A, X, \mathcal{P}, \mathcal{I}_0), Trust(A, X, \mathcal{D}, \mathcal{I}_1), \tag{8.2}$$
$$Valid\langle A, Tran(X, Y, \mathcal{Q}, \mathcal{I}_2), t\rangle \vdash Trust(A, Y, \mathcal{Q}, \mathcal{I}_2)$$

Rule (8.1) states that Alice (A) can derive the authenticity of the public key of entity Y if (a) she believes in the authenticity of certificate authority X with property set $\mathcal{P}$, (b) she believes in the trustworthiness of X for issuing certificates over domain $\mathcal{D}$ and (c) there is a valid certificate issued from X to Y. The property set $\mathcal{Q}$ in the certificate must be an element of the property domain $\mathcal{D}$ of X. It is important to note that the set $\mathcal{P}$ refers to the properties of the certificate authority itself, while the domain $\mathcal{D}$ describes which properties a certificate authority can assign within a certificate it issues. Furthermore, the evaluation time t has to be within the time interval $\mathcal{I}$ that defines the certificate's validity time window.

Similarly, rule (8.2) permits Alice to derive trust to an entity Y, if (a) she believes in the authenticity of certificate authority X with property set $\mathcal{P}$, (b) she believes in the trustworthiness of X for issuing certificates over domain $\mathcal{D}$ and (c) there is a valid trust transfer from X to Y. The property set $\mathcal{Q}$ in the trust transfer must be an element of the property domain $\mathcal{D}$ of X. Also, the evaluation time t has to be within the time interval $\mathcal{I}$ of the trust transfer statement.

Alice will apply these inference rules on the set of statements S that is her initial view $View_A$. This view describes whom Alice believes to be authentic and trustworthy. It also describes which certificates have been issued.

The set $\overline{S}$ denotes the *closure* of the set S after repeatedly applying these inference rules. The set $\overline{S}$ therefore includes all statements derivable from S. The *derived view* of Alice at evaluation time t, notation $\overline{View_A(t)}$, refers to the set of statements derivable from $View_A$ at time t. It is defined as follows:

$$\overline{View_A(t)} : t \mapsto \overline{S}$$

A statement s is considered *valid* if it is derivable at evaluation time t: $s \in \overline{View_A(t)}$. If a statement is not derivable, it is considered *invalid*.

Explicit Revocation

Marchesini [131] also extended the calculus to support explicit certificate revocation by means of a certificate revocation list.

A certificate revocation list (CRL) can be modeled as a special type of certificate: the CRL is signed by the issuing certificate authority and contains a list of revoked certificates as information. The CRL also has a time interval during which it is considered active. In a real-world revocation list this is indicated by the fields "this update" and "next update" as specified in the CRL standard [45].

Within the calculus, a CRL can be expressed as:

$$Cert(X, \emptyset, \mathcal{L}, \mathcal{I})$$

where X refers to the issuing certificate authority, $\mathcal{L}$ refers to the list of revoked certificates and $\mathcal{I}$ specifies the validity time interval. The empty set $\emptyset$ indicates that a CRL is not associated with the public key of a certain entity.

Before using a certificate revocation list, Alice has to derive its authenticity at evaluation time t using inference rule (8.1), such that:

$$Aut(X, \emptyset, \mathcal{L}, \mathcal{I}) \in \overline{View_A(t)}$$

When using rule (8.1), the certificate validity template has to be used for evaluating whether the revocation list is valid or not. The instantiation of this template, e. g., $Valid\langle A, Cert(X, \emptyset, \mathcal{L}, \mathcal{I}), t \rangle$, has to ensure that $t \in \mathcal{I}$ and that the issuer signature on the CRL is valid.

Once the authenticity of the certificate revocation list has been derived, it can be used by Alice when verifying a certificate. Given a certificate revocation list $Aut(X, \emptyset, \mathcal{L}, \mathcal{I}_1) \in \overline{View_A(t)}$, Alice will consider the certificate $Cert(X, Y, \mathcal{P}, \mathcal{I}_2)$ being *revoked* if $Cert(X, Y, \mathcal{P}, \mathcal{I}_2) \in \mathcal{L}$.

Although not addressed in [131], explicit revocation based on the online certificate status protocol (OCSP) can be modeled similarly. The statement $Cert(X, \emptyset, \mathcal{L}, \mathcal{I})$ can also refer to an OCSP server response $\mathcal{L}$ provided by certificate authority X that is considered to be valid at time interval $\mathcal{I}$. Similar to the CRL, no public key is associated to the OCSP server response.

An OCSP response stating that a certificate $Cert$ has been *revoked* is modeled as $Cert(X, Y, \mathcal{P}, \mathcal{I}_2) \in \mathcal{L}$. An OCSP response stating that a certificate is *valid* is modeled as $Cert(X, Y, \mathcal{P}, \mathcal{I}_2) \notin \mathcal{L}$. Alice first has to derive the authenticity of the OCSP response $\mathcal{L}$ at evaluation time t though, such that $Aut(X, \emptyset, \mathcal{L}, \mathcal{I}_1) \in \overline{View_A(t)}$. This is achieved using inference rule (8.1). The certificate validity template has to ensure that $t \in \mathcal{I}$ and that the OCSP response $\mathcal{L}$ is validly signed.

8.1.1.2. Example

In order to illustrate the calculus, an example is presented in the following. It is based on [131, Section 3.3] and relies on standard X.509 identity certificates.

The example consists of the two entities Alice and Bob and two certificate authorities, where the certificate authority Y is a subordinate to certificate authority X. An illustration of this setting is provided in Figure 8.2.

Initially, Alice only believes in the authenticity of her trust anchor, the certificate authority X. This is expressed by the statement $Aut(A, X, \mathcal{P}, \mathcal{I}_0)$, saying that she believes in the authenticity of the public key of X during time interval $\mathcal{I}_0$. A set of properties $\mathcal{P}$ is bound to that public key. In the illustration, the authenticity is shown as solid line from A to X. Alice also believes that X is trustworthy for issuing certificates with properties from domain $\mathcal{D}_0$ during time interval $\mathcal{I}_0$. This is expressed as $Trust(A, X, \mathcal{D}_0, \mathcal{I}_0)$ and visualized by a dotted line from A to X.

The certificate authority X delegates the subset $\mathcal{D}_1$ of its property domain for time interval $\mathcal{I}_1$ to certificate authority Y. This is expressed by a trust transfer between these two certificate authorities. The statement is $Tran(X, Y, \mathcal{D}_1, \mathcal{I}_1)$, which is visualized by a dotted line from X to Y.

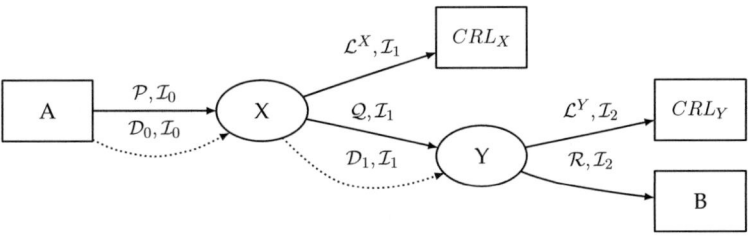

Figure 8.2. A simple example with two certificate authorities.

Alice's initial view also contains two certificates. The first certificate is issued by to Y by X, binding the public key to property Q during time interval $\mathcal{I}_1$. This implements the trust transfer between the two certificate authorities mentioned in the previous paragraph. The statement is $Cert(X, Y, Q, \mathcal{I}_1)$ and is visualized as solid line from X to Y. The second certificate has been issued by Y and binds the property $\mathcal{R}$ during time interval $\mathcal{I}_2$ to the public key of Bob. This is expressed as $Cert(Y, B, \mathcal{R}, \mathcal{I}_2)$ and is visualized as solid line from Y to B.

Finally, there are revocation services provided by certificate authorities X and Y, expressed as $Cert(X, \emptyset, \mathcal{L}^X, \mathcal{I}_1)$ and $Cert(Y, \emptyset, \mathcal{L}^Y, \mathcal{I}_2)$. Both $\mathcal{L}^X$ and $\mathcal{L}^Y$ can refer to either a certificate revocation list or an online certificate status protocol message specifying whether a certificate issued by X or Y has already been revoked during time interval $\mathcal{I}_1$ or $\mathcal{I}_2$. The two respective statements are drawn as solid lines.

Summarized, Alice's initial view is as follows:

$$
View_A = \left\{ \begin{array}{l} Aut(A, X, \mathcal{P}, \mathcal{I}_0), Trust(A, X, \mathcal{D}_0, \mathcal{I}_0), Tran(X, Y, \mathcal{D}_1, \mathcal{I}_1), \\ Cert(X, Y, Q, \mathcal{I}_1), Cert(Y, B, \mathcal{R}, \mathcal{I}_2), \\ Cert(X, \emptyset, \mathcal{L}^X, \mathcal{I}_1), Cert(Y, \emptyset, \mathcal{L}^Y, \mathcal{I}_2) \end{array} \right\}
$$

The view only consists of statements. No validity templates are included as they require a time t that is only present during evaluation when the inference rules are applied.

If Alice attempts to believe in Bob's public key and associated property $\mathcal{R}$, she has to derive the statement $Aut(A, B, \mathcal{R}, \mathcal{I}_2)$ at evaluation time $t \in \mathcal{I}_2$:

$$
Aut(A, B, \mathcal{R}, \mathcal{I}_2) \in \overline{View_A(t)}
$$

In order to derive this statement, Alice first has to establish trust to and the authenticity of the certificate authority Y that issued Bob's certificate. Alice will achieve this by starting from the already existing authenticity of certificate authority X.

Inference rule (8.2) can be used for establishing trust to certificate authority Y. For satisfying the preconditions of the rule, the authenticity and trust with respect to certificate authority X must be valid at evaluation time t. Additionally, the property domain $\mathcal{D}_1$ assigned to certificate authority Y must be a subset of the property domain $\mathcal{D}_0$ of certificate authority X. For the purpose of this example, it is assumed that the trust validity template only has to ensure that the evaluation time t lies within the time interval of the trust transfer $\mathcal{I}_1$.

Hence, assuming that $t \in \{\mathcal{I}_0 \cap \mathcal{I}_1\}, \mathcal{D}_1 \subseteq \mathcal{D}_0$:

$$Aut(A, X, \mathcal{P}, \mathcal{I}_0), Trust(A, X, \mathcal{D}_0, \mathcal{I}_0),$$
$$Valid\langle A, Tran(X, Y, \mathcal{D}_1, \mathcal{I}_1), t\rangle \vdash Trust(A, Y, \mathcal{D}_1, \mathcal{I}_1)$$

Alice's view can therefore be expanded with the trust statement:

$$View_A^1 = View_A \cup \{Trust(A, Y, \mathcal{D}_1, \mathcal{I}_1\}$$

Having established trust to the certificate authority Y, Alice can attempt to infer the authenticity of Y's public key. Before verifying the certificate issued from X to Y, Alice first has to derive the authenticity of the revocation information provided by X. Inference rule (8.1) is used for this purpose. The preconditions of this rule require Alice to have trust to and believe in the authenticity of certificate authority X at evaluation time t. The revocation information $\mathcal{L}^X$ must be a subset of the property domain $\mathcal{D}_0$ of the issuing certificate authority X. For the purpose of this example, it is assumed that the certificate validity template only has to ensure that the signature on the revocation information is valid and that evaluation time t lies within the validity period $\mathcal{I}_1$.

Consecutively, given that $t \in \{\mathcal{I}_0 \cap \mathcal{I}_1\}, \mathcal{L}^X \subseteq \mathcal{D}_0$:

$$Aut(A, X, \mathcal{P}, \mathcal{I}_0), Trust(A, X, \mathcal{D}_0, \mathcal{I}_0),$$
$$Valid\langle A, Cert(X, \emptyset, \mathcal{L}^X, \mathcal{I}_1), t\rangle \vdash Aut(X, \emptyset, \mathcal{L}^X, \mathcal{I}_1)$$

Alice's view can therefore be expanded with the authenticity of the revocation information provided by X:

$$View_A^2 = View_A^1 \cup \{Aut(X, \emptyset, \mathcal{L}^X, \mathcal{I}_1)\}$$

Based on Alice's extended view $View_A^2$, inference rule (8.1) can now be used for deriving the authenticity of the certificate issued by X to Y. The property $\mathcal{Q}$ assigned to Y's public key must be from the property domain $\mathcal{D}_0$ of the issuing certificate authority X. The certificate validity template must ensure that the certificate is valid at evaluation time t. Additionally, the template must also ensure that the certificate has not been revoked by X.

Hence, based on the assumptions $t \in \{\mathcal{I}_0 \cap \mathcal{I}_1\}, \mathcal{Q} \subseteq \mathcal{D}_0, Cert(X, Y, \mathcal{Q}, \mathcal{I}_1) \notin \mathcal{L}^X$:

$$Aut(A, X, \mathcal{P}, \mathcal{I}_0), Trust(A, X, \mathcal{D}_0, \mathcal{I}_0),$$
$$Valid\langle A, Cert(X, Y, \mathcal{Q}, \mathcal{I}_1), t\rangle \vdash Aut(A, Y, \mathcal{Q}, \mathcal{I}_1)$$

Alice's view is expanded to:

$$View_A^3 = View_A^2 \cup \{Aut(A, Y, Q, \mathcal{I}_1)\}$$

Now that both trust and authenticity to certificate authority Y have been established, the authenticity of the certificate revocation list of Y can also be derived. Afterwards, Bob's certificate can be verified.

Inference rule (8.1) can be used for this purpose. The preconditions are fulfilled, as Alice just derived trust to and authenticity of certificate authority Y at time t. The revocation information $\mathcal{L}^Y$ is considered to be a subset of the property domain $\mathcal{D}_1$ of the issuing certificate authority Y. The certificate validity template has to ensure a valid signature on the revocation information and that evaluation time t lies within the validity time interval $\mathcal{I}_2$.

Assuming $t \in \{\mathcal{I}_1 \cap \mathcal{I}_2\}, \mathcal{L}^Y \subseteq \mathcal{D}_1$:

$$Aut(A, Y, Q, \mathcal{I}_1), Trust(A, Y, \mathcal{D}_1, \mathcal{I}_1),$$
$$Valid\langle A, Cert(Y, \emptyset, \mathcal{L}^Y, \mathcal{I}_2), t\rangle \vdash Aut(A, \emptyset, \mathcal{L}^Y, \mathcal{I}_2)$$

Alice's view now also contains the revocation information provided by Y:

$$View_A^4 = View_A^3 \cup \{Aut(A, \emptyset, \mathcal{L}^Y, \mathcal{I}_2)\}$$

Finally, rule (8.1) can be used for establishing the authenticity of Bob's public key. To satisfy the precondition, the property $\mathcal{R}$ assigned to Bob's public key must be an element of the property domain $\mathcal{D}_1$ of the issuing certificate authority Y. The certificate validity template has to ensure that the certificate has a valid signature, that evaluation time t lies within the certificate validity time interval $\mathcal{I}_2$ and that the certificate itself has not been revoked by $\mathcal{L}^Y$.

Hence, given that $t \in \{\mathcal{I}_1 \cap \mathcal{I}_2\}, \mathcal{R} \subseteq \mathcal{D}_1, Cert(Y, B, \mathcal{R}, \mathcal{I}_2) \notin \mathcal{L}^Y$:

$$Aut(A, Y, Q, \mathcal{I}_1), Trust(A, Y, \mathcal{D}_1, \mathcal{I}_1),$$
$$Valid\langle A, Cert(Y, B, \mathcal{R}, \mathcal{I}_2), t\rangle \vdash Aut(A, B, \mathcal{R}, \mathcal{I}_2)$$

The view is therefore further expanded to

$$View_A^5 = View_A^4 \cup \{Aut(A, B, \mathcal{R}, \mathcal{I}_2)\}$$

It is not possible to derive any further statements. Hence, this set corresponds to the closure on Alice's view at evaluation time t:

$$\overline{View_A(t)} = View_A^5 = View_A \cup \left\{ \begin{array}{l} Trust(A, Y, \mathcal{D}_1, \mathcal{I}_1), Aut(A, \emptyset, \mathcal{L}^X, \mathcal{I}_1), \\ Aut(A, Y, Q, \mathcal{I}_1), Aut(A, \emptyset, \mathcal{L}^Y, \mathcal{I}_2), Aut(A, B, \mathcal{R}, \mathcal{I}_2) \end{array} \right\}$$

As the statement $Aut(A, B, \mathcal{R}, \mathcal{I}_2)$ is included in the closure of Alice's view, she is convinced of the authenticity of Bob's public key and the associated property $\mathcal{R}$ at evaluation time $t \in \{\mathcal{I}_0 \cap \mathcal{I}_1 \cap \mathcal{I}_2\}$.

8.2. Calculus Extensions

Maurer's original calculus and the extended version by Marchesini is not capable of modeling cross-certification. The calculus can also not be used for modeling the extended identity certificates presented in Chapter 7. For this reason, extensions to the calculus will be presented in order to address these issues.

8.2.1. Extension to support Cross-Certification

In cross-certification, a certificate authority X issues a certificate to another, non-subordinate certificate authority Y. Such a cross-certificate would permit Alice to establish a certification path from her trust anchor X to a certificate issued by a foreign certificate authority Y. Cross-certification is needed for the inter-domain verification, e. g. as done for Bob's extended identity certificate in Section 8.3.

Within the calculus, the ability to establish trust and authenticity to other certificate authorities and their property domains is provided by the $Tran$ and $Cert$ statements. However, both are inadequate for modeling a bridge certificate authority as shown in the following.

In cross-certification, two certificate authorities with disjoint property domains are "connected". Each certificate authority is authoritative for its respective domain. Within the calculus, based on a cross-certificate, Alice can attempt to extend her view from an initial certificate authority X with property domain $\mathcal{Q}$ to another certificate authority Y with property domain $\mathcal{R}$. The two property domains are disjoint, $\mathcal{Q} \cap \mathcal{R} = \emptyset$.

The already existing trust transfer statement is only useful for delegating already existing trust. Rule (8.2) for deriving trust by means of the $Tran$ statement has the restriction $\mathcal{Q} \subseteq \mathcal{D}$. This implies that a certificate authority X can only delegate a property domain $\mathcal{Q}$ that is a subset of the property domain $\mathcal{D}$ of X. The same restriction applies to rule (8.1) for processing a $Cert$ statement. A certificate issued by certificate authority X can only include a property set $\mathcal{Q}$ that is a subset of the property domain $\mathcal{D}$ of X. The restriction $\mathcal{Q} \subseteq \mathcal{D}$ can not be satisfied within a cross-certification setting though, as the property domain and set $\mathcal{Q}$ and $\mathcal{D}$ of the two two certificate authorities are disjoint.

This shortcoming can be solved by introducing a trust expansion statement with an associated template and two additional inference rules.

Statements and Validity Templates

The new statement and the associated validity template are defined as follows:

- **Trust expansion** $Exp(X, Y, \mathcal{D}, \mathcal{I})$: X performs a trust expansion, therefore stating that entity Y is trustworthy for issuing certificates over domain $\mathcal{D}$ during time interval $\mathcal{I}$.

- **Trust Expansion Validity Template** $Valid\langle A, E, t\rangle$: A beliefs that trust expansion E is valid at evaluation time t, according to the definition of validity appropriate for E's format.

The *trust expansion* permits Alice to extend her view with a certificate authority that is authoritative for a property domain for which her initial trust anchors (certificate authorities) are not authoritative. In contrast to the existing trust statement, the property domain $\mathcal{D}$ within the trust expansion statement is not related with the property domain of an already trusted certificate authority. It is up to the already trusted certificate authorities of Alice to specify the trust expansion for a new certificate authority.[1] The graphical representation for the new statement is equivalent to the one for the $Tran$ statement shown in Figure 8.1d.

A *trust expansion validity template* is used for evaluating a trust expansion, similar to the one used for the trust statement in the original calculus. The template will usually be instantiated with two restrictions. First, the evaluation time t has to be within the time period $\mathcal{I}$ of the trust expansion. Second, the property domain $\mathcal{D}$ of the new certificate authority must not intersect with the property domain of any already trusted certificate authority– this is called *collision freeness*.

Definition 8.1. *Given the view of Alice (A) at evaluation time t, a trust expansion $Exp(X, Y, \mathcal{D}, \mathcal{I})$ is considered being collision free if and only if the following condition holds.*

$$\forall A, \mathcal{Q}, t \in \mathcal{I}, \not\exists Z : Trust(A, Z, \mathcal{Q}, \mathcal{I}) \in View_A(t), \mathcal{Q} \cap \mathcal{D} \neq \emptyset$$

Definition 8.1 states that a trust expansion is collision free if there does not already exist a trusted certificate authority Z in Alice's view whose property domain $\mathcal{Q}$ conflicts with the property domain of the prospective new certificate authority. Collision freeness ensures that a certificate authority that should be added to Alice's view can not issue certificates that are in conflict with certificates issued by an already trusted certificate authority. In this context, "conflict" refers to the property domains of the involved certificate authorities.

The trust expansion statement and associated validity template only permit to derive trust for a certificate authority. The authenticity of this new certificate

---

[1]This is in line with real-world establishment of bridge certificate authorities [135]. Certificates for these entities are issued by certificate authorities and not by any other entities.

authority can only be derived from a certificate though. This certificate must contain a property set $\mathcal{P}$ assigned from the domain $\mathcal{D}$, with $\mathcal{P} \subseteq \mathcal{D}$. Such a certificate is called a cross-certificate; the notation is the same as for any other certificate, e.g., $Cert(X,Y,\mathcal{P},\mathcal{I})$.

Inferencing

The new inference rules for deriving additional statements from a trust expansion statement and a cross-certificate are as follows:

$$\forall X,Y, t \in \{\mathcal{I}_0 \cap \mathcal{I}_1\}, \mathcal{D} \cap \mathcal{Q} = \emptyset :$$
$$Aut(A, X, \mathcal{P}, \mathcal{I}_0), Trust(A, X, \mathcal{D}, \mathcal{I}_1), \tag{8.3}$$
$$Valid\langle A, Exp(X, Y, \mathcal{Q}, \mathcal{I}_2), t \rangle \vdash Trust(A, Y, \mathcal{Q}, \mathcal{I}_2)$$

$$\forall X,Y, t \in \{\mathcal{I}_0 \cap \mathcal{I}_1 \cap \mathcal{I}_2\}, \mathcal{R} \subseteq \mathcal{Q} :$$
$$Aut(A, X, \mathcal{P}, \mathcal{I}_0), Trust(A, X, \mathcal{D}, \mathcal{I}_1), \tag{8.4}$$
$$Trust(A, Y, \mathcal{Q}, \mathcal{I}_2), Valid\langle A, Cert(X, Y, \mathcal{R}, \mathcal{I}_3), t \rangle \vdash Aut(A, Y, \mathcal{R}, \mathcal{I}_3)$$

Rule (8.3) can be used by Alice to extend her trust to a certificate authority that is not a subordinate of another, already trusted certificate authority. In more detail, Alice can derive trust to a certificate authority Y based on the following conditions: if she believes in the authenticity and trust of another certificate authority X and if X provides a valid trust expansion to Y. The property domains of X and Y must be disjoint.

With rule (8.4), the authenticity of a certificate authority can be established. Alice can derive the authenticity of the public key of certificate authority Y based on the following conditions: if she believes in the authenticity and trust of another certificate authority X; if she already has trust to Y; if there is a valid certificate issued from X to Y. The property set $\mathcal{R}$ assigned in the certificate must be an element of the property domain $\mathcal{Q}$ of Y. This certificate is a cross-certificate, as it contains a property set for whom the issuing certificate authority is not authoritative.

Just as with the original calculus, a trust expansion statement or a cross-certificate are considered valid if they can be derived from Alice's initial view $View_A$.

Example

In the following, an example based on the new trust expansion statement is presented. In order to focus on the usage of the new statement, validity template and inferencing rules, certificate revocation will be ignored in this example.

An illustration of the scenario is provided in Figure 8.3. The involved entities are the same as in the example in Section 8.1.1.2. There are only two differences.

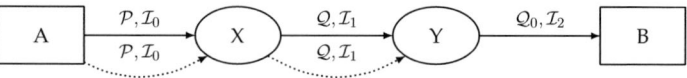

Figure 8.3. Example with two certificate authorities using cross-certification.

First, the statement between certificate authorities X and Y is not a trust transfer, but instead a trust expansion. Second, the certificate issued by X to Y is a cross-certificate.

Alice initially trusts and believes in the authenticity of her trust anchor X with property set and domain $\mathcal{P}$. The certificate authority X expands trust to another domain $\mathcal{Q}$ for which the certificate authority Y is authoritative. A cross-certificate issued from X to Y implements the trust expansion. Bob receives his certificate from the certificate authority Y with a property $\mathcal{Q}_0$ assigned from the domain $\mathcal{Q}$.

The initial view of Alice is therefore:

$$View_A = \left\{ \begin{array}{l} Aut(A, X, \mathcal{P}, \mathcal{I}_0), Trust(A, X, \mathcal{P}, \mathcal{I}_0), \\ Exp(X, Y, \mathcal{Q}, \mathcal{I}_1), Cert(X, Y, \mathcal{Q}, \mathcal{I}_1), Cert(Y, B, \mathcal{Q}_0, \mathcal{I}_2) \end{array} \right\}$$

For simplicity, correlated authenticity and trust statements are specified as being valid within the same time interval. The set of properties assigned in the cross-certificate issued by X to Y is identical with the domain specified in the trust expansion from X to Y. It is assumed that the domains of the two certificate authorities X and Y are disjoint, that is, $\mathcal{P} \cap \mathcal{Q} = \emptyset$.

If Alice attempts to believe in the authenticity of Bob's public key and the associated property $\mathcal{Q}_0$, she has to derive the statement $Aut(A, B, \mathcal{Q}_0, \mathcal{I}_2)$ at evaluation time $t \in \mathcal{I}_2$:

$$Aut(A, B, \mathcal{Q}_0, \mathcal{I}_2) \in \overline{View_A}(t)$$

In order to derive this statement, Alice first has to establish trust to and authenticity of the certificate authority Y that issued Bob's certificate.

Inference rule (8.3) can be used for extending trust. It is assumed that the trust and authenticity to certificate authority X is valid at evaluation time t. Also, the property domains of X and Y do not intersect. The preconditions of inference rule (8.3) are then satisfied. For the purpose of this example, it is assumed that the trust expansion validity template has to ensure that the evaluation time t lies within the time interval $\mathcal{I}_1$ of the trust transfer. The template also has to ensure that the trust expansion statement is collision free with respect to already trusted certificate authorities, cf. Definition 8.1. The only certificate authority trusted by Alice so far is X, whose property domain P is disjoint with $\mathcal{Q}$.

Hence, given $t \in \{\mathcal{I}_0 \cap \mathcal{I}_1\}, \mathcal{P} \cap \mathcal{Q} = \emptyset$:

$$Aut(A, X, \mathcal{P}, \mathcal{I}_0), Trust(A, X, \mathcal{P}, \mathcal{I}_0),$$
$$Valid\langle A, Exp(X, Y, \mathcal{Q}, \mathcal{I}_1), t \rangle \vdash Trust(A, Y, \mathcal{Q}, \mathcal{I}_1)$$

Alice's view therefore now includes the trust statement:

$$View_A^1 = View_A \cup \{Trust(A, Y, \mathcal{Q}, \mathcal{I}_1)\}$$

Having expanded trust to the foreign certificate authority Y, Alice can now attempt to infer the authenticity of Y's public key. Based on $View_A^1$, Alice can use inference rule (8.4) based on the (cross-)certificate issued by X to Y. To fulfill the preconditions of the inference rule, Alice must have trust to and believe in the authenticity of certificate authority X at evaluation time t. Trust to the new certificate authority Y and its domain $\mathcal{Q}$ has just been derived for time t. Finally, it has to be ensured that the property set of Y's public key is a subset of the domain of Y. In this example, these two sets are actually identical. The certificate validity template has to ensure that the cross-certificate has a valid signature and that the evaluation time t lies within the certificate validity period.

Rule (8.4) is applied, assuming that $t \in \{\mathcal{I}_0 \cap \mathcal{I}_1\}, \mathcal{Q} \subseteq \mathcal{Q}$:

$$Aut(A, X, \mathcal{P}, \mathcal{I}_0), Trust(A, X, \mathcal{P}, \mathcal{I}_0), Trust(A, Y, \mathcal{Q}, \mathcal{I}_1),$$
$$Valid\langle A, Cert(X, Y, \mathcal{Q}, \mathcal{I}_1), t \rangle \vdash Aut(A, Y, \mathcal{Q}, \mathcal{I}_1)$$

Alice now believes in the authenticity of certificate authority Y with domain $\mathcal{Q}$, which is disjoint with the domain of certificate authority X:

$$View_A^2 = View_A^1 \cup \{Aut(A, Y, \mathcal{Q}, \mathcal{I}_1)\}$$

Now, inference rule (8.1) can be used for deriving the authenticity of Bob's public key and its associated property. The preconditions of the rule can be fulfilled if the certificate is valid at evaluation time t and by having the property assigned to Bob be a subset of the domain of Y. The certificate validity template has to ensure that the signature on the certificate is valid and that evaluation time t is within the certificate validity period.

Hence, assuming that $t \in \{\mathcal{I}_1 \cap \mathcal{I}_2\}, \mathcal{Q}_0 \subseteq \mathcal{Q}$

$$Aut(A, Y, \mathcal{Q}, \mathcal{I}_1), Trust(A, Y, \mathcal{Q}, \mathcal{I}_1),$$
$$Valid\langle A, Cert(Y, B, \mathcal{Q}_0, \mathcal{I}_2), t \rangle \vdash Aut(A, B, \mathcal{Q}_0, \mathcal{I}_2)$$

The closure is therefore:

$$\overline{View_A(t)} = View_A \cup \big\{\ Trust(A, Y, \mathcal{Q}, \mathcal{I}_1), Aut(A, Y, \mathcal{Q}, \mathcal{I}_1), Aut(A, B, \mathcal{Q}_0, \mathcal{I}_2)\ \big\}$$

Alice therefore believes in the authenticity of Bob's public key and the assigned property $\mathcal{Q}_0$ at evaluation time $t \in \{\mathcal{I}_0 \cap \mathcal{I}_1 \cap \mathcal{I}_2\}$.

8.2.2. Calculus Extension for supporting Extended Identity Certificates

How an extended identity certificate, as defined in Section 7.3, is modeled within the calculus is described in the following.

The difference to standard identity certificates is that the extended certificates contain a set of properties instead of only a single element (identity). Hence, it is also necessary to modify inference rule (8.1).

An extended identity certificate is constructed iteratively, such that several properties $p_i^{X_j}$ are included, assigned by different certificate authorities X_j, $0 < j \le m$, where m is the total number of certificate authorities. It is possible that a certificate authority X_j assigns more than a single property p_i. At the end of this construction process, a local certificate authority X_0 (e.g. the local authority of Alice) will sign and issue Bob's certificate for use within the local domain of X_0. The certificate is then $Cert(X_0, B, \{p_1^{X_1}, \ldots, p_i^{X_j}, \ldots, p_n^{X_n}\}, \mathcal{I}_0)$. The local certificate authority X_0 does not assign a property. The property set within the certificate contains several properties assigned by different certificate authorities. Examples for such certificates are those shown in Figures 7.4c and 7.6 for use with the SeNERO protocol (cf. Section 7.3).

The property set $\mathcal{P}$ of a certificate $Cert(X_0, B, \mathcal{P}, \mathcal{I}_0)$ now contains elements assigned by different authorities. The authenticity statement $Aut(A, B, \mathcal{P}, \mathcal{I}_0)$ can therefore not be derived anymore based on inference rule (8.1), as the authenticity of a certificate $Cert(X_0, B, \mathcal{P}, \mathcal{I})$ issued by certificate authority X_0 with domain $\mathcal{D}$ can only be inferred if $\mathcal{P} \subseteq \mathcal{D}$. This condition is not fulfilled by the set $\mathcal{P} = \{p_1^{X_1}, \ldots, p_i^{X_j}, \ldots, p_n^{X_n}\}$, as there is no property $p_i^{X_j}$ for which holds, $p_i^{X_j} \in \mathcal{D}, 0 < i \le n, 0 < j \le m$.

Two additional inference rules are specified in the following that extend inference rule (8.1) to support the statement for an extended identity certificate.

$$\forall X, Y, t \in \{\mathcal{I}_0 \cap \mathcal{I}_1\}, \mathcal{Q} \subset \mathcal{D}, \mathcal{Q} = \{p_1, \ldots, p_n\}, \nexists p_i, i \in \{0, \ldots, n\} : p_i \in \mathcal{Q}, p_i \in \mathcal{D}$$
$$Aut(A, X, \mathcal{P}, \mathcal{I}_0), Trust(A, X, \mathcal{D}, \mathcal{I}_1), \tag{8.5}$$
$$Valid\langle A, Cert(X, Y, \mathcal{Q}, \mathcal{I}_2), t\rangle \vdash Aut(A, Y, \mathcal{Q}, \mathcal{I}_2)$$

$$\forall X, Y, t \in \{\mathcal{I}_0 \cap \mathcal{I}_1\}, \mathcal{Q} \subset \mathcal{D}, \mathcal{Q} = \{p_1, \ldots, p_n\}, \exists p_i, i \in \{0, \ldots, n\} : p_i \in \mathcal{Q}, p_i \in \mathcal{D}$$
$$Aut(A, X, \mathcal{P}, \mathcal{I}_0), Trust(A, X, \mathcal{D}, \mathcal{I}_1), \tag{8.6}$$
$$Valid\langle A, Cert(X, Y, \mathcal{Q}, \mathcal{I}_2), t\rangle \vdash Aut(A, Y, \mathcal{Q}, \mathcal{I}_2)$$

Rule (8.5) is used when the issuing certificate authority X has not assigned any property p_i to the certificate. More detailed, there must not exist any property p_i within the certificate property set $\mathcal{Q}$ that is also an element of the domain $\mathcal{D}$ of the issuing certificate authority.

Rule (8.6) is used when the issuing certificate authority X has assigned at least one property p_i to the certificate. More detailed, there must be at least one property p_i within the certificate property set $\mathcal{Q}$ that is also an element of the domain $\mathcal{D}$ of the issuing certificate authority.

Each individual certificate authority X_j also provides revocation information $\mathcal{L}^{X_j}$ that indicates whether a property $p_i^{X_j}$ has already been revoked. The revocation information $\mathcal{L}^{X_0}$ provided by the local certificate authority X_0 indicates whether the certificate has been revoked within the local domain of X_0.

In the remainder of this chapter, X_0 always refers to the local certificate authority of Alice. This certificate authority issues and signs Bob's certificate after all properties have been added. For Alice's certificate, this certificate authority assigns all properties and issues her certificate.

8.2.3. Certificate Validity Template for Extended Identity Certificates

The certificate validity template $Valid\langle A, C, t\rangle$ has to be properly specified for use with the statement of an extended identity certificate. Alice has two options for the verification:

1. Local verification: Alice only verifies the certificate information provided by her local certificate authority (X_0). This includes the outermost signature of the certificate C, generated by the local certificate authority Alice relies on the fact that the properties $p_i^{X_j}$ assigned by other certificate authorities have already been validated by her local certificate authority before issuing the certificate. The certificate revocation status is only checked based on the

209

revocation information provided by Alice's local certificate authority (e. g. $\mathcal{L}^{X_0}$).

2. Inter-domain verification: Alice verifies every individual property $p_i^{X_j}$ listed in the property set $\mathcal{P}$ of certificate C. The revocation status is checked for every individual property $p_i^{X_j}$ based on the revocation information $\mathcal{L}^{X_j}$ issued by each individual authority. This is then followed by a local verification of the certificate, as specified above.

Only the local verification provides Alice with the advantage of not requiring any inter-domain operations with a foreign certificate authority. For completeness, both the local and the inter-domain templates will be used in the verification in Sections 8.3 and 8.4.

Template for Local Verification

The certificate validity template for a local verification (option 1), where only information provided by the issuing certificate authority X_0 is validated, is specified in the following.

$$\forall X_0, n, t \in \mathcal{I}_0, \mathcal{P} = \{p_i^{X_j} \mid 0 < i \le |\mathcal{P}|, 0 \le j \le n\} :$$
$$Valid\langle A, C, t\rangle, \text{ where } C = Cert(X_0, B, \mathcal{P}, \mathcal{I}_0)$$
$$\text{evaluates to } valid \text{ if and only if:} \qquad (8.7)$$
$$Trust(A, X_0, \mathcal{D}_0, \mathcal{I}_1) \in View_A(t),$$
$$Aut(A, X_0, \mathcal{P}_0, \mathcal{I}_2) \in View_A(t),$$
$$Aut(A, \emptyset, \mathcal{L}^{X_0}, \mathcal{I}_3) \in View_A(t),$$
$$\forall p_i^{X_0} \in \mathcal{P} : p_i^{X_0} \in \mathcal{D}_0,$$
$$C \notin \mathcal{L}^{X_0}, t \in \{\mathcal{I}_0 \cap \mathcal{I}_1 \cap \mathcal{I}_2 \cap \mathcal{I}_3\}$$

The template verifies that Alice has trust to and believe in the authenticity of certificate authority X_0 that issued the certificate. It is also necessary to establish the authenticity of the revocation information provided by X_0. In case the issuing certificate authority X_0 assigned one or several properties to the property set of the certificate, these properties must be elements of the domain of X_0. In case no properties have been assigned by X_0, no action is required. Furthermore, the certificate must not have been revoked by X_0. E. g., considering the example in Figure 7.4c, the serial number S_0 of the certificate should not be specified as being revoked. One more requirement is not formally expressed within the calculus: the certificate C must have been validly signed by the issuing certificate authority X_0.[2] E. g., based on the example in Figure 7.4c, the signature σ_3 generated by X must be valid.

---

[2]This kind of requirement has also not been formally expressed within the templates of the original calculus.

Template for Inter-Domain Verification

The certificate validity template for an inter-domain verification (option 2), where every individual property is verified, is defined as follows.

$$\forall n, t \in \mathcal{I}_0, \mathcal{P} = \{p_i^{X_j} \mid 0 < i \leq |\mathcal{P}|, 0 \leq j \leq n\}:$$

$Valid\langle A, Cert(X_0, B, \mathcal{P}, \mathcal{I}_0), t\rangle$ evaluates to *valid* if and only if: $\qquad(8.8)$

$$
\begin{aligned}
\text{case } |\mathcal{P}| \geq 1: \quad & p_i^{X_j} \in \mathcal{P}_j, \\
& Trust(A, X_j, \mathcal{D}_j, \mathcal{I}_1) \in View_A(t), \\
& Aut(A, X_j, \mathcal{P}_j, \mathcal{I}_2) \in View_A(t), \\
& Aut(A, \emptyset, \mathcal{L}^{X_j}, \mathcal{I}_3) \in View_A(t), \\
& p_i^{X_j} \notin \mathcal{L}^{X_j}, p_i^{X_j} \in \mathcal{D}_j, t \in \{\mathcal{I}_0 \cap \mathcal{I}_1 \cap \mathcal{I}_2 \cap \mathcal{I}_3\}, \\
& Valid\langle A, Cert(X_0, B, \mathcal{P} \setminus \{p_i^{X_j}\}, \mathcal{I}_0), t\rangle \\
\text{case } |\mathcal{P}| = 0: \quad & Valid\langle A, Cert(X_0, B, \emptyset, \mathcal{I}_0), t\rangle
\end{aligned}
$$

The inter-domain verification is a *recursive* operation, iterating over each individual property contained within the property set $\mathcal{P}$. Alice starts with verifying the property $p_i^{X_j}$ that has been assigned by certificate authority X_j. If the property is valid, it is removed from the property set $\mathcal{P}$ of the certificate and the verification continues with the statement $Cert(X_0, B, \mathcal{P} \setminus \{p_i^{X_j}\}, \mathcal{I}_0)$. This is repeated until all properties of the set $\mathcal{P}$ have been successfully validated. An empty set is then used to represent the property set $\mathcal{P}$. In the final step, Alice performs the verification based on the template for local verification, as specified in (8.7).

For the verification of each individual property $p_i^{X_j}$, Alice will only consider the property being valid if she has both trust to and believe in the authenticity of certificate authority X_j that assigned the property. The authenticity of the revocation information provided by X_j must have also been derived. The property itself should not have been revoked. E. g., based on the example certificate shown in Figure 7.4c, for property q the serial number S_1 must not be listed as being revoked within the revocation information $\mathcal{L}^Y$. The templates also ensures that assigned property is an element of the domain $\mathcal{D}_j$ of the certificate authority X_j that assigned the property. Additionally, the signature σ_p^i generated by certificate authority X_j for the property must also be valid. E. g., based on the example in Figure 7.4c, for property q the signature σ_p^1 generated by Y must be valid. Similar to the validity template of the original calculus, the constraint with respect to signature verification is not formally expressed within the calculus.

The inter-domain verification can only be performed if Alice is able to infer trust to and authenticity of the certificate authorities that assigned the individual properties. The extensions defined in Section 8.2.1 for modeling trust expansion and cross-certification are used for this purpose.

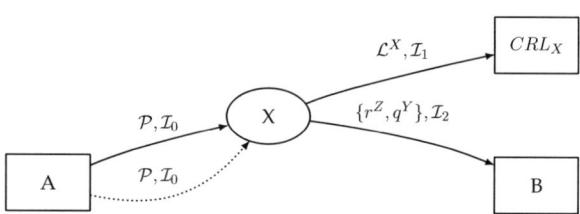

Figure 8.4. Local verification of Bob's extended identity certificate by Alice.

8.3. Proof for Bob's Certificate

In the following, the extended identity certificates, as defined in Section 7.3 for use with the SeNERO protocol, will be verified with the Maurer calculus.

In this section, the certificate of the mobile router is verified. The verification is based on a model describing the point of view of Alice (correspondent router). Given the extended identity certificate of Bob (mobile router), the authenticity of the public key and its associated properties will be inferred by Alice. The verification is performed for the certificate shown in Figure 7.4c, based on the general trust scenario illustrated in Figure 7.2.

8.3.1. Proof for Local Verification

The proof performed in the following is based on the local verification where Alice only verifies the validity of the signature and revocation information provided by her local certificate authority X. This corresponds to the intended usage of an extended identity certificate.

The graph representation of Alice's initial view is provided in Figure 8.4. Initially, Alice only has trust to and believes in the authenticity of certificate authority X with domain $\mathcal{P}$. There is also certificate revocation information provided by that certificate authority. Apart from this, there is only the certificate issued by X to Bob, containing the two properties assigned by Y and Z. The certificate does not include any property from X.

The certificate authority X only issues the certificate $Cert(X, B, \{r^Z, q^Y\}, \mathcal{I}_2)$ if the property assignments within the certificate are valid. Alice can therefore assume that each property and associated signature has already been successfully verified by her certificate authority X. Hence, Alice only has to verify that the certificate has been validly issued and not been revoked by X.

Given Alice's following initial view,

$$View_A = \left\{ \begin{array}{l} Aut(A, X, \mathcal{P}, \mathcal{I}_0), Trust(A, X, \mathcal{P}, \mathcal{I}_0), Cert(X, \emptyset, \mathcal{L}^X, \mathcal{I}_1), \\ Cert(X, B, \{r^Z, q^Y\}, \mathcal{I}_2) \end{array} \right\},$$

in order to believe in Bob's public key and associated properties, she has to derive the appropriate authenticity statement:

$$Aut(A, B, \{r^Z, q^Y\}, \mathcal{I}_2) \in \overline{View_A(t)}$$

Alice first has to infer the authenticity of the revocation information $\mathcal{L}^X$ using rule (8.1). This requires Alice to have trust to and believe in the authenticity of certificate authority X at evaluation time t. The revocation information $\mathcal{L}^X$ is required to be a subset of the domain $\mathcal{P}$. To satisfy the certificate validity template, the signature on the revocation information must be valid and the evaluation time t has to be within the validity period of the revocation information. Summarized, given that $t \in \{\mathcal{I}_0 \cap \mathcal{I}_1\}, \mathcal{L}^X \subseteq \mathcal{P}$:

$$\begin{array}{c} Aut(A, X, \mathcal{P}, \mathcal{I}_0), Trust(A, X, \mathcal{P}, \mathcal{I}_0), \\ Valid\langle A, Cert(X, \emptyset, \mathcal{L}^X, \mathcal{I}_1), t\rangle \vdash Aut(X, \emptyset, \mathcal{L}^X, \mathcal{I}_1) \end{array}$$

Alice's view is therefore:

$$View_A^1 = View_A \cup \{Aut(X, \emptyset, \mathcal{L}^X, \mathcal{I}_1)\}$$

It is now possible to verify whether Bob's certificate has been validly issued by X. Alice will ignore the properties assigned by the certificate authorities Y and Z within the verification process. Instead, she will derive the authenticity of Bob's public key based on the trust and believe in authenticity of certificate authority X. No properties have been assigned to the certificate by X, hence inference rule (8.5) can be used. Assuming that $t \in \{\mathcal{I}_0 \cap \mathcal{I}_1 \cap \mathcal{I}_2\}, r^Z \notin \mathcal{P}, q^Y \notin \mathcal{P}$:

$$\begin{array}{c} Aut(A, X, \mathcal{P}, \mathcal{I}_0), Trust(A, X, \mathcal{P}, \mathcal{I}_0), \\ Valid\langle A, Cert(X, B, \{r^Z, q^Y\}, \mathcal{I}_2), t\rangle \vdash Aut(A, B, \{r^Z, q^Y\}, \mathcal{I}_2) \end{array}$$

The template for local verification (8.7) is used for validating the certificate $C = Cert(X, B, \{r^Z, q^Y\}, \mathcal{I}_2)$. The template instantiation looks as follows:

$$Trust(A, X, \mathcal{P}, \mathcal{I}_0) \in View_A^1,$$
$$Aut(A, X, \mathcal{P}, \mathcal{I}_0) \in View_A^1,$$
$$Aut(A, \emptyset, \mathcal{L}^X, \mathcal{I}_1) \in View_A^1,$$
$$C \notin \mathcal{L}^X, t \in \{\mathcal{I}_0 \cap \mathcal{I}_1 \cap \mathcal{I}_2\}$$

Trust and authenticity of the certificate authority X must be present at evaluation time. Similarly, the authenticity of the revocation information provided by X must also be present at evaluation time. None of the properties listed in Bob's certificate has been assigned by the issuing certificate authority X – hence they do not have to be considered in the evaluation. It is assumed that Bob's certificate has not been revoked. The requirement for the outermost signature σ_3, cf. Figure 7.4c, to be valid is not formally expressed within the calculus.

Closure

Based on the valid certificate statement, the authenticity of Bob's public key can be derived and the closure on Alice's view is as follows:

$$\overline{View_A(t)} = View_A^1 \cup \{ Aut(A, B, \{r^Z, q^Y\}, \mathcal{I}_2) \}$$

Alice therefore believes in the authenticity of Bob's public key and the assigned properties r^Z, q^Y at evaluation time $t \in \{\mathcal{I}_0 \cap \mathcal{I}_1 \cap \mathcal{I}_2\}$.

The proof also showed that Alice is able to perform the verification relying only on the trust anchor of her local domain, the certificate authority X. The believe in authenticity of Bob's public key and associated properties is based on Alice's confidence in certificate authority X to have verified the individually assigned properties before issuing the certificate.

8.3.2. Proof for Inter-Domain Verification

The proof performed in the following uses the template for inter-domain verification (8.8), which involves every certificate authority that assigned a property to Bob's certificate.

This is modeled within the calculus as follows. An accompanying illustration is provided in Figure 8.5. Initially, Alice only believes in the authenticity of her trust anchor, which is the certificate authority X with domain $\mathcal{P}$. This certificate authority performs a trust expansion to the certificate authorities Y and Z with domains $\mathcal{Q}$ and $\mathcal{R}$. The trust expansion is complemented by cross-certificates issued by X to these certificate authorities. There is also a certificate issued by X to Bob, containing the two properties assigned by Y and Z. Each certificate authority also provides certificate revocation information.

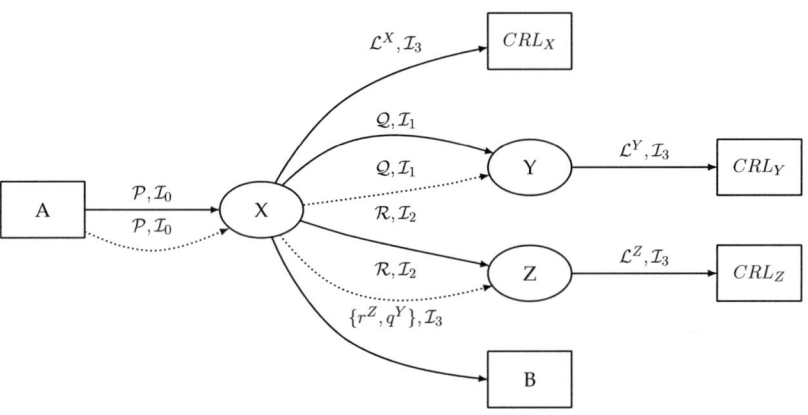

Figure 8.5. Inter-domain verification of Bob's extended identity certificate by Alice.

Alice's initial view is therefore:

$$
View_A = \left\{ \begin{array}{l} Aut(A, X, \mathcal{P}, \mathcal{I}_0), Trust(A, X, \mathcal{P}, \mathcal{I}_0), \\ Exp(X, Y, \mathcal{Q}, \mathcal{I}_1), Cert(X, Y, \mathcal{Q}, \mathcal{I}_1), Exp(X, Z, \mathcal{R}, \mathcal{I}_2), Cert(X, Z, \mathcal{R}, \mathcal{I}_2), \\ Cert(X, B, \{r^Z, q^Y\}, \mathcal{I}_3), \\ Cert(X, \emptyset, \mathcal{L}^X, \mathcal{I}_3), Cert(Y, \emptyset, \mathcal{L}^Y, \mathcal{I}_3), Cert(Z, \emptyset, \mathcal{L}^Z, \mathcal{I}_3) \end{array} \right\}
$$

If Alice attempts to believe in Bob's public key and the associated properties q and r, she has to derive the following authenticity statement at evaluation time t:

$$
Aut(A, B, \{r^Z, q^Y\}, \mathcal{I}_3) \in \overline{View_A(t)}
$$

As this proof is for the inter-domain verification, Alice will also verify the individual properties r and q. This requires to derive trust and authenticity of the certificate authorities Y and Z.

Rule (8.3) can be used for extending trust to certificate authority Y. To satisfy the preconditions of the rule, it is assumed that trust and authenticity of certificate authority X is valid at evaluation time t. The domains of X and Y are assumed to be disjoint. To satisfy the trust expansion validity template, it is assumed that evaluation time t lies within the time period $\mathcal{I}_1$ of the trust expansion.

Using rule (8.3) and given that $t \in \{\mathcal{I}_0 \cap \mathcal{I}_1\}, \mathcal{Q} \cap \mathcal{P} = \emptyset$:

$$Aut(A, X, \mathcal{P}, \mathcal{I}_0), Trust(A, X, \mathcal{P}, \mathcal{I}_0),$$
$$Valid\langle A, Exp(X, Y, \mathcal{Q}, \mathcal{I}_1), t\rangle \vdash Trust(A, Y, \mathcal{Q}, \mathcal{I}_1)$$

Alice's view therefore now includes the trust statement for Y:

$$View_A^1 = View_A \cup \{Trust(A, Y, \mathcal{Q}, \mathcal{I}_1)\}$$

When attempting to derive the authenticity of Y's public key, Alice has to verify that the certificate of Y issued by X has not been revoked. Inference rule (8.1) must therefore first be used to infer the authenticity of the revocation information $\mathcal{L}^X$. The preconditions of this rule require Alice to have trust to and believe in the authenticity of certificate authority X at evaluation time t. The revocation information $\mathcal{L}^X$ is required to be a subset of the domain $\mathcal{P}$. To satisfy the certificate validity template, the signature on the revocation information must be valid and the evaluation time t has to be within the validity period of the revocation statement.

Summarized, given that $t \in \{\mathcal{I}_0 \cap \mathcal{I}_3\}, \mathcal{L}^X \subseteq \mathcal{P}$:

$$Aut(A, X, \mathcal{P}, \mathcal{I}_0), Trust(A, X, \mathcal{P}, \mathcal{I}_0),$$
$$Valid\langle A, Cert(X, \emptyset, \mathcal{L}^X, \mathcal{I}_3), t\rangle \vdash Aut(A, \emptyset, \mathcal{L}^X, \mathcal{I}_3)$$

This expands Alice's view to:

$$View_A^2 = View_A^1 \cup \{Aut(A, \emptyset, \mathcal{L}^X, \mathcal{I}_3)\}$$

As the authenticity of the revocation information of X has been inferred, Alice can now derive the authenticity of Y's public key based on the certificate issued by X. Inference rule (8.4) is used for this purpose. The preconditions of this rule are assumed to be satisfied. At evaluation time t, Alice has trust to and believe in the authenticity of certificate authority X. The trust to the new certificate authority Y with domain $\mathcal{Q}$ has been derived in $View_A^1$. The property set of Y listed within the cross-certificate issued by X is identical to the domain in the trust statement for Y. To satisfy the certificate validity template, it is assumed that the cross-certificate has a valid signature, that the evaluation time t lies within the certificate validity period and that the certificate has not been revoked by X.

Rule (8.4) can therefore be applied, assuming that $t \in \{\mathcal{I}_0 \cap \mathcal{I}_1\}, \mathcal{Q} \subseteq \mathcal{Q}, Cert(X, Y, \mathcal{Q}, \mathcal{I}_1) \notin \mathcal{L}^X$:

$$Aut(A, X, \mathcal{P}, \mathcal{I}_0), Trust(A, X, \mathcal{P}, \mathcal{I}_0),$$
$$Trust(A, Y, \mathcal{Q}, \mathcal{I}_1), Valid\langle A, Cert(X, Y, \mathcal{Q}, \mathcal{I}_1), t\rangle \vdash Aut(A, Y, \mathcal{Q}, \mathcal{I}_1)$$

Alice now believes in the authenticity of the certificate authority Y with domain $\mathcal{Q}$:

$$View_A^3 = View_A^2 \cup \{Aut(A, Y, \mathcal{Q}, \mathcal{I}_1)\}$$

Trust and authenticity of the certificate authority Z can be established in a similar way. First, using inference rule (8.3) for establishing trust of the certificate authority Z with the assumptions $t \in \{\mathcal{I}_0 \cap \mathcal{I}_2\}, \mathcal{R} \cap \mathcal{P} = \emptyset$:

$$Aut(A, X, \mathcal{P}, \mathcal{I}_0), Trust(A, X, \mathcal{P}, \mathcal{I}_0),$$
$$Valid\langle A, Exp(X, Z, \mathcal{R}, \mathcal{I}_2), t\rangle \vdash Trust(A, Z, \mathcal{R}, \mathcal{I}_2)$$

The authenticity of the revocation information provided by X has already been inferred. The authenticity of Z can therefore be immediately derived with rule (8.4). The certificate validity template has to ensure that the certificate has not been revoked and that it has been validly signed. The certificate template also has to ensure collision freeness: the domain $\mathcal{R}$ of the prospective new certificate authority Z must be disjoint from the domain $\mathcal{Q}$ of Y that is now also trusted by Alice.
[3]

Hence, assuming $t \in \{\mathcal{I}_0 \cap \mathcal{I}_2\}, \mathcal{R} \subseteq \mathcal{R}, Cert(X, Z, \mathcal{R}, \mathcal{I}_2) \notin \mathcal{L}^X, \mathcal{R} \cap \mathcal{P} = \emptyset, \mathcal{R} \cap \mathcal{Q} = \emptyset$:

$$Aut(A, X, \mathcal{P}, \mathcal{I}_0), Trust(A, X, \mathcal{P}, \mathcal{I}_0), Trust(A, Z, \mathcal{R}, \mathcal{I}_2),$$
$$Valid\langle A, Cert(X, Z, \mathcal{R}, \mathcal{I}_2), t\rangle \vdash Aut(A, Z, \mathcal{R}, \mathcal{I}_2)$$

Alice's view is now:

$$View_A^4 = View_A^3 \cup \{Trust(A, Z, \mathcal{R}, \mathcal{I}_2), Aut(A, Z, \mathcal{R}, \mathcal{I}_2)\}$$

After authenticity of Y and Z have been established, the revocation information of these two certificate authorities can also be inferred using rule (8.1). The assumptions are that evaluation time t is within the individual time intervals and that the signatures on the revocation information are valid.

Given $t \in \{\mathcal{I}_1 \cap \mathcal{I}_3\}, \mathcal{L}^Y \subseteq \mathcal{Q}$:

$$Aut(A, Y, \mathcal{Q}, \mathcal{I}_1), Trust(A, Y, \mathcal{Q}, \mathcal{I}_1),$$
$$Valid\langle A, Cert(Y, \emptyset, \mathcal{L}^Y, \mathcal{I}_3), t\rangle \vdash Aut(A, \emptyset, \mathcal{L}^Y, \mathcal{I}_3)$$

Similarly, assuming $t \in \{\mathcal{I}_2 \cap \mathcal{I}_3\}, \mathcal{L}^Z \subseteq \mathcal{R}$:

---

[3]When establishing authenticity for Y, it was only necessary to ensure that the domains of X and Y are disjoint, as X was the only trusted certificate authority at this time. This requirement was covered by the precondition of the inference rule.

$$Aut(A, Z, \mathcal{R}, \mathcal{I}_2), Trust(A, Z, \mathcal{R}, \mathcal{I}_2),$$
$$Valid\langle A, Cert(Z, \emptyset, \mathcal{L}^Z, \mathcal{I}_3), t\rangle \vdash Aut(A, \emptyset, \mathcal{L}^Z, \mathcal{I}_3)$$

Alice's view therefore now also includes the revocation information provided by Y and Z:

$$View_A^5 = View_A^4 \cup \{Aut(A, \emptyset, \mathcal{L}^Y, \mathcal{I}_3), Aut(A, \emptyset, \mathcal{L}^Z, \mathcal{I}_3)\}$$

Alice can now attempt to derive the authenticity of Bob's public key. Bob's certificate has been issued by X, but no property has been assigned by X within that certificate. Hence, inference rule (8.5) is used.

Assuming that $t \in \{\mathcal{I}_0 \cap \mathcal{I}_1 \cap \mathcal{I}_2 \cap \mathcal{I}_3\}, r^Z \notin \mathcal{P}, q^Y \notin \mathcal{P}$:

$$Aut(A, X, \mathcal{P}, \mathcal{I}_0), Trust(A, X, \mathcal{P}, \mathcal{I}_0),$$
$$Valid\langle A, Cert(X, B, \{r^Z, q^Y\}, \mathcal{I}_3), t\rangle \vdash Aut(A, B, \{r^Z, q^Y\}, \mathcal{I}_3)$$

The certificate validity template for inter-domain verification, specified in (8.8), is used for evaluating $C = Cert(X, B, \{r^Z, q^Y\}, \mathcal{I}_3)$. As there are two properties assigned to the certificate, the recursion has three levels. The first level ($|\{r^Z, q^Y\}| = 2$) starts with the evaluation of property q^Y:[4]

$$|\{r^Z, q^Y\}| = 2 : \quad q^Y \in \mathcal{Q},$$
$$Trust(A, Y, \mathcal{Q}, \mathcal{I}_1) \in View_A^5,$$
$$Aut(A, Y, \mathcal{Q}, \mathcal{I}_1) \in View_A^5,$$
$$Aut(A, \emptyset, \mathcal{L}^Y, \mathcal{I}_3) \in View_A^5,$$
$$q^Y \notin \mathcal{L}^Y, q^Y \in \mathcal{Q}, t \in \{\mathcal{I}_1 \cap \mathcal{I}_3\},$$
$$Valid\langle A, Cert(X, B, \{r^Z\}, \mathcal{I}_3), t\rangle$$

Trust and authenticity to certificate authority Y must have been derived in Alice's view. Similarly, the authenticity of the certificate revocation information must have also been derived. It is assumed that the property q^Y has not been revoked and that it is an element of the domain $\mathcal{Q}$. The evaluation time t has to be within the time intervals $\mathcal{I}_1$ and $\mathcal{I}_3$. Not formally expressed within the calculus is that the signature σ_p^1 inside the property extension field, generated by Y, has to be valid, cf. Figure 7.4c. Assuming that all these conditions are satisfied, the recursion continues with the second level ($|\{r^Z\}| = 1$) for evaluating the property r^Z:

---

[4]The processing order of the properties can be arbitrary. q^Y will be used as the first property in our verification. The result is equivalent to using r^Z as first property.

$$|\{r^Z\}| = 1 : \ r^Z \in \mathcal{R},$$
$$Trust(A, Z, \mathcal{R}, \mathcal{I}_2) \in View_A^5,$$
$$Aut(A, Z, \mathcal{R}, \mathcal{I}_2) \in View_A^5,$$
$$Aut(A, \emptyset, \mathcal{L}^Z, \mathcal{I}_3) \in View_A^5,$$
$$r^Z \notin \mathcal{L}^Z, r^Z \in \mathcal{R}, t \in \{\mathcal{I}_2 \cap \mathcal{I}_3\},$$
$$Valid\langle A, Cert(X, B, \emptyset, \mathcal{I}_3), t\rangle$$

Trust and authenticity to the certificate authority Z and the revocation information provided by Z must have been derived in Alice's view. The property r^Z must not have been revoked and it must be an element of the domain $\mathcal{R}$. The evaluation time t has to be within the time intervals $\mathcal{I}_2$ and $\mathcal{I}_3$. Although not expressed within the calculus, the signature σ_p^2 generated by Z has to be valid.

Assuming that all conditions are met, the recursion then continues with the last level ($|\emptyset| = 0$). The certificate validity template for local verification (8.7) is now used, as all properties have already been processed:

$$|\emptyset| = 0 : \ Trust(A, X, \mathcal{P}, \mathcal{I}_0) \in View_A^5,$$
$$Aut(A, X, \mathcal{P}, \mathcal{I}_0) \in View_A^5,$$
$$Aut(A, \emptyset, \mathcal{L}^X, \mathcal{I}_3) \in View_A^5,$$
$$C \notin \mathcal{L}^X, t \in \{\mathcal{I}_0 \cap \mathcal{I}_3\}$$

No properties are left anymore for processing at this stage. Only the issuing information is now verified. Trust and authenticity to the certificate authority X and the revocation information provided by X must be within Alice's view. It is assumed that the certificate has not been revoked and that the evaluation time t is within the time intervals $\mathcal{I}_0$ and $\mathcal{I}_3$. Not formally expressed within the calculus is requirement for the final signature σ_3 generated by X, to be valid, cf. Figure 7.4c. All conditions have then been satisfied.

Closure

Each level of the recursion evaluates to valid. Hence, the entire certificate can be considered valid and the authenticity of Bob's public key can be inferred. The closure is therefore:

$$\overline{View_A(t)} = View_A^5 \cup \{ \ Aut(A, B, \{r^Z, q^Y\}, \mathcal{I}_3) \ \}$$

Alice therefore believes in the authenticity of Bob's public key and the assigned properties r, q at evaluation time $t \in \{\mathcal{I}_0 \cap \mathcal{I}_1 \cap \mathcal{I}_2 \cap \mathcal{I}_3\}$.

The proof also showed that Alice has to perform inter-domain operations for this type of verification. That is, she has to derive the authenticity of foreign certificate authorities and also use the revocation services of these authorities, which are located outside her local domain.

8.4. Proof for Alice's Certificate

In the following, the extended identity certificate for Alice (correspondent router), as defined in Section 7.3.2, will be verified. Alice will use the certificate when attempting to authenticate to Bob (mobile router). The verification is based on a model describing the point of view of Bob. Given Alice's extended identity certificate, the authenticity of the public key and the associated properties will be derived by Bob.

The verification is performed for the certificate shown in Figure 7.6 and the general trust scenario illustrated in Figure 7.2.

8.4.1. Proof for Local Verification

The proof performed in the following is based on the local verification where Bob will only verify the validity of the signature and revocation information provided by the local certificate authority of Alice. This is the intended usage of Alice's extended identity certificate.

The graph representation of Bob's initial view is provided in Figure 8.6. Initially, Bob only has trust to and believe in the authenticity of certificate authority X with domains $\mathcal{P}$ and $\mathcal{R}_0$. This certificate authority is Alice's local trust anchor that also provides revocation information. There is also the certificate issued by X to Alice, containing the two properties r^X and p^X assigned by X.

The assignment of the property $r^X \in \mathcal{R}_0$ to Alice is possible due to the delegation $\mathcal{R}_0$ that X received from the certificate authority Z, cf. Section 7.3.2. This delegation is verified by Bob prior to authenticating to Alice, during pre-verification phase (e. g. during pre-flight phase). This is not performed in the following, as this verification corresponds to the runtime operation performed by Bob when Alice authenticates to him.

Bob's initial view is as follows:

$$ View_B = \left\{ \begin{array}{l} Aut(B, X, \mathcal{P}, \mathcal{I}_0), Trust(B, X, \mathcal{P}, \mathcal{I}_0), \\ Aut(B, X, \mathcal{R}_0, \mathcal{I}_2), Trust(B, X, \mathcal{R}_0, \mathcal{I}_2), \\ Cert(X, \emptyset, \mathcal{L}^X, \mathcal{I}_1), Cert(X, A, \{r^X, p^X\}, \mathcal{I}_3) \end{array} \right\}, $$

The authenticity of Alice's public key has to be derived:

$$ Aut(B, A, \{r^X, p^X\}, \mathcal{I}_2) \in \overline{View_A(t)} $$

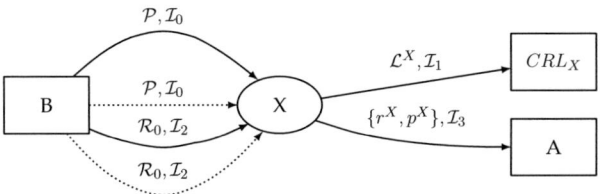

Figure 8.6. Local verification of Alice's extended identity certificate by Bob.

It is first necessary to infer the authenticity of the revocation information $\mathcal{L}^X$ using rule (8.1).

It is assumed that Bob has trust to and believe in the authenticity of certificate authority X at evaluation time t. The revocation information $\mathcal{L}^X$ is required to be a subset of the domain $\mathcal{P}$. To satisfy the certificate validity template, the signature on the revocation information must be valid and the evaluation time t has to be within the validity period of the revocation information. Using rule (8.1) and assuming that $t \in \{\mathcal{I}_0 \cap \mathcal{I}_1\}, \mathcal{L}^X \subseteq \mathcal{P}$:

$$Aut(B, X, \mathcal{P}, \mathcal{I}_0), Trust(B, X, \mathcal{P}, \mathcal{I}_0),$$
$$Valid\langle A, Cert(X, \emptyset, \mathcal{L}^X, \mathcal{I}_1), t \rangle \vdash Aut(X, \emptyset, \mathcal{L}^X, \mathcal{I}_1)$$

Bob's view is therefore:

$$View_B^1 = View_B \cup \{Aut(B, \emptyset, \mathcal{L}^X, \mathcal{I}_1)\}$$

The authenticity of Alice's certificate can now be inferred. As the issuing certificate authority X assigned properties to the certificate, inference rule (8.5) must be used. It is assumed that $t \in \{\mathcal{I}_0 \cap \mathcal{I}_1 \cap \mathcal{I}_2 \cap \mathcal{I}_3\}, r^X \in \mathcal{R}_0$:[5]

$$Aut(B, X, \mathcal{P}, \mathcal{I}_0), Trust(B, X, \mathcal{P}, \mathcal{I}_0),$$
$$Valid\langle A, Cert(X, A, \{r^X, p^X\}, \mathcal{I}_3), t \rangle \vdash Aut(B, A, \{r^X, p^X\}, \mathcal{I}_3)$$

The validity of the certificate $C = Cert(X, A, \{r^X, p^X\}, \mathcal{I}_3)$ has to be evaluated. The verification is performed based on the template for local verification (8.7):

---

[5] As both properties r^X, p^X are assigned by the issuing certificate authority, the processing order used within the validity template for establishing authenticity can be arbitrary. r^X will be used as first property in the verification. The result is equivalent to using p^X as first property.

$$Trust(B, X, \mathcal{P}, \mathcal{I}_0) \in View_B^1,$$
$$Aut(B, X, \mathcal{P}, \mathcal{I}_0) \in View_B^1,$$
$$Trust(B, X, \mathcal{R}_0, \mathcal{I}_2) \in View_B^1,$$
$$Aut(B, X, \mathcal{R}_0, \mathcal{I}_2) \in View_B^1,$$
$$Aut(B, \emptyset, \mathcal{L}^X, \mathcal{I}_1) \in View_B^1,$$
$$p^X \in \mathcal{P}, r^X \in \mathcal{R}_0$$
$$C \notin \mathcal{L}^X, t \in \{\mathcal{I}_0 \cap \mathcal{I}_1 \cap \mathcal{I}_2 \cap \mathcal{I}_3\}$$

Trust and authenticity of certificate authority X with domains and property sets $\mathcal{P}$ and $\mathcal{R}_0$ have already been included in Bob's initial view. The authenticity of the certificate revocation information has been derived for $View_B^1$. It is assumed that Alice's certificate has not been revoked by X. The properties assigned within Alice's certificate are elements of the property sets $\mathcal{P}$ and $\mathcal{R}_0$ of the certificate authority X. The evaluation time t is assumed to be within the individual time intervals $\mathcal{I}_0, \mathcal{I}_1, \mathcal{I}_2, \mathcal{I}_3$. Not expressed within the calculus is the requirement for the outermost signature σ_3 generated by X to be valid. It is assumed that all these conditions are satisfied.

Closure

Based on the valid certificate statement, the authenticity of Alice's public key and the assigned properties can be derived. The closure on Bob's view is as follows:

$$\overline{View_B(t)} = View_B^1 \cup \{ Aut(B, A, \{r^X, p^X\}, \mathcal{I}_3) \}$$

Bob therefore believes not only in the authenticity of Alice's public key but also in the authenticity of the assigned properties r^X, p^X at evaluation time $t \in \{\mathcal{I}_0 \cap \mathcal{I}_1 \cap \mathcal{I}_2 \cap \mathcal{I}_3\}$.

8.4.2. Proof for Inter-Domain Verification

The proof performed in the following uses the template for inter-domain verification (8.8), where every certificate authority that is involved with Bob's properties is involved.

This is modeled within the calculus as follows. An illustration is provided in Figure 8.7. In the initial view, Bob has trust to and believe in the authenticity of the certificate authorities X and Z. The certificate authority Z delegates a part of its property space (IP address space) to certificate authority X. Alice's certificate has been issued by certificate authority X. Revocation information is also provided by both certificate authorities.

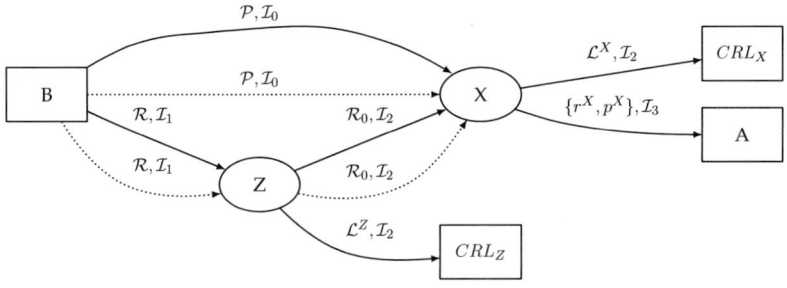

Figure 8.7. Inter-domain verification of Alice's extended identity certificate by Bob.

Summarized, Bob's initial view is as follows:

$$ViewB = \left\{ \begin{array}{l} Aut(B, X, \mathcal{P}, \mathcal{I}_0), Trust(B, X, \mathcal{P}, \mathcal{I}_0), \\ Aut(B, Z, \mathcal{R}, \mathcal{I}_1), Trust(B, Z, \mathcal{R}, \mathcal{I}_1), \\ Tran(Z, X, \mathcal{R}_0, \mathcal{I}_2), Cert(Z, X, \mathcal{R}_0, \mathcal{I}_2), \\ Cert(X, A, \{r^X, p^X\}, \mathcal{I}_3), \\ Cert(X, \emptyset, \mathcal{L}^X, \mathcal{I}_2), Cert(Z, \emptyset, \mathcal{L}^Z, \mathcal{I}_2) \end{array} \right\}$$

The property spaces $\mathcal{P}$ and $\mathcal{R}_0$ are both bound to certificate authority X. The public key in the statement $Aut(B, X, \mathcal{P}, \mathcal{I}_0)$ can be either identical or different from the public key in the certificate statement $Cert(Z, X, \mathcal{R}_0, \mathcal{I}_2)$. The specific choice does not influence the calculus model.

If Bob attempts to believe in Alice's public key and the associated properties r and p, he has to derive the following authenticity statement at evaluation time t:

$$Aut(B, A, \{r^X, p^X\}, \mathcal{I}_3) \in \overline{View_A(t)}$$

As this proof is for the inter-domain verification, Bob will validate the individual properties r and p. This requires Bob to derive the authenticity of the revocation information and the delegation $\mathcal{R}_0$ from Z to X.

Inference rule (8.1) can be used to infer the authenticity of the revocation information $\mathcal{L}^X$. This requires Bob to have trust to and believe in the authenticity of certificate authority X at evaluation time t. The revocation information $\mathcal{L}^X$ is required to be a subset of the domain $\mathcal{P}$. To satisfy the certificate validity template, the signature on the revocation information must be valid and the evaluation time t has to be within the validity period of the revocation information.

223

Summarized, given that $t \in \{\mathcal{I}_0 \cap \mathcal{I}_2\}, \mathcal{L}^X \subseteq \mathcal{P}$:

$$Aut(B, X, \mathcal{P}, \mathcal{I}_0), Trust(B, X, \mathcal{P}, \mathcal{I}_0),$$
$$Valid\langle B, Cert(X, \emptyset, \mathcal{L}^X, \mathcal{I}_2), t\rangle \vdash Aut(B, \emptyset, \mathcal{L}^X, \mathcal{I}_2)$$

Similarly, the authenticity of the revocation information $\mathcal{L}^Z$ can be inferred with rule (8.1). Assuming that $t \in \{\mathcal{I}_1 \cap \mathcal{I}_2\}, \mathcal{L}^Z \subseteq \mathcal{R}$:

$$Aut(B, Z, \mathcal{R}, \mathcal{I}_1), Trust(B, Z, \mathcal{R}, \mathcal{I}_1),$$
$$Valid\langle B, Cert(Z, \emptyset, \mathcal{L}^Z, \mathcal{I}_2), t\rangle \vdash Aut(B, \emptyset, \mathcal{L}^Z, \mathcal{I}_2)$$

This expands Bob's view to:

$$View_B^1 = View_B \cup \{Aut(B, \emptyset, \mathcal{L}^X, \mathcal{I}_2), Aut(B, \emptyset, \mathcal{L}^Z, \mathcal{I}_2)\}$$

In the next step, Bob can verify the trust transfer from Z to X. Trust can be established by using rule (8.2). The validity template has to ensure that the evaluation time lies within the time interval of the trust transfer.

Hence, assuming that $t \in \{\mathcal{I}_1 \cap \mathcal{I}_2\}, \mathcal{R}_0 \subseteq \mathcal{R}$:

$$Aut(B, Z, \mathcal{R}, \mathcal{I}_1), Trust(B, Z, \mathcal{R}, \mathcal{I}_1)$$
$$Valid\langle B, Tran(Z, X, \mathcal{R}_0, \mathcal{I}_2), t\rangle \vdash Trust(B, X, \mathcal{R}_0, \mathcal{I}_2)$$

Bob's view is further expanded to:

$$View_B^2 = View_B^1 \cup \{Trust(B, X, \mathcal{R}_0, \mathcal{I}_2)\}$$

Bob can now infer the authenticity of the certificate issued by Z, implementing the trust delegation to X. This is achieved by using rule (8.1). The certificate validity template has to ensure that a valid signature is present on the certificate and that the certificate itself has not been revoked. Based on the assumptions $t \in \{\mathcal{I}_1 \cap \mathcal{I}_2\}, \mathcal{R}_0 \subseteq \mathcal{R}, Cert(Z, X, \mathcal{R}_0, \mathcal{I}_2) \notin \mathcal{L}^Z$:

$$Aut(B, Z, \mathcal{R}, \mathcal{I}_1), Trust(B, Z, \mathcal{R}, \mathcal{I}_1),$$
$$Valid\langle B, Cert(Z, X, \mathcal{R}_0, \mathcal{I}_2), t\rangle \vdash Aut(B, X, \mathcal{R}_0, \mathcal{I}_2)$$

Bob's view is now:

$$View_B^3 = View_B^2 \cup \{Aut(B, X, \mathcal{R}_0, \mathcal{I}_2)\}$$

The authenticity of Alice's public key can now be inferred. As the properties have been assigned by the issuing certificate authority X, inference rule (8.6) has to be used.

Assuming that $t \in \{\mathcal{I}_0 \cap \mathcal{I}_2 \cap \mathcal{I}_3\}, r^X \in \mathcal{R}_0, p^X \in \mathcal{P}$:

$$Aut(B, X, \mathcal{R}_0, \mathcal{I}_2), Trust(B, X, \mathcal{R}_0, \mathcal{I}_2),$$
$$Valid\langle B, Cert(X, A, \{r^X, p^X\}, \mathcal{I}_3), t\rangle \vdash Aut(B, A, \{r^X, p^X\}, \mathcal{I}_3)$$

The certificate validity template for inter-domain verification specified in (8.8) is used for evaluating $C = Cert(X, A, \{r^X, p^X\}, \mathcal{I}_3)$. As there are two properties assigned to the certificate, the recursion has three levels. The first level $(|\{r^X, p^X\}| = 2)$ starts with the evaluation of the property r^X:[6]

$$|\{r^X, p^X\}| = 2 : \quad r^X \in \mathcal{R}_0,$$
$$Trust(B, X, \mathcal{R}_0, \mathcal{I}_2) \in View_B^3,$$
$$Aut(B, X, \mathcal{R}_0, \mathcal{I}_2) \in View_B^3,$$
$$Aut(B, \emptyset, \mathcal{L}^X, \mathcal{I}_2) \in View_B^3,$$
$$r^X \notin \mathcal{L}^X, r^X \in \mathcal{R}_0, t \in \{\mathcal{I}_2 \cap \mathcal{I}_3\},$$
$$Valid\langle A, Cert(X, A, \{p^X\}, \mathcal{I}_3), t\rangle$$

Trust and authenticity of certificate authority X must be contained in Bob's view. Similarly, the authenticity of the revocation information must also be contained in Bob's view. It is assumed that the property r^X has not been revoked. E. g., the serial number S_2 must not be listed in the revocation information, cf. Figure 7.6. The property has to be an element of the domain $\mathcal{R}_0$. The evaluation time t has to be within the time intervals $\mathcal{I}_2$ and $\mathcal{I}_3$. Although not formally expressed in the calculus, the signature σ_p^2 generated by X has to be valid. Assuming all these conditions have been fulfilled, the recursion continues with the next level $(|\{p^X\}| = 1)$.

$$|\{p^X\}| = 1 : \quad p^X \in \mathcal{P},$$
$$Trust(B, X, \mathcal{P}, \mathcal{I}_0) \in View_B^3,$$
$$Aut(B, X, \mathcal{P}, \mathcal{I}_0) \in View_B^3,$$
$$Aut(B, \emptyset, \mathcal{L}^X, \mathcal{I}_2) \in View_B^3,$$
$$p^X \notin \mathcal{L}^X, p^X \in \mathcal{P}, t \in \{\mathcal{I}_0 \cap \mathcal{I}_2 \cap \mathcal{I}_3\},$$
$$Valid\langle A, Cert(X, A, \emptyset, \mathcal{I}_3), t\rangle$$

Trust and authenticity of certificate authority X and the authenticity of the revocation information provided by X must have been derived in Bob's view. It is assumed that the property p^X has not been revoked. E. g., the serial number S_1 is not listed in the revocation information, cf. Figure 7.6. The property has to be an element of the domain $\mathcal{P}$. The evaluation time t has to be within the time

---

[6]As both properties r^X, p^X are assigned by the issuing certificate authority, the processing order of the properties can be arbitrary. r^X will be used as the first property in the verification. The result is equivalent to using p^X as first property.

intervals $\mathcal{I}_0, \mathcal{I}_2, \mathcal{I}_3$. Not formally expressed within the calculus is the requirement for the signature σ_p^1 generated by X to be valid.

Assuming that all these requirements are fulfilled, the recursion then continues with the last level ($|\{\emptyset\}| = 0$). The certificate validity template for local verification (8.7) is now used as all properties have already been processed:

$$|\emptyset| = 0 : \quad Trust(B, X, \mathcal{P}, \mathcal{I}_0) \in View_B^3,$$
$$Aut(B, X, \mathcal{P}, \mathcal{I}_0) \in View_B^3,$$
$$Aut(B, \emptyset, \mathcal{L}^X, \mathcal{I}_2) \in View_B^3,$$
$$C \notin \mathcal{L}^X, t \in \{\mathcal{I}_0 \cap \mathcal{I}_2 \cap \mathcal{I}_3\}$$

No properties are left anymore for processing at this stage. Only the issuing information is verified. Trust and authenticity of the certificate authority X and the revocation information must have been derived in Bob's view. It is assumed that the certificate has not been revoked. Not expressed within the calculus is the requirement for the outermost signature σ_3 generated by X to be valid, cf. Figure 7.6. It is assumed that all these conditions have been satisfied.

Closure

As each level of the recursion evaluates to valid, the entire certificate can be considered valid and the authenticity of Alice's public key can be derived. The closure is therefore:

$$\overline{View_B(t)} = View_B^3 \cup \{ \ Aut(B, A, \{r^X, p^X\}, \mathcal{I}_3) \ \}$$

Bob therefore believes in the authenticity of Alice's public key and the assigned properties r, p at evaluation time $t \in \{\mathcal{I}_0 \cap \mathcal{I}_2 \cap \mathcal{I}_3\}$.

8.5. Summary

Maurer's calculus [131, 133] has been introduced as a tool for verifying identity certificates. The calculus has been extended to support modeling of both cross-certificates and extended identity certificates. These extensions are a contribution of this thesis.

Based on this extended calculus, the extended identity certificates defined for use with the SeNERO protocol have been verified. It was shown that Alice (correspondent router) can derive the authenticity of the public key of Bob (mobile router) and its associated properties, the identity and the mobile network prefix. Similarly, it was also shown that Bob can derive the authenticity of Alice's public key and associated properties, the identity and the correspondent router prefix.

It was shown that authenticity can be established in two ways. First, based on the local verification, Alice/Bob is only required to have trust and authenticity to the local certificate authority. This approach does not require inter-domain operations with certificate authorities located outside the local domain. This is also the intended usage mode of the certificate extension. In the second approach, based on inter-domain verification, Alice/Bob is required to establish trust and authenticity to all involved certificate authorities. This requires inter-domain operations with different certificate authorities and their revocation services.

9. Summary and Outlook

The aeronautical communications environment will require a protocol for supporting IP mobility across different wireless access technologies. A network layer mobility protocol has the advantage of being transparent to network nodes, such that applications can remain mobility agnostic. However, it is not sufficient to solely rely on the Network Mobility (NEMO) protocol for supporting a mobile network. This is due to the increased end-to-end communications latency as well as the single point of failure problem. The root of these problems is the need to route all traffic from and to the mobile network via the home agent.

The goal of this thesis was therefore the development of a NEMO route optimization protocol that permits establishing a direct routing path between the airborne (mobile) router and a correspondent router located within the correspondent network where correspondent nodes are located. The SeNERO protocol defined within this thesis relies on a public key infrastructure and has been designed for use within the closed aeronautical environment supporting ATS communications. The protocol is secure with respect to certain attacks, efficient in terms of handover signaling overhead and does not rely on the home agent as single point of failure. The protocols in the related work usually suffer from at least one problem within these areas.

For addressing the public key infrastructure related problems of modeling the air traffic control communications environment and single point of failure, a distributed trust anchor architecture has been introduced. This eliminates the need for a global trust anchor during authentication at runtime. The extension for X.509 identity certificates defined within this thesis implements this architecture. When used in the SeNERO protocol, a correspondent router can validate a mobile router's certificate by only relying on the trust anchor located in the same correspondent network. The same applies for the verification of a correspondent router's certificate by the mobile router.

9.1. Summary

A survey of NEMO route optimization protocols has been conducted, with the result that a correspondent router based approach, where a tunnel for traffic forwarding is established between a mobile router and a correspondent router, is the most adequate approach for the safety related aeronautical communications environment. This protocol provides several benefits, which are (1) a short end-to-end communications delay, (2) an optimized route to several correspondent nodes provided by a single correspondent router simultaneously and (3) transparency to the end-systems in the mobile network and on the ground. The correspondent router does not suffer from a single point of failure problem either – the failure of a correspondent router only affects correspondent nodes located within the same correspondent network. Communication with correspondent nodes located in other networks, served by different correspondent routers, is still possible. This is not the case for the basic NEMO protocol, where routing from and to the mobile router is not possible anymore in case of home agent failures. Within this thesis, security deficiencies have been identified for the original correspondent router protocol that prevent its usage within a safety related communications environment. Also, the original protocol requires a reachable home agent for establishing the direct routing path to the correspondent router.

An *improved correspondent router protocol* – SeNERO – was therefore defined that provides the advantages of increased security, reduced handover delay and reduced signaling overhead. Furthermore, the new protocol does not rely on a home agent anymore, that has to be considered being a single point of failure. SeNERO is unique in offering all these properties, which is not the case for the related work. The authentication method used within SeNERO relies on X.509 certificates that authenticate the IP address prefixes of mobile router and correspondent router. Asymmetric cryptography is therefore used within the initial authentication. In subsequent authentications, only symmetric cryptography is used, based on a session key established between mobile router and correspondent router.

For the *security evaluation*, a threat model was specified to support a detailed security analysis of mobility/route optimization protocols. Based on this model, it was shown that the new protocol resolves the mobile network prefix and correspondent router prefix hijacking attacks that were identified for the original correspondent router protocol.

A *performance improvement* was shown for the handover latency and signaling overhead when comparing SeNERO to the original correspondent router protocol. For the *handover latency*, the analytical results showed a latency improvement of 9–50% for SeNERO, depending on the scenario. The same holds for the simulation results with an improvement in the range of 12%–51%. These results were also confirmed by the test-bed based evaluation that showed an improvement of 13–51%. Additional simulations were performed using the aeronautical wireless link technology L-DACS 1. This allowed to study the impact of a varying radio cell load upon the handover latency. More detailed, the three investigated scenarios covered the range from small to medium up to overload traffic situations. It was shown that SeNERO performs better throughout all scenarios, although the performance improvement decreases with an increased radio cell load. While a 81% improvement can be achieved in a situation with a small radio cell load, this performance advantage decreases to 58% and 32% for the medium and overload scenarios. A reduced handover latency is important for safety related communications, as a shorter latency decreases the number of packets dropped during a handover. The *signaling overhead* of the original correspondent router protocol, while initially small, was shown to increase over time due to periodic signaling. SeNERO has a high initial overhead that remains constant over time. It was shown that the new protocol is more bandwidth efficient if an optimized path between a mobile router and correspondent router has to be kept alive for more than 20 minutes. As this is usually the case for ATS communications, the new protocol can be considered being more bandwidth efficient within the aeronautical setting.

SeNERO resolves the *single point of failure* represented by the home agent by using certificates instead of signaling message exchanges via the home agent for prefix authentication.[1] This requires a public key infrastructure with a certificate authority (trust anchor) that is authoritative for IP prefix assignments and trusted by both mobile router and correspondent router. This would constitute another single point of failure. In addition, this approach would not reflect the air traffic control communications environment, where the decision on who can receive a certificate and authenticate within a country or region should be subject to the decision of said country or region.

This issue has been resolved by the X.509 identity certificate extension defined within this thesis. It introduces a distributed architecture that replaces the single global trust anchor with a distributed set of local trust anchors. Such a local trust anchor should be operated by each country or region where an aircraft has to perform authentication operations. An extended identity certificate contains several properties (such as the identity and an IP address prefix) assigned by different certificate authorities. Signatures generated by these authorities bind

---

[1]This only applies to mobile (air) initiated communications. For correspondent node (ground) initiated communications, a home agent is still needed for providing initial reachability to the mobile network.

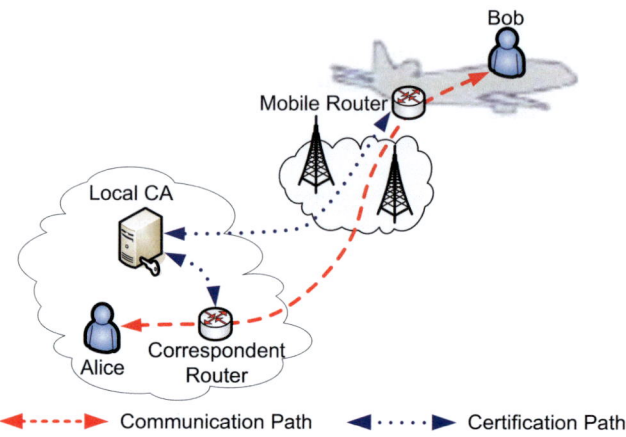

Figure 9.1. Direct communication path between between mobile router and correspondent router, authenticated by relying on local certificate authorities (CAs).

the properties to the public key of the certificate holder. Certificate authorities located within the correspondent networks, so called local certificate authorities, issue and sign the these certificates containing the assigned properties. Verifiers within the same network/trust domain as the local certificate authority can then validate a certificate issued by a local certificate authority based on the signature and revocation information provided by the local certificate authority only. No inter-domain operations with any other certificate authority are therefore necessary for the verifier at runtime. When used with SeNERO, a correspondent router can verify a mobile router's certificate by only relying on the certificate authority that is located within the correspondent router's network domain. The same holds for the verification of the correspondent router's certificate by the mobile router. During the preconfiguration (pre-flight) phase, the aircraft (mobile router) only has to verify the validity of the certificate of the correspondent router's local certificate authority and its delegation certificates. When performing route optimization signaling, the mobile router can verify the correspondent router certificate by relying on the correspondent router's local certificate authority only. An illustration for this is provided in Figure 9.1. This distributed architecture eliminates the single point of failure problem that is present for other approaches. The non-availability of a local certificate authority only prevents authentication operations within the domain represented by this certificate authority, but does not affect other domains.

An *additional advantage* of the extended certificate model is that the mobile router can only authenticate to the correspondent router with a certificate signed and issued by the correspondent router's local certificate authority. The correspondent router does not have to use any trust anchors except for the local one. This certificate authority will in turn only have to trust other certificate authorities for assigning properties from domains for whom these are authoritative. Hence, the decision on who can authenticate within a country or region (local domain) is with the certificate authority of this country or region.

Maurer's calculus was *extended* to support modeling cross-certification and the extended identity certificates. Based on this calculus, the authenticity of a public key and its associated properties can be inferred from the perspective of the verifier, the mobile router or correspondent router. The extended identity certificates, as defined for use within the SeNERO protocol, have been *verified* based on this approach. This was performed based on both a local and an inter-domain verification. In the local verification, the logical inferencing only requires the local but no foreign certificate authorities. In the inter-domain verification, the inferencing does require inter-domain operations with foreign certificate authorities for verifying every individual property assignment or delegation. Either way, the authenticity of the mobile router's and correspondent router's public keys and associated properties – identity and IP address prefixes – have been successfully derived.

9.2. Outlook

The route optimization problem addressed within this thesis addresses a "flat" architecture, where mobile network node and correspondent node are directly attached to mobile router and correspondent router. This assumption is valid for the aeronautical safety related domain, but might not be valid for the passenger domain (APC). Here, the so called *NEMO nesting problem* could appear, where a (personal) mobile router is attached to another (airborne) mobile router. Packets originating from a mobile network node attached to the nested mobile router then have to traverse two mobile routers and consecutively two home agents. This not only increases end-to-end latency but also overhead, due to several layers of IP-in-IP tunneling. A significant amount of research has already been conducted in this area [127, 148, 188, 189].

Mobile multihoming is considered being an important area for future wireless networks, not only for the aeronautical environment, but also for wireless communications based on mobile phones [3]. Multihoming can be easily supported by SeNERO. If the mobile router has multiple network interfaces and associated care-of addresses available, a care-of key would have to be obtained for each of these addresses from the correspondent router. Multiple tunnels via the different care-of addresses could then be established between mobile router and correspondent router. In case the currently used tunnel becomes unavailable, traffic can be switched to another care-of address. Such a scheme would increase the availability of end-to-end communications, which is of high interest for safety related communications.

If at least two care-of addresses are available at the mobile router, it would be possible to route different traffic flows via different addresses simultaneously. This requires development of appropriate Quality of Service (QoS) driven decision algorithms that map traffic flows with their individual requirements to the available wireless network interfaces and access networks that possess different characteristics (e. g. latency, bandwidth, cost). Related work in this area [11, 40, 179, 206] usually only considers a single mobile host instead of a mobile network or the number of decision algorithm parameters is constrained to either signal strength or bandwidth. It would be more interesting to consider a larger variety of parameters, such as delay, cost and provider preference as it has been done in [121].

While the protocol defined within this thesis provides a smaller latency for establishing a direct routing path between mobile router and correspondent router, the overall *handover latency* experienced by a mobile router could be further reduced.[2] If (near) real-time data has to be forwarded, it becomes imperative to minimize delay and resulting packet loss during a handover. In general, the issue of handover latency reduction has been well studied for host mobility in the Mobile IPv6 context [221, 224], but not as extensively for a network mobility protocol such as NEMO [16]. Multihoming can be used to achieve this goal by implementing a make-before-break handover strategy [90, 168]. While data traffic is currently being routed via a certain network interface, another interface can be configured before the currently used one becomes unavailable. Such a strategy would be especially useful in conjunction with sophisticated layer 2 triggers that indicate a prospective imminent loss of radio connectivity. This could be achieved by means of the IEEE 802.21 standard [102, 169], which can provide link layer information collected from different wireless technologies in a uniform way to a mobility management protocol. Apart from make-before-break strategies, it is also possible to optimize the handover latency using link specific properties. One such example for reducing the NEMO handover latency when using the IEEE 802.16e wireless link has been proposed in [42].

Detailed *security* aspects for the future aeronautical communications system have not yet been well studied, except for link specific security [220]. The need for security has been identified, but not yet resolved. This includes both general aspects [197], but also specific problems such as the definition of identities for

---

[2]Mobility signaling is one out of three components contributing to the overall handover latency.

different purposes, e. g., permanent identity such as vehicle identification number and less persistent identities such as flight identity or flight number [27]. Another issue is how to secure position information that is broadcasted by aircraft [181]. However, security related work usually focuses on security management aspects [192] or on generic "cyber security" architectures [219]. More detailed work on security for protocols and applications will have to be performed in the future.

A. Notation

Symbol	Explanation
$|X|$	Cardinality of set X
$\emptyset$	Empty set
$\mathbb{N}$	Set of natural numbers
ρ	Revocation status of a certificate
θ	Name of a certificate authority
$A \rightarrow B$	Message from A to B
$A \mid B$	Concatenation of A and B
$Cert(X, A, p)$	Certificate issued by X for A containing property p
$Cert(X_n, A, \{(X_i, p_i)\})$	Certificate issued by X_n for A containing property p_i assigned by X_i
K_X^{PUB}	Public key of entity X
K_X^{PRIV}	Private key of entity X
K	Symmetric cryptographic key
N_X	Nonce X
$\mathcal{I}_S$	Index to secret key within list of keys S
$\mathcal{C}_X$	Certificate of entity X
$\mathcal{S}$	Strictly increasing sequence number
$\mathcal{T}$	Timestamp with current date and time

A. Notation

Symbol	Explanation
$\mathcal{A}_{MR}, \mathcal{A}_{CR}$	Cryptographic algorithms supported by MR, CR
$K\{M\}$	Message M encrypted with key K
$K[M]$	Message M with HMAC or signature from key K
$H(X)$	One-way hash function with input X
MNP, CRP	Mobile Network Prefix, Correspondent Router Prefix
S	Serial number of a certificate

B. Protocols to Support IP Mobility

A variety of protocols exist that could be used for supporting mobility of mobile hosts or mobile routers in IP based networks. In the following, these protocols are investigated and their individual strengths and weaknesses identified. This investigation is performed based on a particular set of requirements.

It becomes apparent that no protocol can fulfill all requirements. Nevertheless, the network mobility (NEMO) protocol is identified as the most suited one, although it suffers from one problem that remains to be solved: end-to-end latency, which is referred to as the route optimization problem.

B.1. Mobility Requirements

The reader should already be familiar with the IP mobility problem (see Section 2.2.6) and the aeronautical communications and network environment as presented in Section 2.1.

In the following inherent, primary and secondary requirements are specified that have to be fulfilled by a mobility protocol for use in the aeronautical environment. In the following, the word "aircraft" refers to a complete mobile network, consisting of an airborne router and at least one network prefix. Several end-systems (mobile network nodes) are attached to this airborne router.

The inherent requirements that must be completely fulfilled by all candidates are as follows:

1. Session continuity: this property provides a persistent IP address for use to higher layer protocols, even in case of handovers.

2. Mobile network support: mobility should not only be provided for a single mobile host, but for a complete on-board network. More specifically, instead of providing a single IP address (as the case for the previous requirement), one or several persistent network prefixes should be provided to the mobile network nodes.

"Session continuity" is automatically fulfilled by all mobility protocols investigated later. It is therefore not mentioned anymore in the final comparison.

The primary requirements that should be fulfilled by the candidate protocols are as follows[1]:

1. (Mobile) Multihoming: the aircraft should be capable of routing data simultaneously over different interfaces/paths from the aircraft to the ground (e.g. stream X via a satellite and stream Y via a terrestrial network). This requirement covers both load-balancing and fault-tolerance. The latter addresses the important issue of reliability/availability: in case of failure of one interface/path, packets can be routed over another interface/path.

2. Security 1 (masquerading): an attacker must not be able to claim the constant addresses/prefixes of an aircraft, e.g. by means of man-in-the-middle attacks.

3. Security 2 (DoS): the mobility protocol itself should not introduce any new denial of service vulnerabilities.

4. End-to-end delay: the communication delay between the peers (end systems on the aircraft and the ground) should be kept minimal.

5. (Routing) Scalability: the impact of the mobility protocol on the global routing infrastructure should be kept to a minimum, meaning that frequent route announcements/withdrawals for every individual aircraft should be avoided.

6. Applicability to aeronautical administrative communication/aeronautical passenger communication: specifies whether the solution is also applicable to non-safety related services. This indicates whether the protocol stack on the end-systems has to be modified in order to support mobility. Especially for the passenger domain it is unlikely that popular, frequently visited web servers in the public Internet will upgrade their protocol stacks with mobility extensions.

Secondary requirements are desirable and their fulfillment is a bonus:

1. Efficiency 1: the overhead incurred by the mobility protocol itself should be limited. The number of round trip times needed for mobility related signaling should therefore be kept minimal.

---

[1]The order in which the requirements are listed is not prioritized.

2. Efficiency 2: the overhead imposed upon every individual packet with data traffic from the mobile network nodes and correspondent nodes should be limited. The number of additional protocol headers, needed to support mobile routing of end-to-end data, should therefore be kept minimal.

3. Convergence time: a new routing path from and to the mobile network (e.g. because a new wireless interface has been activated) should become usable for packet forwarding within the shortest possible amount of time. While convergence time is also influenced by the number of exchanged signaling messages as described by *Efficiency 1*, this requirement is restricted to the time it takes to propagate the new mobility state throughout the (routing) system.

4. Support for ground-initiated communications: end-systems on the ground should be capable of sending packets to an aircraft they have not yet communicated with. This means that a routing path to the current location of an aircraft has to be available for these nodes.

It is preferable to have a single protocol (family) as a solution for both the safety and the non-safety domains. This is taken into account by the primary requirement "Applicability to AAC/APC". The reason for this requirement is that a single protocol family used in both domains allows for easier maintenance and reduces costs.

B.2. Protocol Options

Protocols for providing IP mobility are also discussed in [123, 165], with a focus on the aeronautical environment in [97]. This investigation is different from the previous ones by assessing the protocols based on the numerous requirements that have been introduced. While the work performed in [97] also specifies certain requirements, many of them are high level. The protocol analysis presented in the following is performed with a higher degree of detail.

From a general perspective, the mobility problem can be solved by a solution that is located on the link, network, transport or application layer.

A solution on the link layer is access technology specific. However, the aeronautical communications environment – the aeronautical telecommunications network – is a heterogeneous environment consisting of different wireless links (cf. Section 2.1.3). This requires providing mobility among different technologies, therefore ruling out the link layer approach and raising the need for a solution located at least on the network layer.

Application layer solutions, for example by using the Session Initiation Protocol [41, 160], require that applications are made mobility aware, e. g. by relying on the SIP protocol. Apart from the burden imposed on application developers, another serious problem is with non-safety related services. All existing airline information systems would have to be updated. Also, applications on passenger-owned devices as well as in the public Internet would have to be modified as well. This rules out the application layer approach for very practical reasons.

This investigation therefore focuses on protocols on the network and transport layer. Five different protocol approaches have been identified that can be categorized as follows:

- Routing protocol based approach (network layer), with the example of the Border Gateway Protocol.
- Tunneling based approaches (network layer), with the examples of the IPsec and Mobile IP protocol families.
- A transport protocol approach, with the example of the Stream Control Transmission Protocol.
- Locator/identifier split (between network and transport layer), with the example of the Host Identity Protocol.

These protocols are investigated in the following. Their suitability to support mobile communications in the aeronautical telecommunications network is assessed with regard to the requirements specified in Section B.1.

B.2.1. Border Gateway Protocol

While routing protocols are not classical IP mobility protocols, they can nevertheless solve the problem of routing in a mobile environment.

The Border Gateway Protocol Version 4 (BGPv4) [173] is the inter-domain routing protocol mainly used in the Internet. BGP is used between autonomous systems for exchanging information on routing paths to specific destination prefixes. Routing information is distributed to neighboring routers that update their routing tables and forward the routing information to other selected routers.

BGP has already been used in the past for providing (IPv4) Internet connectivity for aeronautical passenger communication via satellite links. This solution approach is presented in [54] and is based on dynamic homing, in opposite to the more common static homing used in the Internet.

The operation of this solution is shown in Figure B.1. Each aircraft receives a /24 prefix that is announced via BGP by the ground station the aircraft is currently attached to. Each ground station is an autonomous system with its own AS number and its own BGP router/speaker. When the aircraft moves and performs a handover to a different ground station, the old ground station withdraws the /24 prefix of that aircraft while the new ground station will start announcing the aircraft prefix from its own autonomous system. Packets destined to the aircraft are then routed to the new autonomous system/ground station.

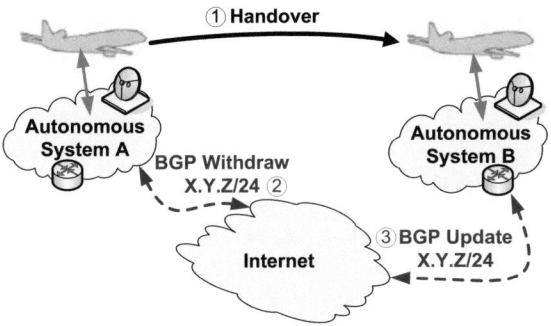

Figure B.1. BGP route announcements by ground stations.

Frequent route announcements and withdrawals lead to route dampening, causing the route in question to not be accepted anymore nor advertised to neighbors by other BGP routers. With a handover occurring only once every 4-8 hours for an aircraft, dampening did not become a problem according to [54]. However, tests showed that with shorter time intervals this might become a problem. This could become an issue, as handovers between terrestrial technologies of the aeronautical telecommunications network are supposed to occur more frequently then with satellites.

Another critical aspect of BGP is convergence time. As mentioned in [54], it took about one minute for the major backbone networks in the Internet to update their routing tables according to the new route. The duration for smaller "outlying" networks to converge was 30-60 minutes.

Analysis

Session continuity (inherent): the aircraft receives a persistent prefix (for example an IPv4-based /24 as in [54]) that is always announced by the current base station of the aircraft. This requirement is therefore fulfilled, as end-systems receive their addresses from this stable prefix.

Mobile Network support (inherent): fulfilled since the aircraft receives a complete mobile network prefix instead of a single IP address.

Multihoming (primary): BGP multihoming is an established technique in the fixed Internet. However, this form of multihoming is usually restricted to either "simple" load-balancing or to destination-based routing decisions. While there are possibilities to include at least the source address of packets into the routing decision [19], the problem of routing individual traffic flows (e.g. based on the used transport protocol and port numbers) over specific interfaces/paths still remains unsolved.

Security 1 (primary): the problems of BGP with respect to security have been thoroughly investigated [34]. One of the key problems is that BGP routers can advertise prefixes that do not even belong to them – an attacker can advertise a prefix owned by someone else and therefore attract the traffic belonging to the other entity. Secure BGP (S-BGP) [117] is one proposal that provides a solution to this problem, although at the expense of an increase in convergence time [34]. S-BGP relies on a public key infrastructure (PKI) and certificates that authorize the owner to manage a certain IP address space. Announced BGP information is then signed by a private key that can be verified by the recipient based on the public key in the certificate, therefore ensuring the authenticity of announced routes. To secure the full routing system, all BGP speakers have to implement S-BGP. Further investigations would be needed to identify whether S-BGP has to be adapted to work with dynamic homing.

Security 2 (primary): The only aspect of S-BGP that might be regarded as problematic is the increase in CPU and memory consumption. There is not enough experience with S-BGP available to properly assess this aspect though.

End-to-end delay (primary): BGP always provides a shortest-path route from the end-systems on the ground to the aircraft, as routes are calculated via the base station that currently advertises the aircraft prefix(es). The exact meaning of "shortest-path" is defined by the metric of the routing protocol.

Scalability (primary): an inherent property of BGP are frequent route announcements and withdrawals from the new and old points of attachment of an aircraft. As the aeronautical telecommunications network will be separated from the public Internet and has its own BGP routing core, scalability might not become a problem within this environment. However, the non-safety related domains are routed over the public Internet and the use of BGP would therefore cause negative impacts upon the routing tables. Scalability is linear with the number of mobile nodes, with regard to the number of route announcements and withdrawals.

Applicability to AAC/APC (primary): the protocol stack on end-systems remains unaffected as BGP exchanges are performed by either the airborne router or the ground station.

Convergence time (secondary) within the aeronautical telecommunications network is not as much an issue as it is for the AAC/APC domains, due to the smaller number of autonomous systems and routes compared to the public Internet.

Efficiency 1 (secondary): within the real-world system of [54], BGP route updates were announced by the ground stations. In this case, the aircraft only has to provide its identity and its prefix to the ground station, which then performs BGP announcements on behalf of the aircraft. Another option, different from [54], would be to put the BGP speaker on-board the aircraft. The signaling, that is based on transmission control protocol, then has to be performed over the wireless link. This implies 1.5 round trip times for establishing the transmission control protocol connection and at least additional 1.5 round trip times for the BGP signaling.

Efficiency 2 (secondary): the size of end-to-end payload packets remains unchanged.

Support for ground-initiated communications (secondary): as soon as a base station starts advertising the aircraft prefix, a route to the aircraft becomes available and traffic would be properly routed to the aircraft.

B.2.2. IPsec

IPsec [116] is a well known protocol providing confidentiality, data integrity and data source authentication. These services are provided by maintaining a shared state between the two communication peers, also called security association. The security association consists of information related to the IP addresses of the two communication peers, cryptographic algorithm identifiers and keys, etc. Establishing such a security association manually would not be scalable, hence the Internet Key Exchange (IKEv2) protocol [112] provides the means to create and manage them dynamically. IKE mutually authenticates the two peers, based on either pre-shared secrets, certificates or the Extensible Authentication Protocol [2].

IPsec is commonly used in virtual private network settings, where an IP-in-IP tunnel is established after the security association has been established. If one of the two IPsec peers moves to a different network and configures a new IP address, the established security associations would not be usable anymore. For this reason, the IKEv2 Mobility and Multihoming protocol (MOBIKE) [57] extends IKEv2 with mobility support. The protocol is usually used between a mobile node and its (fixed) security gateway that assigns a persistent IP address to the mobile node from its own address pool, as shown in Figure B.2. MOBIKE allows one peer (the mobile node) to change the IP address of a security association and to signal this change to the security gateway. In addition, the peer can also transparently move all traffic flows from one interface/IP address to another one.

Analysis

Session continuity: in the process of setting up the initial security association via IKE, the airborne router can request the assignment of a static, fixed IP address from the gateway. Traffic destined to or originating from the mobile network

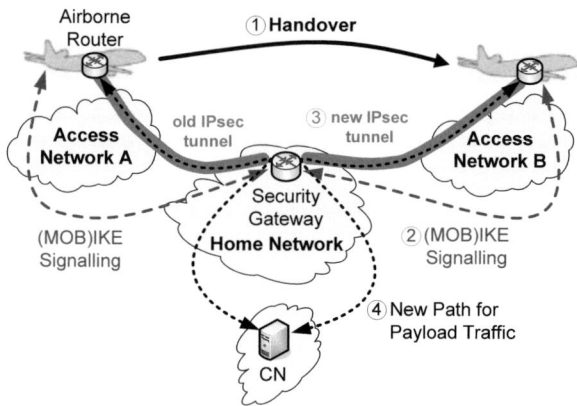

Figure B.2. Signaling between airborne router and IPsec security gateway.

will therefore always be routed via this gateway, with whom the mobile router establishes an IPsec tunnel. In case the mobile router moves to a different access network, a MOBIKE message exchange updates the security association(s) and ensures that the gateway forwards traffic via the IPsec tunnel to the mobile router's new location. The new location is the IP address that the airborne router configures in the new access network (e.g. in Figure B.2, the IP address is first from access network A and after the handover from access network B).

Mobile Network support: instead of acquiring a single address during the establishment of the initial security association with IKE, the airborne router could request a network prefix from the gateway (e.g. a /24 as it was the case for BGP). This way, the mobility of a complete mobile network could be supported.

Multihoming: while MOBIKE provides the means to use different network interfaces, it is limited to using them in a sequential way. Using several interfaces simultaneously to route different data flows over different interfaces is not supported.

Security 1: a mutual authentication within IKE is performed between the gateway and the airborne router, based on pre-shared secrets, certificates or the Extensible Authentication Protocol. This ensures that the gateway forwards traffic to only the correct airborne router.

Security 2: a limited vulnerability of IKE are CPU-exhaustion attacks. The protocol defines a cookie-based mechanism that can be activated if necessary and thereby reduces this threat.

End-to-end delay: the security gateway is a pivotal node that is always traversed by packets exchanged between the mobile network and its communication peers on the ground. If the distance between airborne router and gateway increases, the overall end-to-end latency will also increase.

Scalability: mobility events are only signaled to the security gateway; the routing tables in the routing infrastructure therefore remain unchanged. The security gateway or a BGP speaker in the gateway network only has to advertise a single aggregated prefix via BGP that includes the addresses of all its registered airborne routers (this is called an *aggregate*). Scalability is therefore linear with the number of aggregates, with regard to the entries in the routing tables.

Applicability to AAC/APC: the protocol stack on end-systems remains unaffected as the airborne router transparently tunnels all traffic to the security gateway.

Convergence time: when the airborne router moves to a different network, it notifies the gateway of its new address. As data is always routed via the security gateway, the successful completion of this notification ensures that data is immediately routed to the new location.

Efficiency 1: when moving to a different network, the airborne router needs 1 round trip time of signaling with MOBIKE to inform the gateway of its new location.

Efficiency 2: the use of IPsec usually implies integrity protection and allows for additional encryption. Even if no cryptographic algorithms are specified, the additional headers increase the overhead for every end-to-end payload packet. In addition to that, the overhead of a complete IP header is added to every payload packet as an IPsec tunnel is used. The IPsec transport mode, while eliminating the additional header, would not be able to provide mobility.

Support for ground-initiated communications: as data is always routed via the security gateway that is always notified by the airborne router of its current location, traffic can be immediately forwarded to the mobile network.

B.2.3. NEMO

The Network Mobility (NEMO) protocol [50] is an extension to Mobile IPv6 (MIPv6) [108]. NEMO extends the concept of a mobile host to that of a mobile router (MR) with one or several mobile network prefixes. As soon as the mobile router attaches to a foreign network it registers the IP address acquired from the access network – the care-of address – with its home agent (HA) that is located in the home network. A bi-directional tunnel is created between mobile router and home agent for forwarding traffic between the nodes of the mobile network and the communication peers on the ground. This is also shown in Figure B.3.

247

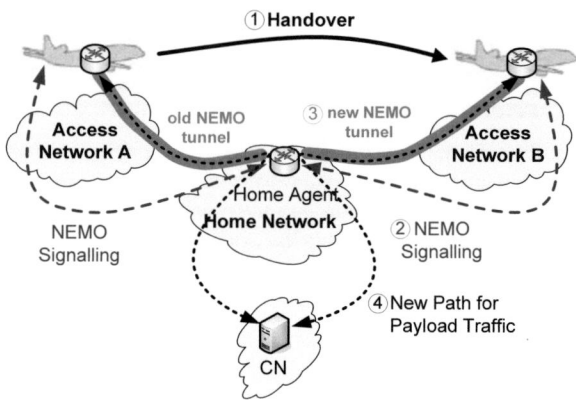

Figure B.3. Signaling between mobile router and home agent.

Analysis

Session continuity: similar to the IPsec solution (cf. Section B.2.2), the home agent provides a mobile node with a persistent IP address – called the Home Address (HoA) – from its own network. Traffic is therefore always routed via the home agent that forwards it to the current location of the mobile node.

Mobile Network support: NEMO extends Mobile IPv6 by introducing a mobile router that has one or several mobile network prefixes. These prefixes are topologically a part of the home network. End-systems that attach to the mobile router configure their addresses based on the mobile network prefix advertised by the mobile router and can therefore remain mobility agnostic.

Multihoming: the possibility to register several care-of addresses with the home agent is specified in [213]. In addition, [207] specifies a policy exchange protocol that can be used to setup forwarding rules for certain traffic flows, taking into account the additional care-of addresses. Detailed traffic selectors can be used to identify a flow, based on IP or higher layer protocol fields such as source/destination address, port numbers, etc. The mobile router sends its current policy to the home agent which sets up forwarding to the mobile router accordingly. This allows for simultaneously routing traffic flows over different interfaces, on the routing path from the mobile router to the home agent as well as on the path from the home agent to the mobile router.

Security 1: mobile router and home agent perform a mutual authentication between each other based on IKEv2 [49]. This ensures that the home agent forwards packets only to the valid mobile router.

Security 2: with the authentication between mobile router and home agent being based on IKEv2, the problem of CPU exhaustion attacks as already discussed for IKE in Section B.2.2 applies here as well.

End-to-end delay: NEMO causes sub-optimal routing where traffic always traverses the home agent. If the distance between mobile router and home agent increases, the overall end-to-end latency also increases.

Scalability: the MR signals its current location to the home agent that updates its routing state accordingly. BGP routing tables remain unchanged as the home network is always advertising an aggregated prefix via BGP that includes all the mobile network prefixes. Scalability is therefore linear with the number of aggregates, with regard to the number of announced prefixes.

Applicability to AAC/APC: the protocol stack on end-systems remains unaffected as traffic is transparently tunneled between mobile router and home agent.

Convergence time is equal to the time it takes the mobile router to signal the new location to the home agent, who will then immediately forward traffic to the mobile router's new care-of address.

Efficiency 1: it takes the mobile router 1 round trip time to signal the new location/care-of address to the home agent.

Efficiency 2: the tunnel between the mobile router and the home agent inflicts an overhead of a full IP header upon every payload packet.

Support for ground-initiated communications: as it was the case for the IPsec-based approach, payload traffic is always routed via the home agent. As the mobile router signals its care-of address(es) to the home agent, traffic can always be forwarded to the mobile router's current location.

B.2.4. SCTP

The problem of mobility is directly impacting the transport layer, where active sessions break due to the simultaneous usage of the IP address as an identifier and locator. One might therefore regard the transport layer as a more proper location for a solution to the mobility problem [56]. An approach that is different from the previous ones is therefore to solve the problem on the transport layer itself. There are proposals for adding mobility extensions to the appropriate protocols, such as TCP-R [70] or M-UDP [33].

In the following, a closer look will be taken at the Stream Control Transmission Protocol (SCTP) [198]. It has been chosen over other protocols such as TCP-R or M-UDP because of the additional features it provides.

SCTP is a connection-oriented transport layer protocol comparable to the transmission control protocol, but with additional features such as multihoming. The original SCTP specification allows specifying several IP addresses during connection setup time only. This limitation has been removed with [200] where newly configured IP addresses can be dynamically added to or deleted from an SCTP association by one of the two communication peers. This is particularly useful for a mobile node where IP addresses appear and disappear due to handovers between different access networks.

Being a transport layer protocol, SCTP is running on the end-systems that are communicating with each other.

Analysis

Session continuity: in case the mobile node moves to a different network where it configures a new IP address, it can dynamically add this new address to the SCTP connection ("association") by performing a "failover". Afterwards, data can be exchanged using the new association.

Mobile Network support: SCTP, as a transport layer protocol, is running on the end hosts and as such is not able to support network mobility, where a mobile router manages mobility on behalf of the mobile network nodes.

Multihoming: while dynamically adding or removing IP addresses can be utilized for mobility, the original intention was to provide multihoming functionality. The SCTP multihoming however supports only redundancy but not load-balancing. While several IP addresses can be associated to a single SCTP association, only one address (the *primary* address) can be used to transmit packets.

Security 1: SCTP is vulnerable with regard to an attacker hijacking an already established association between two communication peers [199]. This enables an attacker to hijack traffic of a mobile node.

Security 2: there do exist vulnerabilities within SCTP that can be exploited to send large volumes of unwanted traffic to a victim. E.g., by providing an additional false address to the SCTP association. The attacker can later force the other SCTP peer to use this address and redirect all traffic to it. These attacks can be either mitigated or the probability to successfully mount an attack at least be minimized. This can be achieved by properly implementing SCTP or choosing proper protocol parameters. [199].

End-to-end delay: SCTP associations are bound to the addresses that are locally available on the two communication peers. The end-to-end delay therefore corresponds to the shortest route between the IP addresses of the two peers.

Scalability: adding or deleting IP addresses to or from SCTP associations is only signaled between the end systems. Therefore there is no impact on the routing infrastructure.

Applicability to AAC/APC: end-systems have to implement SCTP and applications also have to use this protocol in order to have mobility support.

Convergence time is equal to the time the respective SCTP messages need to signal the availability of a new IP address to the communication peer.

Efficiency 1: signaling consumes 1 round trip time for adding a new IP address to the SCTP association.

Efficiency 2: by solving the problem on the transport layer, SCTP does not incur any additional overhead to payload packets.

Support for ground-initiated communications: the attempt of a communication peer on the ground to establish a SCTP connection to a mobile node will fail due to the unknown current location of the mobile node.

B.2.5. HIP

Another, more radical, approach for supporting mobility is the locator-identifier split, where a new shim layer between the network and the transport layer is introduced. This layer also introduces a new namespace on top of the IP address space. The identifiers within this namespace are globally unique and associated to a mobile node. Higher layers (e.g. the transmission control protocol) are not binding anymore to an IP address (the locator), but instead to the new identifier from the shim layer. Several different approaches exist based on these identifiers, for example LIN6 [132] or the Host Identity Protocol (HIP) [151].

In HIP, Host Identity Tags (HITs - the identifiers) are mapped to the available IP addresses (locators) with the help of IPsec. The HITs are generated from the public key and therefore cryptographically bound to it. Only the owner of the corresponding private key can make use of the related HIT in the HIP protocol exchanges. If the HIP enabled mobile node attempts to communicate with a HIP correspondent node, a message exchange is initiated to establish a common session. This session is based on the HITs of the two nodes and the IP addresses they want to use for message exchanges. In case one peer moves to a new location, it signals the new IP address to the other peer. The HIP modules on both nodes can then update their state and map the HIT to the new IP address. In case the mobile node is multihomed, the HIT can have a mapping to several IP addresses.

HIP also provides Rendezvous Servers (RVS). Mobile nodes register with an arbitrary RVS and then update their entries in the Domain Name System (DNS) to include the address of this server. A correspondent node attempting to contact the mobile node performs a DNS lookup based on the mobile node's domain name and thereby retrieves the address of the RVS. The contact initiation from the correspondent node is sent to the RVS from where it can be forwarded by the RVS to the current location of the mobile node.

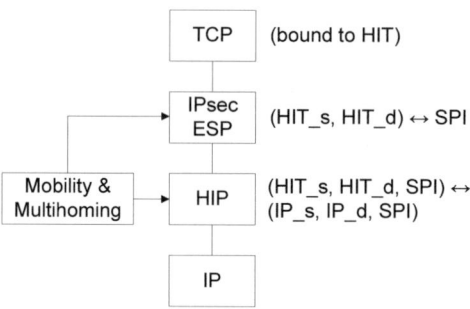

Figure B.4. Host Identity Protocol with mapping to lower and higher layers at mobile node and correspondent node. A Host Identity Tag (HIT) is present for both source ("HIT_s") and destination ("HIT_d"). The Security Parameters Index (SPI) uniquely identifies an IPsec Encapsulated Security Payload (ESP) security association. "IP_s" and "IP_d" refer to source and destination IP address respectively.

The relationship of HIP to other layers of the protocol stack is shown in Figure B.4.

Analysis

Session continuity: As soon as the mobile node moves and configures a new IP address, HIP updates its (HIT, IP address) mappings and signals this change to the correspondent node. The upper layers are not negatively affected as they are bound to the HIT, which remains unchanged.

Mobile Network support: a solution for network mobility support in HIP is proposed in [156]. The mobile network nodes are required to implement HIP and delegate rights to a HIP-enabled mobile router that performs HIP signaling on behalf of the mobile network nodes.

Multihoming: the multihoming support in HIP is focused on providing failover functionality. Simultaneous usage of different interfaces, e.g. for load-balancing, has not been supported at the time of writing. HIP can therefore not fully meet this requirement.

Security 1: HIP relies on authentication and authorization schemes to protect the HIP message exchanges, including signatures. If these mechanisms are used, an attacker – including man-in-the-middle– can not impersonate a node or claim traffic of a node.

Security 2: There is a limited vulnerability to memory and computational exhaustion attacks where an attacker floods a HIP-enabled node with a large amount of HIP signaling messages.

End-to-end delay: traffic is exchanged directly between communication peers. End-to-end delay therefore corresponds to the shortest route between the two peers.

Scalability: HIP does not modify the routing system but instead introduces a new identifier space. Scalability issues are therefore not related to the routing infrastructure, but to the rendezvous servers.

Applicability to AAC/APC: end-systems must have HIP implemented in their network stack. In addition they must delegate rights to the mobile router to enable mobile network support.

Convergence time is equal to the time it takes the mobile node to perform the HIP signaling exchange that updates the (HIT, IP address) mapping at the correspondent node. The only disadvantage is that the signaling has to be performed every time communication of a new (mobile node, correspondent node) pair is initiated.

Efficiency 1: establishing a common HIP state between a mobile node and a correspondent node takes 2 round trip times; updating this state after movement of the mobile node consumes 1.5 round trip times.

Efficiency 2: as HIP uses IPsec to exchange traffic between its two communication peers, overhead is present for every payload packet. However, HIP does not use a IP-in-IP tunnel, but instead relies on IPsec transport mode. This only adds a small IPsec related header instead of an additional IP header.

Support for ground-initiated communications: the initial reachability of a mobile node within HIP can only be provided with the help of the rendezvous server. Scalability, with regard to number of DNS entries, is linear with the number of mobile nodes.

B.3. Grading Of Protocol Options

The discussion of all the various protocols in the previous section shows that there is no optimal solution that is capable of fulfilling all requirements "out of the box". In the following, a summary is provided of how the requirements are graded and how they are fulfilled by each protocol. Table B.1 shows the comparison of all protocols in a more compact manner.

The grading of the property *Multihoming* is either completely fulfilled ($\oplus\oplus$), fulfilled with limitations ($\oplus/\odot$) or not fulfilled ($\ominus$). The latter is applied if load-balancing is not supported.

Protocol	BGP	IPsec	NEMO	SCTP	HIP
Session Continuity	⊕⊕	⊕⊕	⊕⊕	⊕⊕	⊕⊕
Mobile Network Support	⊕⊕	⊕⊕	⊕⊕	⊖	⊕⊕
Multihoming	⊙	⊖	⊕⊕	⊖	⊙
Security 1	⊕⊕	⊕⊕	⊕⊕	⊖	⊕⊕
Security 2	⊕/⊙	⊙	⊙	⊙	⊙
End-to-end delay	⊕⊕	⊖	⊖	⊕⊕	⊕⊕
Scalability	⊖	⊕	⊕	⊕⊕	⊙
Applicability to AAC/APC	⊕⊕	⊕⊕	⊕⊕	⊖	⊖
Convergence time	⊙	⊕⊕	⊕⊕	⊕⊕	⊕
Efficiency 1	⊖	⊕	⊕	⊕	⊙
Efficiency 2	⊕	⊖⊖	⊖	⊕	⊙
Ground-initiated comms.	⊕⊕	⊕⊕	⊕⊕	⊖	⊕

Table B.1. Mobility requirements fulfillment of all candidate approaches. Grading can be either completely fulfilled/optimal (⊕⊕), basically fulfilled/fair (⊕), with limitations/average (⊙) or unsupported/poor (⊖).

Security 1 is either completely fulfilled (⊕⊕), or not fulfilled (⊖). *Security 2* has the additional grading levels (⊕/⊙) and (⊙). The first grading indicates that vulnerabilities exist but the probability for an attacker to exploit them is very small, given that certain precautions are taken. The additional grading levels indicate that a vulnerability has been sufficiently addressed.

The *end-to-end delay* can be either optimal (⊕⊕) or sub-optimal (⊖). The latter applies if packets are routed via a fixed node on the ground, instead of routing on the direct path between the two communication peers.

Scalability always refers to the entries in the BGP routing tables, except for HIP that only creates entries in the DNS. (⊖) indicates linear scalability with number of mobile nodes and (⊕) indicates linear scalability with number of aggregated prefixes. Finally, (⊙) for HIP is scalability with number of mobile nodes, but graded better because it only impacts the DNS. The DNS entry of a mobile node is only stored at a single DNS server. This is in contrast to individual entries for mobile nodes in BGP routing tables that have to be present in *every* BGP router in the routing core.

Applicability to AAC/APC is either possible (⊕⊕) or not possible (⊖).

Convergence time is either limited to the time it takes to signal the new location to a single node (⊕⊕), influenced by DNS lookup and forwarding of the initial packet by a rendezvous server (⊕) or depending on the convergence time of the global routing tables (⊙) for a network of limited size, such as the aeronautical telecommunications network.

The gradings of the individual protocols for *Efficiency 1* and *Efficiency 2* are relative to each other.

Ground-initiated communications is either fully supported (⊕⊕), supported with a dependency on the DNS (⊕) or not supported at all (⊖).

Summary

With respect to the primary requirements, a major issue is the need to implement HIP within the end-systems. This causes difficulties for already existing non-safety related airline systems (aeronautical administrative communication) and makes it infeasible for deployment within the passenger domain (aeronautical passenger communication), where public web servers in the Internet would have to be upgraded. Also, the multihoming capability of HIP would have to be further developed. HIP is therefore unable to fulfill one primary requirement.

SCTP, does not provide full multihoming support. Another critical aspect is the fact that the protocol can only support a mobile host, but is unable to provide mobility for a complete mobile network. While it might be possible to add mobile network support to this solution approach, the fact that both TCP and UDP without any mobility extensions are the most frequently used protocols in the public Internet, makes the transport layer approach infeasible for the non-safety related domains (aeronautical administrative communication/aeronautical passenger communication). Summarized, SCTP is unable to fulfill one inherent, three primary and one secondary requirement.

BGP has problems with providing multihoming on a per-flow granularity level. While S-BGP raises security to an acceptable level, there might be reasons for concern with the increase in CPU and memory consumption. The major problem of BGP – scalability – becomes problematic for the non-safety related domains (aeronautical administrative communication/aeronautical passenger communication) that are based on the public Internet. The operation of BGP as a mobility protocol [54] even caused concerns in the Internet Engineering Task Force (IETF). In total, BGP is unable to completely fulfill one and only partially fulfills another primary requirement.

The remaining two options are IPsec and Mobile IPv6/NEMO. Both protocols are very similar to each other. IPsec suffers from problems with end-to-end latency, overhead inflicted on payload traffic as well as the lack of multihoming capabilities with respect to simultaneous usage of several interfaces. An advantage of IPsec would be the implicitly provided packet-level security for the higher layers. Unfortunately, this feature can not be exploited within a mobile network architecture where the mobile router establishes a tunnel with a security gateway: the IPsec security association would not provide end-to-end security. On the other hand, the NEMO protocol, as part of the Mobile IP protocol family, is a generic mobility protocol providing a multitude of features, but also suffers from problems with payload traffic overhead and end-to-end delay.

A one-to-one comparison between IPsec and NEMO shows that the latter has advantages over the former in two properties: multihoming and, albeit only on a minor level, overhead. IPsec and NEMO fail to meet two and one primary requirement respectively.

A close look at Table B.1 shows that, taking into account all gradings, NEMO is the highest rated solution. It is therefore argued that this protocol is the most feasible solution for the aeronautical environment.

B.4. Conclusion

A number of options has been investigated that can be used to provide IP mobility. These protocols were assessed with regard to the specific aeronautical requirements that have been introduced. The conclusion was that NEMO is capable of fulfilling more requirements "out of the box" than any other protocol.

Despite this conclusion, it might nevertheless be possible to extend some of the other protocol options to such an extend that they are capable of fulfilling all requirements. It is argued though that it is more meaningful to start with the protocol that already fulfills most of the requirements and then address the remaining issues of this protocol.

The only problem of NEMO is the provision of a small end-to-end latency, as all traffic between the mobile network and the ground communication peers is routed via the home agent. Section 3 provides a survey of related work that aims on extending NEMO in order to solve this problem. As these proposal have their deficiencies, Section 4 – the core of this thesis – proposes a route optimization protocol that is suitable for a safety related environment, especially ATS communications.

C. SeNERO Protocol Message Structures & Options

C.1. Overview

In the following, a more detailed view on the individual SeNERO signaling messages is provided. This includes both the overall structure of the four messages used in the SeNERO signaling procedure as well as the individual options (fields) inside each message.

The IPv6 header has been omitted in the following figures for brevity. The generic mobility header that is present in all message, as defined in [50, 108], has been gray colored. This allows simply identifying those options that had to be added in order to support the SeNERO route optimization signaling.

The mobility header is located at the very top of every message and consists of five fields (e. g. Figure C.1a):

- Payload Proto: the next header of the IPv6 packet, succeeding the mobility header (not in use in SeNERO).
- Header Len: specifies the length of the entire message.
- MH Type: specifies the type of the mobility message (e. g. care-of test init, binding update, etc.).
- Reserved: reserved field for future use.
- Checksum: contains a checksum for the entire message.

The content of certain options is described using the variable definitions that have been used in Section 4.4.

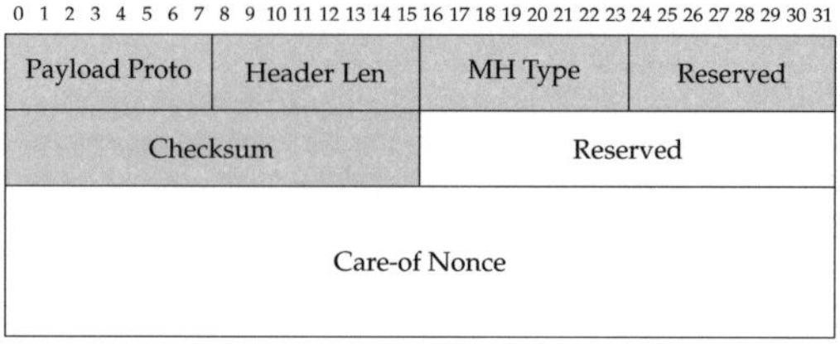

0 1 2 3 4 5 6 7 8 9 10 11 12 13 14 15 16 17 18 19 20 21 22 23 24 25 26 27 28 29 30 31

Payload Proto	Header Len	MH Type	Reserved
Checksum		Reserved	
Care-of Nonce			

(a) Care-of test init.

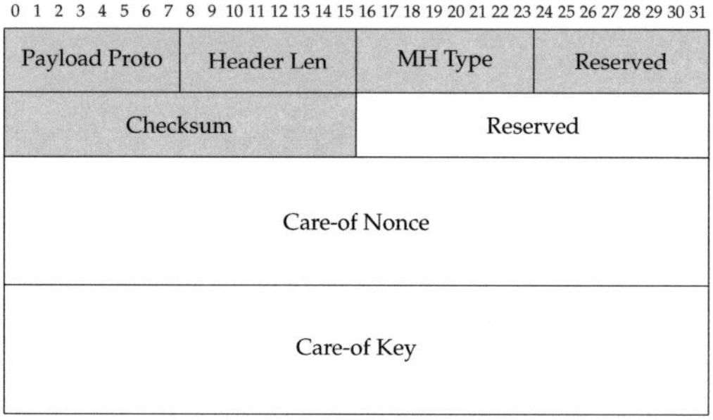

0 1 2 3 4 5 6 7 8 9 10 11 12 13 14 15 16 17 18 19 20 21 22 23 24 25 26 27 28 29 30 31

Payload Proto	Header Len	MH Type	Reserved
Checksum		Reserved	
Care-of Nonce			
Care-of Key			

(b) Care-of test.

Figure C.1. Protocol headers of care-of test messages.

C.2. Care-of Test Messages

The care-of test init and care-of test messages are shown in Figure C.1. They are equivalent to those that have already been defined in Mobile IPv6 [108] for supporting route optimization between a mobile host and a correspondent node.

Apart from the generic mobility header, the care-of test init (cf. Figure C.1a) only includes the *Care-of Nonce* option, which contains the nonce N_C with a length of 64 bits.

The care-of test (cf. Figure C.1b) additionally includes the care-of key K_C that is stored inside the "*Care-of Key*" field. The length of this key is 64 bits.

C.3. Initial Binding Messages

The initial binding update and binding acknowledgement messages, shown in Figures C.2 and C.3 respectively, are the largest messages of the entire SeNERO protocol.

Apart from the mobility header both messages also share a common binding message header with several options. These fields, already defined in Mobile

IPv6 [108] and NEMO [50], have also been gray colored within the figures. These are as follows:

- Sequence Number: an unsigned integer for matching a binding update with its returned binding acknowledgement.
- A, H, L, K: flags indicating certain protocol actions (for more details see [108]).
- Reserved: reserved field for future use.
- Lifetime: indicates the remaining lifetime of a mobility binding. Once the lifetime expires (value equal to zero) the binding has to be deleted.

Binding Update

The option carrying the mobile network prefix ("*Mobile Network Prefix*") is equivalent to what has already been specified in the NEMO Basic Support protocol [50] and has a length of 160 bits. The *care-of nonce* option is equivalent to the one used in the care-of test messages.

The index $\mathcal{I}_S$ to the secret key S_C^i, used by the correspondent router as input to the calculation of the care-of key K_C, is stored inside the option "*CR Secret Key Index*".

The already existing definition of a *Timestamp* option from the Proxy Mobile IPv6 specification [77] has been reused. The timestamp itself has a size of 64 bits: the first 48 bits contain the integer number of seconds while the remaining 16 bits indicate the number of 1/65536 fractions of a second.

The "*Mobile Router Certificate*" is a variable length option containing the certificate $\mathcal{C}_{MR}$ of the mobile router.

The option "*Cryptographic Algorithm Identifiers - Mobile Router*" contains the cryptographic algorithms proposed by the mobile router ($\mathcal{A}_{MR}$). This option contains three subfields for specifying signature, encryption and HMAC algorithms. Each field has a length of 8 bits, therefore supporting up to 255 different algorithms. E. g., for the signature algorithm a value of 4 could indicate "ECDSA with the P-384 curve and SHA-384" while a value of 5 could indicate "RSA with SHA-1".

The "*Mobile Router Certificate*" is a variable length option containing the certificate $\mathcal{C}_{MR}$ of the mobile router.

"*Digital Signature*" is a variable length option containing the signature that has been calculated over the binding update message using the mobile router's private key.

The option "*Binding Authorization Data*" has already been specified in the Mobile IPv6 protocol [108] and carries the first 96 bits of the HMAC output, which is truncated, calculated from the care-of key K_C.

The final *padding* field ensures that the binding update message has a length that is a multiple of 64 bits.

259

Binding Acknowledgement

The binding acknowledgement message differs from the binding update only in a few fields.

The correspondent router prefix is carried inside the *"Correspondent Router Prefix"* option that is equivalent to the mobile network prefix option in terms of structure. It has a length of 160 bits.

The *"Permanent Home Key"* option carries the permanent home key K_{PH} that has a length of 64 bits. Due to the key being transported in encrypted form, this field has a variable length that depends on the used encryption algorithm.

The *"Correspondent Router Certificate"* option carrying the certificate C_{CR} of the correspondent router is also a variable length option.

Finally, the *"Cryptographic Algorithm Identifiers"* option appears twice, indicating which algorithms have been proposed by each mobile router and correspondent router.

"Digital Signature" is a variable length option containing the signature that has been calculated over the binding acknowledgement message using the correspondent router's private key.

The representation of the binding acknowledgement in Figure ?? does not show any padding. In reality, depending on the variable length fields, this might however be necessary.

C.4. Subsequent Binding Messages

The subsequent binding update and binding acknowledgement messages only differ in one options. The structure of these messages is shown in Figure C.4.

Besides the generic mobility header and the common binding message header, the binding update is carrying a 64 bit care-of nonce N_C, the secret key index I_S and the HMAC at the end.

The binding acknowledgement only carries the care-of nonce N_C and the HMAC.

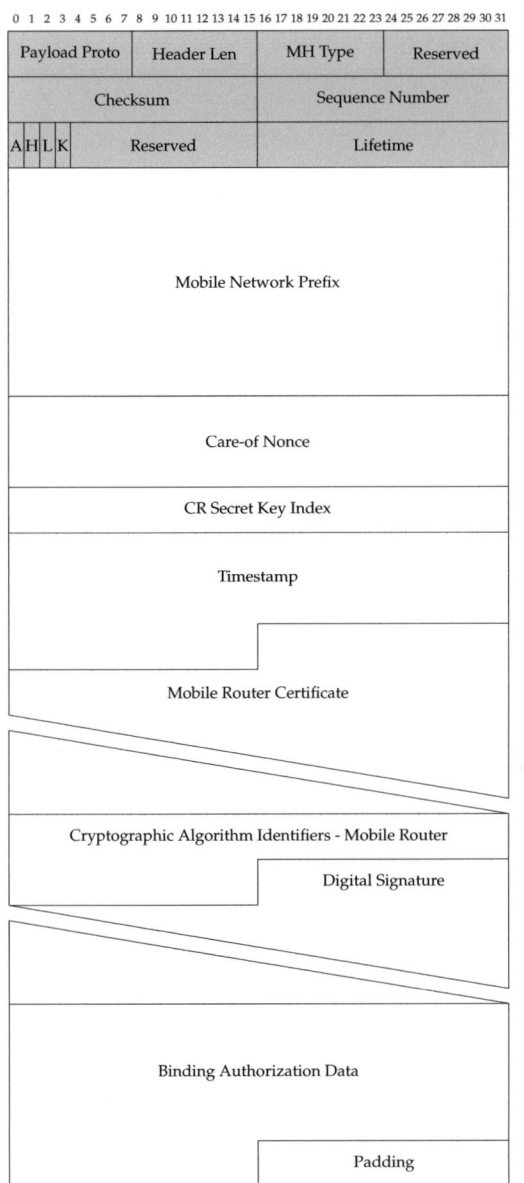

Figure C.2. Protocol header of initial binding update message.

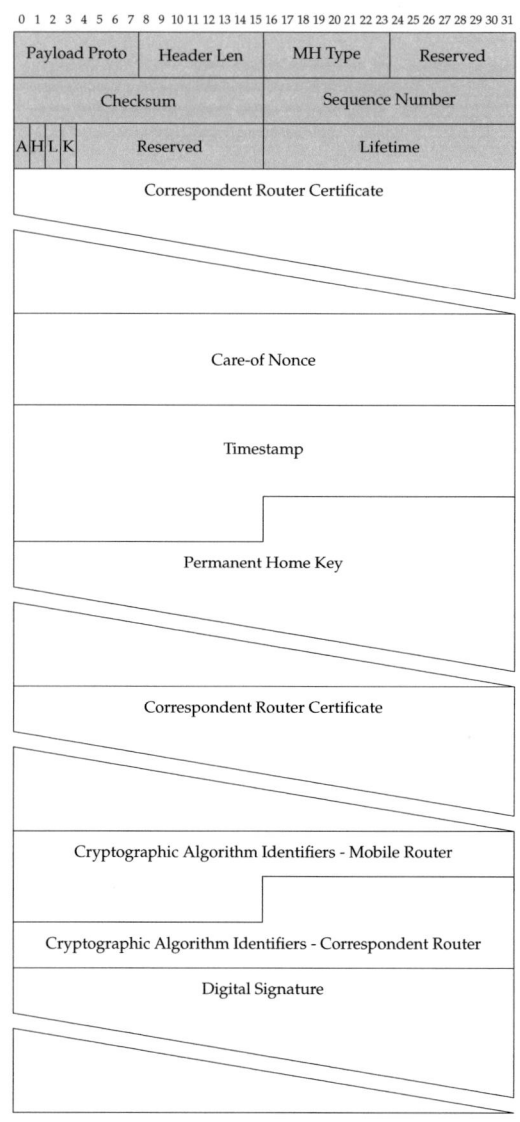

Figure C.3. Protocol header of initial binding acknowledgement message.

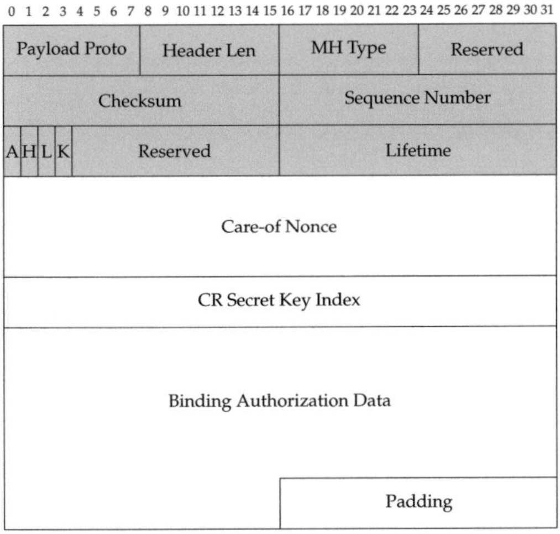

(a) Binding Update.

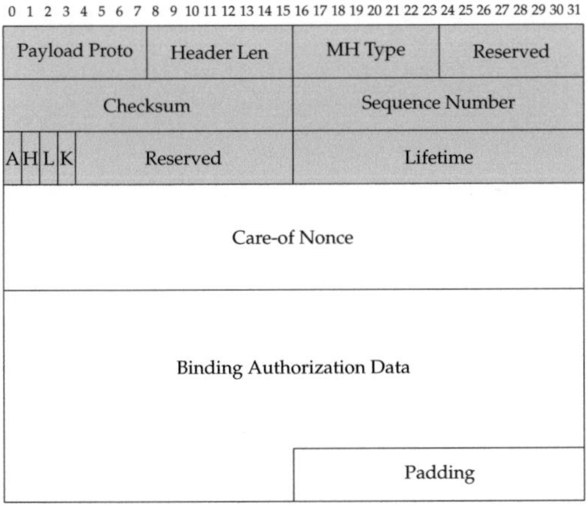

(b) Binding Acknowledgement.

Figure C.4. Protocol headers of subsequent binding update/acknowledgement messages.

D. Handover Evaluation Statistics

The definition of the statistical parameters as well as a comprehensive listing of all test-bed and simulation results is provided on the following pages. The definitions of the parameters are mostly from [32, Section 16.3]. These definitions also apply to the discussion of the results within Chapter 6.

D.1. Statistical Parameters

The **mean** $\overline{x}$, considering n different measurement values x_i, is defined as:

$$\overline{x} = \frac{1}{n} \sum_{i=1}^{n} x_i$$

The variance s^2 is defined as:

$$s^2 = \frac{1}{n-1} \sum_{i=1}^{n} (x_i - \overline{x})^2$$

The **standard deviation** s is directly derived from the variance:

$$s = \sqrt{s^2}$$

The **median** $\tilde{x}$, also called the 50 percentile or $q_{0.5}$, is calculated as follows, considering the discrete case with n measurement results:

$$\tilde{x} = \begin{cases} x_{m+1}, & \text{if } n = 2m + 1 \\ \frac{x_{m+1} + x_m}{2}, & \text{if } n = 2m \end{cases}$$

The 25 and 75 percentiles ($q_{0.25}$ and $q_{0.75}$) can be obtained similarly afterwards: given that the median is the element x_i, then calculating the medians of the lists $[x_1, x_{i-1}]$ and $[x_{i+1}, x_{n-1}]$ provides $q_{0.25}$ and $q_{0.75}$ respectively.

The **interquartile range (IQR)** measures the statistical dispersion and is calculated as the difference between the 75 and 25 percentiles:

$$IQR = q_{0.75} - q_{0.25}$$

The **minimum** and **maximum** are the smallest and largest elements of the measurement results, excluding the outliers:

$$min = \min \left\{ \{x_1, \ldots, x_n\} \setminus outliers_{low} \right\}$$
$$max = \max \left\{ \{x_1, \ldots, x_n\} \setminus outliers_{high} \right\}$$

The outliers are elements that are either larger or smaller then a certain threshold:

$$outliers_{high} = \left(x_i \mid 0 < i \leq n, \ x_i > q_{0.75} + w \cdot IQR \right)$$
$$outliers_{low} = \left(x_i \mid 0 < i \leq n, \ x_i < q_{0.25} - w \cdot IQR \right)$$

A value of $w = 1.5$ corresponds to approximately $\pm 2.7 s^2$ and 99% coverage if the data is normally distributed.

The **confidence interval** for the mean value is defined in the following. If the number of measurement results is not sufficiently large ($n > 100$), the interval has to be calculated based on Student's t-distribution with $m = n - 1$ degrees of freedom and the quantile $t_{\alpha/2;n-1}$ of the t-distribution:

$$\mu = \overline{x} \pm \frac{s}{\sqrt{n}} t_{\alpha/2;n-1}$$

The t-distribution $f_s(t)$ with m degrees of freedom and an error probability α is defined as:

$$f_s(t) = \frac{1}{\sqrt{m\pi}} \frac{\Gamma(\frac{m+1}{2})}{\Gamma(\frac{m}{2})} \frac{1}{(1 + \frac{t^2}{m})^{\frac{m+1}{2}}} \qquad \text{where } \Gamma(m) = (m-1)!$$

An example for $f_s(t)$ with 30 degrees of freedom is shown in Figure D.1. It can be seen that the t-distribution is already close to the uniform distribution. The

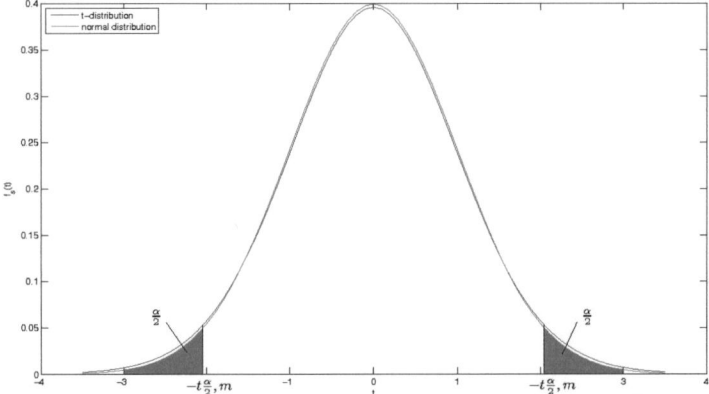

Figure D.1. Student's t-distribution with $m = 30$. The figure also shows the uniform distribution for comparison.

figure further shows the two-sided 99.75 percentiles on each side – the colored space therefore refers to values that have a 5% probability of being smaller or larger than the quantiles.

The confidence interval used in this Appendix is always based on the 95 percentile. It can therefore be said that the probability for the mean value $\bar{x}$ lying within the confidence interval is 95%.

D.2. Test-bed Results

The number of measurements n is equal to 30. The results for the original correspondent router protocol are provided in Table D.3, while the SeNERO results are in Tables D.1 and D.2. The distribution of the results is shown in Figures D.2 and D.2.

D.3. Simulation Results I

The number of measurements n is equal to 60. The results for the original correspondent router protocol are provided in Table D.6. The SeNERO results are in Tables D.4 and D.5. The occurrence distribution of the results is provided in Figure D.3.

Scenario	$\bar{x}$	s	Confidence	$q_{0.25}$	$\tilde{x}$	$q_{0.75}$	Min.	Max.
Europe	625.43	62.83	[601.97, 648.89]	585	619	619	528	746
Asia	626.97	68.47	[601.40, 652.53]	590	619	667	504	757

Table D.1. Statistical properties of test-bed results for the initial authentication signaling in SeNERO. Values in milliseconds.

Scenario	$\bar{x}$	s	Confidence	$q_{0.25}$	$\tilde{x}$	$q_{0.75}$	Min.	Max.
Europe	576.17	42.2	[560.40, 591.93]	557	577.5	597	510	654
Asia	574.3	45.6	[557.26, 591.34]	538	575	600	495	683

Table D.2. Statistical properties of test-bed results for subsequent authentication signaling in SeNERO. Values in milliseconds.

Scenario	$\bar{x}$	s	Confidence	$q_{0.25}$	$\tilde{x}$	$q_{0.75}$	Min.	Max.
Europe	660.03	63.55	[636.30, 683.76]	619	664.5	692	529	798
Asia	1165.53	61.41	[1142.60, 1188.46]	1116	1162	1191	1073	1290

Table D.3. Statistical properties of test-bed results for original correspondent router protocol. Values in milliseconds.

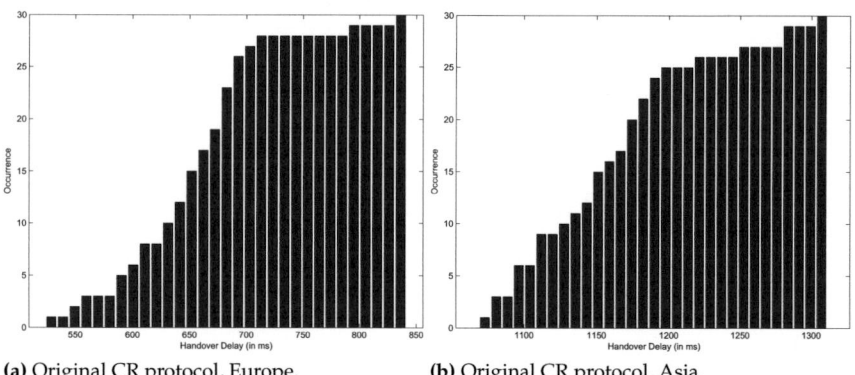

(a) Original CR protocol, Europe.　　　　　**(b)** Original CR protocol, Asia.

Figure D.2. Cumulative distribution of handover delays for original correspondent router protocol, as obtained from the test-bed. The x-axis indicates the handover delay and the y-axis the number of obtained measurements.

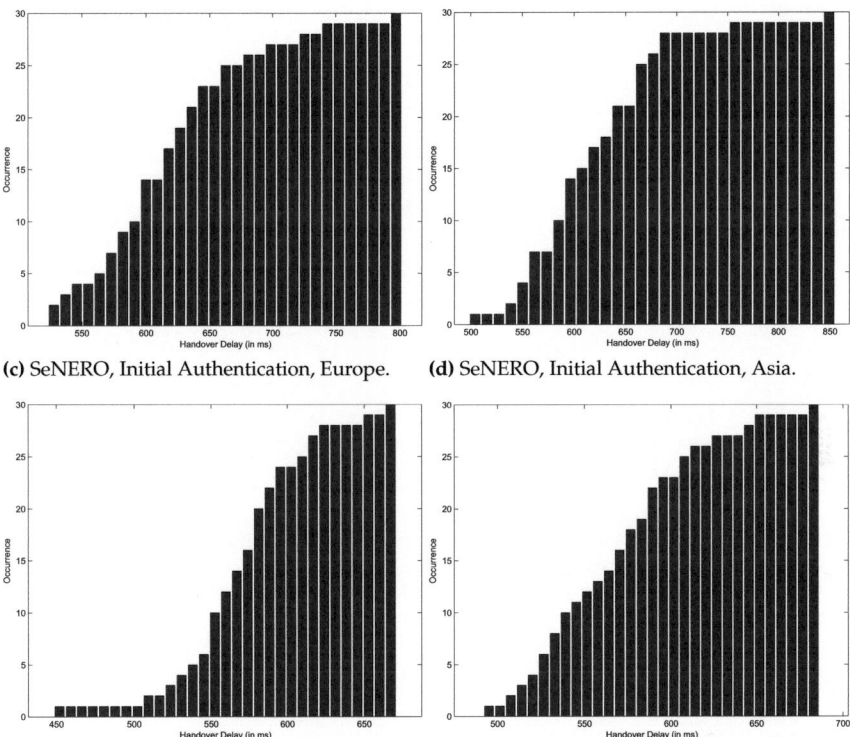

(c) SeNERO, Initial Authentication, Europe.

(d) SeNERO, Initial Authentication, Asia.

(e) SeNERO, Subsequent Authentication, Europe.

(f) SeNERO, Subsequent Authentication, Asia.

Figure D.2. Cumulative distribution of handover delays for SeNERO, as obtained from the test-bed. The x-axis indicates the handover delay and the y-axis the number of obtained measurements.

D.4. Simulation Results II

The number of measurements n is equal to 40. The results for the original correspondent router protocol are provided in Tables D.9 and D.12. The SeNERO results are in Tables D.7, D.8 and D.10, D.11.

Latency to Home	$\overline{x}$	s	Confidence	$q_{0.25}$	$\tilde{x}$	$q_{0.75}$	Min.	Max.
18	571.0	49.1	[558.3,583.7]	539.6	570.7	609.8	441.3	682.1
28	561.6	51.4	[548.3,574.9]	528.8	560.5	594.6	449.4	663.6
38	569.1	53.3	[555.4,582.9]	539.2	562.0	599.9	463.8	678.4
48	575.3	48.7	[562.8,587.9]	541.5	579.2	606.4	457.0	658.0
58	585.3	49.4	[572.5,598.1]	551.0	577.5	621.8	470.7	723.8
68	560.3	49.6	[547.5,573.1]	516.4	569.5	598.8	439.0	655.1
78	556.8	49.0	[544.1,569.4]	520.6	551.1	594.0	475.9	661.9
88	566.4	48.7	[553.8,578.9]	532.9	568.2	598.6	455.0	696.1
98	555.1	48.7	[542.5,567.7]	518.1	550.1	584.3	455.9	662.4
108	571.1	59.5	[555.7,586.4]	534.4	570.1	612.3	441.7	698.3
118	594.1	52.0	[580.7,607.6]	551.8	593.7	630.2	487.7	707.2
128	566.9	60.7	[551.2,582.6]	528.6	562.8	595.8	435.1	681.4
138	569.9	45.8	[558.1,581.7]	539.6	569.6	599.7	474.8	673.7
148	563.6	47.5	[551.3,575.8]	542.8	563.6	591.0	470.3	620.1
Global	569.0	51.8	[565.5,572.5]	535.2	567.8	603.3	422.2	698.3

Table D.4. Statistical properties of simulation results for the initial authentication signaling in SeNERO. Values in milliseconds.

Latency to Home	$\overline{x}$	s	Confidence	$q_{0.25}$	$\tilde{x}$	$q_{0.75}$	Min.	Max.
18	571.0	47.9	[558.7,583.4]	538.9	569.9	608.9	440.4	681.3
28	559.0	50.1	[546.1,571.9]	529.7	560.7	591.8	448.6	662.8
38	568.3	51.4	[555.0,581.6]	533.2	559.3	599.1	462.9	677.5
48	577.5	51.1	[564.3,590.7]	539.8	580.7	608.3	456.2	672.1
58	583.5	51.7	[570.2,596.9]	550.1	576.6	623.9	440.5	689.9
68	558.5	48.1	[546.1,571.0]	517.4	567.1	596.5	438.1	654.2
78	554.9	51.1	[541.7,568.1]	519.7	546.4	594.4	445.1	661.1
88	566.3	48.0	[553.9,578.7]	532.1	568.3	597.8	454.1	695.3
98	560.3	48.3	[547.8,572.8]	524.1	559.4	590.5	463.2	661.6
108	571.1	57.2	[556.3,585.9]	536.5	569.2	615.0	476.6	695.1
118	590.9	52.1	[577.4,604.4]	550.9	596.2	626.9	452.3	706.4
128	566.2	59.0	[551.0,581.4]	529.8	559.9	594.9	434.2	680.6
138	567.9	46.4	[555.9,579.9]	538.2	565.2	598.8	474.0	680.8
148	559.8	41.4	[549.1,570.5]	533.9	565.0	590.1	469.4	634.5
Global	568.2	51.0	[564.8,571.7]	534.3	567.8	603.2	421.3	706.4

Table D.5. Statistical properties of simulation results for the subsequent authentication signaling in SeNERO. Values in milliseconds.

Latency to Home	$\bar{x}$	s	Confidence	$q_{0.25}$	$\tilde{x}$	$q_{0.75}$	Min.	Max.
18	837.6	418.9	[729.4,945.8]	589.4	646.2	700.4	500.4	733.5
28	831.5	382.2	[732.8,930.3]	644.1	675.1	718.2	549.2	739.7
38	717.7	126.6	[685.0,750.4]	666.8	709.5	736.4	612.7	795.0
48	739.9	142.6	[703.1,776.7]	689.7	713.2	761.8	620.0	837.1
58	780.2	53.6	[766.3,794.0]	746.6	771.7	823.2	635.9	904.1
68	816.4	53.9	[802.5,830.3]	782.5	823.3	858.7	697.6	920.6
78	856.3	50.5	[843.2,869.4]	818.0	858.2	884.8	732.5	953.0
88	894.3	54.8	[880.1,908.4]	857.9	901.4	931.9	769.8	991.8
98	942.6	49.9	[929.7,955.5]	912.5	941.4	970.0	830.6	1023
108	970.3	40.4	[959.8,981.7]	942.1	971.5	996.0	890.3	1038
118	1022.8	40.3	[1012,1033]	1006	1026	1052	935.6	1100
128	1056.7	52.1	[1043,1070]	1022	1064	1087	944.1	1167
138	1084.4	52.2	[1071,1098]	1044	1083	1121	1004	1222
148	1133.6	56.4	[1119,1148]	1094	1142	1169	1008	1260

Table D.6. Statistical properties of simulation results for original correspondent router protocol. Values in milliseconds.

Latency to home	$\bar{x}$	s	Confidence	$q_{0.25}$	$\tilde{x}$	$q_{0.75}$	Min.	Max.
18	600.0	319.1	[576.6,623.3]	387.7	505.4	715.2	285.5	1206.6
28	596.2	336.4	[571.6,620.9]	383.3	496.3	672.3	279.3	1087.6
38	591.6	293.8	[570.1,613.1]	388.3	501.6	690.5	279.6	1135.9
48	606.3	310.0	[583.6,628.9]	391.2	501.1	712.3	280.4	1184.2
58	598.6	318.6	[575.3,621.9]	391.1	503.0	686.1	279.0	1109.1
68	611.6	340.7	[586.6,636.5]	389.7	502.7	700.2	278.9	1162.8
78	600.3	305.5	[578.0,622.7]	393.1	503.7	705.1	279.5	1168.6
88	605.2	336.2	[580.7,629.8]	390.4	500.8	695.7	279.3	1148.4
98	606.3	310.7	[583.6,629.1]	395.8	506.4	698.8	280.1	1144.1
108	606.8	327.7	[582.8,630.8]	388.9	508.2	716.6	279.9	1190.6
118	611.9	352.8	[586.1,637.7]	392.6	505.9	687.7	279.2	1130.0
128	597.3	329.1	[573.2,621.4]	390.0	504.6	683.7	279.5	1121.0
138	622.5	360.8	[596.1,648.9]	392.9	501.8	713.2	283.8	1128.8
148	635.4	370.8	[608.3,662.6]	393.1	508.0	718.1	280.0	1195.9

Table D.7. Statistical properties of extended simulation results for SeNERO, initial authentication, grouped by home network delay. Values in milliseconds.

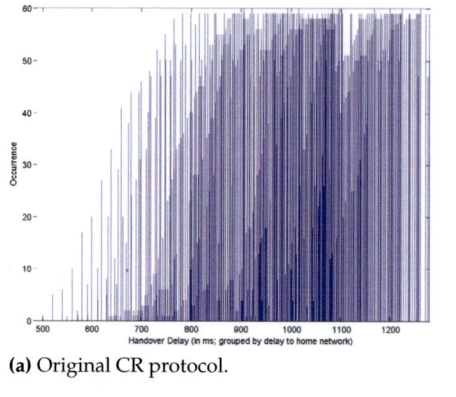

(a) Original CR protocol.

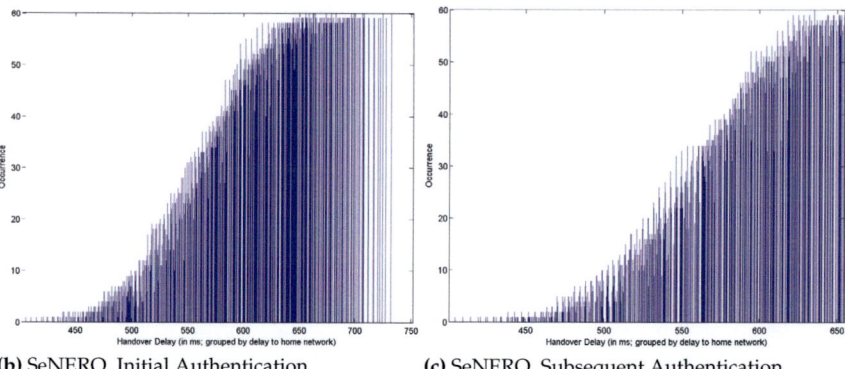

(b) SeNERO, Initial Authentication.   **(c)** SeNERO, Subsequent Authentication.

Figure D.3. Cumulative distribution of handover delays for original correspondent router protocol and SeNERO, as obtained from the simulations. The x-axis indicates the handover delay and the y-axis the number of measurements obtained for the specific delay.

Latency to home	$\overline{x}$	s	Confidence	$q_{0.25}$	$\tilde{x}$	$q_{0.75}$	Min.	Max.
18	565.1	266.1	[545.4,584.9]	378.7	494.5	657.1	206.5	1065.0
28	568.0	280.3	[547.2,588.8]	375.1	482.3	664.4	211.1	1097.9
38	567.8	284.3	[546.7,588.9]	383.3	485.9	669.8	205.1	1087.9
48	552.9	253.0	[534.2,571.7]	377.7	473.3	646.2	211.4	1027.7
58	562.4	265.5	[542.7,582.1]	379.6	480.2	652.0	205.1	1051.6
68	561.3	255.1	[542.4,580.2]	378.1	479.8	673.1	204.2	1091.4
78	556.2	277.3	[535.7,576.8]	377.3	480.6	633.4	205.7	1015.3
88	565.1	254.8	[546.2,584.0]	378.7	495.3	672.3	208.0	1103.9
98	552.3	241.7	[534.3,570.2]	376.5	488.9	655.1	211.8	1060.1
108	572.2	278.8	[551.5,592.9]	377.0	491.2	665.4	213.5	1094.8
118	565.2	268.2	[545.3,585.0]	377.8	491.9	667.9	206.8	1100.6
128	574.9	293.2	[553.2,596.6]	377.1	486.5	680.0	216.1	1131.2
138	577.1	304.2	[554.6,599.7]	382.3	488.5	654.8	210.7	1057.2
148	568.9	269.5	[548.9,588.9]	381.0	484.3	686.6	210.0	1144.0

Table D.8. Statistical properties of extended simulation results for SeNERO, subsequent authentication, grouped by home network delay. Values in milliseconds.

Latency to home	$\overline{x}$	s	Confidence	$q_{0.25}$	$\tilde{x}$	$q_{0.75}$	Min.	Max.
18	620.2	263.2	[600.7,639.7]	441.9	539.9	699.8	329.6	1083
28	655.2	262.5	[635.7,674.6]	492.7	577.4	744.4	329.5	1111
38	678.7	264.6	[659.1,698.3]	496.8	595.1	775.5	388.0	1189
48	715.5	245.0	[697.3,733.6]	552.6	630.2	796.3	446.0	1158
58	778.6	293.4	[756.8,800.3]	609.8	700.7	866.0	452.4	1242
68	799.9	296.5	[777.9,821.9]	614.0	713.3	873.8	509.1	1258
78	831.6	236.2	[814.1,849.1]	669.1	759.9	914.3	567.6	1277
88	893.9	281.0	[873.0,914.7]	725.9	815.9	979.3	567.5	1355
98	918.2	290.7	[896.7,939.7]	732.9	833.8	1002	631.4	1401
108	969.8	308.7	[946.9,992.6]	790.6	880.2	1030	685.7	1380
118	1011	281.0	[989.9,1032]	843.6	930.7	1098	685.2	1474
128	1044	292.9	[1022,1066]	855.7	950.9	1118	753.3	1508
138	1074	249.9	[1055,1093]	916.0	996.4	1152	808.7	1495
148	1122	268.0	[1103,1142]	967.6	1055	1205	808.5	1562

Table D.9. Statistical properties of extended simulation results for original correspondent router protocol, grouped by home network delay. Values in milliseconds.

Dummy Nodes	$\bar{x}$	s	Confidence	$q_{0.25}$	$\tilde{x}$	$q_{0.75}$	Min.	Max.
0	331.0	52.2	[326.7,335.3]	295.1	315.2	335.4	278.9	394.9
10	390.5	47.2	[386.6,394.4]	360.2	377.7	394.2	337.0	416.9
20	393.8	50.2	[389.6,397.9]	361.3	380.2	397.5	337.0	420.9
30	402.9	71.0	[397.0,408.8]	361.7	384.6	415.0	337.2	494.3
40	413.7	87.5	[406.4,421.0]	367.1	387.7	432.0	337.9	526.0
50	433.2	114.2	[423.7,442.6]	371.6	399.5	467.2	337.4	606.6
60	462.5	125.6	[452.1,473.0]	387.3	433.5	503.8	337.5	669.6
70	513.5	189.8	[497.8,529.3]	413.1	462.8	553.9	339.9	763.6
80	524.6	200.5	[507.9,541.2]	407.8	481.5	568.4	339.9	803.3
90	577.1	238.9	[557.3,596.9]	448.1	529.5	630.3	339.8	900.5
100	613.4	249.6	[592.7,634.1]	481.3	552.2	670.4	360.3	949.0
110	674.1	261.6	[652.4,695.8]	519.4	608.4	763.0	360.0	1128
120	713.2	294.7	[688.7,737.6]	541.3	632.4	811.2	339.6	1199
130	796.1	318.7	[769.6,822.5]	580.7	722.0	932.6	352.2	1414
140	826.2	333.3	[798.5,853.9]	589.0	754.1	961.2	357.4	1519
150	882.2	407.8	[848.3,916.0]	641.2	796.5	976.7	361.8	1480
160	927.5	409.9	[893.4,961.5]	662.6	838.5	1074.3	346.7	1691
170	1041	485.2	[1000,1081]	726.8	916.5	1232	371.1	1959

Table D.10. Statistical properties of extended simulation results for SeNERO, initial authentication, grouped by number of dummy nodes. Values in milliseconds.

Dummy Nodes	$\bar{x}$	s	Confidence	$q_{0.25}$	$\tilde{x}$	$q_{0.75}$	Min.	Max.
0	262.8	52.1	[258.5,267.2]	227.0	247.0	268.3	204.2	328.3
10	380.8	49.0	[376.7,385.0]	348.3	365.8	385.1	327.4	411.1
20	380.7	49.1	[376.5,384.8]	349.2	365.7	385.1	327.4	410.5
30	394.7	83.3	[387.7,401.7]	352.2	372.8	400.1	327.8	470.8
40	400.3	76.0	[393.9,406.6]	355.6	376.8	416.8	327.5	506.7
50	430.4	174.7	[415.7,445.1]	362.4	388.5	460.2	327.7	604.8
60	454.5	121.0	[444.3,464.6]	380.6	426.9	496.1	328.4	668.8
70	493.6	164.4	[479.8,507.4]	407.0	455.4	535.4	329.0	717.4
80	492.2	146.1	[479.9,504.5]	396.9	458.6	552.4	330.4	783.9
90	544.8	186.6	[529.1,560.5]	438.5	500.6	595.4	332.1	824.9
100	588.2	201.2	[571.2,605.1]	467.3	537.3	657.4	365.2	939.0
110	629.2	234.9	[609.4,648.9]	488.6	574.6	701.2	334.8	1015.5
120	658.7	218.1	[640.3,677.0]	512.9	604.5	746.1	341.9	1091.7
130	728.3	260.4	[706.4,750.2]	546.8	661.9	850.4	337.5	1282.5
140	777.0	295.0	[752.1,801.8]	587.4	723.7	890.0	327.9	1332.9
150	796.1	286.3	[772.0,820.1]	594.2	742.9	941.8	336.2	1462.5
160	824.4	270.4	[801.7,847.1]	630.3	788.9	966.4	356.3	1468.6
170	932.8	355.7	[902.9,962.7]	683.4	872.9	1089.5	372.8	1696.5

Table D.11. Statistical properties of extended simulation results for SeNERO, subsequent authentication, grouped by number of dummy nodes. Values in milliseconds.

Dummy Nodes	$\bar{x}$	s	Confidence	$q_{0.25}$	$\tilde{x}$	$q_{0.75}$	Min.	Max.
0	610.4	169.5	[596.2,624.7]	469.8	609.3	741.2	329.5	928.7
10	669.9	160.4	[656.4,683.4]	526.1	660.2	796.8	386.3	988.0
20	681.5	160.7	[668.0,695.0]	553.6	673.0	830.1	392.4	1002
30	702.2	198.3	[685.6,718.9]	560.3	693.9	831.9	387.7	1032
40	705.0	174.7	[690.3,719.7]	565.2	698.1	843.7	386.1	1070
50	723.4	199.4	[706.7,740.2]	572.8	706.4	852.8	386.8	1106
60	767.2	227.4	[748.0,786.3]	599.8	747.7	897.2	408.0	1153
70	802.7	239.7	[782.6,822.8]	634.0	787.8	922.0	389.1	1230
80	812.3	221.7	[793.6,830.9]	658.4	802.4	940.0	452.9	1241
90	860.6	269.7	[837.9,883.3]	699.1	840.5	966.0	395.2	1270
100	863.3	233.9	[843.6,882.9]	711.6	849.3	980	399.5	1327
110	915.5	262.6	[893.4,937.6]	752.2	886.2	1035	427.9	1455
120	945.5	285.8	[921.4,969.5]	766.1	932.6	1078	457.8	1541
130	1008	297.8	[982.9,1033]	809.9	981.2	1150	457.4	1628
140	1019	275.2	[996.3,1043]	831.5	1011	1166	500.5	1665
150	1107	360.5	[1076,1137]	900.6	1052	1239	518.6	1687
160	1137	372.5	[1106,1168]	909.7	1088	1262	533.3	1776
170	1243	444.4	[1205,1280]	968.7	1156	1368	502.0	1964

Table D.12. Statistical properties of extended simulation results for original correspondent router protocol, grouped by number of dummy nodes. Values in milliseconds.

E. Procedures For Discovering a Correspondent Router

Before a mobile router can engage in route optimization signaling with a correspondent router, the mobile router first has to learn of the correspondent router's address. The original protocol relied on a procedure where a discovery-request message is sent to a correspondent node. The correspondent router, who has to be located on the routing path between mobile router and correspondent node, will intercept this message and return an appropriate discovery-response message.

There are alternatives to this discovery approach though, which allow to use a correspondent router that is not located on the direct routing path to the correspondent node. These are presented in the following. A discussion can also be found in the IETF draft [23].

E.1. Preconfiguration

The probably simplest approach is to keep a pre-configured list of correspondent routers at the mobile router. This list would have entries in the form of $(CRP, CR\ Address)$, where CRP refers to the correspondent router prefix and $CR\ Address$ is the address the mobile router should use for route optimization signaling with the correspondent router.

When routing packets to a correspondent node, the mobile router checks whether there is a correspondent router with a prefix that matches the correspondent node address. In case an appropriate correspondent router is available from the correspondent router list, the mobile router can start performing route optimization

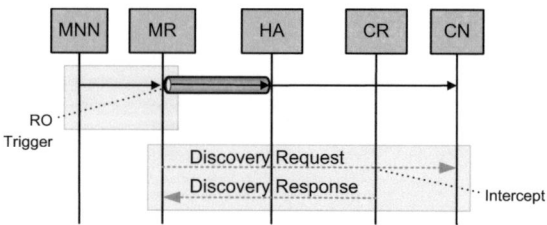

Figure E.1. Discovery of a correspondent router.

signaling with the *CR Address* that is associated with the respective correspondent router prefix.

The advantage of this approach is that no additional signaling is necessary to locate a correspondent router. The disadvantage is that the mobile router has to be regularly supplied with a recent, global list of correspondent routers.

E.2. Discovery Request-Response

The following mechanism is based on what has been proposed in the original correspondent router protocol (cf. Section 3.1.5). The original mechanism has been extended with a nonce for security reasons though.

This discovery procedure will be triggered by an appropriate packet arriving at the mobile router (cf. Section 4.6). An illustration is also provided in Figure E.1.

The mobile router will send a discovery request message to the address of the correspondent node with whom the mobile network node is exchanging packets with:

$$MR \rightarrow CN \, (Disc - Req): \; N_D \qquad (E.1)$$

The message contains a nonce N_D. The correspondent router, located on the routing path to the correspondent node, intercepts this discovery request message and responds with a discovery response message:

$$CR \rightarrow MR \, (Disc - Rsp): \; N_D \qquad (E.2)$$

The nonce N_D from the request is copied to the response message. After receiving the response message, the mobile router will know that this correspondent router is providing route optimization for that particular correspondent node.

A disadvantage of this approach is the lack of any advanced security mechanism, as no authentication is performed. This can be compensated by an authentication in the route optimization signaling that is started afterwards though. A latter au-

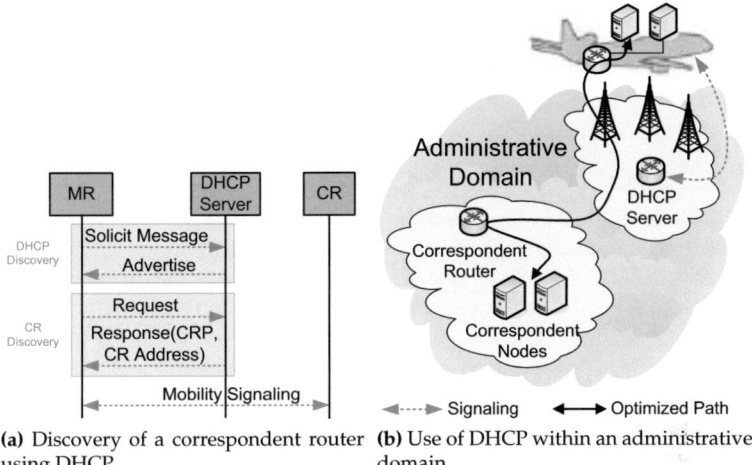

(a) Discovery of a correspondent router using DHCP. **(b)** Use of DHCP within an administrative domain.

Figure E.2. DHCP based correspondent router discovery.

thentication can then thwart an attack on the discovery procedure for the purpose of supporting a subsequent masquerading attack.

The advantage of this approach is that a correspondent router can be detected on demand, without requiring prior configuration.

E.3. DHCP-based Approach

The Dynamic Host Configuration Protocol is usually used for address configuration. It can however also be used to retrieve the address of a correspondent router. The only constraint is that only a correspondent router can be discovered that is located within the same administrative domain as the DHCP server.

The signaling of the proposed method is illustrated in Figure E.2a. As soon as the mobile router attaches to an access network, the local DHCP server will be discovered by means of the solicit-advertise message pair, as specified in [53]. Afterwards, the mobile router can use a modified request message to retrieve the address and prefix of the local correspondent router. The mobile router can then perform the route optimization signaling with this correspondent router, establish a tunnel and route packets to local correspondent nodes via the local correspondent router. This is also illustrated in Figure E.2b.

An advantage of this approach is that signaling only has to be performed with a local node, the DHCP server. The mobile router might even already know the DHCP server address if its care-of address has been configured by means of DHCP – only a single round trip time of signaling is then required for discovering the correspondent router parameters. Furthermore, DHCP security [53] can be used for protecting the message exchange(s).

A disadvantage is that a DHCP server can only provide network information for the local administrative domain, which is associated to the current access network of the mobile router. Hence, only information on a local correspondent router can be supplied to the mobile router. As a consequence, optimized routing can only be provided to local correspondent nodes that are within the same domain as the DHCP server. The discovery of correspondent routers serving correspondent nodes in other domains still has to rely on a different mechanism.

E.4. DNS-based Approach

Another possibility is to use the domain name system (DNS) for discovering the correspondent router that is associated with a certain correspondent node. By using the DNS security extensions [13], called DNSSEC, security can also be provided to the discovery procedure.

For each correspondent node, there must be a DNS entry mapping its domain name to its IPv6 address and vice versa. The DNS information of each correspondent node will be extended with a service resource record (SRV RR) that indicates which correspondent router is assigned to this particular correspondent node.

The SRV RR can be used to specify the server location for a specific protocol and domain [76]. It is suitable for new protocols and services, instead of creating new protocol-specific records and thereby overloading the DNS specification. The format of the SRV RR for a route optimization entry in the direct DNS tree is as follows:

```
_dnssecnemo._ro.cn.domain.atn.   TTL IN SRV Priority Weight 0
cr.domain.atn.
```

This specifies that NEMO route optimization for the correspondent node with the domain name cn.domain.atn is available. This entry lists cr.domain.atn the as domain name of the associated correspondent router.

The discovery procedure using the SRV RR is as follows: the mobile router can learn the correspondent node's address from the packets exchanged with the mobile network node. The mobile router will then send a DNS query to a DNS server, asking for the NEMO RO SRV RR for the address of that particular correspondent node.

An example for a reverse DNS entry that provides such a resource record for a particular correspondent node is provided in Table E.1: the IPv6 address

```
$ORIGIN 0.0.0.0.0.0.0.0.8.b.d.0.1.0.0.2.ip6.addr.

_dnssecnemo._ro.e.f.0.0.0.0.0.0.0.0.0.0.0.0.0.0.0.0
TTL IN SRV 0 5 0 cr.domain.atn.

_dnssecnemo._ro.e.f.0.0.0.0.0.0.0.0.0.0.0.0.0.0.0.0
TTL IN RRSIG SRV 5 3 TTL .. (
Sig. Lifetime;
Keytag foo.com.
AK5utJ6OvtJGKL23.= ) ; Signature

@ 7200 IN DNSKEY 256 3 5 (
AQUTY76rthQWE435KBCBkjeruhg./);
```

Table E.1. An example for a reverse DNS zone entry with a SRV RR.

2001:db8::fe of the correspondent node is provided in the beginning. This is followed by the SRV RR _dnssecnemo._ro that provides the domain name cr.domain.atn for the correspondent router. Afterwards, the DNSSEC specific records with the signature and the used key are listed.

When the mobile router receives a response from the DNS server with these entries, the message itself can be verified with help of the embedded signature. Afterwards, the mobile router can retrieve the IPv6 address for the cr.domain.atn by means of another DNS query-response message exchange; route optimization signaling can then be started.

An advantage of this approach is the possibility to obtain the responsible correspondent router for every correspondent node in the global network. In addition, by relying on DNSSEC, security is also provided: both the authenticity and integrity of the DNS response that associates a correspondent node with a correspondent router can be verified.

A disadvantage is the increased signaling load: the mobile router has to communicate with a DNS server to retrieve the SRV RR and the IPv6 address of the correspondent router. This not only increases latency due to requiring additional round trip times of signaling, but also increases the signaling overhead.

From the ground network perspective, the size of the DNS databases also increases as a _dnssecnemo._ro SRV RR has to be added to every individual correspondent node's DNS entry.

E.5. Summary

Every presented approach can be useful, depending on the deployment scenario. Correspondent router discovery should therefore not be exclusively based on a single mechanism. Instead, it is suggested that all discovery mechanisms should be available for implementation, subject to local decision making by the respective network operator.

The security provided by the different mechanisms varies: it is possible to make use of the DNS security extensions for the DNS based system. A DHCP-based discovery can make use of DHCP security, although its limitations should be considered. A security mechanism for the discovery request-response would have to be developed. For the additional discovery mechanisms discussed in [23], such as CR-resolver servers or an anycast mechanism, no security mechanisms are available either.

SeNERO therefore provides mutual authentication to ensure that route optimization will only be performed with a legitimate correspondent router. SeNERO does not make any assumptions on how a correspondent router is discovered and what kind of security the used mechanism provides, if at all.

Bibliography

[1] 3GPP. Mobility management based on Dual-Stack Mobile IPv6. TS 24.303, 3rd Generation Partnership Project (3GPP), September 2009.

[2] B. Aboba, L. Blunk, J. Vollbrecht, J. Carlson, and H. Levkowetz. Extensible Authentication Protocol (EAP). IETF RFC 3748, June 2004.

[3] T. Ahmed, S. Antoine, Song Dong, and D. Barankanira. Multi Access Data Network Connectivity and IP Flow Mobility in Evolved Packet System (EPS). In *IEEE Wireless Communications and Networking Conference (WCNC)*, April 2010.

[4] Air Transport Association. Aviation Industry Standards for Digital Information Security. Revision 2009.1.

[5] Airbus. Global Market Forecast 2011-2030, September 2011.

[6] Airlines Electronic Engineering Committee (AEEC). ARINC Report 651-1: Design Guidance for Integrated Modular Avionics, November 1997.

[7] Airlines Electronic Engineering Committee (AEEC). ARINC Specification 664-1: Aircraft Data Network, Part 1, Systems Concepts and Overview, January 2002.

[8] Airlines Electronic Engineering Committee (AEEC). ARINC Specification 653: Avionics Application Standard Software Interface, Part 1, Required Services, October 2003.

[9] Airlines Electronic Engineering Committee (AEEC). ARINC Specification 822: Aircraft/Ground IP Communication, October 2003.

[10] Airlines Electronic Engineering Committee (AEEC). ARINC Report 811: Commercial Aircraft Information Security Concepts of Operation and Process Framework, December 2005.

[11] T. Alpcan, J.P. Singh, and T. Basar. A Robust Flow Control Framework for Heterogenous Network Access. In *5th International Symposium on Modeling and Optimization in Mobile, Ad Hoc and Wireless Networks and Workshops (WiOpt)*, April 2007.

[12] G. Appenzeller, L. Martin, and M. Schertler. Identity-Based Encryption Architecture and Supporting Data Structures. IETF RFC 5408, January 2009.

[13] R. Arends, R. Austein, M. Larson, D. Massey, and S. Rose. Resource Records for the DNS Security Extensions. IETF RFC 4034, March 2005.

[14] J. Arkko, J. Kempf, B. Zill, and P. Nikander. SEcure Neighbor Discovery (SEND). IETF RFC 3971, March 2005.

[15] J. Arkko, C. Vogt, and W. Haddad. Enhanced Route Optimization for Mobile IPv6. IETF RFC 4866, May 2007.

[16] S. Ayaz, F. Hoffmann, C. Sommer, R. German, and F. Dressler. Performance Evaluation of Network Mobility Handover over Future Aeronautical Data Link. In *IEEE Global Telecommunications Conference (GLOBECOM)*, December 2010.

[17] Serkan Ayaz, Felix Hoffmann, Ulrich Epple, Reinhard German, and Falko Dressler. Performance evaluation of network mobility handover over future aeronautical data link. *Computer Communications*, 35(3):334 – 343, 2012.

[18] F. Azzedin and M. Maheswaran. Evolving and managing trust in grid computing systems. In *IEEE Canadian Conference on Electrical and Computer Engineering (CCECE)*, volume 3, pages 1424 – 1429, 2002.

[19] Marcelo Bagnulo, Alberto García-Martínez, Juan Rodríguez, and Arturo Azcorra. The Case for Source Address Dependent Routing in Multihoming. In *Quality of Service in the Emerging Networking Panorama: Fifth International Workshop on Quality of Future Internet Services (QofIS)*, pages 237–246, 2004.

[20] R. Baldessari, A. Festag, and J. Abeille. NEMO meets VANET: A Deployability Analysis of Network Mobility in Vehicular Communication. In *Proceedings of 7th International Conference on ITS Telecommunications (ITST 2007)*, pages 375–389, Sophia Antipolis, France, June 2007.

[21] Elaine Barker. *Recommendation for key management. Part 1: General*. NIST special publication; 800-57. Computer security. National Institute of Standards and Technology, March 2007.

[22] M.S. Ben Mahmoud, N. Larrieu, and A. Pirovano. A performance-aware public key infrastructure for next generation connected aircrafts. In *29th IEEE/AIAA Digital Avionics Systems Conference (DASC)*, October 2010.

[23] C. Bernardos, M. Calderon, and I. Soto. Correspondent Router based Route Optimisation for NEMO (CRON). IETF Internet-Draft (work in progress) draft-bernardos-mext-nemo-ro-cr-00, July 2008. URL http://tools.ietf.org/html/draft-bernardos-mext-nemo-ro-cr-00.

[24] Dimitri Bertsekas and Robert Gallager. *Data Networks*. Prentice-Hall Inc., 1987. ISBN 0-13-196825-4.

[25] Kemal Bicakci, Bruno Crispo, and Andrew S. Tanenbaum. How to incorporate revocation status information into the trust metrics for public-key certification. In *Proceedings of the 2005 ACM symposium on Applied computing*, SAC '05, pages 1594–1598, 2005.

[26] Marcus Biella, Bettina Birkmeier, Bernd Korn, Christiane Edinger, Sebastian Tittel, and Dirk Kügler. Operational Feasibility of Sectorless ATM. In *The International Conference of the European Aerospace Societies (CEAS)*, October 2011.

[27] B. Blanchette. Global identity issues that impact network security for NextGen. In *Integrated Communications, Navigation and Surveilance Conference (ICNS)*, May 2011.

[28] Andrey Bogdanov, Dmitry Khovratovich, and Christian Rechberger. Biclique Cryptanalysis of the Full AES. In *17th Annual International Conference on the Theory and Application of Cryptology and Information Security (ASIACRYPT)*, December 2011.

[29] Joppe W. Bos, Onur Özen, and Jean-Pierre Hubaux. Analysis and Optimization of Cryptographically Generated Addresses. In *Proceedings of the 12th International Conference on Information Security (ISC)*, pages 17–32, Berlin, Heidelberg, 2009. Springer-Verlag.

[30] Colyn Boyd and Anish Mathuria. *Protocols for Authentication and Key Establishment*. Information Security and Cryptography. Springer, 2003. ISBN 3-540-43107-1.

[31] Philippa J. Broadfoot and Andrew P. Martin. A Critical Survey of Grid Security Requirements and Technologies. Technical Report RR-03-15, Oxford University Computing Laboratory, August 2003.

[32] I. N. Bronstein, K.A. Semendjajew, G. Musiol, and H. Mühlig. *Taschenbuch der Mathematik*. Verlag Harri Deutsch, Frankfurt am Main, 7. edition, 2008.

[33] K. Brown and S. Singh. M-UDP: UDP for Mobile Networks. In *ACM Computer Communication Review*, pages 60–78, 1996.

[34] K. Butler, T.R. Farley, P. McDaniel, and J. Rexford. A survey of bgp security issues and solutions. *Proceedings of the IEEE*, 98(1):100 –122, jan 2010. doi: 10.1109/JPROC.2009.2034031.

[35] M. Calderon, C.J. Bernardos, M. Bagnulo, and I. Soto. Securing route optimisation in NEMO. In *Third International Symposium on Modeling and Optimization in Mobile, Ad Hoc, and Wireless Networks (WIOPT)*, pages 248 – 254, April 2005.

[36] M. Calderon, C. Bernardos, M. Bagnulo, I. Soto, and A. de la Oliva. MIRON: Mobile IPv6 Route Optimization for NEMO. *IEEE Journal on Selected Areas*

in Communications (J-SAC), issue on Mobile Routers and Network Mobility, 24 (9):1702–1716, Sept 2006.

[37] Zhen Cao, Hui Deng, Yuanchen Ma, and Po Hu. Integrating Identity Based Cryptography with Cryptographically Generated Addresses in Mobile IPv6. In *Proceedings, Part II, Computational Science and Its Applications – ICCSA 2007*, volume 4706 of *Lecture Notes in Computer Science*. Springer, 2007.

[38] David W Chadwick. Authorisation Using Attributes from Multiple Authorities. In *IEEE International Workshops on Enabling Technologies*, pages 326–331, Los Alamitos, CA, USA, 2006. IEEE Computer Society.

[39] Peter Chapin, Christian Skalka, and X. Sean Wang. Authorization in Trust Management: Features and Foundations. *ACM Computing Surveys*, 40(3): 1–48, 2008.

[40] K. Chebrolu and R. Rao. Communication using multiple wireless interfaces. In *IEEE Wireless Communications and Networking Conference (WCNC)*, volume 1, pages 327 – 331, March 2002.

[41] Tuan-Che Chen, Jyh-Cheng Chen, and Zong-Hua Liu. Secure Network Mobility (SeNEMO) for Real-Time Applications. *IEEE Transactions on Mobile Computing*, 10(8):1113 –1130, August 2011.

[42] Ming-Chin Chuang and Jeng-Farn Lee. A lightweight mutual authentication mechanism for network mobility in IEEE 802.16e wireless networks. *Computer Networks*, 55(16):3796 – 3809, 2011.

[43] David D. Clark. The design philosophy of the DARPA Internet Protocols. *SIGCOMM Computer Communication Review*, 25(1):102–111, January 1995.

[44] Erin Cody, Raj Sharman, Raghav H. Rao, and Shambhu Upadhyaya. Security in grid computing: A review and synthesis. *Decision Support Systems*, 44:749–764, March 2008.

[45] D. Cooper, S. Santesson, S. Farrell, S. Boeyen, R. Housley, and W. Polk. Internet X.509 Public Key Infrastructure Certificate and Certificate Revocation List (CRL) Profile. IETF RFC 5280, May 2008.

[46] J.A.R.P. de Carvalho, H. Veiga, P. Gomes, C.F.F.P.R. Pacheco, N. Marques, and A.D. Reis. Laboratory performance of wi-fi point-to-point links: A case study. In *Wireless Telecommunications Symposium (WTS)*, April 2009.

[47] S. Deering and R. Hinden. Internet Protocol, Version 6 (IPv6) Specification. IETF RFC 2460, December 1998.

[48] Luc Deneufchatel. L-DACS 2 Development - Status and Preliminary Specification. In *EUROCONTROL Innovative Research Workshop & Exhibition*, March 2008.

[49] V. Devarapalli and F. Dupont. Mobile IPv6 Operation with IKEv2 and the Revised IPsec Architecture. IETF RFC 4877, April 2007.

[50] V. Devarapalli, R. Wakikawa, A. Petrescu, and P. Thubert. Network Mobility (NEMO) Basic Support Protocol. IETF RFC 3963, January 2005.

[51] W. Diffie and M. Hellman. New directions in cryptography. *IEEE Transactions on Information Theory*, 22(6):644 – 654, nov 1976.

[52] Danny Dolev and Andrew Chi-Chih Yao. On the security of public key protocols. *IEEE Transactions on Information Theory*, 29(2):198–207, 1983.

[53] R. Droms, J. Bound, B. Volz, T. Lemon, C. Perkins, and M. Carney. Dynamic Host Configuration Protocol for IPv6 (DHCPv6), July 2003.

[54] Andrew L. Dul. Global ip network mobility using border gateway protocol. www.quark.net/docs/Global_IP_Network_Mobility_using_BGP.pdf, March 2006. Boeing White Paper.

[55] W. Eddy, W. Ivancic, and T. Davis. Network Mobility Route Optimization Requirements for Operational Use in Aeronautics and Space Exploration Mobile Networks. IETF RFC 5522, October 2009.

[56] W.M. Eddy. At what layer does mobility belong? *IEEE Communications Magazine*, 42(10):155 – 159, October 2004.

[57] P. Eronen. IKEv2 Mobility and Multihoming Protocol (MOBIKE). IETF RFC 4555, June 2006.

[58] EUROCAE. Safety And Performance Requirements (SPR) For Aeronautical Information Services (AIS) And Metereological (MET) Data Link Services. Number Rev. 3.0, 5 2010.

[59] Eurocontrol. LINK 2000+ Network Planning Document, May 2007. Edition 3.4.

[60] Eurocontrol. Long-Term Forecast: IFR Flight Movements 2010-2030, December 2010. STATFOR, the Eurocontrol Statistics and Forecast Service.

[61] Eurocontrol/FAA Future Communication Study. Communications Operating Concept and Requirements for the Future Radio System, May 2007. COCR version 2.0.

[62] S. Farrell, R. Housley, and S. Turner. An Internet Attribute Certificate Profile for Authorization. IETF RFC 5755, January 2010.

[63] Federal Aviation Administration (FAA). 14 cfr part 25, special conditions: Boeing model 787-8 airplane; systems and data networks security protection of airplane systems and data networks from unauthorized external access, April 2007. URL http://edocket.access.gpo.gov/2007/pdf/07-1838.pdf. last visited: 2nd November 2011.

[64] Federal Aviation Administration (FAA). Review of Web Applications Security and Intrustion Detection in Air Traffic Control Systems. Report Number: FI-2009-049, May 2009. URL http://www.oig.dot.gov/sites/dot/files/pdfdocs/ATC_Web_Report.pdf.

[65] Federal Aviation Administration (FAA). Special conditions: Boeing model 747-8 airplanes, systems and data networks security-isolation or protection from unauthorized passenger domain systems access, September 2010. URL http://federalregister.gov/a/2010-30993. last visited: 2nd November 2011.

[66] U. Feige, A. Fiat, and A. Shamir. Zero-knowledge proofs of identity. *Journal of Cryptology*, 1:77–94, August 1988.

[67] Directorate-General for Research, Directorate General for Mobility Innovation, and Transport. *Flightpath 2050 – Europe's Vision for Aviation, Report of the High Level Group on Aviation Research*. European Commission, 2011. ISBN 978-92-79-19724-6.

[68] H. Forsgren, K. Grahn, J. Karlsson, T. Karvi, and G. Pulkkis. Securing Control Signaling in Mobile IPv6 with Identity-Based Encryption. In *IEEE EUROCON (Region 8)*, St. Petersburg, Russia, May 2009. IEEE.

[69] Amy Friedlander, Allison Mankin, W. Douglas Maughan, and Stephen D. Crocker. DNSSEC: A Protocol Toward Securing The Internet Infrastructure. *Communications of the ACM*, 50:44–50, June 2007.

[70] D. Funato, K. Yasuda, and H. Tokuda. TCP-R: TCP mobility support for continuous operation. In *Proceedings of the International Conference on Network Protocols (ICNP)*, Washington, DC, USA, 1997. IEEE Computer Society.

[71] T. Gaska, B. Werner, and D. Flagg. Applying virtualization to avionics systems – The integration challenges. In *29th IEEE/AIAA Digital Avionics Systems Conference (DASC)*, October 2010.

[72] L. Graglia, B. Favennec, and A. Arnoux. Vocalise: assessing the impact of data link technology on the R/T channel. In *The 24th Digital Avionics Systems Conference (DASC)*, October 2005.

[73] T. Graupl, M. Ehammer, and C.-H. Rokitansky. L-DACS 1 data link layer design and performance. In *Integrated Communications, Navigation and Surveillance Conference (ICNS)*, pages 1 –12, May 2009.

[74] Thomas Gräupl and Max Ehammer. LDACS1 data link layer evolution for ATN/IPS. In *30th IEEE/AIAA Digital Avionics Systems Conference (DASC)*, October 2011.

[75] I. Guardini, E. Demaria, and M. La Monaca. Mobile IPv6 deployment opportunities in next generation 3GPP networks. In *Proceedings of 16th IST Mobile and Wireless Communications Summit*, 2007.

[76] A. Gulbrandsen, P. Vixie, and L. Esibov. A DNS RR for specifying the location of services (DNS SRV). IETF RFC 2782, February 2000.

[77] S. Gundavelli, K. Leung, V. Devarapalli, K. Chowdhury, and B. Patil. Proxy Mobile IPv6. IETF RFC 5213, August 2008.

[78] B. Haindl, M. Sajatovic, M. Ehammer, T. Gräupl, M. Schnell, U. Epple, and S. Brandes. L-DACS 1 System Definition Proposal: Deliverable D2. In *EUROCONTROL*, February 2009.

[79] Georg Hampel and Vladimir Kolesnikov. Securing Host-Based Mobility and Multi-Homing Protocols against On-Path Attackers. *Journal of Communications*, 6(1):101–114, 2011.

[80] Heise. Ausmaß der Cyber-Attacke auf das Pentagon größer als bisher bekannt, March 2008. URL http://www.heise.de/newsticker/meldung/ Ausmass-der-Cyber-Attacke-auf-das-Pentagon-groesser-als-bisher-bekannt-188938. html. last visited: 8th November 2011.

[81] Heise. Hotspot über den Wolken, November 2010. URL http://www.heise. de/newsticker/meldung/Hotspot-ueber-den-Wolken-1144984.html. last visited: 7th November 2011.

[82] Heise. Systeme der Bundesregierungs unter Angriff, Sep 2011. URL http://www.heise.de/newsticker/meldung/ Regierungscomputer-vermehrt-im-Visier-auslaendischer-Geheimdienste-1336391. html. last visited: 8th November 2011.

[83] Heise. RSA-Hack könnte Sicherheit von SecurID-Tokens gefährden, March 2011. URL http://www.heise.de/security/meldung/ RSA-Hack-koennte-Sicherheit-von-SecurID-Tokens-gefaehrden-1210245. html. last visited: 8th November 2011.

[84] Heise. Hacker-Angriff auf US-Beobachtungssatelliten, October 2011. URL http://www.heise.de/newsticker/meldung/ Hacker-Angriff-auf-US-Beobachtungssatelliten-1368627.html. last visited: 8th November 2011.

[85] Heise. USA legen Verteidigungsstrategie für den Cyberspace vor, July 2011. URL http://www.heise.de/security/meldung/ USA-legen-Verteidigungsstrategie-fuer-den-Cyberspace-vor-1279764. html. last visited: 8th November 2011.

[86] Heise. 2012: das Jahr, in dem die dicken Drohnen kommen, Dec 2011. URL http://www.heise.de/newsticker/meldung/ 2012-das-Jahr-in-dem-die-dicken-Drohnen-kommen-1400782.html. last visited: 2nd January 2012.

[87] Stephen Hemminger. Network Emulation with NetEm. In *Linux Conference Australia*, April 2005.

289

[88] R. Hinden and S. Deering. Internet Protocol Version 6 (IPv6) Addressing Architecture. IETF RFC 3513, April 2003.

[89] Julien Holstein and Dave Coombs. Public Key Infrastructure (PKI) – Obstacles to implementation. In *ATA e-Business Forum*, June 2011. Montreal, Canada.

[90] Md. Shohrab Hossain, Mohammed Atiquzzaman, and William Ivancic. Performance Evaluation of Multihomed NEMO. In *IEEE International Conference on Communications (ICC)*, June 2012. Ottawa, Canada.

[91] M.S. Hossain, M. Atiquzzaman, and W.D. Ivancic. Security vulnerabilities and protection mechanisms of mobility management protocols. In *IEEE Aerospace Conference*, March 2011.

[92] S.L. Hunt, P. Platt, T.A. Evans, P.D. Ryan, M. Ehammer, and T. Brikey. NEWSKY Security Concept, Oct 2009. Deliverable D15 of NEWSKY project.

[93] G. Huston, M. Rossi, and G. Armitage. Securing BGP – A Literature Survey. *IEEE Communications Surveys & Tutorials*, 13(2):199 –222, 2011.

[94] Internet Assigned Numbers Authority (IANA). Internet Protocol Version 6 Address Space, October 2011. URL http://www.iana.org/assignments/ipv6-address-space/ipv6-address-space.xml. last visited: 01.10.2011.

[95] ICANN. Icann's first dnssec key ceremony for the root zone, June 2010. URL http://www.icann.org/en/announcements/announcement-2-07jun10-en.htm. last visited: 3rd February 2011.

[96] ICAO Aeronautical Communications Panel, WG F. Off-Board Communications for Vehicle Health Management. http://www.icao.int/anb/panels/acp/wgdoclist.cfm?MeetingID=266, December 2009. 21st meeting of the working group F, Bangkok, Thailand.

[97] ICAO Aeronautical Communications Panel, WG I. Analysis of Candidate Mobility Solutions, June 2007. 13th meeting of the working group N-SWG1, Montreal, Canada.

[98] IEEE. *IEEE Standard for Local and Metropolitan Area Networks: Overview and Architecture (IEEE Std 802-2001, Revision of IEEE Std 802-1990)*. Institute of Electrical and Electronics Engineers, Inc., February 2002.

[99] IEEE. *Wireless LAN Medium Access Control (MAC) and Physical Layer (PHY) Specifications (IEEE Std 802.11-2007)*. Institute of Electrical and Electronics Engineers, Inc., June 2003.

[100] IEEE. *IEEE Standard for Local and metropolitan area networks. Physical and Medium Access Control Layers for Combined Fixed and Mobile Operation in Li-*

censed Bands (IEEE Std 802.16e-2005). Institute of Electrical and Electronics Engineers, Inc., February 2006.

[101] IEEE. *IEEE Standard for Local and metropolitan area networks. Part 3: Carrier Sense Multiple Access with Collision Detection (CSMA/CD) Access Method and Physical Layer Specifications (IEEE Std 802.03-2008).* Institute of Electrical and Electronics Engineers, Inc., December 2008.

[102] IEEE. *IEEE Standard for Local and metropolitan area networks. Part 21: Media Independent Handover Services (IEEE Std 802.21-2008).* Institute of Electrical and Electronics Engineers, Inc., January 2009.

[103] International Civil Aviation Organization. Machine Readable Travel Documents (Doc 9303), 2006. Sixth edition.

[104] International Civil Aviation Organization. Manual on the Aeronautical Telecommunications Network (ATN) using Internet Protocol Suite (IPS) Standards and Protocols (Doc 9896), 2010. 1st edition.

[105] ITU-T. Rec. X.690, ASN.1 encoding rules: Specification of basic encoding rules (BER), canonical encoding rules (CER), and distinguished encoding rules (DER), July 2002.

[106] ITU-T. G.114, General Recommendations on the transmission quality for an entire international telephone connection – One-way transmission time, May 2003.

[107] A. Jahn, M. Holzbock, J. Muller, R. Kebel, M. de Sanctis, A. Rogoyski, E. Trachtman, O. Franzrahe, M. Werner, and Fun Hu. Evolution of aeronautical communications for personal and multimedia services. *IEEE Communications Magazine*, 41(7):36 – 43, July 2003.

[108] D. Johnson, C. Perkins, and J. Arkko. Mobility Support in IPv6. IETF RFC 6275, July 2011.

[109] B. Kamali. An overview of VHF civil radio network and the resolution of spectrum depletion. In *Integrated Communications Navigation and Surveillance Conference (ICNS)*, May 2010.

[110] W. Kampichler and D. Eier. Satellite based voice communication for air traffic management and airline operation. In *Integrated Communications, Navigation and Surveillance Conference (ICNS)*, May 2011.

[111] Jonathan Katz and Yehuda Lindell. *Introduction to Modern Cryptography.* Cryptography and Network Security. Chapman & Hall/CRC, 6000 Broken Sound Parkway NW, Suite 300, Boca Raton, FL 33487-2742, 2008. ISBN 978-1-58488-551-1.

[112] C. Kaufman. Internet Key Exchange (IKEv2) Protocol. IETF RFC 5996, September 2010.

[113] Charlie Kaufman, Radia Perlman, and Mike Speciner. *Network Security: Private Communication in a Public World*. Prentice-Hall, Inc., Upper Saddle River, NJ, USA, 11th printing edition, November 2007. ISBN 0-13-046019-1.

[114] S. Kent. IP Authentication Header. IETF RFC 4302, December 2005.

[115] S. Kent. IP Encapsulating Security Payload (ESP). IETF RFC 4303, December 2005.

[116] S. Kent and K. Seo. Security Architecture for the Internet Protocol. IETF RFC 4301, December 2005.

[117] S. Kent, C. Lynn, and K. Seo. Secure Border Gateway Protocol (S-BGP). *IEEE Journal on Selected Areas in Communications (J-SAC)*, 18(4):582–592, April 2000.

[118] Cheeha Kim. S-RO: Simple Route Optimization Scheme with NEMO Transparency. In *Information Networking, Convergence in Broadband and Mobile Networking (ICOIN)*, volume 3391 of *Lecture Notes in Computer Science*. Springer, 2005.

[119] Jung-Doo Koo, Seong-Hoon Oh, and Dong-Chun Lee. Authenticated route optimization scheme for network mobility (NEMO) support in heterogeneous networks. *International Journal of Communication Systems*, 23:1252–1267, September 2010.

[120] Rajeev S. Koodli and Charles E. Perkins. *Mobile Internetworking with IPv6: Concepts, Principles and Practices*. Wiley-Interscience, 2007. ISBN 978-0-471-68165-6.

[121] G. Koundourakis, D.I. Axiotis, and M. Theologou. Network-based access selection in composite radio environments. In *IEEE Wireless Communications and Networking Conference (WCNC)*, pages 3877 –3883, March 2007.

[122] A. Kukec, M. Bagnulo, and A. de la Oliva. CRYPTRON: CRYptographic Prefixes for Route Optimization in NEMO. In *IEEE International Conference on Communications (ICC)*, June 2010.

[123] Deguang Le, Xiaoming Fu, and Dieter Hogrefe. A review of mobility support paradigms for the Internet. *IEEE Communications Surveys & Tutorials*, 8(1):38–51, 2006.

[124] Franck Le and Stefano M Faccin. IPv6 address ownership solution based on zero-knowledge identification protocols or based on one time password. Patent, June 2009. US 7546456.

[125] Yong Lee, Goo Yeon Lee, and Hwa Jong Kim. Design and Performance Evaluation of a Scalable Authentication Protocol in Mobile IP. In *Second International Conference on Communications and Networking in China (CHINACOM), 2007*, pages 1069 –1073, August 2007.

[126] Albert Levi, M. Ufuk Caglayan, and Cetin K. Koc. Use of nested certificates for efficient, dynamic, and trust preserving public key infrastructure. *ACM Transactions on Information and System Security (TISSEC)*, 7:21–59, February 2004.

[127] Hyung-Jin Lim, Moonseong Kim, Jong-Hyouk Lee, and Tai-Myoung Chung. Route Optimization in Nested NEMO: Classification, Evaluation, and Analysis from NEMO Fringe Stub Perspective. *IEEE Transactions on Mobile Computing*, 8(11):1554–1572, 2009.

[128] J. Loughney. IPv6 Node Requirements. IETF RFC 4294, April 2006.

[129] C. Lynn, S. Kent, and K. Seo. X.509 Extensions for IP Addresses and AS Identifiers. IETF RFC 3779, June 2004.

[130] G. Malkin. RIP Version 2. IETF RFC 2453, November 1998.

[131] John Marchesini and Sean Smith. Modeling Public Key Infrastructures in the Real World. In *2nd European PKI Workshop: Research and Applications (EuroPKI)*, volume 3545 of *Lecture Notes in Computer Science*, pages 118–134. Springer, 2005.

[132] Arifumi Matsumoto, Kenji Fujikawa, Yasuo Okabe, Fumio Teraoka, Mitsunobu Kunishi, Masataka Ohta, and Masahiro Ishiyama. Multihoming Support based on Mobile Node Protocol LIN6. In *Proceedings of the 2003 Symposium on Applications and the Internet Workshops (SAINT'03 Workshops)*, page 204, Washington, DC, USA, 2003. IEEE Computer Society.

[133] Ueli Maurer. Modelling a Public-Key Infrastructure. In E. Bertino, editor, *European Symposium on Research in Computer Security – ESORICS '96*, volume 1146 of *Lecture Notes in Computer Science*, pages 325–350. Springer-Verlag, September 1996.

[134] Alfred J. Menezes, Paul C. van Oorschot, and Scott A. Vanstone. *Handbook of Applied Cryptography*. CRC Press, 1997.

[135] Gabriel López Millán, Manuel Gil Pérez, Gregorio Martínez Pérez, and Antonio F. Gómez Skarmeta. PKI-based trust management in inter-domain scenarios. *Computers & Security*, 29(2):278 – 290, 2010.

[136] Ilya Mironov. Hash functions: Theory, attacks, and applications. Technical Report MSR-TR-2005-187, Microsoft Research, November 2005. URL http://research.microsoft.com/en-us/people/mironov/hash_survey.pdf.

[137] Gabriel Montenegro and Claude Castelluccia. Crypto-based identifiers (CBIDs): Concepts and applications. *ACM Transactions on Information and System Security (TISSEC)*, 7(1):97–127, 2004.

[138] P.C. Moore, W.R. Johnson, and R.J. Detry. Adapting Globus and Kerberos for a Secure ASCI Grid. In *ACM/IEEE Supercomputing Conference*, pages 54

– 54, November 2001.

[139] C. Morlet, N. Ricard, and S.F. Rodriguez. Options for the Iris satellite-based datalink. In *Integrated Communications, Navigation and Surveilance Conference (ICNS)*, May 2011.

[140] J. Moy. OSPF Version 2. IETF RFC 2328, April 1998.

[141] Andreas Müller, Georg Carle, and Andreas Klenk. Behavior and classification of NAT devices and implications for NAT traversal. *IEEE Network*, 22 (5):14–19, 2008.

[142] M. Myers, R. Ankney, A. Malpani, S. Galperin, and C. Adams. X.509 Internet Public Key Infrastructure Online Certificate Status Protocol - OCSP. IETF RFC 2560, June 1999.

[143] T. Narten, E. Nordmark, W. Simpson, and H. Soliman. Neighbor Discovery for IP version 6 (IPv6). IETF RFC 4861, September 2007.

[144] Anil Nerode and Richard A. Shore. *Logic for Applications*. Springer, 1997. ISBN 9780387948935.

[145] NEWSKY Project. NEWSKY Operational Requirements Document, January 2008. Deliverable D08 of NEWSKY project.

[146] NEWSKY Project. Technology Screening and Characterisation for Integration in NEWSKY Network, April 2008. Deliverable D09 of NEWSKY project.

[147] C. Ng and J. Hirano. Securing Nested Tunnels Optimization with Access Router Option. IETF Internet-Draft (work in progress) draft-ng-nemo-access-router-option-01, July 2004. URL http://tools.ietf.org/html/draft-ng-nemo-access-router-option-01.

[148] C. Ng, F. Zhao, M. Watari, and P. Thubert. Network Mobility Route Optimization Solution Space Analysis. IETF RFC 4889, July 2007.

[149] P. Nikander, J. Arkko, T. Aura, and G. Montenegro. Mobile IP version 6 (MIPv6) route optimization security design. In *IEEE Vehicular Technology Conference (VTC Fall)*, volume 3, pages 2004 – 2008, October 2003.

[150] P. Nikander, J. Arkko, T. Aura, G. Montenegro, and E. Nordmark. Mobile IP Version 6 Route Optimization Security Design Background. IETF RFC 4225, December 2005.

[151] Pekka Nikander, Andrei Gurtov, and Thomas R. Henderson. Host Identity Protocol (HIP): Connectivity, Mobility, Multi-homing, Security, and Privacy over IPv4 and IPv6 Networks. *IEEE Communications Surveys & Tutorials*, 12 (1):24 –38, 2010.

[152] NIST. *Advanced Encryption Standard (AES) (FIPS PUB 197)*. National Institute of Standards and Technology, November 2001.

[153] NIST. *Secure Hash Standard (SHA) (FIPS PUB 180-2)*. National Institute of Standards and Technology, August 2002.

[154] NIST. *The Keyed-Hash Message Authentication Code (HMAC) (FIPS PUB 198)*. National Institute of Standards and Technology, March 2006.

[155] NIST. *Digital Signature Standard (DSS) (FIPS PUB 186-3)*. National Institute of Standards and Technology, June 2009.

[156] Szabolcs Novaczki, Laszlo Bokor, Gábor Jeney, and Sándor Imre. Design and Evaluation of a Novel HIP-Based Network Mobility Protocol. *Journal of Networks (JNW)*, 3(1):10–24, 2008.

[157] NTT Communications Europe Website. Performance Statistics, February 2009. URL http://www.eu.ntt.com/en/products/global-network/transit/sla-of-global-ip-network.html. last visited: 1st October 2012.

[158] Philippe Oechslin. Making a faster cryptanalytic time-memory trade-off. In *23rd Annual International Cryptology Conference (CRYPTO 2003)*, volume 2729 of *Lecture Notes in Computer Science*, pages 617–630. Springer, August 2003.

[159] M.L. Olive, R.T. Oishi, and S. Arentz. Commercial aircraft information security-an overview of arinc report 811. In *25th IEEE/AIAA Digital Avionics Systems Conference*, pages 1 –12, October 2006.

[160] Sangheon Pack, Kunwoo Park, Aekyoung Kwon, and Yanghee Choi. SAMP: scalable application-layer mobility protocol. *IEEE Communications Magazine*, 44(6):86 –92, June 2006.

[161] P. Papadimitratos, L. Buttyan, T. Holczer, E. Schoch, J. Freudiger M. Raya, Z. Ma, F. Kargl, A. Kung, and J.-P. Hubaux. Secure Vehicular Communication Systems: Design and Architecture. *IEEE Communcations Magazine*, 46 (11):100–109, November 2008.

[162] Joon S. Park and Ravi Sandhu. Smart Certificates: Extending X.509 for Secure Attribute Services on the Web. In *In Processinds Of 22nd National Information Systems Security Conference (NISSC)*, pages 18–21, 1999.

[163] Joon S. Park, Ravi Sandhu, and Gail-Joon Ahn. Role-based access control on the web. *ACM Transactions on Information and System Security (TISSEC)*, 4:37–71, February 2001.

[164] V. Patel and T. McParland. Public key infrastructure for air traffic management systems. In *20th IEEE/AIAA Digital Conference Digital Avionics Systems Conference (DASC)*, October 2001.

[165] Eranga Perera, Vijay Sivaraman, and Aruna Seneviratne. Survey on network mobility support. *SIGMOBILE Mobile Computing and Communications Review*, 8(2):7–19, 2004.

[166] C. Perkins. Securing Mobile IPv6 Route Optimization Using a Static Shared Key. IETF RFC 4449, June 2006.

[167] R. Perlman. An overview of PKI trust models. *IEEE Network*, 13(6):38 –43, November/December 1999.

[168] Henrik Petander and Eranga Perera. Measuring and improving the performance of network mobility management in IPv6 networks. *IEEE Journal on Selected Areas in Communications (J-SAC)*, 24:1671–1681, 2006.

[169] E. Piri and K. Pentikousis. Towards a GNU/Linux IEEE 802.21 Implementation. In *IEEE International Conference on Communications (ICC)*, June 2009.

[170] Ying Qiu, Jianying Zhou, Feng Bao, and Robert H. Deng. Using Certificate-based Binding Update Protocol to Hide the Movement of Mobile Nodes in MIPv6. In *Vehicular Technology Conference (VTC Spring)*, pages 828–830, 2006.

[171] M. Raya, P. Papadimitratos, and J.-P. Hubaux. Securing Vehicular Communications. *IEEE Wireless Communications*, 13(5):8–15, October 2006.

[172] Ken Reid. Towards a common understanding creating the network-centric environment. In *ICAO Worldwide Symposium on Enabling the Net Centric Information Environment*, Montreal, Canada, June 2008.

[173] Y. Rekhter, T. Li, and S. Hares. A Border Gateway Protocol 4 (BGP-4). IETF RFC 4271, January 2006.

[174] Kui Ren, Wenjing Lou, Kai Zeng, Feng Bao, Jianying Zhou, and Robert H. Deng. Routing optimization security in Mobile IPv6. *Computer Networks*, 50:2401–2419, September 2006.

[175] E. Rescorla and B. Korver. Guidelines for Writing RFC Text on Security Considerations. IETF RFC 3552, July 2003.

[176] Certicom Research. Standards for efficient cryptography, SEC 1: Elliptic curve cryptography, May 2009. URL http://www.secg.org/download/aid-780/sec1-v2.pdf. Version 2.0.

[177] R. L. Rivest, A. Shamir, and L. Adleman. A method for obtaining digital signatures and public-key cryptosystems. *Communications of the ACM*, 21: 120–126, February 1978.

[178] Richard V. Robinson, Mingyan Li, Scott A. Lintelman, Krishna Sampigethaya, Radha Poovendran, David von Oheimb, and Jens-Uwe Bußer. Impact of public key enabled applications on the operation and maintenance of commercial airplanes. In *AIAA Aviation Technology Integration, and Operations (ATIO) Conference*, September 2007.

[179] Pablo Rodriguez, Rajiv Chakravorty, Julian Chesterfield, Ian Pratt, and Suman Banerjee. MAR: a commuter router infrastructure for the mobile

Internet. In *Proceedings of the 2nd international conference on Mobile systems, applications, and services*, MobiSys, pages 217–230. ACM, 2004.

[180] K. Sampigethaya, R. Poovendran, L. Bushnell, Mingyan Li, R. Robinson, and S. Lintelman. Secure wireless collection and distribution of commercial airplane health data. *IEEE Aerospace and Electronic Systems Magazine*, 24(7): 14 –20, jul 2009.

[181] K. Sampigethaya, R. Poovendran, S. Shetty, T. Davis, and C. Royalty. Future e-enabled aircraft communications and security: The next 20 years and beyond. *Proceedings of the IEEE*, 99(11):2040 –2055, November 2011.

[182] Frederic Saugnac. e-Operations – A350 full digital aircraft. In *Air Transport IT Summit 2010*, June 2010. Brussels, Belgium.

[183] Eurocontrol/FAA Future Communication Study Evaluation Scenarios. Future Communications Infrastructure – Technology Investigations, May 2007. Appendix of ACP/1-WP/21.

[184] Jochen Schiller. *Mobile Communications*. Pearson Education Limited, Edinburgh Gate, Harlow CM20 2JE, UK, 2. edition, 2003. ISBN 0321123816.

[185] Bruce Schneier. Description of a New Variable-Length Key, 64-Bit Block Cipher (Blowfish). In *Fast Software Encryption, Cambridge Security Workshop Proceedings*, volume 809 of *Lecture Notes in Computer Science*, pages 191–204, Cambridge, UK, December 1993. Springer-Verlag.

[186] SESAR Joint Undertaking. High-Level SWIM A-G Architecture and Functional Requirement Specification, September 2010. Deliverable D02 of project 9.19, edition 00.01.00.

[187] SESAR Joint Undertaking. Analysis of Aeronautical Spectrum Utilization and Impact Assessment, March 2011. Deliverable D01 of project 15.1.6, edition 00.03.00.

[188] A.Z.M. Shahriar and M. Atiquzzaman. Evaluation of Prefix Delegation-Based Route Optimization Schemes for NEMO. In *IEEE International Conference on Communications (ICC)*, June 2009.

[189] A.Z.M. Shahriar, M. Atiquzzaman, and W. Ivancic. Performance of Prefix Delegation-Based Route Optimization Schemes: Intra Mobile Network case. In *IEEE International Conference on Communications (ICC)*, May 2010.

[190] A.Z.M. Shahriar, M. Atiquzzaman, and W. Ivancic. Route optimization in network mobility: Solutions, classification, comparison, and future research directions. *IEEE Communications Surveys & Tutorials*, 12(1):24 –38, 2010.

[191] Adi Shamir. Identity-based cryptosystems and signature schemes. In *Proceedings of CRYPTO 84 on Advances in cryptology*, pages 47–53, New York,

NY, USA, 1985. Springer-Verlag New York, Inc.

[192] Mark Shaughnessy and Jeff Morrow. Security Architecture and Management Considerations for FAA NextGen. In *Integrated Communications, Navigation and Surveillance Conference (ICNS)*, May 2011.

[193] R. Shirey. Internet Security Glossary, Version 2. IETF RFC 4949, August 2007.

[194] Single European Sky ATM Research (SESAR). European Air Traffic Management Master Plan, March 2009. Edition 1.

[195] Hesham Soliman. *Mobile IPv6: Mobility in a Wireless Internet*. Addison Wesley Longman Publishing Co., Inc., Redwood City, CA, USA, 2004. ISBN 0201788977.

[196] William Stallings. *Cryptography and Network Security*. Prentice Hall, Upper Saddle River, NJ 07458, fourth edition, 2006. ISBN 0-13-187316-4.

[197] Bob Stephens. Security Challenges for the 21st Century. In *ATA e-Business Forum*, October 2007.

[198] R. Stewart. Stream Control Transmission Protocol. IETF RFC 4960, September 2007.

[199] R. Stewart, M. Tuexen, and G. Camarillo. Security Attacks Found Against the Stream Control Transmission Protocol (SCTP) and Current Countermeasures. IETF RFC 5062, September 2007.

[200] R. Stewart, Q. Xie, M. Tuexen, S. Maruyama, and M. Kozuka. Stream Control Transmission Protocol (SCTP) Dynamic Address Reconfiguration. IETF RFC 5061, September 2007.

[201] Symantec. Trends for 2010. *Internet Security Threat Report (ISTR)*, April 2011.

[202] Technical Department of European Network and Information Security Agency (ENISA). Risk Management: Implementation principles and Inventories for Risk Management/Risk Assessment methods and tools, June 2006. Deliverable D1.

[203] R. Thomas. ISP Security BOF, NANOG 28, June 2003. URL http://www.nanog.org/mtg-0306/pdf/thomas.pdf.

[204] S. Thomson, T. Narten, and T. Jinmei. IPv6 Stateless Address Autoconfiguration. IETF RFC 4862, September 2007.

[205] Kentaroh Toyoda, Yuta Kamiguchi, Shinichiro Inoue, and Iwao Sasase. Efficient Solution to Decrease the Effect of DoS Attack against IP Address Ownership Proof in Mobile IPv6. In *IEEE 20th International Symposium on*

Personal, Indoor and Mobile Radio Communications (PIMRC), Toronto, Canada, September 2011.

[206] M.-A. Tran, P.-N. Tran, and N. Boukhatem. Strategy Game for Flow/Interface Association in Multi-Homed Mobile Terminals. In *IEEE International Conference on Communications (ICC)*, May 2010.

[207] G. Tsirtsis, H. Soliman, N. Montavont, G. Giaretta, and K. Kuladinithi. Flow Bindings in Mobile IPv6 and Network Mobility (NEMO) Basic Support. IETF RFC 6089, January 2011.

[208] Peter Tuggey. Hello, I'm On the Plane! In *WAEA Conference & Educational Workshops (CEW)*. World Airline Entertainment Association, April 2009. Kuala-Lumpur.

[209] András Varga and Rudolf Hornig. An overview of the OMNeT++ simulation environment. In *Proceedings of the 1st international conference on Simulation tools and techniques for communications, networks and systems & workshops (Simutools)*, pages 1–10, Brussels, Belgium, 2008.

[210] Christian Vogt. A Comprehensive and Efficient Handoff Procedure for IPv6 Mobility Support. In *Proceedings of the IEEE International Symposium on a World of Wireless, Mobile and Multimedia Networks, Niagara Falls, NY, USA*, June 2006.

[211] Son T. Vuong and Peng Fu. A security architecture and design for mobile intelligent agent systems. *SIGAPP Applied Computing Review*, 9:21–30, September 2001.

[212] R. Wakikawa, S. Koshiba, K. Uehara, and J. Murai. ORC: Optimized Route Cache Management Protocol for Network Mobility. In *IEEE 10th International Conference on Telecommunications (ICT)*, volume 2, pages 1194 – 1200, 23 February–1 March 2003.

[213] R. Wakikawa, V. Devarapalli, G. Tsirtsis, T. Ernst, and K. Nagami. Multiple Care-of Addresses Registration. IETF RFC 5648, October 2009.

[214] R. Wakikawa, R. Kuntz, Z. Zhu, and L. Zhang. Global HA to HA Protocol Specification. IETF Internet-Draft (work in progress) draft-wakikawa-mext-global-haha-spec-02, September 2011. URL http://tools.ietf.org/html/draft-wakikawa-mext-global-haha-spec-02.

[215] Ryuji Wakikawa, Guillaume Valadon, and Jun Murai. Migrating home agents towards internet-scale mobility deployments. In *CoNEXT '06: Proceedings of the 2006 ACM CoNEXT conference*, New York, NY, USA, 2006. ACM.

[216] Xiaoyun Wang, Yiqun Lisa Yin, and Hongbo Yu. Finding Collisions in the Full SHA-1. In *Advances in Cryptology (CRYPTO'05)*, pages 17–36, August 2005.

[217] J. P. Watt, Oluwafemi Ajayi, Jipu Jiang, Jos Koetsier, and Richard O. Sinnott. A Shibboleth-Protected Privilege Management Infrastructure for e-Science Education. In *Sixth IEEE International Symposium on Cluster Computing and the Grid (CCGrid 2006)*, pages 357–364, May 2006.

[218] Klaus Wehrle, Mesut Günes, and James Gross. *Modeling and Tools for Network Simulation*. Springer-Verlag, Berlin, Heidelberg, 1st edition, June 2010. ISBN 978-3-642-12330-6.

[219] James H. Williams and T.L. Signore. National airspace system security cyber architecture. Technical report, MITRE, Februrary 2011. URL http://www.mitre.org/work/tech_papers/2011/10_4169/10_4169.pdf.

[220] S. Wilson. The network security architecture and possible safety benefits of the AeroMACS network. In *Integrated Communications, Navigation and Surveilance Conference (ICNS)*, May 2011.

[221] Gaogang Xie, Ji Chen, Hongxia Zheng, Jianhua Yang, and Yu Zhang. Handover Latency of MIPv6 Implementation in Linux. In *IEEE Global Communications Conference (GLOBECOM)*, pages 1780–1785, 2007.

[222] Tie yan Li, Huafei Zhu, and Kwok yan Lam. A Novel Two-Level Trust Model for Grid. In *International Conference on Information and Communications Security (ICICS)*, pages 214–225. Springer, 2003.

[223] H Yang, E Osterweil, D Massey, S Lu, and L Zhang. Deploying Cryptography in Internet-Scale Systems: A Case Study on DNSSEC. *IEEE Transactions on Dependable and Secure Computing*, 8(5):656 –669, sept.-oct. 2011. ISSN 1545-5971.

[224] Mi-Jeong Yang, Kyung-Yul Cheon, Ae-Soon Park, Young-Hwan Choi, and Sang-Ha Kim. Seamless Handover Using FMIPv6 with Effective Tunnel Management Scheme. In *IEEE Global Communications Conference (GLOBECOM)*, November 2008.

[225] Ilsun You. A Ticket Based Binding Update Authentication Method for Trusted Nodes in Mobile IPv6 Domain. In *EUC Workshops: Emerging Directions in Embedded and Ubiquitous Computing*, volume 4809 of *Lecture Notes in Computer Science*. Springer, 2007.

[226] Faqir Zarrar Yousaf, Christian Bauer, and Christian Wietfeld. An accurate and extensible mobile IPv6 (xMIPV6) simulation model for OMNeT++. In *Simutools '08: Proceedings of the 1st international conference on Simulation tools and techniques for communications, networks and systems & workshops*, 2008.

[227] John Zao, Joshua Gahm, Gregory Troxel, Matthew Condell, Pam Helinek, Nina Yuan, Isidro Castineyra, and Stephen Kent. A public-key based secure mobile IP. *Wireless Networks*, 5:373–390, October 1999.

[228] Zhenkai Zhu, Ryuji Wakikawa, and Lixia Zhang. SAIL: A scalable approach for wide-area IP mobility. In *IEEE Conference on Computer Communications Workshops (INFOCOM Workshops)*, pages 367 –372, April 2011.

Index